What Makes an Elite Pitcher?

ALSO BY WARREN N. WILBERT
AND FROM MCFARLAND

*A Cunning Kind of Play: The Cubs-Giants
Rivalry, 1876–1932* (2002)

*The Best of Baseball: The 20th Century's
Greatest Players Ranked by Position* (2001)

*Rookies Rated: Baseball's Finest
Freshman Seasons* (2000)

What Makes an Elite Pitcher?

Young, Mathewson, Johnson, Alexander, Grove, Spahn, Seaver, Clemens, and Maddux

WARREN N. WILBERT

Foreword by Robin Roberts

McFarland & Company, Inc., Publishers
Jefferson, North Carolina, and London

Illustations supplied by B & W Photos, Brace Photography, and the personal collections of C. Paul Rogers, III; William Hageman; and Warren N. Wilbert.

LIBRARY OF CONGRESS CATALOGUING-IN-PUBLICATION DATA

Wilbert, Warren N.
    What makes an elite pitcher? : Young, Mathewson, Johnson, Alexander, Grove, Spahn, Seaver, Clemens, and Maddux / Warren N. Wilbert.
      p.   cm.
    Includes bibliographical references and index.

    ISBN 0-7864-1456-1 (softcover binding : 50# alkaline paper) ∞

    1. Pitchers (Baseball) — Rating of — United States.   2. Pitching (Baseball) — Statistics.   I. Title.
GV871.W53   2003
796.357'092'2 — dc21   2003006894

British Library cataloguing data are available

©2003 Warren N. Wilbert. All rights reserved

No part of this book may be reproduced or transmitted in any form or by any means, electronic or mechanical, including photocopying or recording, or by any information storage and retrieval system, without permission in writing from the publisher.

Cover photograph: Cy Young of the 1908 Boston Red Sox
(George Grantham Bain Collection, Library of Congress)

Manufactured in the United States of America

McFarland & Company, Inc., Publishers
  Box 611, Jefferson, North Carolina 28640
    www.mcfarlandpub.com

To the Kohler Greyhounds

ACKNOWLEDGMENTS

Those of us who belong to the Society for American Baseball Research usually rely on one another to help along with bits and pieces (and some of those bits and pieces are substantial contributions, by the way) of research or information that go into authoring a book about a team, a player, a pennant race or some other facet of the grand old game. I'm grateful to each of them, and to the others mentioned who have given of their time, talent and support to help put this book between covers. They include:

Saberites Bill Deane, Pete Palmer, Hank Thomas, Robin Roberts, Dr. C. Paul Rogers, Bill James, Al Kermisch (now deceased), Steve Gietschier, John Zajc, the good people at Retrosheet and Dave Smith.

Special thanks to Bill Hageman, a dear friend, who helped not only with counsel and support, but with two rare photos, one of "Iron Man" Joe McGinnity and one of "Big Ed" Reulbach.

And *very* special thanks to a loving and supportive family, with an extra word of thanks to grandson Alan, who helped so much with some of those important numbers and lists.

CONTENTS

Acknowledgments	vii
Foreword by Robin Roberts	xi
Introduction	1
1. Cy Young	5
2. Christy Mathewson	39
3. Walter Johnson	76
4. Pete Alexander	129
5. Lefty Grove	158
6. Warren Spahn	200
7. Tom Seaver	238
8. Roger Clemens	280
9. Greg Maddux	309
10. Fall Classics	345
Notes	357
Appendix A: Ratings from the Total Pitcher Index	363
Appendix B: Selected Career Statistics	365
Bibliography	367
Index	371

FOREWORD
by Robin Roberts

Warren Wilbert's book *What Makes an Elite Pitcher?* strikes a special chord with a former ballplayer like me. When I pitched in the Major Leagues from 1948 to 1966, the game was simpler than it is today. For most of that time, only sixteen teams made up the Major Leagues, and for the first 10 years of my career there were no big league teams west of St. Louis. We played a 154 game season with no interleague play, which meant that teams played each other 22 times a year. Needless to say, suiting up to play another club 22 times built rivalries between teams and between individual players on those teams.

In those days clubs generally used a four-man rotation with three regular starting pitchers. The fourth starter would often rotate among pitchers who would sometimes pitch in long relief. As a result, the regular starters pitched every fourth day, on three days rest. The series were often three games in length so a starter would pitch a game in virtually every series his team played. I had a run of twenty-plus win years and in those seasons I often pitched the opening game of a series against the opposition's ace. I was frequently matched against fellows like Don Newcombe, Warren Spahn, Sal Maglie or other outstanding pitchers. With only 16 teams and three regular starters on a team, the competition was tough.

Playing each team so many times also meant that the starting pitchers were constantly matched against the top hitters. For example, I believe it is accurate to say that I faced Jackie Robinson more than any other pitcher during Jackie's ten-year major league career. I knew each time I faced Jackie that I was in for a battle. Sometimes he won, sometimes I won, but it was a competition that I enjoyed.

Warren Wilbert has captured those kinds of rivalries for nine of our

Robin Roberts

greatest pitchers of all time. How did Walter Johnson fare against Ty Cobb? How did Christy Mathewson do against Honus Wagner? How did I do against Spahnie? Grove vs. Gomez or Seaver vs. Carlton? The answer is here. I guarantee that you will enjoy the journey.

Robin Roberts

INTRODUCTION

Ed Linn led off his story about one of baseball's ultimate rivalries mincing no words: "I don't care what anybody says, there is no rivalry on the face of the earth that can compare with the Yankees vs. the Red Sox."[1] Mr. Linn, the adept New Englander whose every last drop of blood was Boston Carmine, spoke from up-close-and-personal experience with pinstriped and red-stockinged ball players, and his point is rather persuasively made in his lively account of the drama-laden, hotly contested New York–Boston rivalry.

Had he been at Yankee Stadium on May 28, 2000, he would have had the rare privilege of witnessing one of the more scintillating renewals of the storied and captivating Yankee–Red Sox saga. On this occasion Roger Clemens squared off against Pedro Martinez, and the two went at each other with the razor sharp precision of two highly skilled surgeons. Inning after inning the two zipped through the batting order, setting down the enemy with deadly dispatch as they strung up a scoreboard full of goose eggs.

Finally, in the top of the ninth, Trot Nixon, whose name was made for baseball heroics but whose career featured few of them, put a charge on a Clemens heater and sent it off into the stadium's far reaches. The two-run shot left it up to Martinez the Magnificent, who promptly took care of Red Sox business to preserve a hard-fought 2 to 0 spine-tingler.

Referred to as a throw-back, the game was hashed and re-hashed in the media, and in glowing terms. Who said the ol' 1 to 0 and 2 to 1 games no longer "filled the bill"? A crowd of 55,339 on hand that day knew they had been witness to something very special and would no doubt have anted up, and gladly, to see more of the same.

The Martinez-Clemens confrontation brings this book's review of the elite hurlers of the 20th century into sharp perspective. When two legends go *mano a mano* the potential for "a game to remember" is very, very high.

What happened, for example, when Cy Young and Walter Johnson met, or when Christy Mathewson faced Mordecai "Three Finger" Brown, or when Tom Seaver crossed swords with Lefty Carlton?

Perhaps Pete Alexander against Dazzy Vance? Or Warren Spahn facing Robin Roberts? And for you latter day fans: how about checking on the Greg Maddux vs. Orel Hershiser or Dwight Gooden matchups? Those kinds of confrontations are what this book is all about. Just ahead are encounters with dozens of pitching greats, many of whom are in the Hall of Fame, some of whom soon will be, and still others who probably should be.

Many of these superlative hurlers, beginning with Cy Young, whose American League career coincided with the beginning of the 20th century, and continuing through the century to Greg Maddux and Roger Clemens, who closed it out, serve as pivot points for a cluster of pitching greats they faced during their careers. Cy Young, for example, is matched against each Hall of Famer he opposed (as is each of the featured pitchers, as well as several of the best hurlers listed among the top 300 moundsmen, all time, in Palmer's TPI listing[2]). That basic format is followed for each of the pitching greats who spread-eagle the 20th century.

The *Total Baseball Encyclopedia*'s top 300 TPI listing is, further, the basic touchstone for sorting out those who are worthy of comparison with the artists assembled in this review. The complete listing, found in Appendix A, presents only the very best, and from that list each of the greats is paired with his contemporaries, both Hall of Famers and pitching luminaries just a notch below Hall of Fame status (a status that has been, and will no doubt remain, debatable).

The 2001 edition of the *Total Baseball Encyclopedia* lists nine outstanding pitchers among the game's top 300 whose names you will *not* find mentioned in this review. They include Hoyt Wilhelm, ranked at number 15 all time; John Franco, number 39; Goose Gossage, number 44; the Eck, Dennis Eckersley (50); Kent Tekulve (77); Rollie Fingers (81); the recently retired John Wetteland (84); Tom Henke (87); and Roberto Hernandez (98). These nine are the top ranked among the game's relievers. Those rankings may change in the century ahead, but through the close of the twentieth century, they were the pacemakers among those indispensable late-inning game savers. Because the focus here is on starters only, there will be no appearances out of the pen from among the assemblage of hurling greats in this book.

Finally, our Mound Maestros are matched with contemporaries from opposing leagues who were named to the Hall of Fame and who pitched against them in the World Series.[3] That makes for some interesting matchups — for example, Christy Mathewson vs. Albert "Chief" Bender, or Warren Spahn vs. Whitey Ford.

Earl Weaver, the feisty little majordomo of those famous Baltimore teams of the '70s, was once asked by a Los Angeles sportswriter what he felt was the relationship between pitching and winning or losing. His answer, quoted in the June 16, 1978, *Los Angeles Times*, was, "Nobody likes to hear it because it's dull, but the reason you win or lose is darn near always the same ... pitching."

That same sentiment has been expressed over and over by countless numbers of managers, and in many different ways. There may be an infinite number of ways of handling the pitchers, of using one system or another, or of developing a strategy that exploits the best each pitcher brings to the staff, but on one thing there seems to be unanimous agreement: winning or losing ball games starts 60 feet, 6 inches from home plate. The select few who have entered the charmed circle of enshrinement at Cooperstown because of their surpassing artistry as past masters of the pitching arts, always were, and always will be, the foundation pieces of every manager's hopes, schemes and dreams for a pennant winner.

From "Cy" to "Tom Terrific," and from "the Big Train" to "the Rocket," and on to all the other mound masters in this book whose careers tower over even their Hall of Fame pitching compadres, these extraordinary hurlers, in a stellar orbit unique even among Cooperstown's worthies, have made mind-bending contributions to the record book and, perhaps more interestingly, have enriched baseball's fascinating lore with stories and incidents that make for retelling around Hot Stove gatherings on a cold winter's night.

This review celebrates their awesome achievements.

1. CY YOUNG

Major League Career:	Won	Lost	Pct.
Cleveland (NL)	241	135	.641
St. Louis (NL)	45	35	.563
Boston (AL)	192	112	.632
Cleveland (AL)	29	29	.500
Boston (NL)	4	5	.444
Career Totals	511	316	.618

Young was elected to the Baseball Hall of Fame in 1937

In 1921 the city of Cleveland celebrated its 125th anniversary. One of the Forest City's festive events that year was an Old Timers game headed by an all-star cast of former diamond heroes. Among them, the brightest star was Denton True Young, the beloved Buckeye they called Cy. The aging star, by this time a paunchy, middle-aged citizen, led his team to victory with a two-inning, starting effort featuring no runs, a pair of strikeouts, and enough zip on what was left of his quick one to remind a capacity crowd of the way things once were. Out there on the hill he was doing what he used to do best, enduring, all the while slipping his high hard one and his breaking stuff past the hitters.

As a matter of fact, through an unparalleled Hall of Fame career that went on and on through 22 seasons, an incredible 7,356 innings pitched and a mind-numbing 511 victories, that was exactly what Cy did best: endure. And further, he persisted with a consistency that was as reliable as the sun rising in the East. When it came to pitching, this fellow did more of it, and more of it better over a longer period of time, than anyone else before or since, and that takes into account more than 130 seasons of professional baseball.

The legendary Cy Young.

He was indeed a hurler set apart. Consider this: it would take a modern-day pitcher 29 years at 250 innings pitched per year (a busy season by modern reckoning) to amass over 7,000 innings, and at 18 wins a season (again, a very solid number considering the conduct of our contemporary pitching game), no less than 28-plus seasons. Considering that the usual number of starts for the number one and two staff hurlers is between 30 and

1. Cy Young

35, it would take better than 23 seasons to rack up a career total of 815 starting assignments, the number Cy accumulated, to say nothing of the number of games he completed, an astounding 749 (that's no less than 92 percent!), which, at the rate of the present 10 or 12 completions a year, would take the better part of Mr. Lincoln's four score and seven.

Those gargantuan numbers get us off to an auspicious start with our celebrated 20th century pitching heroes, the first and foremost of whom was on hand also for the initial season of the American League in 1901. Coincidentally, the second of these elite twirlers, Christy Mathewson, started his stellar career with six appearances in 1900 before logging his first 20-game season in his rookie season, 1901. How better to start than at the very beginning of the century with two of the game's greatest!

Over one-third of the 58 pitchers in the Hall of Fame at the close of the 20th century (the exact numbers are 21 and .3621 percent) wore uniforms during Cy Young's career. He actually squared off against ten of them during the 20th century, each of whom thus merits a closer look. The ten are: Grover Cleveland Alexander; Albert "Chief" Bender; Happy Jack Chesbro; Walter Johnson; Adrian "Addie" Joss; the Iron Man, Joe McGinnity; Edward "Gettysburg Eddie" Plank; George "Rube" Waddell; Big Ed Walsh; and that sly Ol' Fox, Clark Griffith. It's worth noting that Alexander, Johnson, Mathewson (who was active during 12 of Young's years), and Young himself form a quartet of Famers who ride herd on the top four all-time Total Pitching Index spots: Johnson, first at 91.4, is followed by Young, with 78.0; Alexander, 64.6; and Mathewson, 62.9. Greg Maddux (60.0) and Roger Clemens (57.5), both of whom bridged the 20th and 21st centuries, will probably alter this prestigious list before calling it a career. But neither will change the 1–2, Johnson and Young rankings. Between them these six illustrious twirlers form imposing 20th century bookends of pitching excellence.

To complete the list of distinguished pitchers who challenged Young, George Mullin has been added. He will be remembered as the Tiger ace who headed Detroit's 1907–09 pennant-winning pitching staffs. Handsome Harry Howell, who toiled in relative obscurity with St. Louis' second-division ball clubs of the early 1900s and Guy "Doc" White, whose puzzling southpaw slants helped Chicago's White Sox win the 1906 American League championship, surprising the baseball world with a shocking World Series conquest of their crosstown arch-enemies, the Frank Chance–led Cubs, complete the list.

White, with a career TPI of 20.1, ranking number 101 on the list of baseball's top 300 hurlers; Howell, 16.6, at number 144; and Mullin, 14.5, at number 168, were Young's most challenging, non–HOF competitors during the American League phase of his career. Note too, that these three bettered the rankings of Chief Bender, Jack Chesbro, Jim Galvin, Don Sutton, Rube Marquard and Jim Bunning, each a Cooperstown choice. Let the games begin. A baker's dozen of these titans are about to lock horns with the Legendary One, Cy Young.

During Cy Young's amazing 22-year career, 21 Famers were active. Each is listed below, though only those who appeared against him in the 20th century will be reviewed. The chronological arrangement of this list also serves to establish the review order, a pattern followed throughout the book. The Cy Young matchup list:

Name/HOF Year	Debut/Career Yrs.	TPI/All Time Pitcher Ranking
Jim Galvin/1965	May 22, 1875/1875–1892	13.0/201
Mickey Welch/1973	May 1, 1880/1880–1892	15.1/158t
Charley Radbourne/1939	May 5, 1880/1880–1891	29.5/39t
Tim Keefe/1964	August 6, 1880/1880–1893	38.1/20
John Clarkson/1963	May 2, 1882/1882–1896	46.0/11
Amos Rusie/1977	May 9, 1889/1889–1901	39.8/16
"Kid" Nichols/1949	April 23, 1890/1890–1906	57.5/7t
Clark Griffith/1946	April 11, 1891/1891–1914	28.3/45
"Rube" Waddell/1946	Sept 8, 1897/1897–1910	24.4/69
Vic Willis/1995	April 30, 1898/1898–1910	21.2/88t
Harry Howell	October 10, 1898/1898–1910	16.6/144
Joe McGinnity/1946	April 18, 1899/1899–1908	18.8/113t
Jack Chesbro/1946	July 12, 1899/1899–1909	10.9/238t
Christy Mathewson/1936	July 17, 1900/1900–1916	62.9/4
Guy "Doc" White	April 22, 1901/1901–1913	20.1/101
Eddie Plank/1946	May 13, 1901/1901–1917	26.9/53
"Addie" Joss/1978	April 26, 1902/1902–1910	25.8/60
George Mullin	May 4, 1902/1902–1915	14.5/168t
Mordecai Brown/1949	April 19, 1903/1903–1916	35.3/23
"Chief" Bender/1953	April 20, 1903/1903–1925	14.4/170
Ed Walsh/1946	May 7, 1904/1904–1917	44.9/12
Walter Johnson/1936	August 2, 1907/1907–1927	91.4/1
"Rube" Marquard/1971	Sept 25, 1908/1908–1925	-2.3/NR
"Pete" Alexander/1938	April 15, 1911/1911–1930	64.3/3

Cy Young versus Clark C. Griffith (1869–1955)

Griffith was elected to the Baseball Hall of Fame in 1946

Although the Ol' Fox and Cy hooked up only four times in the American League (they were National League foes during the 1890s), they pitched in the thick of hotly contested pennant races. Griffith's White Sox, the first American League pennant winners, were dethroned by Connie Mack's 1902 winners, who were in turn sternly tested by a Boston club that went on to win it all, as well as the game's first World Series title, in 1903.

Throughout those crucial early years of the American League, Boston, Philadelphia and Chicago were among the powerful forces leading the way, both in the front office and on the field of play. Clark Griffith, with sufficient evidence (at least from this corner) to warrant his Hall of Fame niche as a pitcher (to say nothing of his managerial and executive abilities), was a huge force during that pivotal time in the league's formative years.

During his highly successful tour of duty in the major leagues,

The Ol' Fox, Clark Griffith.

Clark Griffith crafted a string of six straight 20-game seasons, notching a career-high 26 for Cap Anson's Colts in 1895. Chicago's sharp-eyed franchise president, Charley Comiskey, took note of Anson's ace. Desirous of putting a Chicago name in the White Sox lineup, Comiskey offered him a deal he couldn't refuse, putting the wily righthander in charge of the Pale Hose. Between them, the two, both inclined toward the audacious, helped put not only the Chicago team, but the league itself on the baseball map.

Clark Griffith's career was spread over 23 years, seven teams, and three major leagues, finally coming to a close on October 7, 1914, in Boston, where the Ol' Fox took the hill for the last time in 1914's season-ending game. He was only a few weeks away from his 45th birthday, but still had enough left to get by the last inning of a game that Washington won by an 11 to 4 margin. Babe Ruth was one of Washington's opposing pitchers, and Tris Speaker, playing the outfield and first base, also got in on the last-day fun by pitching an inning himself. Griffith used his usual mix of trick and quick pitches, with scuffed and moistened deliveries that accounted for the ground balls and whiffs that marked his pitching throughout a career that saw victories three out of every five times he took the hill, as he won 237 games against 146 losses.

Matched against Cy Young, however, he wasn't nearly as successful. Griffith might have been foxy out there on the mound, but Boston's ace was just plain better, beating the colorful banty hurler three times out of four. Still, that doesn't take all that much away from one of baseball's most dedicated and provocative personalities. Although Young, a White Sox nemesis, beat back Chicago's challenges regularly, the Ol' Fox did turn in a gem against Boston's non pareil on June 10, 1902, when he beat the Pilgrims 3 to 2, stranding the tying run in the top of the ninth at Chicago's West Side grounds.

The Young-Griffith Log:

May 23, 1902	Boston 6, Chicago 0	Young WP, Griffith LP
June 10, 1902	Chicago 3, Boston 2	Griffith WP, Young LP
June 3, 1903	Boston 9, New York 3	Young WP, Griffith LP
June 22, 1907	Boston 12, New York 3	Young WP, Griffith LP

Cy Young versus George Edward "Rube" Waddell (1876–1914)
Waddell was elected to the Baseball Hall of Fame in 1946

As the old bromide goes: "They threw away the mold after this one came along." George Edward Waddell, the Original Rube, eccentric extraordinaire, adds a special spice to the parade of moundsmen who matched pitches — and wits (yes, Waddell was cunning as well as quick) — with Master Young. The two hooked up 14 times, and Connie Mack's zany southpaw took the measure of Young eight times, losing but four, with three no-decisions and a 13-inning tie that ranks among Waddell's better career outings.

Rube was a handful, all right, whether out on the town, in front of (or behind) the bar at one of Philadelphia's watering holes, at the firehouse, or when Mr. Mack stationed him on the mound. Especially on the mound. When Rube was on his game there weren't many who could do much of anything with him. Possessed of blinding speed and near faultless control, baseball's first strikeout king posted 131 wins, averaging nearly 22 a season for the Athletics during the six prime seasons of his career.

It was a given that there was something special in store when Young and Waddell crossed swords.

Rube Waddell, one of baseball's first great flamethrowers.

Five of their games resulted in shutouts. Additionally, there were five tilts in which the losing team registered three runs or less. In one other, a July 4th marathon that gave almost 13,000 Red Sox fans two games for the price of one, Young and Waddell matched goose eggs for 13 innings before the A's pushed over a pair of runs in the top of the 20th to win, 4 to 2. But the gem of the Waddell-Young encounters was recorded by the old master himself in the form of the American League's first perfect game on May 5, 1904. Not even "Rube" could cope successfully with that one!

At Boston, May 5, 1904

Philadelphia	AB	H	PO	A	Boston	AB	H	PO	A
Hartsel, lf	1	0	0	0	Dougherty, lf	4	1	1	0
Hoffman, lf	2	0	2	1	Collins, 3b	4	2	2	0
Pickering, cf	3	0	1	0	Stahl, cf	4	1	3	0
Davis, 1b	3	0	5	0	Freeman, rf	4	1	2	0
L. Cross, 3b	3	0	4	1	Parent, ss	4	2	1	4
Seybold, rf	3	0	2	0	LaChance, 1b	3	1	9	0
Murphy, 2b	3	0	1	2	Ferris, 2b	3	1	0	3
M. Cross, ss	3	0	2	3	Criger, c	3	1	9	0
Schreckengost, c	3	0	7	0	Young, p	3	0	0	2
Waddell, p	3	0	0	1					
Totals	27	0	24	8	Totals	32	10	27	9

Line Score	Philadelphia	000	000	000	0–0–1
	Boston	000	001	20x	3–10–0

2BH	Collins, Criger
3BH	Stahl, Freeman, Ferris
DP	Hoffman, Schreckengost; L. Cross, Davis
K	Young 8; Waddell 6
BB	None
Umpire	Dwyer
Time	1:25
Att.	10,267

The perfect game, with two other no-hitters, became a part of the Young–Hall of Fame legacy. His career numbers were not merely Fame-worthy. They were staggering, finding their way to the top of the list in more than a dozen career and single season categories. A sampling includes: Games Started and Completed, Games Won and Lost, Innings Pitched, Pitching Runs, Wins Above Team and League, and 20-game seasons. Those lofty number ones are buttressed by rankings in the top ten in Shutouts and Total Pitching Index, and top 15 in Fewest Walks/game, Games Pitched and Strikeouts.

As for Mr. Waddell, there were also several entries in the record book.

One would have to list as number one, and unbreakable, his record for chasing fires in Philadelphia and other cities around the league. But there were also a number of the more conventional kind, to wit: Top 50 ratings in Opponents' On Base percentage and Opponents Batting Average, Strikeouts per game (7.04 during his 13 year career, which included two very brief seasons of less than 50 innings pitched between them), Hits per Game, Pitching Wins, and a noteworthy number six ranking, all time, with his career 2.16 Earned Run Average. Remember, too, that Rube was the southpaw who set the original Strikeout record in 1904 with 349, a mark that still ranks way up there in the number 17 spot. All of that and 13 years of fun and games with his favorite carousing pal and battery mate, catcher Ossee Schreckengost. He might have given the saintly Mr. Mack fits, but he also gave the Mackmen a solid crack at winning the tough ones. And more often than not, he did.

The Young-Waddell Log

Sept 12, 1902	Boston 5, Philadelphia 4	Young WP, Waddell LP
Sept 15, 1902	Philadelphia 9, Boston 2	Waddell WP, Young LP
Sept 19, 1902	Philadelphia 6, Boston 4	Waddell WP, Young LP
April 25, 1904	Philadelphia 2, Boston 0	Waddell WP, Young LP
May 5, 1904	Boston 3, Philadelphia 0	Young WP, Waddell LP
June 22, 1904	Boston 7, Philadelphia 5	Young WP, Waddell LP
June 30, 1904	Boston 4, Philadelphia 3	Young WP, Waddell LP
July 4, 1905*	Philadelphia 4, Boston 2	Waddell WP, Young LP
July 7, 1905	Philadelphia 2, Boston 1	Waddell WP, Young LP
Sept 8, 1905	Philadelphia 5, Boston 3	Waddell WP, Young LP
April 25, 1906	Philadelphia 5, Boston 0	Waddell WP, Young LP
Sept 14, 1906	Philadelphia 4, Boston 0	Waddell WP, Young LP
Sept 9, 1907†	Boston-Philadelphia, 0–0 tie	Young and Waddell CG

On July 8, 1902, in their first meeting, both Young and Waddell were used as relief pitchers in a game won by Philadelphia, 22 to 6.

Cy Young versus Harry Howell (1876–1956)

Handsome Harry Howell was fated to a career filled with some downright lousy ball clubs behind him. The Handsome One nonetheless pitched well consistently, brilliantly on occasion, and badly seldom enough to warrant high ranking among his contemporaries. During baseball's deadball era, when bunts and scratch, in-field grounders were such a significant part of the game, Howell excelled as one of the very best fielding pitchers of the day.

---

*In this 20-inning game both Waddell and Young pitched complete games.
†A 13-inning game called because of darkness.

Arriving in St. Louis the same year the town celebrated the Louisiana Purchase with a World's Fair and Exposition, the smallish spitballer settled down to five straight seasons of the kind of pitching that would ordinarily have put him in the 20-game winner's circle. Unfortunately, the most he could muster under the circumstances was an 18–18 standoff for the 1908 Brownies. Beginning in 1904 with an ERA of 2.19, he added 1.98, 2.11, 1.93 and 1.89 ERAs in successive seasons before his retirement in 1909. His career 2.74 ERA netted him a spot among the top 75 hurlers in the game's history.

Locking horns with Cy Young 11 times during his career, Howell managed to wrest an even-up, 5–5 reading from the masterful Red Sox veteran. That was about as much as one could hope for — even if there had been a strong club behind him. Five of the 11 matches between them resulted in victory margins of two runs or less. Among them, two

Handsome Harry Howell, early 1900s workhorse.

stand out: a 2 to 0 shutout at Boston in which Howell spaced seven hits, walked but one hitter and picked up the only run he needed in the seventh stanza when shortstop Bill "Wagon Tongue" Keister, who had doubled at the Red Sox' spacious Huntington Grounds (it was 635 feet to the center field wall, mind you), scored shortly after on a Steve Brodie single; and the other, another 2 to 0 shutout, this one administered by Young at St. Louis in the stifling Mound City heat of August 29, 1905. Cy, supported by two first-inning runs on a Jimmy Collins triple, shut the Browns down on six hits, benefiting from two Boston twin-killings. The old master whiffed nine and walked but one. The box score of the 1905 tilt follows:

At St. Louis, August 29, 1905

Boston	R	H	PO	A	St. Louis	R	H	PO	A
Burkett, lf	0	1	0	0	Stone, lf	0	1	1	0

Parent, ss	1	0	2	1	Rockenfield, 2b	0	1	5	2
Stahl, cf	1	0	1	0	Frisk, rf	0	0	0	0
Collins, 3b	0	2	1	2	Wallace, ss	0	1	2	4
Freeman, rf	0	0	0	0	Jones, 1b	0	1	11	0
Grimshaw, 1b	0	1	11	0	Gleason, 3b	0	0	0	1
Ferris, 2b	0	0	3	3	Koehler, cf	0	1	1	0
Criger, c	0	0	9	0	Spencer, c	0	0	7	2
Young, p	0	0	0	6	Howell, p	0	1	0	7
Totals	2	4	27	12	Totals	0	6	27	16

Line Score				
Boston	200	000	000	2-4-0
St. Louis	000	000	000	0-6-2

2BH	Stone	DP	Ferris, Parent, Grimshaw; Collins, Grimshaw
3BH	Collins	BB	Howell 4, Young 1
SH	Frisk	K	Howell 7, Young 9
SB	Parent	E	Rockenfield, Wallace

You may have noticed that Young and Howell had a hand in 29 of the 54 put-outs in that glittering pitching exhibition in the Mound City, 16 by way of strike-outs and another 13 by throwing out baserunners. For the two it was business as usual, as with the successful twirlers of the deadball era. Spitball (Howell's) and breaking ball pitchers (Young) kept infielders busy. Known today as groundball pitchers, they routinely went through nine innings with no more than ten balls hit over or through the infield. That, of course, put a premium on fifth infielder responsibilities, and Handsome Harry, as noted, took a backseat to none in this regard.

Howell's numbers occupy top ranking among pitchers all time, as, for example, his second place ranking in career chances per game (3.61), a number two position with his 2.84 assists per game, and number 59 with a career Earned Run Average of 2.74. Not always blessed with solid hitting and decent defensive support, he still managed to win 131 of his 277 decisions. One of those 131 victories came at the expense of Cy Young on August 8, 1901, when Howell, then with Baltimore (the franchise moved to New York for the 1903 season), slammed the door at Boston, throwing a seven-hit shutout at Young and Company, as he turned in his best effort during the 11-game series between the two pitchers.

The Young-Howell Log:

July 3, 1901	Boston 9, Baltimore 1	Young WP, Howell LP
August 5, 1901	Boston 3, Baltimore 1	Young WP, Howell LP
August 8, 1901	Baltimore 2, Boston 0	Howell WP, Young LP
July 29, 1903*	New York 15, Boston 14	Howell WP, Young LP

*Howell won this game in relief. The loss was charged to Young.

July 16, 1905	Boston 5, St. Louis 2	Young WP, Howell LP
August 29, 1905	Boston 2, St. Louis 0	Young WP, Howell LP
May 14, 1906	St. Louis 11, Boston 1	Howell WP, Young LP
July 14, 1906	St. Louis 3, Boston 1	Howell WP, Young LP
June 17, 1907	Boston 3, St. Louis 1	Young WP, Howell LP

On April 18, 1901, in the first meeting between Young and Howell, Baltimore beat Boston, 12 to 6, as Howell went the route and Young appeared in relief without a decision.

On July 10, 1903, Boston beat New York, 10 to 5. Young was the winning pitcher. Howell had a no-decision game, appearing in relief.

Cy Young versus Joe McGinnity (1871–1929)

McGinnity was elected to the Baseball Hall of Fame in 1946

When John J. McGraw stormed out of the American League in 1902 to resume his National League career as the Giants' manager, the Iron Man left with him. That ended, after only two engagements, what might have been a series of most interesting duels between Cy and Joe McGinnity. The two first met as American Leaguers on April 28 at Baltimore (they were also Senior Circuit competitors in 1899 and 1900), where Boston's Chick Stahl clubbed two triples to lead the Pilgrims to a 7 to 3 victory over the Orioles. The final encounter ran afoul of a McGraw tantrum that finally ended in Umpire Tom Connolly's ejection of the fiery Oriole commander, and a forfeit of what was at that point a 9 to 4 game in the eighth inning, with Boston ahead. As a result, Young emerged from the two games with a 2–0 record.

"The Iron Man," Joe McGinnity.

The Young-McGinnity Log:

April 28, 1902	Boston 7, Baltimore 3	Young WP, McGinnity LP
June 28, 1902	Game forfeited to Boston, 9 to 0	Young WP, McGinnity LP

Cy Young versus John "Happy Jack" Chesbro (1874–1931)
Chesbro was elected to the Baseball Hall of Fame in 1946

Before the well ran dry in 1908, Jack Chesbro put together a compact but exceptional run at the record book, winning almost 200 games within a ten year span. A master spitballer, he turned in three consecutive 20-game seasons before capping his Hall of Fame career with a monster year that carried the New York Highlanders to within a spitball pitch of the 1904 pennant. The well chronicled game, played at Boston (Big Bill Dinneen, not Cy Young, was Chesbro's mound foe that fateful day) at the close of the season, broke the hearts of New Yorkers and, poignantly, of Chesbro himself, as the Pilgrims' Lou Criger, Cy Young's favorite receiver, tallied the winning run on "the spitball that got away."

There was, of course, much more than that single, albeit disastrous game, to the stocky hurler's career, especially those critically important New York–Boston games that set off one of the most famous American League rivalries. It should be noted that it was Jack Chesbro who shut down the Pilgrims only two days before the disastrous afternoon of October 10, by a 3 to 2 score, allowing Boston only four hits in an equally crucial spine-tingler. That one was his 41st—and record-setting—conquest of the season. The game was also fairly representative of the Young-Chesbro matches, usually won by the fellow they called Happy Jack.

After dropping his first encounter in 1903 with Young, a decisive 6 to 1 loss in the first game of a Highland Park twinbill, Chesbro bounced back after two 1903 no-decisions, in which the teams split, to open his fantastic 1904 record-setter with an 8 to 2 win

Master Spitballer Jack Chesbro.

over Boston at New York. From that point on, Happy Jack had far the better of it, beating Boston's ace in the hole four out of their last five meetings. That upped his career record to 5 and 2 against one of baseball's greatest.

On May 9, 1908, Young and Chesbro opposed one another for the last time in a Boston thriller that the Yankees won, 2 to 1, marking the fourth time in their nine-game series that the winning team had squeaked out a one-run victory. This one was, for all practical purposes, over in the second inning when New York got to Cy for a pair of tallies and Boston closed out the inning with a singleton. The story of the game was told in the opening paragraph of the *New York Times'* coverage:

> Getting away in the second inning to a good start the Yankees [ed: a.k.a. Highlanders at that point in the franchises history] to-day inflicted the second consecutive defeat on the Boston team and retained their lead in the American League championship race. As though to emphasize their victory, the visitors took the measure of "Cy" Young, the veteran twirler. It was his first defeat this year, and he "died hard" fighting against an adverse fate up to the last. It was not as much the superiority of their playing that won for the Yankees as their ability to make their hits count at opportune times. Young outpitched Chesbro, but the latter was fortunate in keeping the hits well distributed.

The Young-Chesbro Log

July 23, 1903	Boston 6, New York 1	Young WP, Chesbro LP
April 14, 1904	New York 8, Boston 2	Chesbro WP, Young LP
June 25, 1904	New York 5, Boston 3	Chesbro WP, Young LP
April 14, 1906	New York 2, Boston 1	Chesbro WP, Young LP
June 22, 1907	Boston 12, New York 2	Young WP, Chesbro LP
August 27, 1907	New York 5, Boston 1	Chesbro WP, Young LP
May 9, 1908	New York 2, Boston 1	Chesbro WP, Young LP

On July 25, 1903, Boston beat New York 7 to 5 (Young, WP in relief), and Chesbro received a no-decision in his appearance and on July 29, 1903, in a game won by New York, 15 to 14, Chesbro relieved but received no-decision, and Young was the LP.

Cy Young versus Christopher "Christy" or "the Big Six" Mathewson (1880–1925)

Mathewson was elected to the Baseball Hall of Fame in 1936

The only meeting between "the Big Six" and "Cy" Young, two of the three titans (the three include Young, Alexander and Mathewson) among National League hurlers, occurred on September 12, 1911, during the last weeks of Cy Young's star-studded career. The problem for Young, though pitching in front of partisan Boston fans, was that he was on the home lap of his career, a bit too beefy to maneuver with the youngsters in the game; and despite the magic of his name and pitching persona, there were no more miracles left in that once dominating right arm. There was another formidable complication: Christy Mathewson. Nonetheless, one can imagine the crowd stirring in anticipation of what turned out to be the only Mathewson-Young confrontation. Those who witnessed the spectacle at Boston's South End Grounds on a sun-splashed, late summer day knew exactly how singular the cut of this game would be, no matter the winner. Though it wasn't much of a game (the Giants disposed of the Old Master quickly, and probably mercifully, within the first two innings, Matty himself rubbing the salt deep with a run on the front end of a double steal), it did provide the fans that day — and the record book — with one of those priceless Hall of Fame match-ups baseball buffs savor.

Baseball idol Christy Mathewson.

A note on those last several weeks in the National League as Young closed out his career is in order. Waived by Cleveland in August of 1911, he made his first start on the 22nd against Cincinnati, only to find that the Redlegs, as well as others, were licking their chops at the prospect of facing the aged twirler. The Reds that day knocked Cy out of the box with an eight run splurge over the first three innings of the game. It was the first of five losses he sustained in the last six weeks of the campaign. But if the Senior Circuit clouters thought Young would go silently into the night, they were at least somewhat mistaken. He won his 511th and last game, still taking his regular turn right on down to the end of the season, on September 22 leading his Boston Rustlers (a.k.a. Braves in later years) to a choice, 1 to 0 victory over Pittsburgh. The win was one of four he fashioned in those last farewells to the National League and to baseball.

As for the legendary Mathewson, a more complete account follows just ahead when his brilliance will be reviewed against an array of NL worthies during his scintillating career.

Cy Young versus Guy "Doc" White (1879–1969)

Doc White was a multi-talented portsider who marched to his own drum beat, bedeviling hitters with a variety of pitches that came to the plate from sidearm and overhanded deliveries. This lefty was a control freak who, with all his breaking stuff, nonetheless managed to find the corners with maddening consistency, maneuvering around the big sticks with the precision of a college graduate with a major in medicine, which, by the by, was what Dr. White, a "Painless Parker" at the turn of the century, was. But the White portfolio also contained hit tunes, sermons for the "Sawdust Trail," an uncanny knack for a good business deal, a round of minor league managing and administrating on the executive level, as well as teaching and coaching. Phew! There's enough there for one of those colorful adventures just waiting to be written.

Alas, when the doctor was in, the Red Sox turned out to be rather ordinary "patients," and succumbed regularly to his wicked slants. So did Cy Young, who managed nary a win in five tries, though he did come awfully close in the very last encounter between the two in the midst of the nerve-wracking 1908 pennant race. On that occasion, the game, played on September 28, was decided by darkness rather than by either White or Young, and wound up in a 2 to 2 tie. Since it was the last time the two met, it closed out their record at 4 and 0 in favor of the Merry Troubadour, Guy White. Among all of the crack hurlers, Hall of Fame and otherwise, only the incomparable Mathewson was able to go undefeated against Young, and he, of course, met the Boston legend only once. With a few more 20-game seasons — there was only one, that 27 game, 1907 sparkler — Doc might well have been measured for a niche at Cooperstown. He was, all things considered, almost that good. Here are some of the reasons why: in August of 1906 he worked

Doc White, musician, dentist, poet, sawdust trail preacher and southpaw ace of the 1906 champs.

his way through 45 consecutive innings of scoreless baseball, winning a record-setting five straight shutouts while allowing but 18 base hits. That wasn't too much of a good thing either. You will undoubtedly remember that 1906 was the "Miracle on the South Side" year for the White Sox, and every win was a dire necessity as the Pale Hose stormed to the pennant on the wings of an improbable 19 game winning streak. It was during that same August, of course, that Doc ran up his record-setting skein.

There is more. A year later we find him running a string of 65 consecutive innings without issuing a base on balls. Then, too, the lean lefty finished his career with a miserly 2.39 ERA, good enough for a number 18 ranking, all time. And to cap the White achievements, it should be noted that he registered the highest single-season Clutch Pitching Index, 152.84[1] in 1904, in the game's history.

Small wonder Cy Young encountered serious difficulty in those White match-ups. We'll discover a bit later on that Big Ed Walsh was another of that Sox pitching staff who proved to be very, very bothersome. Between the two, they took the measure of Boston's, and later Cleveland's, number one, Mr. Young, with dismaying regularity.

The Young-White Log:

August 26, 1905	Chicago 2, Boston 1	White WP, Young LP
August 2, 1906*	Chicago 3, Boston 0	White WP, Young LP
August 17, 1906†	Chicago 4, Boston 3	White WP, Young LP
Sept 27, 1907‡	Chicago 4, Boston 2	White WP, Young ND
Sept 28, 1908§	Tie game, 2 to 2	(10 innings)

Cy Young versus Edward S. "Gettysburg Eddie" Plank (1876–1925)

Plank was elected to the Baseball Hall of Fame in 1946

Connie Mack's pitching staffs during the deadball era were the envy of the American League, blessed with uncommon wealth in savvy, natural abilities, depth and a bewildering array of styles and deliveries. The first two

---

*With this 3 to 0 shutout the White Sox began their 19-game winning streak.

†White relieved Frank Owen in this game at Boston, becoming the pitcher of record when the White Sox broke a 3 to 3 tie in the top of the ninth with the run that won the game.

‡Young relieved starting pitcher Harry Morgan, pitching the ninth inning. Morgan was the losing pitcher, having left the game with Boston behind, 3 to 2. Consequently, Young received a no-decision.

§In the air-tight 1908 pennant race, this tie game was crucial to the White Sox. It ended in a 2 to 2 tie, called because of darkness at Chicago's West Side Grounds. Young went the distance. White came into the game in the fourth inning and finished the game.

hurlers cut from that kind of cloth were both southpaws, Mack's "Odd Couple," the uninhibited free spirit, Rube Waddell, and the serious-minded Gettysburg College grad, Eddie Plank. They won regularly, shut the door on surging ball clubs and piled up 267 wins for the A's during their six seasons together in Philadelphia, winning 51 times alone in 1904 to make the Athletics the only team with a pair of left-handed, 25-plus winners in the 20th century.

Plank, notorious for his fussing and fidgeting between pitches, ran off four 20-game seasons in a row (1902–1905), added another in 1907, and two more for those Mack juggernauts of 1911 and '12. Out of 20 decisions, Plank and Waddell managed to break even at 10-10 with Young. During those 20 ball games the A's averaged one run better than Boston, and save one wild affair that resulted in a 22 to 8 win for the A's, in which both Young and Waddell appeared as relievers, the average score of the twenty Plank-Waddell and Young match-ups would have been 4 to 3. Moreover, in six of the Plank-Young duels the losing team mustered two runs or less in 11 meetings.

Connie Mack's ace portsider, "Gettysburg Eddie" Plank.

On September 10, 1904, Young and Plank hooked up in a 1 to 0 classic at Philadelphia, with over 14,000 in attendance who sat in on a thrilling, 13-inning heart-stopper. The game was won by Gettysburg Eddie himself with a rifle shot down the right field line, with two out, that scored the Athletics' second baseman, Danny Murphy. The box score of one of 1904's best ball games looked like this:

At Philadelphia, September 10, 1904

Boston	AB	H	PO	A	Philadelphia	AB	H	PO	A
Selbach, lf	5	1	1	0	Hartsel, lf	5	1	4	0
Parent, ss	5	0	2	5	Pickering, cf	5	0	0	1
Stahl, cf	5	0	1	0	Noonan, 1b	5	1	12	2
Collins, 3b	6	2	1	4	L. Cross, 3b	5	0	3	0
Freeman, rf	5	2	0	0	Seybold, rf	5	0	6	0
LaChance, 1b	5	0	19	0	Murphy, 2b	5	2	2	4

Ferris, 2b	5	2	2	7	M. Cross, ss	4	1	5	3
Criger, c	4	0	12	1	Powers, c	5	1	5	0
Young, p	5	0	0	4	Plank, p	5	1	1	5
Totals	46	7	38*	21	Totals	44	7	39	15

Line Score	Boston	000	000	000	000	0	0–7–0
	Philadelphia	000	000	000	000	1	1–7–3

2BH	Collins	BB	Plank 2, Young 0
3BH	Murphy	K	Plank 1, Young 12
SH	Stahl, M. Cross	Umpire	Connolly
DP	Murphy, Noonan	Time	2:15

Chicago's *Tribune* presented this short summary of the game:

> Philadelphia, Pa., Sept. 10:
>
> In the finest game seen on the local grounds this season the home team in thirteen innings defeated Boston by the score of 1 to 0. Plank won his own game. Murphy in the last inning singled, Monte Cross sacrificed, and Powers was retired at first. Plank hit a fast one over first base to the right field fence, Murphy scoring from second. Young struck out twelve men. Brilliant fielding characterized the game. Attendance, 14,404.

It only took one of Young's seven-hit allotment to ruin what looked like yet another whitewashing during a season in which he led the league with 10. Instead it became Plank's seventh in one of the best seasons of his distinguished career. And distinguished it was, showcasing an ERA of 2.90 or less in 15 of his 17 major league seasons. The final figure on his career ERA was 2.35, ranking him 13 on the all time charts. His career 287.7 Wins Above League5 earned an equally impressive number 18 ranking, and his stingy, .239 Opponents' BA ranks at 65. These are the kind of marks that make for winning in a big way, totaling, finally, 326 wins as against but 194 losses, a better than three out of five average.

Eddie Collins, who played alongside Gettysburg Eddie, said this about Plank: "He was not the fastest, not the trickiest, and not the possessor of the most stuff, but just the greatest." Perhaps not the greatest of them all, but a Hall of Famer among the top three lefties — all time.

The Young-Plank Log:

May 15, 1902	Boston 6, Philadelphia 2	Young WP, Plank LP
May 20, 1902	Boston 2, Philadelphia 1	Young WP, Plank LP
April 24, 1903	Boston 2, Philadelphia 1	Young WP, Plank LP

*Two out when winning run scored.

May 2, 1903	Philadelphia 3, Boston 0	Plank WP, Young LP
August 10, 1903	Boston 7, Philadelphia 2	Young WP, Plank LP
Sept 10, 1904	Philadelphia 1, Boston 0	Plank WP, Young LP
April 27, 1906	Philadelphia 3, Boston 0	Plank WP, Young LP
May 9, 1906	Philadelphia 9, Boston 6	Plank WP, Young LP
July 4, 1908	Boston 4, Philadelphia 3	Young WP, Plank LP
July 25, 1910	Cleveland 4, Philadelphia 3	Young WP, Plank LP

On April 20, 1903, Cy Young was the losing pitcher in a 10 to 7 loss to Philadelphia. Because Eddie Plank was knocked out of the box in the third inning of that game, Chief Bender, who came on in Plank's relief, got credit for the victory as the A's rallied to win.

Cy Young versus Adrian "Addie" Joss (1880–1911)
Joss was elected to the Baseball Hall of Fame in 1978

About the only way a pitcher can improve on a one-hitter is to throw a no-hitter, and Addie Joss did it. Twice. His one-hitter came on the day he debuted as a Cleveland Indian on April 26, 1902, against the St. Louis Browns. That left the young man from Woodland, Wisconsin, a pretty tough act to follow, but the long-armed curve-ball pitcher worked his way through the American League's second season with enough solid pitching to move to the head of Cleveland's pitching corps. By 1905 he was a 20-game winner, and on October 2, 1908, he took on Chicago's ace, Big Ed Walsh, in a white-hot pennant chase that came down to the last day of the season. That was the day Joss picked to turn up the heat a few degrees more with a perfect game that beat the White Sox 1 to 0. The followup to his one-hitter in 1902 took a while in coming, but when it did, it was a masterpiece. That no-no was followed by another in 1910, again at the expense of the Pale Hose.

There were far more than enough low-hit, low-scoring games in Joss' career to mark his candidacy for the Hall of Fame. His career, halted by his untimely death in 1911, was destined to be reckoned as worthy of enshrine-

Cleveland's superb Addie Joss.

ment despite not having met the requisite number of seasons (10) for eligibility. Because some of his numbers border on the unbelievable, and, further, because tubercular meningitis cut short his stellar career, the Veterans Committee, in 1978, finally waived the 10-year requirement and elected him to the Hall.

During the last five Young-Joss matchups the losing team managed to score only five times, with "Addie" coming out on the long end four times. In his seven winning games he allowed Boston batsmen to run up but nine tallies while shutting them out 2 to 0 in 1907 and then 1 to 0 in the last game featuring a Cy Young confrontation, on September 17, 1908.

Two feature games are included from the Joss-Young log. The first, played in the town that hosted the first National Association game in 1871, Fort Wayne, Indiana, was an 11-inning thriller that Boston won, 3 to 1. The second was Joss' brilliant whitewashing of the Young forces as the Indians pushed over a run in the ninth to win 1 to 0 in the last of the great moundsmen's encounters, in 1908. The Fort Wayne box score follows:

At Fort Wayne, Indiana, August 31, 1902

Cleveland	R	H	PO	A	Boston	R	H	PO	A
Bay, cf	0	0	4	0	Dougherty, lf	0	3	2	0
Bradley, 3b	0	3	1	2	Stahl, cf	0	1	2	0
Lajoie, 2b	1	0	2	8	Gleason, 3b	0	1	0	0
Hickman, 1b	0	2	12	0	Freeman, rf	0	0	1	0
Flick, rf	0	0	1	0	Parent, ss	1	1	6	5
McCarthy, lf	0	2	4	0	LaChance, 1b	0	1	14	1
Gochnauer, ss	0	0	3	4	Ferris, 2b	1	4	0	7
Wood, c	0	1	6	0	Criger, c	0	0	7	1
Joss, p	0	0	0	2	Young, p	1	1	1	0
Totals	1	8	33	16	Totals	3	12	33	14

Line Score	Cleveland	100	000	000	00	1–8–3
	Boston	000	010	000	02	3–12–0

2BH	Hickman, Ferris 2, McCarthy 2, Wood, Dougherty		
3BH	Ferris, Bradley	BB	Joss 2, Young 0
SH	Lajoie, Criger	K	Joss 4, Young 7
SB	Stahl, Criger, Ferris	Umpire	Connolly
DP	Lajoie and Gochnauer; Parent and LaChance	Time	2:00

A pitcher capable of posting ERAs under the 2.00 mark will never be out of work. That kind of pitching fetches serious money, the kind Pedro Martinez was paid for his 1.74 ERA in 2000. But observe, please, that in a nine-year, 2,327-inning career, Addie Joss logged a 1.84 ERA, limiting AL ball clubs to less than two earned runs per game five times, and registering a career low of 1.16 in 1908. And his career Ratio[6] stat, a gaudy 8.9, will in all likelihood never be surpassed. Further, Joss was one of the game's finest fielding pitchers, ranking number one, all time, in Assists per Game (3.47), number two in Chances Accepted per Game (3.47) and number three in Total Chances per Game (3.51). Add to all of that his perfect game against the White Sox on October 2, 1908 (he put another no-hitter into the record books on April 20, 1910), and one is left wondering why it took until 1978 for Hall of Fame electors to give him the nod.

Cy Young joined the Indians for the 1909 season, thus bringing to an end the afternoons that featured those classic Joss-Young match-ups. There were 12 in all, each one a complete game effort, winding up in Addie Joss' favor, 7 to 5.

The Young-Joss Log:

June 5, 1902	Boston 3, Cleveland 2	Young WP, Joss LP
June 17, 1902	Cleveland 4, Boston 3	Joss WP, Young LP
August 1, 1902	Cleveland 6, Boston 3	Joss WP, Young LP
August 31, 1902	Boston 3, Cleveland 1	Young WP, Joss LP
May 13, 1903	Cleveland 2, Boston 1	Joss WP, Young LP
July 15, 1903	Boston 4, Cleveland 3	Young WP, Joss LP
July 16, 1904	Boston 13, Cleveland 3	Young WP, Joss LP
Sept 3, 1904	Cleveland 9, Boston 1	Joss WP, Young LP
July 24, 1906	Boston 5, Cleveland 1	Young WP, Joss LP
July 10, 1907	Cleveland 2, Boston 0	Joss WP, Young LP
Sept 20, 1907	Cleveland 4, Boston 1	Joss WP, Young LP
Sept 17, 1908	Cleveland 1, Boston 0	Joss WP, Young LP

Cy Young versus Wabash George Mullin (1880–1944)

The pitching prowess and significant achievements of George Mullin seem to have faded away on the brittle pages of baseball history. Not even in the Motor City, where he remains one of the winningest hurlers in Tiger history to this very day (he's second, with 209 W's, to George "Hooks" Dauss, another of those relatively unheralded yet accomplished pitchers of bygone days), is the name of George Mullin, the burly righthander from Wabash, Indiana, mentioned. And yet here was another of those pitching staff aces who was at the forefront of pennant-winning teams. During Detroit's three-year run atop the Junior Circuit in 1907, '08 and '09, he won 20, then 17, and finally, in 1909, put together a 29 and 8 season that had American League swatsmiths eating out of his hand. That was particularly true in Boston, and no less than Cy Young found the Detroiter a particularly tough competitor.

Burly George Mullin, star hurler for the 1907-08-09 Tigers.

Only once in 13 meetings between the two did the losing team (on that occasion it was Cleveland, for whom Young pitched in 1909) score as many as four runs, and that was in a game that Detroit tied in the seventh and won at the expense of reliever Fred "Cy" Falkenberg, who took over for Young, 5 to 4. Thrice, Young permitted only one Tiger to score, and Mullin did it twice, the final such score registered in a 2 to 1 nail-biter at Detroit during a crucial game in the 1909 pennant race on September 11 that featured a game-saving, barehanded stab, with the bases loaded, by second-sacker Jim Delehanty.

During that 1909 pennant race Mullin faced Young five times, besting Cleveland's slab ace four times, each tilt resulting in a complete game effort for Wabash George, something he did more often than any other Tiger hurler, ringing up 336 in a 14-year career at Detroit. His complete game totals between 1904 and 1907 — 42 in 1904, and 35 each in '05, '06 and '07 — rank among Detroit's top five in a single season; and over the course of 14 seasons with the Tiges' Mr. Mullin logged more complete games than any other Detroit hurler: 336.

He wasn't a Hall of Famer, but George Mullin was a tough nut to crack during the latter stages of Cy Young's career. And Cy Young knew it. They crossed swords 13 times, Young victorious in five of the encounters, and Mullin in seven of them, allowing but two runs per winning effort.

The Young-Mullin Log:

July 18, 1903	Boston 5, Detroit 3	Young WP, Mullin LP
July 5, 1904	Detroit 4, Boston 3	Mullin WP, Young LP
July 19, 1906	Detroit 6, Boston 1	Mullin WP, Young LP
July 26, 1907	Boston 3, Detroit 1	Young WP, Mullin LP
August 15, 1908	Boston 4, Detroit 3	Young WP, Mullin LP
April 28, 1909	Detroit 8, Cleveland 1	Mullin WP, Young, LP

June 29, 1909	Detroit 3, Cleveland 2	Mullin WP, Young LP
July 3, 1909	Cleveland 4, Detroit 1	Young WP, Mullin LP
July 28, 1909	Detroit 5, Cleveland 4	Mullin WP, Young LP
Sept 10, 1909	Detroit 2, Cleveland 1	Mullin WP, Young LP

Young and Mullin met three times before the first game recorded above. On July 28, 1902, in their first meeting, Boston beat Detroit 8 to 1. Mullin (ND) relieved starter Joe Yeager (LP). Young went the distance for the victory. On August 18, 1902, the two teams played to a 4–4 tie, both Mullin and Young turning in complete games without a decision. On June 9, 1903, Detroit beat Boston 9 to 3. Mullin (WP) defeated starter George Winter, who was relieved by Young (ND) in the second inning and finished the game.

Cy Young versus Mordecai Centennial "Three Finger" or "Miner" Brown (1876–1948)

Brown was elected to the Baseball Hall of Fame in 1949

Mordecai Brown was the last Hall of Famer "Cy" Young faced during his career. The historic matchup took place on September 25, 1911, when a soggy day in Chicago provided the backdrop for a scheduled doubleheader that, because of wet grounds that were worked over by the grounds crew at the old West Side Park right up until game time, wound up being a single game. The *New York Times* inserted this note in its coverage of the game:

> Cy Young, the veteran pitcher, worked for Boston, pitching his first game on the West Side grounds, and got a warm reception from the small crowd.

In the only match-up between these two Hall of Fame luminaries, Cy went all the way, finally losing the game in the ninth when Chicago's defending National League champs pushed across a run to win the game by a 6 to 5 count. Surviving a three-run first, the old Boston veteran settled down while his teammates managed to tie the score at four with a two-run fifth.

The Braves tied the score with a run in the top of the ninth as they rallied to dispose of Leonard "King" Cole, who in 1910 had run up a 20 and 4 log in his rookie year. Cole appeared in relief of starter Lew Richie. When the Braves frisked the King for a tying run, manager Frank Chance called on Three Finger to quell the Braves' surge, and he did, picking the Save as the Cubs coaxed home the winning run with one out in the bottom of the ninth.

In terms of Cy Young's fabulous career, the loss was his 312th. Just four days before his Chicago loss, Young had brushed aside Babe Adams and the Pirates in a 1 to 0 game, reminiscent of his earlier days, that put career whitewash number 76 in the record book (the shutout spots Young at number four behind Johnson [110], Alexander [90], and Mathewson [79]). One more disappointment, on October 6, at the hands of Brooklyn, would close out the loss column at 313, a number that ranks right at the top of the list in the game's history. But then, there would also be 511 wins, light years removed from his nearest challenger, Walter Johnson, who won 417 — still a stunning number, yet almost 100 shy of the Master's orbital total.

As for Mordecai Brown, the appearance against Denton True Young makes for a glossy portfolio credential, if only for a passing moment on a heavy weather day in the Windy City. Although it lasted only for an inning, it did provide the few West Side faithful who attended the game that day with a one-of-a-kind memory to pass along to the next generation. And a pretty good one at that!

Cy Young versus Charles Albert "Chief" Bender (1884–1954)

Bender was elected to the Baseball Hall of Fame in 1953

His first name was Charles but he didn't use it, preferring Albert. His nickname was Chief, stemming from his Chippewa background, and although he was polite about it, he didn't acknowledge that, either. Instead, he autographed baseballs and scorecards Albert Bender. Nevertheless, the baseball world always has, and no doubt always will refer to Connie Mack's number one money pitcher — and respectfully — as Chief Bender.

Albert Bender. Mr. Mack called him Albert; the players called him Chief.

Bender, who came along in 1903 to complete an incredible Hall of Fame threesome (Eddie Plank came first in 1901 and Rube Waddell followed in 1902), was Plank's lefthanded counterpart, a brainy, cunning curveball pitcher whose forte seemed to be low-hit, pressure-packed wins when Mack's A's needed them most. In fact, the venerable Philadelphia manager was quoted in the 1989, 50th Anniversary Hall of Fame Yearbook as saying: "If I had all the men I've ever handled and they were in their prime and there was one game I wanted to win above all others, Albert would be my man."

Aside from the two White Sox stars Doc White and Big Ed Walsh, none gave Cy Young a tougher afternoon than Chief Bender. The two went at it eight times over a five-season spread, and Young was fortunate to come away with a pair of victories, one of them in relief (on May 29, 1907, when he entered the game for the ninth inning after the Red Sox put up a five-spot to edge ahead of the Athletics). That chased Bender after he had shut them out through the first eight innings of play, enabling Young to come on for the win. But there were those other times. The Chief shut down the Boston attack regularly as the two teams battled one another during the early 1900s, when first Philadelphia, in 1902, then Boston in 1903 and 1904, and then the Mackmen again in 1905, were routinely running atop the league. The feature attraction from among the Young-Bender duels, each of which was a miniature clinic of its own, is a Bender victory at Philadelphia on June 26, 1906. The game hinged on one pitch in the bottom of the seventh that was undoubtedly not where Cy wanted to put it, and Captain Harry Davis jumped on it for a two-run homer that put Bender in the winner's circle, 3 to 1. The box score follows.

Boston at Philadelphia, June 26, 1906

Boston	R	H	PO	A	Philadelphia	R	H	PO	A
Parent, ss	0	1	1	4	Hartsel, lf	1	2	2	0
Stahl, cf	1	1	3	0	Lord, cf	1	2	3	0
Freeman, 1b	0	1	8	1	Davis, 1b	1	1	6	2
Selbach, lf	0	1	1	0	Seybold, rf	0	3	1	0
Ferris, 2b	0	0	4	2	Murphy, 2b	0	2	2	3
Hayden, rf	0	0	2	0	Schreckengost, c	0	0	7	1
Morgan, 3b	0	1	0	2	Cross, ss	0	1	5	1
Armbruster, c	0	0	5	1	Knight, 3b	0	1	0	3
Young, p	0	0	0	1	Bender, p	0	1	1	0
Totals	1	5	24	11	Totals	3	13	27	10

Line Score	Boston	000	100	000	1–5–0
	Philadelphia	000	010	20x	3–13–2

2BH	Bender
3BH	Hartsel
HR	Davis
SB	Selbach, Lord
SH	Davis, Freeman
LOB	Boston 5, Philadelphia 9
DP	Cross, Murphy and Davis
K	Young 4, Bender 6
BB	Young 0, Bender 2
Umpires	Hurst and Connor
Time	1:50

On May 12, 1910, Chief Bender threw a no-hitter at the Indians as Cy Young and his teammates watched Freddy Link absorb a 4 to 0 masterpiece. The game featured Bender's famous "nickel curve," which he had been using more regularly from the 1908 season forward. Initially, the pitch caused quite a stir. It wasn't a fastball, though it approached the plate at a pretty good clip. And it wasn't a hard-breaking curveball. It was "somewhere in between," and served the A's' top righthander well, helping him to drop his ERA to a microscopic 1.75 in 1908, followed by a 1.66 in 1909 and a career-low 1.58 in 1910. The final reading on his career ERA was 2.46, earning him a number 23 ranking, all time. One of baseball's more cerebral pitchers, he recorded a spectacular 17 and 3 record for the pennant-winning Athletics in 1914. His winning percentage of .850 that season is a solid 19th in the record book.

The Young-Bender series was, in truth, a Bender show, the tall A's righthander winning five times against a single defeat. That's often the way things went, no matter his foe. His enshrinement at the Hall took place in 1953 and testifies to his impressive achievements.

The Young-Bender Log:

April 20, 1903	Philadelphia 10, Boston 7	Bender WP, Young LP
August 6, 1903	Philadelphia 4, Boston 3	Bender WP, Young LP
April 14, 1905	Philadelphia 3, Boston 2	Bender WP, Young LP
July 7, 1905	Philadelphia 2, Boston 1	Bender WP, Young LP
June 26, 1906	Philadelphia 3, Boston 1	Bender WP, Young LP
May 30, 1907	Boston 6, Philadelphia 4	Young WP, Bender LP

On June 22, 1904, Boston beat Philadelphia 7 to 5, as Young (WP) defeated Rube Waddell, who started. Bender relieved Waddell (ND).

On September 14, 1907, in the last encounter between Young and Bender, both started and were relieved. With a run in the seventh inning, the A's won, 7 to 6. Jimmy Dygert got the win and Charles "Tex" Pruiett got the loss.

Cy Young versus Big Ed Walsh (1881–1959)
Walsh was elected to the Baseball Hall of Fame in 1946

Between them, Doc White and Ed Walsh made life miserable for Cy Young. Young managed but one conquest of Chicago's Pale Hose, losing 10 times to the two crack White Sox hurlers. The only victory Young managed to wrestle from the two came in a 14 inning gem in which he beat the Sox 2 to 1 on August 7, 1907. It marked the first time Walsh was used in a Boston-Chisox game. Young went the route that day, and Walsh entered the game in the eighth inning, relieving Nick Altrock. Big Ed must have remembered that day because the next time around he shut the door on the Carmine, firing a five-hit shutout. Then came one of those games that brought out the famous

1. Cy Young

Manager Ray Schalk called on his old friend and battery mate Big Ed Walsh (right) in 1928 to come back to the White Sox to coach the pitchers, one of whom was Walsh's son, Ed Jr.

Walsh strut as he mesmerized the Cleveland Indians with a one-hitter on June 20, 1909. It was his fourth straight over Cleveland's ancient mariner. Walsh went on to beat Young twice more, the finale coming during Cy's last American League days, on June 30, 1911, in Cleveland, as the Sox touched up Young for eight big ones, providing Walsh with his sixth victory in seven tries overall.

There was, however, a last-laugh scenario for Cy Young, and it came some 20 years after that 8 to 1 loss in Cleveland. This one was sheer entertainment, without the pressures of a pennant race. It was, in fact, one of those all-star classics, a gathering of old timers who somehow managed to get through nine innings without any drastic effect on either their weary bones or baseball psyche. The game was billed as a charity game benefiting crippled children. Played in Boston on September 7, 1930, the dream-teams—one the All Bostons, and the other the All Stars—squared off at Fenway Park with two of the game's greatest, Cy Young and Big Ed Walsh, starting on the mound. The old fellow, by this time 63 but still willing, disposed of the All Stars in the top of the first inning without permitting a run. Boston fans had seen that before, of course, and roared their approval.

In the bottom half of the opening stanza the All Bostons got to Big Ed, by this time 49, but also in decent shape by virtue of his coach's position with the White Sox, for two runs. The official scorer had seen enough. The old feller would be declared the winning pitcher if the All Bostons could hang on and beat the All Stars. The baseball gods had undoubtedly decreed that this was to be Cy's Day, and the All Bostons won 8 to 4. Walsh also went the second inning, but Young knew a good thing when he saw it and left as the winner, having warmed the hearts of his many fans once again. Here's the box score of that star-studded game:

At Boston, September 7, 1930

All Stars	AB	R	H	PO	All Bostons	AB	R	H	PO
Cobb, cf	3	0	0	2	Hooper, rf	5	1	3	3
Paskert, cf	2	0	0	0	J. Collins, 3b	1	1	0	2
Clarke, cf	2	1	1	1	Gardner, 3b	2	0	0	0
Oldring, lf	2	0	0	2	Engle, 3b	1	0	1	0
Strunk, lf	1	0	0	2	Yerkes, 3b	2	1	2	0
E. Collins, 2b	1	0	1	0	Speaker, cf, 2b	5	1	3	3
Evers, 2b	1	0	0	0	Lewis, lf	4	2	3	2
Wagner, ss	2	0	1	0	Parent, ss	2	0	2	0
Baker, 3b	4	0	0	0	Janvrin, ss	3	0	0	2
Bradley, 2b	1	0	1	0	LaChance, 1b	1	0	0	1
McInnis, 1b	3	2	0	2	Tenney, 1b	1	0	1	1
Altrock, 1b	1	0	0	5	Hoblitzell, 1b	3	0	0	11
Bransfield, 1b	1	0	0	1	Ferris, 2b	1	0	0	0
Roush, rf	3	1	2	0	Sweeney, 1b	1	1	0	1
Mann, rf	2	0	1	0	Shean, 2b	2	0	1	0
Barry, ss	3	0	2	2	Carrigan, c	0	0	0	0
Archer, c	2	0	0	2	Madden, c	0	0	0	0
Bresnahan, c	1	0	1	2	Gowdy, c	1	0	1	1
Mitchell, c	0	0	0	0	Young, p	0	0	0	0
Walsh, p	1	0	1	0	Dinneen, p	0	0	0	0
Coombs, p	1	0	1	0	Rudolph, p	1	0	1	0
Doyle, 2b	2	0	0	2	Wood, p, cf	1	0	0	0
Tesreau, p	1	0	0	1	Tyler, p	1	1	1	0
Bender, p	0	0	0	0	Bedient, p	1	0	0	0
					Freeman, ph	1	0	0	0
					Donovan, ph	1	0	1	0
					Hendrickson, ph	1	0	0	0
					Duffy, ph	1	0	0	0
					Cobb, ph*	1	0	0	0
Totals	40	4	12	24	Totals	44	8	20	27

Line Score				
All Stars	012	010	000	4–14–1
All Bostons	203	000	30x	8–20–2

*Ty Cobb pinch hit for Dave Shean, thus playing for both teams.

2BH	Mann, Lewis 2, Parent, Gowdy
SB	McInnis, Speaker
DP	McGinnis, Barry and Archer
WP	Young
LP	Walsh
Umpires	Beardon, Moran and Hart

It wasn't always "Hail the Conquering Hero" where Ed Walsh, sometimes called the Big Moose, was concerned. Dick Lindberg, in his story of the White Sox, entitled Stealing First in a Two-Team Town, had this insightful comment about one of the Sox' greatest heroes:

> Comiskey reeled in the biggest prize of them all in 1904 when pitcher Ed Walsh was invited to spring camp in Marlin Springs, Texas. Ed Walsh had toured Wilkes Barre, Newark, and Meridian with little success. His lack of physical conditioning, and an exaggerated pitching windup that allowed opposing players to run the bases at will made this big Irishman from the Pennsylvania coal fields an amusing if not eccentric sight to behold. What saved Walsh from oblivion was his mastery of the spit ball, or "eel ball" as it was then known.

Once his spitter came into play, the course was set on a direct line to Cooperstown. Along the way was that barely believable 1908 season, studded with outlandish numbers like 40 victories, representing 45.5 percent of his team's total wins; 464 innings pitched, including a doubleheader victory over Young's Boston club by scores of 5 to 1 and 2 to 0; and a 1.42 ERA for the season, one of six such sub-2.00 seasons that helped put him on top of the hurler's heap with a career 1.82 ERA, better even than his friend Addie Joss's, whose 1.89 ranks behind Walsh's pace-setting mark. Between 1906 and 1912 he posted seven straight seasons of less-than-10 Ratio readings (his career Ratio mark is 9.2). Those are the kind of records that made for some of those long Young-Walsh afternoons, at least from Cy's vantage point.

The Young-Walsh Log:

August 7, 1907	Boston 2, Chicago 1	Young WP, Walsh LP
June 20, 1908	Chicago 1, Boston 0	Walsh WP, Young LP
August 22, 1908	Chicago 7, Boston 6	Walsh WP, Young LP
May 9, 1909	Chicago 4, Cleveland 2	Walsh WP, Young LP
June 20, 1909	Chicago 4, Cleveland 0	Walsh WP, Young LP
May 30, 1910	Chicago 4, Cleveland 3	Walsh WP, Young LP
June 30, 1911	Chicago 8, Cleveland 1	Walsh WP, Young LP

Cy Young versus Walter Johnson

Johnson was elected to the Baseball Hall of Fame in 1936

Walter Johnson, just one year deep into his legendary career, was matched against "Cy" Young in a relief role on September 1, 1908. In that game Boston took the measure of Washington's Senators, 7 to 3, as Young

Walter Johnson.

went the route, defeating Jesse "Powder" Tannehill, who had started the season as one of Young's stablemates. Another Johnson appearance against Young came in a game played at Cleveland on June 4, 1910. At that point Cy was bearing down on his 500th victory, which came a few weeks later in an 11 inning game at Washington (Johnson didn't pitch in this game) on July 19, as he beat the Senators with a complete game, 5 to 2 win, the loss going to reliever Bob Groom.

The June 4, 1910, matchup was a different story. Walter Johnson, in this appearance against Young, turned in a complete game, beating the Indians 8 to 2 in a game that was nip and tuck through seven innings. At that point, with the Senators ahead 3 to 2, Young left. His reliever, Fred Link, a lefty whose major league career consisted of the 1910 season, was welcomed with a six-run barrage that put the game away for the Senators.

Although those two encounters marked the only times the two icons met, it was nonetheless historic. Walter Johnson was still talking about his victory over Cy Young, in his own humble way, years later. Those fortunate to have been there no doubt remembered — and treasured — that day, as well.

Cy Young versus Grover "Pete" Alexander (1887–1950)

Alexander was elected to the Baseball Hall of Fame in 1937

Closing out a brilliant freshman campaign in which he stunned the National League with league-leading numbers in wins (28), innings pitched (367) and shutouts (7), Pete Alexander was paired with the Boston Braves' Cy Young on September 7, 1911, during Young's last days in the major leagues. It was one of those young-bucks-against-the-old-man games, and it was all that the young Phillies phenom could handle. It wasn't until the eighth inning that a run was scored, and it proved to be the only tally in the game as both twirlers cut

Peter Alexander.

down the hitters with monotonous regularity. Unfortunately for the elderly Boston hero, the run that was scored belonged to Philadelphia. And probably just as significant was Alex's whitewashing, his seventh of the season, crafted on the strength of a sparkling one-hitter. This ball game, too, was "one for the books!" The box score follows.

At Boston, September 7, 1911

Philadelphia	AB	R	H	PO	Boston	AB	R	H	PO
Knabe, 2b	4	0	0	2	Ingerton, 2b	4	0	0	2
Paskert, cf	4	1	1	2	Bridwell, ss	3	0	0	3
Lobert, 3b	3	0	1	1	Jackson, lf	3	0	0	2
Magee, lf	4	0	1	3	Donlin, cf	3	0	0	6
Beck, rf	4	0	1	0	Kaiser, cf	0	0	0	1
Luderus, 1b	4	0	2	13	Miller, rf	3	0	1	1
Walsh, ss	3	0	0	0	McDonald, 3b	3	0	0	1
Carter, c	3	0	0	6	Gowdy, 1b	3	0	0	8
Alexander, p	3	0	0	0	Tenney, 1b	0	0	0	1
					Rariden, c	3	0	0	2
					Young, p	2	0	0	0
					Flaherty, ph	1	0	0	0
Totals	32	1	6	27	Totals	28	0	1	27

Line Score				
Philadelphia	000	000	010	1-6-0
Boston	000	000	000	0-1-0

SB	Paskert, Lobert	K	Young 2, Alexander 7
LOB	Philadelphia 5, Boston 1	Umpires	Klem and Brennan
BB	Young 1, Alexander 0	Time	1:27

Cy Young versus Richard "Rube" Marquard

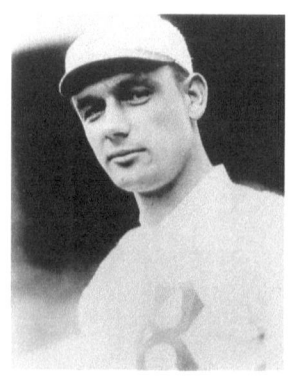

John McGraw's star lefty, Rube Marquard.

Marquard was elected to the Baseball Hall of Fame in 1971

Richard "Rube" Marquard debuted on September 25, 1908, hitting his stride in the 1911 season, when he won 24 games. By the time Cy Young had come back to the National League, only five playing dates between the Giants and Braves remained on the schedule. While the two were on the field of play at the same time, they did not pitch against one another during the two remaining 1911 series between the Giants and Braves. Marquard was much involved with Pete Alexander in a series of encounters that will receive attention when Alexander the Great's extraordinary exploits are reviewed later on.

The Award Has the Right Name

The top ten pitchers in the game, ranked according to TBE's Total Pitching Index, include two, Charles "Kid" Nichols and Cy Young, who stood astride the 19th and 20th centuries. Young, who ranks second only to the game's all time greatest pitcher, Walter Johnson, was such a remarkable hurler that even in his waning years he kept right on logging 20-game seasons, adding to that incredible, critical mass of superior numbers that occasioned naming the award for each season's best pitcher after him. And, blessing heaped upon blessing, he was a gentleman, an icon worthy of icon status among the nation's young and aspiring baseball players.

The Hall of Fame would not be the Hall of Fame without him — Denton True "Cy" Young.

He stood the test of a lot of time as pitchers and baseball careers go. That is not only an accomplishment in and of itself, it is also the very thing that enabled him to pile up one stellar statistic after another. Against an array of Hall of Famers, some of whom rank not all that far off the lofty Young and Johnson pace, he kept his head above water, sometimes winning, sometimes losing, but, as was his manner, persisting through the thick and thin of rallies and scoreless strings of innings, and surviving to take the mound yet another day in front of good, bad, indifferent and exceptional ball players, all of whom had a direct hand in his won-loss record at one time or another.

TBE, in its biographical sketches of the game's top 100 players, had this to say about Young:

How many Cy Youngs would Cy Young have won if the eponymous award had existed when he pitched? Various historians and statisticians have given estimates of three to six, but such assertions are based solely on numbers and ignore the human factor. Because Young was well liked, he might have been voted the award a couple of times even when he wasn't statistically the best pitcher in his league.

Humility in greatness. A rare commodity. That is what characterized Cy Young.

2. Christy Mathewson

Major League Career Totals:	Won	Lost	Pct.
New York (NL)	373	188	.665

Mathewson was elected to the Baseball Hall of Fame in 1936

All the good things said about Christy "Big Six" Mathewson, and there have been many, are true, and some of them are almost too good to be true. Nonetheless, any account of John McGraw's "son" begins there, taking his impeccable behavior, indomitable spirit, intelligence, superb athletic gifts and his decency into consideration. He was a man, in every sense and meaning of the word, who absolutely stood apart as a paragon among contemporaries given to a far more earthy, coarse approach to the game (McGraw himself a prime example)—and life.

However, in this particular review of baseball's pitching colossi, what Mathewson achieved as a pitcher is the prime concern. And, as in the case of Cy Young, the search for evidence of his preeminence inevitably winds up near the top of the all time charts. What makes Mathewson's accomplishments so awesome is the number of high rankings he logged in what amounted to 15 full seasons of major league pitching. He doesn't own a single number one ranking, but Mathewson's name appears regularly among the top ten in career statistics. Young, with 22 seasons; Alexander, with 19 full campaigns; and Johnson, with 20, quite obviously had an edge on the Big Six in longevity. Nonetheless, we find Mathewson in the number two spot in career Assists (1503), number four in Wins Above Team (64.9), tied for fourth in Ratio (9.6) and fifth in ERA at 2.13. These numbers form a rather solid base for making the Mathewson case as a complete pitcher. Those Ratio and Assist numbers make strong statements about his ability to keep men off the bases.

They called him "the Big Six"—Christy Mathewson.

Averaging less than 10 men on base per game reduces, radically, a team's scoring opportunities, and his Assist marks attest to his superior fielding abilities. At the top of his career, between 1905 and 1910, Matty was at or very near the top of the league in giving up the fewest number of hits per game. In fact, his 1909 record of 6.28 hits per game tied him with J. R. Richard (1978) for the 55th spot on the list. It is well to remember, further, that bases on balls, which usually bode evil for a pitcher's effectiveness in shutting down his opponents, play a big part in jeopardizing ERAs. For Christy Mathewson that was no problem. He gave up but 1.59 per game, good for a number 19 ranking all time. All of that makes for fewer runs per game and usually shows up in a pitcher's ERA. Matty's? A stingy 2.13 career mark, good for fifth behind Walsh (1.82); Addie Joss (1.89); Mordecai Brown (2.06), his arch enemy during the halcyon days of the Cubs and Giants; and John Ward (2.10), the famed Providence and Giant Hall of Famer of the 1880s and '90s.

The sampling of numbers above, which will be augmented as the Mathewson matchups with his contemporaries unfold, suffice at this point to suggest that those who opposed one of Pennsylvania's finest sons faced stern testing. Seven Hall of Famers (five more, treated as a unit—Amos Rusie, Burleigh Grimes, Joe McGinnity, Albert "Chief" Bender and Cy Young— are mentioned but didn't appear against Matty) and five other accomplished hurlers have been called on to test the mettle of Bucknell University's most famous baseball alum. The list once again is arranged in chronological order according to the debut dates of the pitchers.

Name/HOF Year	Debut/Career Yrs	TPI/All Time Pitcher Ranking
Charles "Kid" Nichols/1949	Apr 23, 1890/1890–1906	57.5/7(t)
Cy Young/1937	Aug 6, 1890/1890–1911	78.0/2
Jack Taylor	Sep 25, 1896/1896–1907	17.3/130(t)
George "Rube" Waddell/1946	Sep 8, 1897/1897–1910	24.4/69
Vic Willis/1995	Apr 20, 1898/1898–1910	21.2/88
Sam Leever	May 26, 1898/1898–1910	15.4/153(t)
Frank "Noodles" Hahn	Apr 18, 1899/1899–1906	16.0/148
Charles "Deacon" Phillippe	Apr 21, 1899/1899–1911	15.1/158(t)
Jack Chesbro/1946	Jul 12, 1899/1899–1910	10.9/238(t)
Mordecai Brown/1949	Apr 19, 1903/1903–1916	35.3/23
Ed Reulbach	May 16, 1905/1905–1917	17.8/124(t)
Richard "Rube" Marquard/1971	Sep 25, 1908/1908–1925	–2.3/NR
Grover Alexander/ 1938	Apr 15, 1911/1911–1930	64.6/3
Eppa Rixey/1963	Jun 21, 1912/1912–1933	26.6/57

HOF'ers who were in the NL during Mathewson's career but did not appear against him:

Amos Rusie/1963	May 9, 1889/1899–1901	39.8/16
Joe McGinnity/1946	Apr 18, 1899/1899–1908	18.8/113(t)
Albert "Chief" Bender/1953	Apr 20, 1903/1903–1925	14.4/170(t)
Burleigh Grimes/1964	Sep 10, 1916/1916–1934	23.7/74

Christy Mathewson versus Charles "Kid" Nichols (1869–1953)

Nichols was elected to the Baseball Hall of Fame in 1949

Was there ever a time in professional baseball when owners, GMs, players and managers were at peace and satisfied with the way player transactions, contracts, franchise affairs and especially salaries were handled? There may have been, but it would take some serious digging to come up with as much as even several months out of a single year to find peace and quiet in that stress and strife–laden part of the game.

One of the more spectacular instances of complete upheaval in the financial and business end of the game occurred in the 1889–90 formation of the Players League, which arose primarily out of the players' total dissatisfaction and rebellion regarding contracts that reduced them to chattels in the baseball marketplace. The story has been well documented, and the players did get a "league of their own," but it didn't last very long—one season, to be exact.

Into that cauldron of discontent and animosity came three young men. The first, Amos Rusie, debuted amid the recurring rumors that the players had "had it," and were going to do something about their shoddy treatment as professionals. He joined the New York Giants pitching staff in 1889. The second, Cy Young, was contracted by the Cleveland Spiders in 1890. The third, a young Wisconsinite, Charles Augustus Nichols, promptly renamed Kid because he still looked like a teenager, was signed by the Boston Beaneaters in 1890, thus completing a threesome of fireballing, Cooperstown-worthy hurlers who were kings of the hill in their respective franchises for years to come. Interestingly, all three signed National League contracts, bypassing the Players League.

300-game winner Kid Nichols, star righthander of the champion Boston Beaneaters, shown here at his Hall of Fame induction.

Kid Nichols didn't waste any time getting into high gear. He won 27 times in his rookie season, followed that with four straight 30-game seasons, and in each of his first five years twirled more than 400 innings. By the time he called it a day Nichols had pitched more than 5,000 innings (that spots him in the number 11 position all time), and had accomplished that in less than 15 full seasons of play. The final tally on his won-loss record, 361–208, put his winning percentage at .634, another top 25 mark, all time. Though most pitchers during the 1890–1910 era were called on to complete their games, Nichols' .9466 completion rate is really beyond herculean (532 completions in 562 career starts).

Boston's five pennant-winning seasons during the 1890s were fashioned largely on the strength of the Kid's dominant pitching. He logged 30-game seasons in each of those banner years, 30 in 1891, 35 in '92, 34 in '93, and 31 each in 1897 and '98. Two other 30-win seasons, which made seven all told, plus a pair of 20-win seasons, put his final 361 mark in the number six position all time. His Hall of Fame plaque came *after* those of pitchers the likes of Jack Chesbro, Joe McGinnity and Herb Pennock, who were undoubtedly stalwart worthies of the hill but not to be compared with the brilliance of "the Kid."

Each of the Nichols-Mathewson match-ups, save one, came during 1901, Matty's rookie season. The two dueled six times that year, Nichols winning three times and Matty twice, with an August 15 game ending in a 5 to 5 tie in the second game of a twin bill. In their first encounter, Mathewson emerged victorious in a tight 2 to 1 game, for his third major league victory. That was followed by the veteran Nichols' conquest of Mathewson in a 5 to 4 squeaker. Later that summer Nichols bested Matty again in a brilliantly pitched 3 to 0 whitewash that went into the tenth inning before a run was scored. Boston then pushed over the winning runs on Coogan's Bluff in the top of the tenth when Duff Cooley lined a double between VanHaltren and Selbach with the bases loaded.

On October 3, 1904, the two greats met one last time. The game, played at the Polo Grounds before a surprisingly scanty crowd, went to the bottom of the eighth before a Sam Mertes two-bagger drove home a pair of runs that overcame a 1 to 0 lead Boston had scraped together with a free pass, a sacrifice and a single in the sixth stanza, using the typical deadball era formula for scoring a run here and there. Unfortunately for Nichols, who had come out of retirement to pilot the St. Louis Cardinals in 1904, the Mertes double was all Mathewson needed to lock up his 33rd win of the campaign, a 3 to 1 victory. The loss was Nichols' 13th in his last season as a 20-game winner. By that time he had stashed away all the necessary credentials for a call from the Hall. For Matty, the long trail to Cooperstown was just underway.

The Mathewson-Nichols Log:

May 3, 1901	New York 2, Boston 1	Mathewson WP, Nichols LP
July 29, 1901	Boston 5, New York 4	Nichols WP, Mathewson LP

August 1, 1901	New York 9, Boston 8	Mathewson WP, Nichols LP
August 13, 1901	Boston 3, New York 0	Nichols WP, Mathewson LP
August 19, 1901	Boston 11, New York 6	Nichols WP, Mathewson LP
October 3, 1904	New York 3, Boston 1	Mathewson WP, Nichols LP

On August 15, 1901, Boston and New York played to a 5 to 5 tie in the second game of a doubleheader. The game was called after 11 innings due to darkness. Both Mathewson and Nichols pitched complete games.

In the August 1, 1901, game, Nichols relieved Bill Dinneen in the seventh inning, giving up three runs in the bottom of the ninth to lose the game, 9 to 8. Mathewson went the distance for New York.

Christy Mathewson versus John W. "Brakeman Jack" Taylor (1874–1938)

Connie Mack's Milwaukee Brewers wound up their 1898 Western League season in third place, principally because a young Ohioan, Jack Taylor, side-armed his way to a 28 and 14 record, winning the games Milwaukee needed most to stay on the heels of Kansas City's champions. Taylor's record that summer was bound to attract attention. Tommy Burns, Cap Anson's successor, who was in his first season as manager of the team they called the "Orphans" (because the Anson-less White Stockings seemed fatherless without their longtime fixture at the helm), led Chicago to a fourth place finish that year. He brought in Taylor to bolster his sagging pitching corps. That turned out to be a very bright move. Taylor promptly reeled off five complete-game victories to finish out the season, therewith starting out a 10-year career that was marked indelibly by the Taylor trademark — complete games.

Putting aside all the unsavory qualities that also marked his checkered career (he was involved in bribes, Chicago's night-life and with less than respectable companions), there is no gainsaying the fact that this fellow was a tower of pitching reliability. He could be counted on to finish what he started and did so 97 percent of the time. That translates to a mind-bending 279 completions in 287 career starts. It's the one — and usually only — thing for which he is remembered, if his name rings a bell at all.

Even though his career record of 152 wins against 139 losses smacks of pitching mediocrity, and certainly raises no Hall of Fame conjecture, there were those days, and sometimes entire years, that Brakeman Jack or Old Iron Arm, as he was variously called (he apparently worked as a railway line brakeman during the off-season, and Old Iron Arm is a rather obvious nickname) was a formidable if not daunting opponent on the mound. 1902 would be a striking example. During that season his league-leading marks in ERA (1.29) and Shutouts (8) helped keep Chicago's punchless Colts near the .500 mark. And he completed 34 of the (you guessed it) 34 games he started.

On June 13, 1901, Taylor was lifted in the fourth inning of a game against the Giants, which he lost 9 to 4. One week later he completed his next starting assignment and finished his next 187 starts in a row. It's a record that, one can safely say, will never, but never, be broken.

Had Taylor never encountered Christy Mathewson his record would have been much, much better. The two crossed swords 13 times, and Matty won 9 times. In five of those victories Mathewson meted out two or less runs, and on four occasions he beat Taylor by a single run, an indication that though Matty was the heavy-handed winner in their series, the

"Brakeman" Jack Taylor — he finished what he started.

Colts, Cardinals, and later Cubs teams behind Taylor might have put Taylor in the winning column more often had they been able to deal better with Mathewson's assortment of fadeaways, curves, 90 MPH speed and masterful control. But then, many another ball club and many another hurler was frustrated by that same combination. Matty could get downright ornery when his lead was threatened. He was the kind of pitcher, like Robin Roberts many years later, who had to be shelved in a hurry because he simply got stronger and more focused as the game progressed.

One game between the two was tossed out altogether because the Giants had put the May 7, 1902, game under a protest that was upheld by the National League front office. The protest was registered because Giant hitters complained that the mound was too close to home plate. A measurement after the game proved them right. The mound was only 58'6" from home plate. Jack Taylor had turned in a fine 4 to 0 shutout, victimizing both the Giants and Matty, that is, until they brought out the measuring stick. Mathewson was the ultimate winner even in that game, since the loss would never appear on his record.

The Giants also figured in Jack Taylor's last complete game in 1907, beating him 12 to 4. That was followed by a pair of appearances against the Cardinals in a September 2, 1907, doubleheader. Though he wasn't charged with a defeat in either game, he did pitch poorly enough to indicate to the Cubs that the Iron Arm had mined his last in the Bigs. His days of completing one ball game after another on a major league level were over, and he was released a few days later, finishing up his professional career in the minors.

The Mathewson-Taylor Log:

May 15, 1901	New York 4, Chicago 0	Mathewson WP, Taylor LP
July 19, 1901	Chicago 5, New York 2	Taylor WP, Mathewson LP
August 9, 1902	Chicago 8, New York 2	Taylor WP, Mathewson LP
August 18, 1902	New York 5, Chicago 0	Mathewson WP, Taylor LP
May 26, 1903	New York 4, Chicago 3	Mathewson WP, Taylor LP
August 27, 1904	New York 9, St. Louis 3	Mathewson WP, Taylor LP
May 11, 1905	New York 4, St. Louis 0	Mathewson WP, Taylor LP
July 21, 1905	New York 14, St. Louis 2	Mathewson WP, Taylor LP
May 26, 1906	New York 5, St. Louis 4	Mathewson WP, Taylor LP
June 15, 1906	New York 2, St. Louis 1	Mathewson WP, Taylor LP
July 20, 1906	Chicago 6, New York 3	Taylor WP, Mathewson LP
August 4, 1906	New York 7, Chicago 4	Mathewson WP, Taylor LP

On May 7, 1902, New York won its protest over the distance of the pitcher's box to home plate, reversing what would have been a Chicago 4 to 0 victory, with Taylor the winning pitcher and Mathewson the loser. The game was erased from the 1902 record.

Christy Mathewson versus George "Rube" Waddell (1876–1914)

Waddell was elected to the Baseball Hall of Fame in 1946

According to chronological sequence, Rube Waddell appears once again — like that recurring bad penny. This time he's on the list of pitching greats who opposed Christy Mathewson. While the number of appearances against Mathewson was far fewer than against Cy Young — there were only two, both coming in June of 1901— you will no doubt remember that Waddell's career began in the National League with the Louisville Colonels. There for parts of the 1897 and 1899 seasons, and continuing only through the 1901 season before Connie Mack arranged to have him brought to Philadelphia, he managed to leave behind a growing reputation for tom-foolery that kept him on the move from city to city and coast to coast before Mr. Mack got him settled down enough to perform some of his southpaw wonders. It was only then that he began to rack up the super numbers that eventually landed him in a permanent resting place at Cooperstown.

2. Christy Mathewson

After absorbing a 9 to 2 drubbing at the hands of Connie Mack's *bon vivant* on June 15, 1901, the Giant rookie must have thought that one over. The very next — and last — time they encountered one another, Mathewson turned down the screws in a four-hit, 14 to 1 demolition of Chicago's North Siders. The destruction was so complete that Waddell was gone before the fourth inning was over, done in by a sizzling line drive Matty himself drove through the box. Reaching out to flag the liner, Rube's pitching hand got in the way, and though he tried to continue, it was evident that the ol' pitching paw would have none of it. The Giants added another nine tallies to round out their total of 14 after the injured Waddell departed to more friendly confines, no doubt in the company of a few

He started out as a National Leaguer, eccentric even then — George Edward "Rube" Waddell.

friends and a few cool ones to reconsider things. One of the significant things about Mathewson's victory that day was the way he helped himself afield, a skill that he honed to near perfection with the passing years, and which was often overlooked in his career. The Sunday *New York Times* reported his defensive skills this way:

> ...the New Yorks, gingered up by Mathewson's masterful pitching, played a faultless game in the field and left nothing to be desired at the bat...One rooter in the right-field bleacheries enlivened the crowd at intervals, and everyone awoke to cheer Mathewson when he made a particularly good catch of a hard line drive from the bat of Dexter.

Christy Mathewson was among the game's premier "fifth infielders."

That is best summed up in a sabermetric column titled PB — that is, Pitcher's Defense.[7] Any rating for a given season between 2 and 4 is considered excellent. Mathewson logged marks of 4 and better 10 times during his career, adding up to a career 69, which translates to 46 Pitching Wins,[8] earning a number nine rating all time for career PWs in Thorn and Palmer's *TBE*. One of the many dimensions of the pitching art, this phase of Mathewson's game was not left to chance, nor were any of the other pieces and parts that in sum added up to his pitching mastery.

Christy Mathewson versus Victor Gazaway "Vic" Willis (1876–1947)

Willis was elected to the Baseball Hall of Fame in 1996

The *Hall of Fame Yearbook* for 1997 summarized Vic Willis' career as follows:

> Vic Willis was a tall, graceful workhorse with a sweeping curve that made him a strikeout artist. While compiling a 249–205 record, he notched 50 shutouts, a 2.63 ERA and completed 388 of 471 starts. His 45 complete games in 1902 are still the most in the N.L. in the 20th century. He was the mainstay of the staff of the Boston Beaneaters before his trade to Pittsburgh, where he averaged 22 wins a season.

Vic Willis' career numbers (only a choice few of the many superior Willis entries into the record book appear above) jump off the pages at the reader. What was there about this gifted righthander that somehow escaped the attention of the Hall's electors for so many years? His career 21.2 TPI rating is higher than the ratings of such prestigious Famers as Sandy Koufax, Lefty Gomez, Waite Hoyt, Nolan Ryan and still others. Those 50 shutouts mentioned above put him in the 19th slot all time, not to mention the fact that the rangy Willis suffered through 37 low-scoring games that also turned out to be shutouts — at the hands of his opponents. And to dress up the Willis record a tad, here are a few more numbers: his career 2.63 ERA ties him with Cy Young at number 39; 388 Complete Games rank him at 18th; 249 career wins, more than Mordecai Brown, Whitey Ford, "Catfish" Hunter or "Chief" Bender garnered, rank number 40 all time; and his 1906 Clutch Pitching Index[9], 138.7, is number 25. It all adds up to a career of distinguished achievement, and, further, marks Vic Willis as a tough competitor who, when assigned to pitch against Christy Mathewson, might be expected to produce an interesting afternoon of baseball.

The two Famers matched pitches 14 times, producing five Mathewson victories and seven Willis wins. On one occasion Willis relieved "Deacon"

Phillippe, who was charged with a loss to Mathewson, and on another, rain brought a halt to a 2 to 2 tie in the eighth inning of an August 16, 1909, game at Pittsburgh's brand new Forbes Field. That's a pretty even division of labor.

It was during the Pirates' pennant-winning season, 1909, that Mathewson and Willis hooked up four times, no doubt saved for the pressures of a heated pennant race in which the Cubs and Giants both gave chase to the Corsairs. That resulted in a victory for each hurler, a tie game called after the eighth frame, and an August 24 pairing that went to the Giants in which Hooks Wiltse was the winning pitcher, Vic Willis the loser, and Matty the pitcher who was credited with one of his two Saves that season.

Eight-time 20-game winner Vic Willis, elected to the Hall of Fame in 1996.

However, the feature game in this closely matched series occurred on July 17, 1907, when, involved as they usually were in a race for the blue ribbon, the Pirates confronted the Giants at the Polo Grounds. Though both ultimately bowed to Chicago that summer, this particular game kept the Pirates at the heels of the Giants and Chicago's Bruins. In this contest both hurlers were especially effective, not permitting a run until the top of the eighth when the Pirates broke through with a single marker. That was followed in the ninth by Eddie Abbatichio's smash between Seymour and Shannon for an inside the park four base blow to salt the game away for Willis, one of his 21 victories that summer. Willis' 21-game splurge was followed by two more 20-gamers in 1908 and again in 1909, to mark the eighth time he had entered the 20-game winner's circle. The box score of that 1907 gem follows:

At New York, July 17, 1907

Pittsburgh	R	H	PO	A	New York	R	H	PO	A
Anderson, rf	0	0	3	0	Shannon, lf	0	0	2	0
Leach, cf	0	1	2	1	Browne, rf	0	0	3	0
Clarke, lf	0	0	2	0	Devlin, 3b	0	0	2	2
Wagner, ss	0	0	2	1	Seymour, cf	0	0	4	0
Abbatichio, 2b	1	1	3	2	Bresnahan, 1b	0	0	11	0
Nealon, 1b	0	0	7	0	Dahlen, ss	0	0	1	5
Storke, 3b	0	0	1	0	Strang, 2b	0	0	1	1
Gibson, c	1	1	7	1	Bowerman, c	0	2	3	1
Willis, p	0	1	0	1	Mathewson, p	0	0	1	1
Totals	2	4	27	8	Totals	0	2	27	10

Line Score	Pittsburgh	000	000	011	2–4–0
	New York	000	000	000	0–2–3

2BH	Bowerman
Home Run	Abbatichio
SB	Devlin
SH	Mathewson
LOB	Pittsburgh 5, New York 3
BB	Willis 4, Mathewson 0
K	Willis 3, Mathewson 1
Umpires	Rigler and O'Day
Time	1:40

In 1910 the Cardinals picked up Vic Willis, figuring that some world series know-how — and class — would help engender a little more gumption in the moribund St. Louis ball club. Alas, the Willis touch didn't extend quite that far, as the Redbirds wound up in the same seventh place fix they found themselves in the year before. Vic Willis won 9 and lost 12 for the 1910 Cardinals, not nearly enough to entice him back for another season. Remembering those Beaneater and Pirate powerhouses he pitched for in former seasons was no doubt enough to remind him that there was a far piece between the bottom and the top of the league. He knew just what it meant to be on either end of the league, having been one of four 20-game *losers* on one of Boston's worst ball clubs in 1905. Leaving it all behind was beyond doubt a wise decision. Almost nine decades later, his record sullied by losing ball clubs no more, his ticket to Cooperstown acknowledged his truly fine career.

The Mathewson-Willis Log:

July 28, 1903	Boston 5, New York 3	Willis WP, Mathewson LP
August 3, 1903	New York 4, Boston 1	Mathewson WP, Willis LP
Sept 12, 1904	Boston 3, New York 1	Willis WP, Mathewson LP
Sept 7, 1905	New York 3, Boston 0	Mathewson WP, Willis LP
August 21, 1906	Pittsburgh 2, New York 1	Willis WP, Mathewson LP
July 17, 1907	Pittsburgh 2, New York 0	Willis WP, Mathewson LP
June 11, 1908	Pittsburgh 5, New York 2	Willis WP, Mathewson LP
Sept 21, 1908	Pittsburgh 2, New York 1	Willis WP, Mathewson LP
July 12, 1909	New York 3, Pittsburgh 2	Mathewson WP, Willis LP
July 30, 1909	Pittsburgh 3, New York 1	Willis WP, Mathewson LP

May 11, 1907: Mathewson beat Pittsburgh in relief. Willis started this game but Mike Lynch, who relieved him, was charged with the loss.

August 16, 1909: Pittsburgh and New York tied, 2 to 2. Neither Willis nor Mathewson were credited with a decision.

August 24, 1909: New York 4, Pittsburgh 3; Mathewson (Save), Wiltse (WP), and Willis was the losing pitcher.

July 23, 1910: Mathewson was the WP, defeating St. Louis 9 to 2. Willis relieved starter Ed Zmich, who was charged with the defeat.

Christy Mathewson versus Sam "The Goshen Schoolmaster" Leever (1871–1953)

There is a Mystery Guest among the seven mound warriors listed below, each of whom had rather similarly successful careers in the 13-year range that resulted in a winning percentage of .600 or better, at least one 20-game season, and, relatively speaking, around the 2500 innings pitched level. Two of these worthies are Hall of Fame denizens, and another, Randy Johnson, is en route. Here are their career numbers:

	Yrs	W-L	W%	IP	SH	Ratio	OBA	ERA	TPI	20W
Mystery Guest	13	194–110	.660	2660	39	10.6	.245	2.47	15.4	4
Randy Johnson	13*	179–95	.653	2498	28	11.3	.213	3.19	31.8	1
Ron Guidry	14	170–91	.651	2392	26	10.7	.244	3.29	18.5	3
Lefty Gomez (HOF)	14	189–162	.649	2503	28	12.2	.242	3.34	19.9	4
Deacon Phillippe	13	189–109	.634	2607	27	10.1	.253	2.59	15.1	6
Ed Reulbach	13	182–106	.632	2632	40	10.7	.224	2.28	17.8	2†
Bob Lemon (HOF)	13	207–128	.618	2850	31	12.2	.241	3.23	38.4	7
Eddie Rommel	13	171–119	.590	2556	18	12.3	.277	3.54	25.2	2

*Randy Johnson's statistics are complete through the 2000 season.
†Ed Reulbach was a 20-game winner for Newark of the Federal League (1915).

Our Mystery Guest, perched smartly atop this elite group of hurlers, won two out of every three games, tossed 37 shutouts and posted a career ERA of 2.47, which ranks among the top 25 in the history of the game. He broke in with the Pirates, remained with them throughout his 13-year career, and was active between 1898 (he debuted on May 26 that year but pitched in only five games, with a 1 and 0 record) and 1910 — years, as you will recognize, that were among the Pirates' greatest. In fact, Pittsburgh's 1909 world

Sam Leever, Pittsburgh's curveball artist who won 20, four times.

champions boasted a pitching staff of Deacon Phillippe, rookie phenom Babe Adams, Howie Camnitz, Vic Willis, whom we've already met, Lefty Leifeld and, of course, our Mystery Guest (8 and 1 that season), combining for a 90–32 record and a .738 winning percentage.

Despite his glossy career numbers, our Mystery Guest is not well known, and more's the pity. Like many another outstanding pitcher in the history of the game, this fellow somehow didn't break through to the level of the game's greats and remained relatively unknown. But teammates who played behind him, like the little fellow they called Tommy the Wee (Leach, who was with Pittsburgh from 1900 to 1912), the incomparable Hans Wagner, Fred Clarke, his playing-manager, and especially his batterymate, George Gibson, all respected this fellow's ability, his even-handed approach to the game, and his tough, inner fiber. And they all went on record accordingly.

Samuel Leever, The Goshen (Ohio) Schoolmaster, is the name of our Mystery Guest, and his encounters with Christy Mathewson provided Pittsburgh and New York fandom with some razor-edged baseball each time they met. There were 13 engagements, most of which were taut, tense pitching duels. Then too, there was one encounter between Leever and the Giants in 1903 that was part of a record-setting five straight Pittsburgh shutouts, when on June 8 he fashioned the third of the five with a 5 to 0 win (not, however, over Mathewson). In the Mathewson-Leever series of 13 games, the Schoolmaster, a.k.a. "Deacon" because of his subdued and circumspect demeanor, broke even, winning four out of eight decisions. The Big Six, winner of six out of ten decisions, also saved two other New York games and was involved in one, no-decision, appearance. Leever, on the other hand, also appeared in five no-decision games.

One of the more interesting games between the two occurred on May 16, 1904, when the Giants had the Schoolmaster on the ropes after a five-run outburst in the top of the fifth inning at Pittsburgh. In the frame's bottom half, the quiet but determined Schoolmaster was due up with a runner in scoring position when manager Clarke decided to pull him. Not without an argument from Leever, however, who finally broke down the skipper's resistance and followed up his insistence with a run-producing single. That made it 5 to 1 and kept Leever in the game. After holding the Giants scoreless, the Pirates staged a five-run rally of their own, almost decking Mathewson. But both hurlers finished out the game by shutting out their opponents. Final score: Pirates 6, Giants 5, with Leever on the long end. Mathewson, being Mathewson, had his day against Sam Leever, nonetheless, beating him twice via the whitewash route, one of them a super 2 to 0 outing during which he doled out six hits during the season of the first world series (in which Leever and his Pirates were proud participants). Never mind Leever's obscurity. His sterling record brought with it treasured memories few have had — before or since.

The Mathewson-Leever Log:

June 11, 1901	Pittsburgh 4, New York 0	Leever WP, Mathewson LP
August 21, 1904	Pittsburgh 2, New York 0	Leever WP, Mathewson LP
May 20, 1903	New York 2, Pittsburgh 0	Mathewson WP, Leever LP
June 26, 1903	New York 8, Pittsburgh 2	Mathewson WP, Leever LP
May 16, 1904	Pittsburgh 6, New York 5	Leever WP, Mathewson LP
August 20, 1904	New York 5, Pittsburgh 0	Mathewson WP, Leever LP
May 18, 1905	Pittsburgh 7, New York 2	Leever WP, Mathewson LP
June 21, 1906	New York 5, Pittsburgh 4	Mathewson WP, Leever LP
August 24, 1908	New York 4, Pittsburgh 3	Mathewson WP, Leever LP

On June 9, 1905, Mathewson and Leever appeared as relief pitchers without a decision, in a 12 to 6 game won by Pittsburgh. Phillippe was the winning pitcher and McGinnity the loser.

Mathewson and Leever relieved, without a decision, in the July 15, 1905, game won by McGinnity. Mathewson was credited with a Save.

On June 16, 1909, Mathewson beat the Pirates 8 to 2, pitching a complete game. Leever appeared as a relief pitcher without a decision.

On August 24, 1909, "Hooks" Wiltse beat Vic Willis (New York 4, Pittsburgh 3). Leever relieved. Mathewson was credited with a Save.

Christy Mathewson versus Frank G. "Noodles" Hahn (1879–1960)

According to her son, Mrs. Hahn, of Nashville, Tennessee, served up the best noodle soup anyone ever tasted, and young Frank didn't mind letting one and all know about it. Having bragged on mom's soup quite often, it was inevitable that he would be tagged with a nickname like "Noodles," and, of course, the name stuck. But the young lad did more than enjoy noodle soup. Like many another youngster, he was crazy about baseball, and before too long became a good enough lefthanded pitcher to attract the kind of attention that brought professional contract offers with it.

Hahn signed his first contract at the tender age of 16 with the Mobile club of the Southern League in 1895, moving up to the Western League with Detroit in 1897. Before his 20th birthday, he donned a big league uniform, debuting with Cincinnati's Reds in April of 1899. The "slight but ferocious moundsman," as Peter Bjarkman calls the 5'9", 160-pounder in his *Encyclopedia of Major League Baseball* (Carroll and Graf, 1991), a flamethrower with outstanding control, went right to work. The Reds, a fumbling, weak-hitting collection of rather pedestrian ball players, needed all the help they could get, and young Hahn gave them more than they probably deserved, finishing his first season in the Bigs with a splashy 23 and 8 record, leading the league in whiffs, and tossing better than 300 innings with an ERA of 2.68 on a staff that averaged a full run more per nine innings, at 3.68.

Frank Hahn's sophomore season wasn't as noteworthy, as he dropped 20 while winning 16, but he was a marked man, the one hurler on the Cincinnati roster other teams knew would give them a rough afternoon. One of those occurred on July 12, 1900, when he stopped the Phillies cold with a no-hitter, winning 4 to 0 on "Wahoo Sam" Crawford's circuit smash. While his marks weren't as eyecatching as those of his rookie season, he again turned in a league-leading figure in strikeouts and 300-plus innings of work.

1901 was a long season in Cincinnati. The Reds plummeted into the NL basement, losing both often and dismally, but not when young Mr. Hahn took the hill. By this time 22 and well seasoned (with 620 innings of major league pitching under his belt), he was ready to get back into the 20-game winner's bracket, despite the team's faltering efforts behind him. Going into the post–Memorial Day lap, the signpost already pointed south, and not only for the Reds. The Giants, too, no great shakes themselves in the pre–McGraw days, were having their troubles. So when June 8 rolled around that summer, about the only interesting thing to attract fans to Cincinnati's League Park was an intriguing matchup between the two young stars, each of whom gave promise of being around a long time. After a couple of innings of scoreless ball, the Cincinnati's got rolling with a Hahn triple and a sacrifice fly to move into the lead, which they never relinquished. Adding a pair in the fourth and three more in the fifth, they had enough to withstand a three-run Giant rally that died when Noodles pulled himself together to fan Giants catcher John Warner with another run in scoring position. The Reds moved on to a 6 to 4 victory in what would turn out to be a seven game series between the two staff aces.

Hahn went on to record four 20-game seasons in his first five seasons, beating the legendary Mathewson three times during his brief career, while losing the same number. He also beat the Giants in a game started by Tully Sparks (with the Giants briefly) in 1902, that was finished by Matty, though Sparks was tagged with the loss in a 7 to 5 game that Hahn won.

There were two shutouts in the Matty-Hahn series, both administered in 1903. In the first of these on June 13, Mathewson was at his brilliant best, setting down the Reds on but one hit, a single, and beating Hahn 4 to 0. But Noodles caught up with the great one in September, hanging an 8 to 0 shellacking on the Giants in a four-hit exhibition of masterful pitching. The last time the two met, on September 21, 1904, at a time when Hahn's arm was already hurting him, the Reds pulled away from a 4 to 4 tie to win on the strength of a two run rally that beat "the Big Six," 6 to 4.

At the turn of the 20th century there were no MRIs, sophisticated medical treatments, "miracle operations," or the kind of facilities that enable contemporary pitchers to resume pitching after injuries that put an end to the careers of many an athlete during the game's earlier years, Frank Hahn among

Elder statesman Frank "Noodles" Hahn, pitching consultant with the 1939 Reds.

them. It wasn't to be, but it surely would have been interesting to see what Noodles Hahn would have done, not only against Christy Mathewson, but in a 15 to 20 year career. Even pitching for an also-ran, it's even money that he would have been knocking on the door at Cooperstown.

The Mathewson-Hahn Log:

June 8, 1901	Cincinnati 6, New York 4	Hahn WP, Mathewson LP
June 13, 1903	New York 4, Cincinnati 0	Mathewson WP, Hahn LP
Sept 15, 1903	Cincinnati 8, New York 0	Hahn WP, Mathewson LP
July 12, 1904	New York 7, Cincinnati 4	Mathewson WP, Hahn LP
August 30, 1904	New York 3, Cincinnati 1	Mathewson WP, Hahn LP
Sept 21, 1904	Cincinnati 6, New York 4	Hahn WP, Mathewson LP

On June 13, 1902, Tully Sparks (NY) was the starting and losing pitcher. Mathewson relieved Sparks. Hahn was the winning pitcher.

The June 13, 1903, game was a Mathewson one-hitter.

Christy Mathewson versus Charles Louis "Deacon" Phillippe (1872–1952)

During the first dozen years of the 20th century, the NL was utterly dominated by a threesome of powerhouses. The mighty trinity, consisting of Chicago, Pittsburgh and New York, fought desperately to nudge one another out of a pennant flag. Each was successful four times during that span, Pittsburgh in 1901 '02, '03, and '09; New York in 1904, '05, '11, and '12; and Chicago in 1906, '07, '08, and '10. Each of the franchises was blessed with astute management, possessed adequate power and consistency in the batting order, played the game with passion and smarts, and, above all, had the kind of pitching that sent no less than six of their hurlers to the Hall of Fame: Mordecai Brown, Jack Chesbro, Christy Mathewson, Joe McGinnity, "Rube" Waddell[10] and Vic Willis.

In each instance those Famers were joined by a supporting cast of able pitchers, some of whom might well have made it to the Hall with another credential or two. One of this latter group was a gifted righthander by the name of Charles Phillippe, who was called Deacon, a telltale sobriquet given those who toed the line, were temperate, quiet and law-abiding. Since that was such a contrast to most of the ball players of his time, the name Deacon seemed the most appropriate. It's of course well known that there weren't many deacons in professional baseball during the deadball era, so the Phillippes, Mathewsons, Cy Youngs and Eddie Planks were refreshing exceptions.

Deacon Phillippe was a 20-game winner in 1899, his first major league season. His Louisville ball club had Hans Wagner at third and in the outfield, hitting .341, driving home 114 runs and stealing 37 bases, as well as two other 20-game winners in Jesse Tannehill and Sam Leever, and still wound up ninth in the NL's last 12-team race. But owner Barney Dreyfuss refused to break up a promising ball club, turned down some tempting offers, and wound up transferring his franchise to Pittsburgh, where Clarke, Wagner, Phillippe and Company promptly leapfrogged to prominence, capturing the flag in 1901.

During the next three seasons, with New York and Chicago adding important players to their fast-rising clubs, several more significant names were added to the rosters of all three challengers. Mathewson and McGinnity were in place in New York; and out in the Midwest, Three Finger Brown, Carl Lundgren, Jack Taylor and, in 1905, Ed Reulbach joined a fearsome Chicago pitching corps. The three-way race was on. In earnest.

Adding to the luster of this blue chips competition were some 13 Matty-Deacon match-ups between 1901 and 1910. The very first of these provided a foretaste of the sharp-edged competition ahead. On May 19, 1901, with

7,000 on hand at the Polo Grounds, the Giants beat the Pirates 2 to 1, as Matty scattered six hits, three of them of the scratchy, infield variety. But it wasn't until the bottom of the eighth that New York nailed down its win with a run that sent them ahead 2 to 0. In Pittsburgh's last at bat, the Pirates scored but stranded the tying run as Mathewson fanned the final two hitters. Though the two teams wound up on either end of the league that season (New York tied Chicago for seventh place with a wretched 52 and 85 reading), the duels between Phillippe, Willis and Leever and Mathewson, McGinnity, Hooks Wiltse and Red Ames were just ahead, delivering just what might be expected, some of the most interesting and top-level baseball of the deadball era.

Early 1900s Pirates ace who walked only 1.25/game, Charles "Deacon" Phillipe.

During a remarkably consistent career, Phillippe turned in six 20-game seasons before fighting recurring arm problems that reduced his playing time and effectiveness. Two of his last five years were almost entirely lost (he logged only 18 innings in eight outings), but in 1909 and 1910 he turned in a number of scintillating relief appearances that helped the Pirates in some very tight spots. During his last big season, 1910, he came up with several innings of spectacular relief pitching, among them back-to-back gems against New York to beat them twice in three days. Those victories over a Mathewson-led ball club were a long time in coming. The Deacon hadn't won against Matty since a September 20, 1906, 3 to 2 decision, but on Bastille Day of 1910 he was liberated with a 4 to 3 decision and celebrated that one with his July 16 conquest, again in relief, as the Pirates got to Matty for five late-inning tallies, winning 6 to 3. The Deacon scattered four hits, giving up nary a Giant run in seven innings of work.

Though not nearly as successful against Christy Mathewson as he was against other luminaries during his time, Phillippe was one of Pittsburgh's all time heroes. Two of his accomplishments are unavoidable — and usually cited: his miserly 1.25 base on balls ratio per nine innings pitched (issuing but 363 free passes in 2,607 innings of pitching — marking him as the greatest, yes, the greatest control pitcher in the game's modern history), and the fact that he was the first pitcher to win a game in World Series history, a 7 to 3 triumph over Cy Young in 1903. And, yes, he didn't walk a single Boston batter.

The Mathewson-Phillippe Log:

May 21, 1901	New York 2, Pittsburgh 1	Mathewson WP, Phillippe LP
May 19, 1903	New York 4, Pittsburgh 3	Mathewson WP, Phillippe LP
Aug 2, 1905	New York 3, Pittsburgh 1	Mathewson WP, Phillippe LP
Aug 21, 1905	New York 10, Pittsburgh 2	Mathewson WP, Phillippe LP
Sep 25, 1905	New York 10, Pittsburgh 4	Mathewson WP, Phillippe LP
Sep 20, 1906	Pittsburgh 3, New York 2	Phillippe WP, Mathewson LP
May 11, 1907	New York 9, Pittsburgh 6	Mathewson WP, Phillippe LP
Aug 24, 1907	New York 7, Pittsburgh 4	Mathewson WP, Phillippe LP
Jul 14, 1910	Pittsburgh 4, New York 3	Phillippe WP, Mathewson LP
Jul 16, 1910	Pittsburgh 6, New York 3	Phillippe WP, Mathewson LP

Phillippe appeared as a reliever in the following games:

June 9, 1905	Pittsburgh won 12 to 6	Phillippe WP, Mathewson LP
August 9, 1906	New York won 6 to 0	Mathewson WP, Phillippe ND
June 17, 1909	New York won 8 to 2	Mathewson WP, Phillippe ND
August 25, 1909	New York won 3 to 2	Mathewson WP, Phillippe ND
July 14, 1910	Pittsburgh won 4 to 3	Phillippe WP, Mathewson LP
July 16, 1910	Pittsburgh won 6 to 3	Phillippe WP, Mathewson ND

Mathewson appeared in relief for the following games:

May 19, 1903 (WP)
June 9, 1905 (ND)
May 11, 1907 (WP)
June 17, 1909 (WP)
May 23, 1910 (ND)
July 16, 1910 (ND)

Christy Mathewson versus Jack Chesbro (1874–1931)
Chesbro was elected to the Baseball Hall of Fame in 1946

Before moving on to the AL, Jack Chesbro had become a fixture in Pittsburgh's starting rotation, accelerating his victory pace with each passing season.

Hall of Famer Jack Chesbro, who won 20 twice in the NL before jumping to the AL in 1903.

He broke in with six 1899 victories, upped the figure to 15 and then 21 before leading the NL with 28 wins in 1902 as the Pirates won their second straight pennant. By that time Happy Jack had mastered the pitch that took him to the top ranks of NL pitchers — the spitter (and not until the premier spitball pitcher of them all, Ed Walsh, came along, was there a better practitioner of that pitch).

Although there were a limited number of match-ups between them, Jack Chesbro had the privilege of pitching against Cy Young, as noted previously, Christy Mathewson and Walter Johnson. Against Mathewson there were two engagements, each pitcher winning one of them. But the second of the two, at Pittsburgh on July 12, 1902, is worth noting. On that day Chesbro struck out 11 Giants and pinned a 4 to 0 shutout on the Horace Fogel–led club, one of eight he threw that summer, tying him with no less than Mathewson for the league's leadership in 1902. Fogel, it will be remembered, was the fellow who suggested to Christy Mathewson that first base might be a better spot for him. Mathewson, who didn't buy it, tried nonetheless. But that, and a good deal more, soon came to a screeching halt when John McGraw checked into the Giants clubhouse, leading the team for the first time just a week later. For Mathewson and the Giants a new era had begun. Immediately.

The Mathewson-Chesbro Log:

July 4, 1901	New York 5, Pittsburgh 3	Mathewson WP, Chesbro LP
July 12, 1902	Pittsburgh 4, New York 0	Chesbro WP, Mathewson LP

Christy Mathewson versus Mordecai Centennial "Three Finger" or "Miner" Brown (1876–1948)

Brown was elected to the Baseball Hall of Fame in 1949

For those who have more than a nodding acquaintance with the game, there is probably an irresistible urge to pair up one superstar with another. That is, after all, what brought this book about. The reader will no doubt have his own list of pairings. Here is another list that matches the elite pitchers of the 20th century when they were at or very near the apex of their careers:

Cy Young vs. Rube Waddell	Whitey Ford vs. Billy Pierce
Walter Johnson vs. Eddie Plank	Tom Seaver vs. Bob Gibson
Pete Alexander vs. Dazzy Vance	Jim Palmer vs. Nolan Ryan
Lefty Grove vs. Red Ruffing	Roger Clemens vs. Randy Johnson
Carl Hubbell vs. Dizzy Dean	Greg Maddux vs. Dwight Gooden
Warren Spahn vs. Sandy Koufax	

Mordecai "Miner" Brown.

There is one matchup conspicuous by its absence in the list above. That's the one that probably ranks as the number one of them all: Christy Mathewson vs. Three Finger Brown. If not *the* most captivating, it certainly must rank among the top two or three, all time. Through more than 20 near priceless engagements, these two upper echelon Famers waged their own private little war, leading their ball clubs to pennant after pennant while waging sophisticated, nerve-wracking warfare in one tight NL race after another. When it all ended in the late afternoon shadows of Chicago's Weeghman Park on September 4, 1916, in a game when both of these titans struggled and staggered through nine innings to a 10 to 8 New York victory, the curtain rang down on what amounted to an even split in 24 games. That included two Mathewson victories over Brown when the latter was in his freshman season with the Cardinals, a Brown winning streak of eight in a row, and a strong finish by Mathewson, who won six of the last seven decisions in that incredible series of games.

Before even getting into some of the more delicious morsels, a departure in the usual format, with a listing of games in which both pitchers registered decisions:

The Mathewson-Brown Log:

July 9, 1903	New York 4, St. Louis 2	Mathewson WP, Brown LP
August 13, 1903	New York 6, St. Louis 2	Mathewson WP, Borwn LP
June 13, 1904	Chicago 3, New York 2	Brown WP, Mathewson LP
July 23, 1904	New York 5, Chicago 1	Mathewson WP, Brown LP
June 13, 1905*	New York 1, Chicago 0	Mathewson WP, Brown LP

* Mathewson no-hit the Cubs 1 to 0 in a game in which Brown also carried a no-hitter into the New York eighth. New York's winning run came in the top of the ninth.

July 12, 1905	Chicago 8, New York 1	Brown WP, Mathewson LP
July 17, 1906	Chicago 6, New York 2	Brown WP, Mathewson LP
August 18, 1906	Chicago 6, New York 2	Brown WP, Mathewson LP
May 21, 1907	Chicago 3, New York 2	Brown WP, Mathewson LP
June 5, 1907	Chicago 8, New York 2	Brown WP, Mathewson LP
August 2, 1907[†]	Chicago 5, New York 0	Brown WP, Mathewson LP
July 17, 1908	Chicago 1, New York 0	Brown WP, Mathewson LP
August 29, 1908	Chicago 3, New York 2	Brown WP, Mathewson LP
Sept 24, 1908[‡]	New York 5, Chicago 4	Mathewson WP, Brown LP
October 8, 1908[‡]	Chicago 4, New York 2	Brown WP, Mathewson LP
June 8, 1909	New York 3, Chicago 2	Mathewson WP, Brown LP
August 28, 1909	Chicago 6, New York 1	Brown WP, Mathewson LP
Sept 16, 1909	New York 2, Chicago 1	Mathewson WP, Brown LP
Sept 24, 1910	New York 6, Chicago 5	Mathewson WP, Brown LP
May 9, 1911	New York 5, Chicago 3	Mathewson WP, Brown LP
August 7, 1911	Chicago 8, New York 6	Brown WP, Mathewson LP
July 9, 1912	New York 5, Chicago 2	Mathewson WP, Brown LP
July 15, 1913	New York 5, Cincinnati 2	Mathewson WP, Brown LP
Sept 4, 1916[§]	Cincinnati 10, Chicago 8	Mathewson WP, Brown LP

The sum and substance of these two gladiators was quintessential Cooperstown. Both left behind a trail of orbital numbers: Brown's career ERA, 2.06, exceeded only by Ed Walsh and Addie Joss; his 14th spot as a shutout hurler, with 55; a lofty number six position in Ratio, at 9.8; a fine, top-50 ranking in Hits per Game (6.17 in 1908); as well as a high-ranking, single season Ratio in 1908 (7.72, 13th). As for Mathewson, whose statistics have been reviewed throughout this chapter, there are no more telling numbers than those involving several lengthy winning streaks; 76 career shutouts (3rd high); a string of 68 consecutive innings without giving up a base on balls; that gaudy career ERA mark, 2.13, at the heels of the top three career leaders; and the one Matty himself considered to be his career highpoint — his shutout trifecta, 1905 world's championship. In fact, that ERA mark, along with that of the Chicago icon's, gives pause for further consideration. Check these numbers:

[†]On August 17, 1907, Chicago beat New York 3 to 2 in 13 innings. Mathewson was the starter and loser, pitching a complete game. Brown started for Chicago, received no decision, and was relieved in the ninth by the winner, Jack "The Giant Killer" Pfiester. Mathewson had given up only a bunt single through nine innings in this game, only to lose the game on former Giant catcher Johnny Kling's homer in the 13th.

[‡] Mathewson was the winning pitcher in relief in the Sept 24, 1908 game; and Brown won in relief on October 8, 1908, a game which the storied pennant-winner often called the "Merkle Game."

[§]This game, won by the Giants, was the last pitching appearance for both Mordecai Brown and Christy Mathewson.

What Makes an Elite Pitcher?

	ERA-NL	ERA-Brown	ERA-Mat	SH-NL	SH-Brown	SH-Mat
1901	3.33		2.41	70		5
1902	2.79		2.12	101		8
1903	3.27	2.60	2.26	69	1	3
1904	2.73	1.86	2.03	108	4	4
1905	3.00	2.17	1.28	106	4	8
1906	2.63	1.04	2.97	145	9	6
1907	2.47	1.39	2.00	157	6	8
1908	2.35	1.47	1.43	164	9	11
1909	2.60	1.31	1.14	133	8	8
1910	3.03	1.86	1.89	111	6	2
1911	3.40	2.80	1.99	92	0	5
1912	3.20	2.64	2.12	85	2	0
1913	3.20	2.91	2.06	91	1	4
1914	2.79	3.52*	3.00	119	2*	5
1915	3.21	2.09*	3.58	101	3*	1
1916	2.62	3.91	3.01	140	0	1
Career		2.06	2.13		55	79

A final note or two is in order concerning the riveting story of these two Famers, locked so often in down-to-the-end combat. In four out of every five games Brown and Mathewson faced each other, the winning pitcher allowed the losing team two runs or less. In eight of these matches the winning team won by a single run, and in 10 of them the winning team scored four runs or less to win. Incredibly, Brown and Mathewson finished each game in the series. Well, almost. There was that game on August 17 of 1902 that went 13 frames before the Cubs finally beat Matty. But even in that one Mordecai Brown went nine innings before being relieved. Think on those incredible numbers a moment or two!

Picking one unforgettable game out of the entire series was easy for Brown, a game that he was asked about frequently as the years moved on — "The Merkle Game." It was the one game of the Mathewson-Brown series he didn't start, but he was certainly there when in ended! As for Mathewson, that same game was also unforgettable, though it turned out to be as disappointing for him as it was satisfying for Brown. But there was that afternoon of June 13, 1905, when the two young stallions had at it in front of an overflow crowd at Chicago's West Side Grounds. On that day Matty reigned supreme, fighting off a determined Brown effort that held the Giants hitless through seven-plus stanzas with a no-hitter of his own, winning one of 1905's thrillers, 1 to 0. That one might very well have presaged the highlight of his career, that fall's World Series. On that misty day in Chicago, Mathewson had put the handwriting on the wall.

*During the 1914 and 1915 seasons Brown pitched in the Federal League.

Christy Mathewson versus Edward Marvin "Big Ed" Reulbach (1882–1961)

By the time manager Frank Chance gave Ed Reulbach the ball against Christy Mathewson and the Giants on August 10, 1905, the McGrawmen were well on their way to a second straight pennant, having stretched their lead over second place Pittsburgh to eight games and come out winners in nine of the previous 15 encounters with Chicago. Reulbach had already been paired with Giant pitchers four times, coming away with but a single win, a classy 4 to 0 shutout over Joe McGinnity. Now the rookie, who at that point had won 12 out of 20, was sent out to meet the Master, Mathewson, whose 19 and 6 record might just as easily have been 21 and 4 or even 22 and 3 with a break or two.

To make a long story short, the boss man of NL pitchers took the rookie to camp, matching his superb outing pitch for pitch in a game in which Reulbach gave up only four hits, did not issue a free pass, and matched Ks with Matty at six a piece. But Mathewson allowed only three bingles and won his 20th, 1 to 0. It wasn't the only time Matty had broken Chicago hearts that summer. You will recall the no-hitter he tossed at them, beating Three Finger Brown on June 13 by that same paper-thin 1 to 0 margin.

In the final counting, the two of them wound up the season as the league's number one and two hurlers. The order was: Mathewson (9.9 TPI) and then Reulbach (4.8 TPI), just as it was after the final game of their competition against each other between 1905 and 1914 — Mathewson five wins and Reulbach four.

But despite Mathewson's slight edge in head to head competition with Big Ed Reulbach, there was more than enough in their pairings to convince all involved, especially Mathewson, who tendered the Chicago righthander every bit as much respect as he did Mordecai Brown, that here was a pitcher of the first rank, a tough, determined competitor who had both the stuff and the temperament of a winner. And that is what Ed Reulbach turned out to be, winning 182 out of 286 big league decisions, placing him at number 28 on the all time list of pitchers with the highest winning percentage — in his case, .632.

Some years later, wearing the uniform of the Brooklyn Dodgers, Ed Reulbach caught up with Christy Mathewson, turning the tables on that earlier 1 to 0 loss with a 2-zip shutout of his own. This time he narrowed the Giants down to two hits, but this time he was backed by 11 Dodger hits, a couple of them responsible for a pair of runs that decided things in Big Ed's favor.

At New York, September 6, 1913

Brooklyn	AB	R	H	PO	New York	AB	R	H	PO
Moran, rf	4	1	2	3	Snodgrass, cf	4	0	0	2

Cutshaw, 2b	3	0	2	1	Doyle, 2b	4	0	0	3
Collins, lf	4	0	1	1	Fletcher, ss	4	0	0	1
Stengel, cf	3	1	2	2	Burns, lf	3	0	1	1
Daubert, 1b	4	0	1	10	Shafer, 3b	3	0	0	1
Smith, 3b	4	0	2	1	Murray, rf	3	0	1	1
B. Fischer, ss	2	0	1	1	Meyers, c	2	0	0	5
Kirkpatrick, ss	2	0	0	1	Merkle, 1b	3	0	0	13
W. Fischer, c	4	0	0	7	Mathewson, p	1	0	0	0
Reulbach, p	4	0	0	0	McCormick, ph	1	0	0	0
Totals	34	2	11	27	Totals	28	0	2	27

	Line Score	Brooklyn	011	000	000	2–11–1
		New York	000	000	000	0–2–1

2BH	Moran	K	Mathewson 5, Reulbach 5
3BH	Cutshaw	BB	Mathewson 1, Reulbach 1
SB	Snodgrass	HPB	Meyers (Reulbach)
SH	Cutshaw	Umpires	Eason and Brennan
LOB	Brooklyn 7, New York 3	Time	1:26
DP	Doyle and Merkle 2,		
	B. Fischer and W. Fischer,		
	B. Fischer, Cutshaw and Daubert		

Ed Reulbach's 1905 went down as the number 15 rookie season all time (rated at 4.8 TPI), despite a mediocre-appearing 18 and 14 record. Here are some of the reasons for that 4.8: he won two of those 18 victories by scores of 2 to 1, one in St. Louis against Jack Taylor (the same Iron Arm who had a thing about complete games as you will remember) that went 18 innings, and another 2 to 1 winner in Philadelphia against Tully Sparks, who also went the route against Big Ed, this one in 21 innings. That was part of a career low 1.42 ERA that just happens to be the 29th best on record, due in large part to the miniscule 6.42 hits he gave up per nine innings pitched. His four-hit, one-run effort against Matty in that losing 1 to 0 game helped both figures along.

Between 1902 and 1913, years of Chicago glory, there was a 20-game winner on the staff each season. Reulbach contributed to the string with 24 in 1906 and in 1908, and again in 1909 came close with 19. During his sophomore, 1906 season, he posted more spectacular numbers as he limited opposing hitters to a paltry .175 BA, a number five all time listing. That season he logged one, two, and three hit wins, beat Matty 10 to 5 in their only matchup, and led the league in winning percentage at .826, a number #40 all time listing, on the way to a three-year reign as the NL's winning percentage leader. All things considered, Big Ed turned out to be one of Matty's most challenging opponents.

"Big Ed" Reulbach, who pitched the first one-hitter in World Series history in 1906 vs. the White Sox.

The Mathewson-Reulbach Log:

August 10, 1905	New York 1, Chicago 0	Mathewson WP, Reulbach LP
Sept 24, 1906	Chicago 10, New York 5	Reulbach WP, Mathewson LP
August 30, 1909	New York 5, Chicago 0	Mathewson WP, Reulbach LP
August 27, 1910	New York 18, Chicago 9	Mathewson WP, Reulbach LP
July 26, 1912	Chicago 4, New York 3	Reulbach WP, Mathewson LP
Sept 16, 1912	Chicago 4, New York 3	Reulbach WP, Mathewson LP
Sept 6, 1913	Brooklyn 2, New York 0	Reulbach WP, Mathewson LP
Sept 24, 1913	New York 2, Brooklyn 1	Mathewson WP, Reulbach LP
May 4, 1914	New York 4, Brooklyn 3	Mathewson WP, Reulbach LP

Christy Mathewson versus Richard "Rube" Marquard (1886–1980)

Marquard was elected to the Baseball Hall of Fame in 1971

It took the big lefty a while to get there, but when he did, Rube Marquard, who teamed with Christy Mathewson to form McGraw's one-two pitching punch for the Giants' 1911-12-13 pennant winners, did it with all the trimmings. During those three seasons he nailed down 73 wins against but 28 losses for a ball club that almost won four straight trips to the Dance before Boston's miracle-workers derailed them in 1914. That the miracle should never have taken place is another story, although Marquard's sudden descent into oblivion with a nasty 12 and 22 record certainly helps explain New York's abdication from the pennant throne room. And from that point on the career of Mr. Marquard never quite regained its former luster. As a matter of fact, his Hall of Fame credentials seem to be few and far between, although one of them, his 19 game winning streak, a genuinely superhuman effort, is a piece of superb, record-making authentica that had plenty to say about Mr. McGraw's 1912 pennant.

Rube Marquard won a record 19 straight in 1911.

The Matty and Rube show went through almost eight seasons, providing the Coogan's Bluff faithful with one thriller after another. Between them they anted up almost 300 victories (Matty with 195 and Rube with 103) from Marquard's onset in 1908 to his 1915 departure via the trade route to the club he had no-hit earlier in that very same season, Uncle Wilbert Robinson's Dodgers. Fate somehow had decreed that neither Mathewson nor Marquard would be wearing Giant flannels for the 1916 season, and those same Fates must also have decreed that a Cincinnati-Brooklyn matchup between Marquard and Matty would be less than acceptable. Let the record show, therefore, that the two let matters stand on the laurels of their former New York conquests.

Christy Mathewson versus Grover Cleveland "Pete" Alexander (1887–1950)
Alexander was elected to the Baseball Hall of Fame in 1938

There was no way for Christy Mathewson to know it beforehand, but before the 1911 season was history, he would pit his own artistry against that of Cy Young, Three Finger Brown, Pete Alexander and, in the World Series, Chief Bender, and defeat each of them — save one. The exception was Alexander, who in his rookie season was matched with Matty on two occasions, both in relief, neither of which resulted in a decision for the man who by season's end was already being hailed as "the Second Mathewson."

His 1911 performance was among a half dozen extraordinary seasons Christy Mathewson entered into the record books, seasons that made his 1912, 25 and 12 record, 2.12 ERA and league leading .281 Opponents' On Base Percentage look, well, ordinary by comparison. But 1911 was also Pete Alexander's maiden voyage through the hazards of the New Yorks, Pittsburghs and Chicagos of the National League, and he negotiated the journey in grand style with one of the best rookie seasons ever, logging league leading numbers in wins, 28, innings pitched, 367, and in Low Opponents' BA, at .219. He had, in fact, covered the first leg of his journey to Cooperstown that season, following it with another six, pre–World War I seasons of pitching summitry that established him as baseball's preeminent hurler among his contemporaries. By 1915, when he led his Phillies to the World Series, he had already posted a 127–63 record, a harbinger of the final numbers he would bring to the Hall of Fame: 373 (always, it seems, linked with Matty's final tally at the same number) and 208, for a winning percentage of .642, a number that is still good enough, after all these years, to rank among the top 25 in baseball history.

Alexander, whose career against contemporary Famers and other master moundsmen of the 1910s and '20s is up for review momentarily, was in the early stages of his career when he met Matty, who was enjoying the final quarter of his tenure as reigning potentate among NL pitchers. But Alex challenged the Big Six from day one, meeting up with McGraw's ace and besting him four times (as against two setbacks), while moving into the elite ranks of the NL's twirlers.

Among the eight Mathewson-Alexander games, one should be noted as one of the strangest games (it was actually a two-in-one affair) of the 1913 season. The game was played — or, more aptly put, started — on August 30, with Alexander and Mathewson paired as the starting pitchers. It was completed on October 2 after having been called originally as a forfeit in the ninth inning by umpire Bill Brennan, with the Phils leading 8 to 6. After the league offices ruled that the game should be completed at a later date, the two teams teed it up once again on October 2 with one away in the ninth inning, the point at which the game had been interrupted by Brennan. Note the *New York Times* review in its October 3, 1913, sports pages:

> The best the Giants got was the worst of it at the Polo Grounds yesterday with the Phillies, for besides winning the uncompleted game which Umpire Bill Brennan stopped in the ninth inning at Philadelphia on Aug. 30, the Philles also split even on the day's programme of a twofold bill. Philadelphia gets the prodigious Brennan mistake by a score of 8 to 6, the Giants gathered the first tussle of a double-header, 8 to 3, and the Phils absorbed the second clash, a six-inning affair, by a tally of 4 to 3, and everybody is glad that much is over, anyway.
>
> The situation was unique in major league baseball. At 1 o'clock, the two clubs lined up as they were when the officious umpire clogged the game on Aug. 30. There was one Giant down in the ninth, and Red Murray was waving the willow. Murray rolled to Bobby Byrne and was thrown out at first. Chief Meyers rapped a single to right, and Attorney Grant romped for him. Larry McLean was shoved in to bat for Snodgrass and he forced Grant at second, and that was the end of it.

And so the game went into the books as a Philadelphia win. Alex, who started the game in Philadelphia, was chased in the third inning, relieved by spitballer George Chalmers, who was credited with the win. Mathewson, who also started — and completed — his eight innings in Philadelphia (it was unnecessary for him to pitch on October 2), was charged with the loss. The tripleheader (the completion of the August 30 game was followed by a twinbill in which Mathewson again pitched and won), if indeed it might be called that, was the last one staged in major league baseball.

The rest of the Mathewson-Alexander confrontations were far more conventional, although there were no pitching gems of the 1 to 0 or 2 to 1 variety, as might well have been expected.

The Mathewson-Alexander Log:

May 3, 1912	Philadelphia 8, New York 6	Alexander WP, Mathewson LP
June 30, 1913	New York 11, Philadelphia 10	Mathewson WP, Alexander LP
April 17, 1915	Philadelphia 7, New York 1	Alexander WP, Mathewson LP
May 1, 1915	Philadelphia 4, New York 2	Alexander WP, Mathewson LP

The first matchup occurred on May 26, 1911, when Mathewson beat the Phils, 5 to 3, in a relief role. Bill Burns started and was charged with the loss. Alexander was used in relief, with runners on in scoring position, and though he was knicked for the game-winning hit, the runs were charged to Burns.

On July 3, 1911, Philadelphia beat New York 7 to 3. Alexander again relieved Burns in a no-decision appearance. Mathewson was charged with the loss in a complete game effort.

The May 3, 1912, game was a ten-inning game won by Alexander. New York tied the score in the ninth, but reliever Mathewson surrendered two runs in the tenth to get the loss.

On June 30, 1913, New York beat Philadelphia in 10 innings in a game won by Mathewson in relief of Hooks Wiltse. The loss went to Alexander, who had relieved Chalmers. The final score was 11 to 10.

The August 30–October 2, 1913, game is explained above. George Chalmers, in relief of Alexander, was the winning pitcher, Mathewson the loser.

Christy Mathewson versus Eppa "Jephtha" Rixey (1891–1963)

Rixey was elected to the Baseball Hall of Fame in 1963

Eppa Rixey, who will be on much more prominent display for a number of Grover Alexander skirmishes during the latter stages of Ol' Pete's career, encountered Christy Mathewson but once, on May 31, 1913, during his first full season in the majors. That day he was bested 3 to 2, although he gave up only six hits, while his teammates were coming up empty against their old tormentor (Matty put the Phillies away 52 times during his career), finally breaking through with two ninth–inning tallies — too little and too late, as was so often the case when a ball club locked horns with the Big Six.

Between his mid-summer debut in 1912 and 1918, when Alexander and Rixey were in the armed forces, and later with different ball clubs, Eppa "Jephtha" and Alex were teammates, staff fixtures for the able Pat Moran, their manager. Though his first years were hardly indicators of future Hall of Fame residency, he broke through with a 22-win season in 1916, something Moran remembered when later, as manager of the Cincinnati Reds, he brought Rixey back to his hometown to pitch for the Reds.

Rixey and Mathewson were much more alike as personalities than they

Popular Eppa Rixey came off the University of Virginia campus to become a Cincinnati mainstay in a 21-year, Hall of Fame career.

were as pitchers. Mathewson dominated a game, challenging any team any time to get the better of him. Not so Rixey, who, in his own devious, cutesy way, just "hung around" until, perhaps, a base knock here or there would pull him even or maybe win the game while he hung on to win what at one point seemed like another "L." And though both were agreeable sorts, that 3 to 2 loss to Matty back in 1913 pretty much spelled the difference between "just making it" to the Hall, as many might have felt Rixey did, and hiking its standards to pantheon levels, as veritably everyone felt Mathewson did.

Christy Mathewson versus Amos "The Hoosier Thunderbolt" Rusie (1871–1942)

Rusie was elected to the Baseball Hall of Fame in 1977

Amos Rusie, the fireballing hero of the Giants during the 1890s, was more a part of Christy Mathewson's career than one would suspect. Though he didn't appear against Mathewson during the 1901 season, the only year that Rusie and Matty were in the NL at the same time, he was involved in a contractual maneuver that the Giants and Cincinnati Reds negotiated which made the young Mathewson, a pitcher of promise, Giant property, while making the former strikeout whiz a Cincinnati Redleg in 1901. That was the year, it will be remembered, that Rusie tried to make a comeback after having injured his arm in a pickoff play during the 1898 season. But his arm was no longer up to the rigors of major league pitching, and was dead as a doornail. Consequently, so was his career.

During the 1901 season Rusie did pitch against his former ball club, appearing in a relief role on June 9 in a wild ball game ultimately given to the visiting Giants per umpire Bob Emslie's forfeit decree. The game, played before an overflowing throng at Cincinnati's old League Park, was filled with extrabase hits that would otherwise have been easy outs because the crowds surrounding the outfield caused the ground rules to be altered in the face of the over-taxing mob of 17,000 plus who managed to squeeze into the ball park. The game was called in the ninth inning with the Giants ahead 25 to 12, having pummeled William "Silver Bill" Phillips, Barney McFadden and Amos Rusie, who pitched from the fourth through the eighth innings, giving up a monstrous six-spot in the seventh and another pair of runs in his last inning of work before giving way to McFaden. And why was the game not completed?

They called Amos Rusie "the Hoosier Thunderbolt." This Famer was baseball's first "95 mph" fastballer.

Because those Cincinnati fans, like others around the league in those days, took matters into their own hands, milling about and disrupting the game to the extent that umpire Emslie had no choice but to bring it to an end.

That was enough for Cincinnati–and for Rusie. He retired, permanently, after that spectacle. One cannot help but wonder what went through his mind that day — and, more especially, through Christy Mathewson's mind!

Christy Mathewson versus Chief Bender (1884–1954)

Bender was elected to the Baseball Hall of Fame in 1953

Chief Bander moved from the Federal League in 1915 to the Philadelphia Phils in 1916, where he was used in spots and in several relief appearances, picking up seven wins and three saves that year, and posting an 8 and 2 record with two more saves in 1917 on the Alexander-led Phillies pitching staff. None of his appearances were against Mathewson, though the two personable veterans no doubt exchanged a few words here and there as their paths crossed on the field of play.

Christy Mathewson versus Burleigh Grimes (1893–1985)
Grimes was elected to the Baseball Hall of Fame in 1964

The last of baseball's legalized spitball pitchers, Burleigh Grimes.

Burleigh Grimes, who debuted just days after Matty's last major league appearance in Chicago on September 4, 1916, was a rookie up "for a look and a cup of coffee" with the Pittsburgh Pirates at the tail end of the 1916 season. It would be equally interesting to find out what the rookie up from the Birmingham club thought about the first time he saw the Cincinnati manager, the great Mathewson, who by this time was a living legend, in the visiting team's dugout. Although the Reds and Pirates closed out the 1916 series with a three game set, two in Pittsburgh and one in Cincinnati on October first, Mathewson had already made his last and triumphant appearance in Chicago.

Because of his lengthy and much-traveled career, parts of the Burleigh Grimes saga appear in several chapters ahead. Pitching in both leagues, he was active during the careers of Pete Alexander and Lefty Grove, while also pitching against Famer Stan Coveleski in the final game of the 1920 World Series. Old "Boily," as he was known in Brooklyn, where Dazzy Vance and one of the last of the spitballers, Grimes himself, teamed during the '20s, was a colorful addition to any baseball setting. Back in 1916, however, he was just a willing, albeit hardnosed, rookie trying to make it in the Bigs, a place that the mighty Mathewson had enriched beyond measure before Grimes' September 10 debut.

"Big Six" Among the Game's Elite

The view from Olympus is uncluttered. There aren't many around to get in the way of the few who are up there looking down on the rest of the "mere mortals" who have played the game — those who, by comparison, make their awesome deeds so remarkably *sui generis*. Baseball's Pitching Olympians are less than 10 in number. Among them, the Big Six, Christopher Mathewson, a charter member of the Hall of Fame, is one set apart even among these, and for very special reasons. Every commentary on the career of the legendary Giant begins not with the record book — however many and exceptional contributions he made to it — but with the Mathewson persona, his gentlemanly demeanor that stood in such stark contrast to the players of his time. In the long run that demeanor was as instrumental in making the national pastime a thing not only to be enjoyed, but to be respected, as was the Ruthian shot in the arm that catapulted the game into national popularity and prominence when that, like the integrity of Mathewson in his time, was desperately needed.

Nevertheless, a few numbers herewith to remind one and all that there were no lack of entries in baseball's "good book" to warrant his lofty position among his Cooperstown brethren. Be reminded that:

- Not only are Mathewson's career and single season pitching numbers routinely to be found among the game's top ten, his fielding and hitting statistics among pitchers are equally superior.
- Among the game's hurlers, Mathewson's career TPI, 62.9, ranks fourth (21st among all players).
- Matty ranks third in Wins (373) and eighth in W percentage (.665).
- His 79 Shutouts rank third behind Walter Johnson and Grover Alexander.
- In his career, Mathewson walked only 1.59 batters per nine innings pitched.
- In less than 16 full seasons he amassed 421 Pitching Runs, 10th on the all time list.
- Matty's 64.9 Wins Above Team ranks fourth all time.
- His 1503 career Assists, one every third inning, are second all time.
- In 1908 Mathewson threw 11 Shutouts (8th highest); in 1909 his 1.14 ERA earned a number five ranking all time; and his 0.62 Walks per game in 1913 ranks 16th all time, and first in the modern era.
- And finally, sabermetrician Tony Blengino,[11] in his ranking of the most dominant pitchers in the game's history, rates the Big Six number three among the game's top five pitchers, citing his peak period, 1907 to 1909, when he won 86 out of 115 decisions, as one of the greatest of pitching achievements ever, coming at a time when his team overall was just not good enough to unseat the Cubs and Pirates.

Connie Mack has the last word: "Mathewson was the greatest pitcher who ever lived. He had knowledge, judgment, perfect control, and form. It was wonderful to watch him pitch — when he wasn't pitching against you."

3. WALTER JOHNSON

Major League Career Totals:	Won	Lost	Pct.
Washington (AL), 1907–1927	417	279	.599

Johnson was elected to the Baseball Hall of Fame in 1936

The Express came barreling down the line, making no stops except in the big towns, whistling its way through the night full throttle. It was full speed ahead. That's the one they called the Big Train. And after a couple of seasons under the Big Tent, that's what they called Walter Johnson. The name of his game was speed. Blinding, paralyzing speed. And by the time the Big Train had made his final stop, he had rewritten substantial parts of the record book, as well as having carved a niche for himself at the end of the line — Cooperstown. As a matter of fact, he was among the first to get there, right on time, and about as fast as a body could.

It couldn't have happened to a nicer person. Not only was this fella very, very good, he was cut from the Young and Mathewson cloth, a gentle, humble human being who just happened to have the nastiest number one in the game.

By the time the second World War rolled around, the game had been around long enough to have seen a few fireballers come and go. The December 25, 1946, issue of *The Sporting News* ran a feature article on pitchers who burned up the league with the kind of heat that makes batters wince in the on-deck circle. The list stretched all the way back to the Hoosier Thunderball, Amos Rusie, of 1890s fame, and moved on through Donovan, Waddell, Reulbach, Bush, Vance, Grove, Dean and Feller, just to mention a few, all of whom were capable on any given day of blowing just about anybody away — and regularly did.

When it came to naming number one with number one, there was one and only one name that claimed the top spot: Walter Johnson. Shirley Povich, the gifted Cap City baseball scribe who wrote one of the stories in the *TSN* feature, told of the day Johnson came to see Bobby Feller pitch at Griffith Stadium. Asked to comment about the Iowa farm boy's fast one as the game commenced, Johnson replied,

"You can't judge a man's speed in the first inning. He throws mighty fast, but he'll throw faster along about the fourth or fifth after he's really warmed up."

Now it was the fifth inning and Johnson was following intently the pitching of Feller.

The game's greatest pitcher, Walter Johnson.

"He's mighty fast," Johnson repeated, "those are strikeout pitches he's throwing."

Then it was I who put the question to him: "Walter, does he throw that ball as fast as you did?" Squarely on the spot I had put the most modest man in my memory. He looked at me squarely, and then grinned. Truthful belief triumphed over modesty at that point. "No," was Johnson's answer. "I guess I used to throw that thing faster."

Rusie was fast, but those who should have known claimed that Feller was faster. Then there was Johnson. And how about the rest of the 20th century? Don Newcombe, or Sudden Sam McDowell, or Ryne Duren, or Goose

Gossage, or Bob Gibson? And from the more recent era, those who rate the Mr. Swift nod: J. R. Richards, Nolan Ryan, Roger Clemens, or Randy Johnson? On any given day any of the above might have...

Selecting number one Mr. Swift is, of course, risky business. There are, after all, so many variables, so many varying circumstances, and so many ways to line up the numbers in support of personal preferences. From the perspective of this corner, the choice would be the gentleman from Humboldt, Kansas, aware that the reader's favorite may be from among those listed or different altogether.

From among the baker's dozen listed in the following chart, all of them exceptional flamethrowers (only one, Sudden Sam McDowell, is not in the Hall of Fame), at least six or seven of them have been hailed as the Fastest Ever at one time or another, with Bob Feller, Randy Johnson, Lefty Grove, Nolan Ryan — and Walter Johnson usually named at or very near the number one spot.

The numbers cited reflect not only productivity, but the net result of heaving baseballs at more than 95, and even 100-plus miles per hour. The selected fireballers below (another 25 could have been chosen), each of whom had enough control to make excessive speed work, could be expected to keep opposing hitters off the bases better than two-thirds of the time, surrendered far fewer hits than average hurlers, and whiffed batters in huge numbers. That often adds up to low ERAs, winning games at the rate of at least three out of five, and, usually, a Cooperstown plaque. The list is arranged chronologically. Boldface numbers indicate best statistics in this list. The career numbers:

The Mr. Swift List

Nm/Yrs	K's	K's/gm	Hits/gm	Opp. OB%	ERA
John Clarkson, 1882–1894 (12 years)	1978	3.92	8.70	.291	2.81
Amos Rusie, 1889–1901 (10)	1950	4.64	8.07	.319	3.07
Kid Nichols, 1890–1906 (15)	1880	3.34	8.75	.300	2.95
Rube Waddell, 1897–1910 (13)	2316	7.04	7.48	.288	**2.16**
Walter Johnson, 1907–1927 (21)	3509	5.34	7.48	.279	2.17
Lefty Grove, 1925–1941 (17)	2266	5.17	8.79	.311	3.06
Bob Feller, 1936–1956 (18)	2581	6.07	7.69	.319	3.25
Sandy Koufax, 1955–1966 (12)	2396	9.28	6.79	**.276**	2.76
Sam McDowell, 1961–1975 (15)	2453	8.86	7.03	.318	3.17
Steve Carlton, 1965–1988 (24)	4136	7.13	8.06	.308	3.22
Nolan Ryan, 1966–1993 (27)	5714	9.55	**6.56**	.309	3.19
Roger Clemens, 1986* (15*)	3504	8.60	7.61	.295	3.07
Randy Johnson, 1988* (13*)	3040	**10.95**	6.96	.305	3.19

*Incomplete. Statistics through 2000 season.

3. Walter Johnson

In Walter Johnson's case, however, there are some numbers that command respect because they have never been surpassed, nor will they be; and, further, because they reflect the awesome control the man exercised over the flow and outcome of the game. Those stats involve the number of shutouts in which Johnson was involved, both on the winning and losing end. And it is well to remember that in many of these games there was no margin for pitching mistakes that might just tip the balance, netting opponents the one run they needed to win — if for no other reason than the meager Washington attack was so often incapable of scoring enough to overcome even narrow leads. These numbers merit a look and some reflection:

- There were 110 career shutouts, perhaps Johnson's most durable record.
- The 110 represent 26.4 percent of his career victory total, 417.
- 38 of the 110 shutouts, .345 percent, were 1 to 0 victories, an indication not only of the era in which Sir Walter pitched, but the dire need of his low-scoring ball club to shut out their opponents.
- On May 18, 1918, Johnson shut out the White Sox, 1 to 0, in an 18 inning marathon, an extra-inning game shutout record.
- Johnson's record in 1 to 0 games was 38W and 26L, a seemingly low .594 winning percentage, but very close to his career Win percent (.599). Coincidentally, the numbers are the same for 2 to 1 games, making a grand total of 128 one run games by scores of 1 to 0 or 2 to 1. 76 of those were Ws, no less than 18 percent (ca.2/5) of his career total.
- During his career, the Big Train shut out the Philadelphia A's 23 times, a record for shutouts against a single team.

These numbers are part of a pitching portfolio that, in sum, identify him as the most dominating pitcher the game has ever seen, or no doubt ever will see. More of his orbital accomplishments are just ahead in his confrontations with the very best hurlers of his day. The list, arranged chronologically according to debut dates, follows:

Name/HOF Year	Debut/Career Years	TPI/All Time Pitcher Ranking
Cy Young/1937	Aug 6, 1890/1890–1911	78.0/2
Clark Griffith/1946*	Apr 11, 1891/1891–1914	27.4/49
Rube Waddell/1946	Sep 8, 1897/1897–1910	24.4/69
Jack Chesbro/1946	Jul 12, 1899/1899–1901	10.9/239
Eddie Plank/1946	May 13, 1901/1901–1917	26.9/53
Addie Joss/1978	Apr 26, 1902/1902–1910	25.8/60
Chief Bender/1953	Apr 20, 1903/1903–1925	14.4/170
Ed Walsh/1946	May 7, 1904/1904–1917	44.9/12

Eddie Cicotte	Sep 3, 1905/1905–1920	25.4/63
Herb Pennock/1948	May 14, 1912/1912–1934	6.8/NR
Stan Coveleski/1969	Sep 10, 1912/1912–1928	27.0/52
Red Faber/1964	Apr 17, 1914/1914–1933	27.2/51
Babe Ruth/1936	Jul 11, 1914/1914–1935	17.2/135
Carl Mays	Apr 15, 1915/1915–1929	36.6/22
Dazzy Vance/1955*	Apr 16, 1915/1915–1935	27.4/49
Urban Shocker	Apr 24, 1916/1916–1928	25.8/60
Waite Hoyt/1969	Jul 24, 1918/1918–1938	15.1/158
Ted Lyons/1955	Jul 2, 1923/1923–1946	37.1/21
Lefty Grove/1947	Apr 14, 1925/1925–1941	59.7/6
Red Ruffing/1967	May 31, 1925/1925–1947	28.0/47

Cy Young and Walter Johnson

There is something utterly absorbing about contemplating a Young-Johnson matchup. Two of the game's legends doing battle against one another... There have been any number of those titanic confrontations, each of them an occasion unto itself, and even though two of the game's superstars might not have met when each was in his prime, as often was the case, the very sight of two past masters matching pitches, savvy, power, finesse and grit sets imagination aflame. The best of them — and there are Hubbell vs. Dean, Walsh vs. Joss, Koufax vs. Marichal, or Ryan up against Carlton, just to mention a few from among a number of extraordinary possibilities — somehow lose luster when mentioned in the same breath with Young and Johnson. Would that their years had blended better to bring about 10 or more encounters that would certainly have produced a series of ball games worthy of a Grantland Rice writeup!

We are left, instead, with Cy Young's relief appearance against the Senators and the Johnson conquest of Boston's Red Sox during the 1910 season as previously reported. And in the case of two such peerless Famers, those two engagements beat none by far more than the old country mile.

Walter Johnson versus Clark Calvin "Old Fox" Griffith (1869–1955)

Griffith was elected to the Baseball Hall of Fame in 1946

Clark Griffith signed his first professional contract in 1888, moved on to a successful major league career as one of the craftier pitchers of his time,

---

* Although in the league during the Johnson years, Griffith and Vance did not appear against him.

and ultimately became a manager and then the CEO of the Washington Senators, serving in that capacity until his death in 1955. All told, it was a 67-year run, one of the most colorful in baseball's history. Very few served the national pastime longer, or with more distinction. That was duly recognized when he was elected to baseball's pantheon in 1946.

That said, it should be noted that the Griffith-Johnson relationship was to the American League what the McGraw-Mathewson relationship was to the National League. The Old Fox and the Big Train. Some twosome. They carried the Washington franchise on their backs for better than a score of years, and did it with all the selfless determination, professional class, and clever maneuvering necessary to bring, finally, the Big Trophy to the nation's capitol city.

There were no Griffith-Johnson matchups during their playing careers, but it is interesting to note that Walter Johnson came into the AL at a time when Griffith was managing New York and making his last few appearances as a reliever, finishing out the 1907 season (Johnson's rookie year) with four appearances before accepting Cincinnati's managerial reins. Three years later he was back in the AL, this time as the boss-man of the Senators, just in time to manage Washington in 1912, the first of Walter J's 30-win seasons in a year that the Senators bid fair to win the pennant, rising from the shadows of the AL basement in 1911 to a second place finish.

Elected to the Hall as an executive, Clark Griffith might well have been admitted on his pitching prowess.

During the Johnson-Griffith years, the Nationals might not have always been the best in the league, but the likes of Miller Huggins and Connie Mack, managers who knew a thing or two about the game, never took the Senators lightly, not as long as Johnson and Griffith were around.

Luke Sewell, 20-year veteran of baseball's wars, who struggled with Johnson's hummer and toiled for Clark Griffith, catching in 141 of the Senators' pennant winning games in 1933, gets the last word on the Old Fox.

The story begins with an exchange between the two prior to the 1934 season and revolves around Big Luke's salary for the upcoming season. Sewell tells it this way:

> I'd say that anybody who missed playing at least a full year for Clark Griffith missed half his baseball life. Griff was a great character. He'd argue with you over five cents. In 1933 I caught 141 games for him and he wanted to cut me 2500 dollars the next year. I said to him, "Griff, I caught all of your ball games for you. What are you doing?!"
> "Well," he said, "you didn't win the World Series."
> I couldn't help laughing. "You're right," I said. "The Giants beat us in six games."
> We argued about salary, and I said I wasn't going to sign. A day or two before spring training opened in Biloxi, Mississippi, I got a wire from Griff telling me they were going to open the training camp on a certain day and that there was going to be a parade at nine o'clock in the morning. The fire department and the police department and everybody in town was going to be out for it. He said that if I was there in time to ride in the fire engine, he would give me the 2500 dollars back and a thousand-dollar bonus if I caught a certain number of games.
> Well, I've got to tell you, I was sitting on that fire engine at nine o'clock in the morning when the parade started. So you see how Griff would handle things. He knew darned well he had to pay me that money, but in order to salve his pride, he made it look like he was getting something out of me. But he was a great fellow, one of a kind, and I liked him.

Though often the subject of heated debate, and no little consternation among owners, when the last word was said, it usually came out about the way Luke Sewell put it. They liked the Old Fox, too!

Walter Johnson versus George "Rube" Waddell (1876–1914)
Waddell was elected to the Baseball Hall of Fame in 1946

They only matched laser shots twice, did Johnson and Waddell, but when they did, Walter Johnson saw enough to be convinced that, in his own words, "Waddell had more sheer pitching ability than any man I ever saw."[12] Many, of course, said the same thing, and many shared the same frustration over the Eccentric One's off-the-wall approach to life in general, and pitching in particular. But in Dr. Waddell's pitching bag there was heat capable of melting steel — on that everyone agreed. His ace had that Randy Johnson-Lefty Grove velocity, the kind of one-second blur from the mound to the plate that prompts hitters to start their swing during the windup.

It just so happened that under some unusual circumstances — even for

Rube — the ol' heater was aflame on the day in 1908 when Johnson and Waddell did battle. In this particular meeting between the two, Rube, then with the St. Louis Browns, was closer to the end of his major league days than he might have known (the end came in 1910). He wasn't quite the flamethrower he had been, except, of course, if he would reach deep down for some special occasion. The occasion came on September 20 when Johnson's catcher, Mike Kahoe, made the remark that set Waddell on fire, letting the Brownies' lefty know that the Senators were going to tear him apart. It was all Waddell needed to hear, setting him off on a merciless tear that finally wound up in a 17-K, 2 to 1, ten-inning win over the Nationals that even had the veterans muttering before the day was done.

Nor was the other Johnson-Waddell encounter any better for the Senators, or the Big Train. It's hard to say what clicked inside the mind of George Edward Waddell on July 23, 1909, but once again he came out steaming with the mid-summer St. Louis heat and trampled the Senators with a five-hit shutout. Perhaps the very sight of the Senators and Mike Kahoe was all he needed to recall that September afternoon the previous season. Whatever it was, it turned out to be the last great performance of his career, and it put him two up on Walter Johnson, having given the Senators one run in 19 innings in the two Waddell-Johnson matchups. The box score of the 1909 game follows:

At. St. Louis, July 23, 1909

Washington	AB	R	H	PO	St. Louis	AB	R	H	PO
Browne, lf	4	0	0	1	Hartzell, ss	4	1	2	1
Milan, cf	4	0	2	3	Stone, rf	3	3	2	1
Lelivelt, rf	4	0	0	2	Hoffman, cf	4	0	2	0
Unglaub, 2b	4	0	1	0	Griggs, lf	4	0	1	2
Donohue, 1b	4	0	1	5	Jones, 1b	4	1	2	10
Conroy, 2b	3	0	0	2	Williams, 2b	4	0	0	3
McBride, ss	3	0	0	3	Ferris, 3b	4	1	1	5
Street, c	2	0	1	8	Stephens, c	3	0	1	5
Johnson, p	3	0	0	0	Waddell, p	4	0	0	0
Totals	31	0	5	24	Totals	34	6	11	27

Line Score	Washington	000	000	000	0–5–1
	St. Louis	200	011	11x	6–11–12

BH	Hartzell, Jones, Street, Stephens
3BH	Ferris
SH	Stephens
SB	Hoffman, Jone 2, Stone
LOB	Washington 5, St. Louis 6
DP	Ferris and Williams
BB	Johnson 1, Waddell 1

K	Johnson 8, Waddell 7
Umpires	Hurst and O'Laughlin
Time	1:25

Walter Johnson versus John Dwight "Happy Jack" Chesbro

Jack Chesbro, a Hall of Famer in his own right, had the pleasure (though some might qualify that by using the modifier "dubious") of meeting three of the four top hurlers in baseball's history. Those four, it will be recalled, are Cy Young, Christy Mathewson, Pete Alexander and Walter Johnson. Rube Waddell is the other pitcher who took on the same threesome out of that distinguished group (Young, Mathewson and Johnson).

The first of these historic matchups occurred at a time when Walter Johnson was beginning to feel at home under the Big Tent, having just completed his first full season, as September opened during the 1908 season. Over the Labor Day weekend, Washington and New York busied themselves with a four game set at Hilltop Park. Working on three days rest, the Big Train took on Chesbro and his Hilltopper colleagues in a September 4 engagement, brushing them aside with a 3 to 0 six-hitter. Sir Walter followed that one up with another white-washing the next day, this time by a 6 to 0 count. After a day off on Sunday, Johnson returned on the 7th to find Chesbro on the hill once again. In front of more than 12,000 disbelieving New Yorkers he shut down Gotham's bats, administering yet another shutout, a two-hit, 4 to 0 effort that has been ranked among the 25 best games he ever pitched — if for no other reason than that it was the third of three straight shutouts within a span of four days. The feat was immediately recognized as one of baseball's major pitching accomplishments, even as it still is. And what must Jack Chesbro have been thinking beyond *why me?*!

By 1909 it was just about sunset time for Jack Chesbro's much used arm, and before the season was over he had been moved on to Boston for a final appearance or two. One of his four starts for New York was made on June 19. On that day he pitched what was perhaps his last good ball game, but, unfortunately, his opponent was Walter Johnson. In this third and final encounter the Big Train, the game went into the final stanza tied at three before the Nationals cracked it open with a four-run barrage, opening up a 7 to 3 lead. Though Johnson surrendered a last-of-the-ninth run, the New York rally fell far short and Jack Chesbro was charged with one of his defeats in an 0–4 record for the New Yorkers during his final season. One more loss with Boston settled the record at 0 and 5 for his last major league season.

In 21 innings against Walter Johnson, Jack Chesbro's support consisted of three earned runs and nine hits, the kind of pitching that became boilerplate Johnson over the years. That's what Hall of Famers and all the rest of the game's hurlers had to look forward to, and Happy Jack was no exception.

How did Walter Johnson sustain the pace and strain of all the games in which he was involved (his 802 pitching appearances ranks among the top 25, and his 666 starts are 10th all time)? There are several important parts in answering that one, as well as others that were often asked about both the frequency and the speed with which he pitched. But one of the more important is certainly motion and style. On that score his trainer, Mike Martin, had this to say in a February 26, 1927, *Washington Star* interview:

> For him, throwing a ball involves no more labor than snapping your fingers does for you, and as far as his wing is concerned, he will be able to pitch when he is 60.

Mr. Chesbro and the rest of the pitching fraternity should have been so lucky!

Walter Johnson versus Edward Stewart "Gettysburg Eddie" Plank, 1875–1926

Plank was elected to the Baseball Hall of Fame in 1946

Through a decade of superb pitching, Eddie Plank and Walter Johnson dueled, serving up one breathtaking masterpiece after another. The record speaks for itself:

Sep 2, 1907	Philadelphia 3, Washington 2	Plank WP
Oct 4, 1907	Washington 2, Philadelphia 1	Johnson WP
Sep 11, 1908	Washington 2, Philadelphia 1	Johnson WP
Apr 4, 1910	Washington 3, Philadelphia 0	Johnson WP
July 5, 1910	Philadelphia 3, Washington 2	Plank WP
Oct 3, 1911	Washington 2, Philadelphia 0	Johnson WP
Jun 29, 1912	Philadelphia 2, Washington 1	Plank WP
Sep 27, 1912	Washington 5, Philadelphia 4	Johnson, WP
Apr 30, 1913	Washington 2, Philadelphia 0	Johnson WP
Aug 6, 1917	Washington 1, Philadelphia 0	Johnson WP

There were three other occasions, no less tense, on which these two mound masters met. On July 30, 1910, the Athletics got to Barney[13] for a dozen hits, nibbling away until they had built up a 7 to 0 lead going into the top of the ninth, when the Senators suddenly broke loose against starter Chief Bender, scoring four times, loading the bases, and threatening to blow the game wide open. Enter Gettysburg Eddie, who stifled the rally, enabling the A's to escape with a 7 to 5 win. Bender got the W and Plank the Save.

326 wins and a career 2.35 ERA put Eddie Plank in the Hall of Fame.

There was no decision for either Plank or Johnson on May 8, 1914, when the Senators and Athletics beat up on one another, settling for a 9 to 9 tie. Finally, on June 1, 1917, Johnson and Plank went at each other in a game that ended in a 2 to 2 tie after nine. St. Louis, for whom Eddie Plank pitched the last two seasons of his career, won the game with two markers in the tenth inning, though Plank had been removed, giving way to Alan Sotheron, who picked up the victory. Johnson went all the way, absorbing the loss.

Among those awesome encounters three stand out. The first occurred on the very day that the tradition involving the throwing of the ceremonial first ball by the president was inaugurated. The date was April 14, 1910, a pleasant spring day just meant for a ball game in the nation's capitol city. Connie Mack's Athletics, who would go on to win the pennant that season, opposed the Senators, whose opener would be the Big Train. In the first of his 14 Opening Day assignments he was absolutely invincible, tossing a one-hitter that might very well have been baseball's first Opening Day no-hitter, when Frank Baker's fly ball into the roped off section of the overflow crowd was misplayed into a ground rule two bagger. But that didn't dim the brilliance of the duel between Eddie Plank, who also turned in an artful performance, and the flamethrowing Johnson. After scoring a run on two doubles in the first inning, Sir Walter, often used as a pinch hitter during his career, opened up the fifth with a screaming double to center, and scored moments later when his road roomie and lifelong friend, Clyde "Deerfoot" Milan, also doubled. When Milan scored on a sacrifice fly, the Senators had a 3 to 0 lead that turned out to be the final score.

The coda for this snappy Opening Day march came on April 15, when President Taft inscribed the ball he threw out from the presidential box with the words: "To Walter Johnson, with the hope that he may continue to be as formidable as he was in yesterday's game. William H. Taft." That hope was well placed. There would follow 17 seasons of Hall of Fame pitching that blazed new trails in the annals of pitching.

Toward the tail end of the 1912 season, the Senators and Athletics met in Philadelphia to try to do something about second-place in a pennant race already tucked away by Boston's Red Sox. The Mackmen, 2 and 1/2 games behind the second place Nationals, sent Gettysburg Eddie to the mound to face Bobby Groom, who was finishing up a 24 and 13 season, his best career effort by far. In command of a 4 to 1 lead going into the bottom of the ninth, Groom finally wilted, giving up three to send the game into extra stanzas. At that point manager Clark Griffith called on — who else? — the Big Train.

A "new game" started at that point. Two master craftsmen went at it inning after inning until another nine had been played without so much as a hint of another score. Then, in the 19th frame, catcher Alva "Buff" Williams drew a leadoff walk. That was followed by a bunt intended to sacrifice Williams to second, but so well placed was it that it turned out to be Walter Johnson's only hit of the day. With runners on first and second, Danny Moeller's grounder forced Williams at third, leaving Johnson and Moeller aboard. Plank got the grounder he needed from the Senators' next hitter, Eddie Foster, but the usually reliable Eddie Collins threw wildly to Stuffy McInnis, at first trying to complete an inning-ending twin-killing, and Barney himself scored from second, beating the A's and Plank, 5 to 4. Aside from its ending, the game was a microcosm of those typically taut, nerve-wracking duels staged by the two mound maestros.

The third of these scintillating matchups was another history-making event. In a pitching duel the likes of which had become *de rigueur* in a Plank-Johnson faceoff, the St. Louis Browns met the Nationals on August 6, 1917. This one was Eddie Plank's last, and he left the game a winner, despite the fact that he lost it by the heartbreaking score of 1 to 0 — and in the 11th inning, at that. Unfortunately, he ran headlong into what was perhaps Walter Johnson's best ball game of the season. Barney gave up but five scattered hits. Just a few days later the veteran Plank, Old Fuss and Fidget, informed the baseball world that he was retiring. Nearing his 42nd birthday, he had decided that he had had enough. No matter. The niche would be waiting at Cooperstown when the time came. He had nothing left to prove. The box score of that game follows:

At Washington, August 6, 1917

St. Louis	AB	R	H	PO	Washington	AB	R	H	PO
Shotton, lf	4	0	0	4	H. Milan, lf	5	0	2	2
Smith, cf	5	0	0	1	Foster, 2b	4	0	1	2
Sisler, 1b	5	0	0	14	C. Milan, cf	3	0	0	5

Pratt, 2b	4	0	0	3	Rice, rf	4	0	1	2
Sloan, rf	4	0	1	2	Shanks, ss	4	0	0	3
Severeid, c	4	0	2	3	Gharrity, 1b	4	0	0	14
Austin, 3b	4	0	0	3	Leonard, 3b	4	0	0	1
Lavan, ss	4	0	2	1	Ainsmith, c	3	1	1	3
Plank, p	2	0	0	0	Johnson, p	4	0	0	1
Totals	36	0	5	31*	Totals	35	1	5	33

Line Score	St. Louis	000	000	000	00	0-5-0
	Washington	000	000	000	01	1-5-2

2BH	Lavan	BB	Plank 3, Johnson 1
SB	Ainsmith	K	Plank 3, Johnson 3
SH	Plank, Shotton	E	H. Milan, Foster
LOB	St. Louis 6, Washington 6	Umpires	Nallin and Owens
DP	C. Milan and Ainsmith	Time	1:46

Walter Johnson versus Adrian "Addie" Joss (1880–1911)
Joss was elected to the Baseball Hall of Fame in 1978

One of the more revealing statistics about pitching indicates the number of free passes issued per nine innings pitched. That one speaks volumes about a pitcher's mastery of the strike zone. In the game's history, only 29 hurlers have given up *less than one base on balls* per nine innings pitched in an entire season. One of these was Addie Joss, whom you encountered among Cy Young's Hall of Fame competitors. Joss walked only 30 men in 325 innings in 1908, achieving a mind-boggling .083 average. With those kinds of numbers working for him it could be expected that the accompanying Ratio and ERA marks would be equally low. They were. His Ratio stat was a miniscule 7.3, and his ERA that year was a major league–leading 1.16, eighth high all time. Joss' brilliance preceded him wherever he went. Around the league even the top drawer pitchers summoned "a little extra" for the Joss engagements.

So it was a foregone conclusion that Walter Johnson knew he would be up against a master slab artist when matched with Addie Joss, and if he didn't realize it because of his lack of experience (he encountered Joss for the first time during his second season in the majors in September of 1908), there were those among the Senators who would have warned him well in advance.

By 1909 Barney knew his way around the league and was ready for bigger things, but that very season turned out to be the worst season in Barney's career. A 13 and 25 log saddled him with his highest ERA until the 1920 sea-

---

*One out when winning run scored.

son, when everything soared out of sight, baseballs included, as the new bombs-away-era began. It was also a season during which Johnson was victimized a record-setting 10 times by shutouts.

By the time Johnson and Joss were scheduled to face off on August 4, 1909, they had already met in an inaugural match on September 26, 1908 — started, but not completed — by Joss, and finished for Washington by Johnson, who took a 5 to 4 loss in relief. Their second meeting occurred on May 20 in the 1909 season in a game that Johnson won 3 to 2 over Joss in 10 innings; and the way these two went at each other, it was reasonable to anticipate that a shutout might be in store. On August 4, then, Joss and Johnson crossed swords in the first game of a twin bill at Washington's League Park at the intersection of Florida and Trinidad Avenues in the nation's capitol. And, indeed, there was a shutout, a spine-tingling 1 to 0 affair that tolerated but 10 hits, six for the Senators and four for the visiting Naps. But Walter Johnson was not the losing pitcher. On this day Addie Joss was bested by the young sidearmer who threw those blinding bullets past the likes of Hall of Famers Larry Lajoie and Elmer Flick. There were no free passes this day, though Johnson did hit two batsmen, which probably made him that much more effective. The victory was one of 13 he was able to manage during the 1909 campaign, and it was his best outing of the season.

Addie Joss, who pitched a perfect game on October 2, 1908, in the heat of one of the greatest pennant races in the game's history.

There was only one other matchup between Joss and Johnson, this one coming on May 14, 1910, during what proved to be Addie Joss' last year. This time the Cleveland ball club got one more hit than in 1909, but the result was the same, a 1 to 0 ball game that featured airtight pitching, one walk by Joss, and eight Johnson strikeouts (the same as he had contributed to the 1909 ball game). The issue was settled in the first inning when hits by Jack Lelivelt, Kid Elberfeld and Doc Gessler provided the Senators with the only run they needed.

What the future might have provided by way of pitching extravaganzas between these two titans of the mound was left to imagination and conjecture with the sudden passing of the popular Cleveland hurler. Walter Johnson, one of the privileged stars who was asked to participate in baseball's first all-star game, a benefit that was staged for the Addie Joss family on July 24, 1911, wired his acceptance: "I'll do anything they want for Addie Joss' family." That was vintage Johnson for a vintage Hall of Famer.

Walter Johnson versus Albert "Chief" Bender (1884–1954)

Bender was elected to the Baseball Hall of Fame in 1953

Connie Mack's remarkable assemblage of pennant winning teams between 1910 and 1914 was not only built on superior firepower and smart defense. He just happened to have a few Hall of Fame pitchers on hand, not least of which was his favorite go-to guy when the blue chips were being anted up. That fellow was the Chief, Albert Bender. The Carlisle Indian School alum, along with colleagues Eddie Plank, Jack Coombs and Eddie Collins, college grads all, helped guide the Mackmen to the top of the AL heap at a time when Boston, Detroit, Cleveland and Chicago, on occasion, all gave hot chase for the league's honors.

During those heady years in the City of Brotherly Love, Albert, as Mr. Mack was wont to call him, stacked up a glistening .761 winning percentage while tossing his bat-breaking curveballs and late-breaking fastballs at the Junior Circuit's hitters. Winning at crucial times, and usually well rested for those must-win ball games Mack counted on, he came through with a 91–31 record between 1910 and 1914 alone.

While Philadelphia and Boston, in 1912, monopolized the pennant picture, Washington elbowed its way into the flag wars with an entry that was as middling as its capitol was famous. Who knew *any* of the Senators — with one exception? Not many. But the one almost everyone knew was Walter Johnson, who almost single-handedly pulled the Nats up by their bootstraps and had them threatening the league leaders. Beginning in 1912, when Washington wound up in the league's second spot (much to everyone's amazement), Mr. Johnson went about his business with 33 wins, and followed that up with another 36 in 1913, 29 in 1914, and 27 in 1915 to round out a foursome of Hall of Fame years that had his name on the lips of every knowledgeable baseball buff in the country.

Bender-Johnson duels were inevitable under those circumstances. Every team knew that, barring the "blessing" of a rainout or two, they would have to face Big Barney at least once during a series. And Connie Mack would want to have his Chief on tap for that meeting. Bender had been around since 1903, battle-tested and brainy, the ideal mound opponent for Washington's ace. So they squared off seven times between 1907 and 1914, with the following results:

The Johnson-Bender Log:

Aug 17, 1909	Washington 1, Philadelphia 0	Johnson WP, Bender LP
Jul 30, 1910	Philadelphia 7, Washington 5	Bender WP, Johnson LP
Sep 3, 1910	Washington 3, Philadelphia 1	Johnson WP, Bender LP
Jun 19, 1911	Philadelphia 6, Washington 2	Bender WP, Johnson LP
Jun 2, 1914	Philadelphia 4, Washington 2	Bender WP, Johnson LP

On July 1, 1911, and June 25, 1913, Chief Bender appeared against Walter Johnson in a relief role but was not credited with Philadelphia's 13 to 8 and 14 to 2 victories. Walter Johnson was the losing pitcher in both games. Colby Jack Coombs and Bullet Joe Bush were the winners, respectively, in the 1911 and 1913 games.

In the first two engagements between Bender and Johnson, mound duels of the very first order, Sir Walter got the better of it, coming away with a 12-inning 1 to 0 deadball-era classic on August 17, 1909, a typically sticky, hot-as-Hades summer day in Washington. The second Bender-Johnson meeting in 1910 resulted in a 3 to 1 Washington win in which Bender was lifted after only four innings of work, but behind 2 to 1. The A's never made it up, garnering only three hits off Johnson's rifle shots and eight whiffs. Connie Mack saw the handwriting on the dugout wall in the second when the Nationals posted their second run. With the 12-game lead he had over second place New York, it must have seemed prudent to save the big part–Chippewa for another day. Given his 1914 wrecking crew, Mack's prudence, never questioned in any case, was verified at season's end with his fourth pennant in five seasons.

Chief Bender was another of those Famers who had the distinction of meeting Cy Young, Walter Johnson and Christy Mathewson, though the setting for the three Mathewson-Bender encounters was not during the regular season. Two[14] of their three duels took place during the 1911 World Series. In that series, won by the Athletics in six games, Matty led off with a 2 to 1 victory at the Polo Grounds, beating Bender in a tense nail-biter before the largest throng to that date in the Series' history. But the Chief caught up with Mathewson in their next pairing, beating him 4 to 2 at Shibe Park as Philadelphia took a 3 to 1 lead in games. Bender also beat the Giants two days later in the game that won the world's championship for the A's, 13 to 2, at the expense of Red Ames, Hooks Wiltse and Rube Marquard.

A final footnote: The Chief was on the Phillies' pitching staff of 1916 and 1917 with Grover Alexander. The big Native American traveled in some pretty exclusive company, now didn't he?!

Walter Johnson versus Edward "Big Ed" Walsh (1881–1959)
Walsh was elected to the Baseball Hall of Fame in 1946

It was quite an assignment. Walter Johnson, still recovering from the aftereffects of a 16-inning, complete game, 2 to 1 victory over St. Louis on July 28, 1908 (a year when every team in the league battled relentlessly in every game for an edge that might set them apart from the pack), was pressed into service just four days later by manager Joe Cantillon. His foe was the White Sox, who were bunched with the Indians, Browns and the Cobb-led Tigers in a fevered race that ultimately went down to the last game of the season before Detroit would be declared the winner of the 1908 pennant. Chicago's pitching staff was ready for this series, to be played at the Sox' home field, the South Side Grounds, soon to be the site of one of baseball's emerging group of "baseball palaces," Comiskey Park.

So Johnson laced 'em up and took on Big Ed Walsh, the premier spitballer of the day, got the Senators through seven Chicago innings still in contention, albeit on the short end of a 2 to 1 score, and headed into the top of the eighth trying to figure out how to hit Walsh's tantalizing but ever bobbing and weaving out-pitch. Just meeting the ball turned out to be enough, however, because three Pale Hose errors opened the floodgates and the Senators took a 5 to 2 lead into the final frame. Although Walsh and Co. managed to add one more in the bottom of the ninth, there was enough left in the Johnson tank to finish things off, beating the Sox 5 to 3. Two weeks later he polished off Chicago once again in one of those patented 1 to 0 "clinics," this time over the White Sox' talented Doc White, two-hitting them, all of which was part of a streak that put up 11 straight Ws out of 13 possible decisions.

Sir Walter had set sail in his first two Chicago encounters with a pair of mound gems. But by September 19, Big Ed leveled the count with a 1 to 0 "clinic" of his own. And from that point on, Walsh was a Johnson nemesis as the White Sox peeled off five more wins in a row before the Washington Wonder was able to register another win. Although a pair of Washington victories preceded Johnson's next winning decision, the victory he was looking for over Ed Walsh finally came on their very last major league meeting, August 15, 1912, when both entered the game as relievers, Johnson gaining the win and Walsh the loss, in relief of Doc White.

As was the case with Eddie Plank, the Walsh-Johnson matchups produced a series of tight ball games, any one of which might have gone one way or another. It was deadball era baseball at its best, the kind of baseball and the kind of pitching one would expect from two of the Hall's foremost. Here is the record:

The Johnson-Walsh Log:

Aug 1, 1908	Washington 5, Chicago 3	Johnson WP, Walsh LP
Sep 19, 1908	Chicago 1, Washington 0	Walsh WP, Johnson LP
Aug 29, 1909	Chicago 2, Washington 0	Walsh WP, Johnson LP
Aug 23, 1910	Chicago 1, Washington 0	Walsh WP, Johnson LP
May 8, 1912	Chicago 7, Washington 6	Walsh WP, Johnson LP
Aug 15, 1912	Washington 4, Chicago 3	Johnson WP, Walsh LP

Johnson was the starting and losing pitcher in the May 10, 1910, game won by Chicago, 10 to 3. Doc White was the starting and winning pitcher, with relief and a Save for Ed Walsh. Johnson started for Washington and was the loser. Exactly one year later, Chicago beat the Senators 9 to 6 as Johnson was chased in the first inning, receiving the loss, while "Death Valley Jim" Scott came on in relief of Walsh to earn the win.

On May 8, 1912, Ed Walsh relieved Joey Benz and was credited with a win as the Sox beat the Senators 7 to 6. Johnson was the LP.

On August 4, 1912, Washington beat Chicago 3 to 2. Johnson relieved the winner, "Long Tom" Hughes, picking up the Save. Walsh, in relief of White, was the losing pitcher.

A Johnson Special: The Big Train, the Georgia Peach and the Bambino

Two of the game's greatest hitters facing the game's greatest pitcher — an exciting, bound-to-stir-up-your-interest matchup, isn't it?! That most intriguing of

Ed Walsh. They said he could strut while standing still. With *his* numbers he could afford to do a little struttin'.

prospects was one of baseball's stellar attractions for most of the earlier years of the 20th century, as baseball aficionados looked forward to seeing or reading about the celebrated faceoffs that brought together Ty Cobb, Babe Ruth and the legendary Walter Johnson.

Between them, Cobb, who was on hand for Johnson's debut and registered the very first base hit against him on August 2, 1907, and Ruth, whose first appearance against Johnson was as a pinch hitter on October 5 of his 1914, rookie season, were enough to tame any pitcher, no matter what their assortment of pitches and deliveries. Though their style, swing, approach to the game, and personalities were eons apart, their effect on opposing pitchers was virtually the same; when these fellas stepped in, pitchers took a deep breath—fearing the worst, despite giving the two swatmeisters their best shot.

Ty Cobb in the batter's box and Walter Johnson on the mound. Think about it. They certainly did. In their first encounter, Cobb, at 20 and well into his first super season, and Johnson, a strapping teenager whose warmups gave Cobb something to think about, left Washington's fans with something to remember. Leading off the second inning, the Georgia Peach dragged a bunt between first baseman Jim Delehanty and Johnson that was so well placed that Delehanty didn't even attempt a throw. That started off Cobb's day in style, as he went on to destroy the Senators single-handedly, firing two bullets from right field that nailed a pair of potential Washington runs, stealing bases and pounded out two more hits in that day's second game, leading Detroit to a pair of wins, one of which hung the first defeat of Johnson's career, a 3 to 2 loss, on the man who would carry Washington on his shoulders for the next 20 years. That day's exhibition, a strong start for Johnson and a typical afternoon's work of diversified, relentless baseball on Cobb's part, set the stage for a score of years ahead. As it turned out, when Walter Johnson retired in 1927 the curtain came down on a matchup that featured more Cobb at bats against the Big Train than any other pitcher he faced. And, as one might expect, the redoubtable Cobb found a way to hit Johnson better than most of the other players the Big Train faced. The overall average of all players against Johnson was .227, which ranks 23rd, all time. Cobb? He did what he usually did. He hit Johnson for a .367 lifetime average, exactly what his career, number one all time average turned out to be. Mr. Cobb, it will be remembered, had that hitting thing down like no player before or since.

In 368 plate appearances against Johnson, more than any hitter against a single pitcher in the game's history, Ty Cobb's record against Johnson took off some eight seasons deep into the rivalry. The pivotal game that changed the Cobb versus Johnson confrontation dramatically came on August 10, 1915, when a curve ball got away on Sir Walter and beaned Oscar Vitt. Hitting batters always caused undue trauma for Johnson, and this one just happened to come up with Mr. Cobb, a very attentive observer, in a position to see both the beaning and the effect it had on Johnson, which, as usual, was drastic. In one of his cannier adjustments, Cobb, from that moment forward, began crowding the plate, giving Johnson a smaller strike zone. As the count began to swing in his favor, the Georgia Peach would edge back deeper into the batter's box, betting that Johnson would offer up softer touches nearer the heart of the plate. Cobb's calculation was right. As the years went on, his average against Johnson climbed from a .275 reading through the 1914 season to his final .367 average, which factored in a .435 after 1915.

The Georgia Peach, Ty Cobb.

Before turning to the Ruth-Johnson years, a look at Cobb's and Johnson's best individual season, and their record against each other during those years:

Walter Johnson, 1912:

Overall record:	Won 33, Lost 12. W% .733.
League-leading Numbers:	Strikeouts, 303; Ratio, 8.8; ERA, 1.38; Opp. BA, .196; Opp. OB%, .248; **TPI, 11.1.**
Cobb vs. Johnson:	6 for 20, .300 BA in 7 games.
Best gm, Cobb vs. W.J:	August 2, Wash. 4, Det. 0; Cobb, 3 for 4.
Johnson vs. Detroit:	7 games, Won 6, Lost 0, 1 Save.
Outstanding Feat:	Johnson's 16 game winning streak, the 16th win coming against Detroit on August 23; Cobb, 1 for 4.

Ty Cobb, 1917:

Hitting Statistics:	B.A, .383; OB%, .444; S.A, .570.

League-leading Numbers:	B.A; OB%; S.A; Hits, 225; 2BH, 44; 3BH, 24; SB, 55; **TPI, 8.3**.
Cobb vs. Johnson:	14 for 27, .519 B.A. in 7 games.
Best gms, Cobb vs. W.J:	3 for 4 games, June 19 and July 9; 2 for 2 gm. on June 15 with sacrifice and 2 BB.
Outstanding Feat:	35 game hitting streak.

No matter who does the numbers or rankings, the two names at or very near the top of the list of "Greatest and Most" are often Ruth and Cobb — and usually in that order. For example, take *TBE*'s linear measurements, which result in Total Player Rankings: Babe Ruth, 126.1 (number 1, all time), and Ty Cobb, 92.1 (4), just ahead of Walter Johnson's 91.0 (5); or Bill James' Win Shares: Ruth, 758 (1), and Cobb 726 (2); or Runs Created: Ruth, 2849 (1), and Cobb, 2810 (2); or Batting Wins: Ruth, 124.1 (1), and Cobb, 104.0 (3); and finally, Runs Produced: Cobb, 4067 (1), and Ruth, 3673 (3). The sampling makes the point!

But the remarkable, if not next-to-unbelievable, thing about the Bambino's offensive numbers is that they were stacked up within a relatively short span of 14–15 seasons. Before Babe's thunder began to peal across the AL in a full 154–game season, there were those five seasons during which he bid fair to become one of the game's premier southpaws. It is reasonable to assume that if Ruth's potential productivity in those five years were added to his 1920–35 record, he would wind up in the number one career position in Runs (Cobb is number 1), Home Runs, Total Bases, RBI, Runs Created and Extra Base Hits, or six more to go with the 10 already on the books. Simply staggering.

Ruth's career *vis-à-vis* the Johnson years divides, therefore, into two parts involving 15 games (in three of those games he pinch hit against Johnson) in which he was one of Boston's staff aces. During that time Johnson had his number, allowing

Johnson's .433 BA in 1924 is number one all time for pitchers.

but four hits in 30 at bats, including an 0 for 3 pinch hitting record. But when it came to pitching, the Bambino outshone Walter J, winning six and losing only two. Indeed, three of those wins were by a 1 to 0 score, and a fourth by a 2 to 1 margin. Simply Ruthian.

Did the Babe hit .300 and homer more than a few times against Walter Johnson? Guessing no would have brought you closer to the truth than you might have suspected. First, with regard to those home runs. Against the Big Train, a Hall of Famer of the very first order, 97 long ones either left the park or rattled around the far corners of the outfield long enough to make the scoresheet as a four-bagger during a busy career that endured through 5,914.1 innings pitched. That figures out to one for each 61 innings, or roughly one every seven games. That is a very, very low percentage, especially for a fastball pitcher. How hard the ball was thrown didn't matter much to the Sultan of Swat, of course, and after warming to the task, he hit 10 of those 97 between May 7, 1918, and April 20, 1926, one or two of which dented the right field facade of the Stadium's upper deck. Ruth was up and over the .300 mark lifetime against the Senators, but it took him until 1924 to nose his career mark over the magic number for hitters. By that time he was 37 for 120, for a .308 mark.[15] During the last several years of Johnson's career, Ruth, how ever, pumped some life into his average against the Washington Wonder, going 14 for 30 (a .467 B.A.) between 1924 and '27.

There is a marked contrast between Cobb's .300 and Ruth's. Although it was to be expected that the big fellow could do something drastic each time up, the damage came with far less psychic stress. One mighty swoosh and the damage was done. None of this drag bunting, base stealing, and jockeying for every inch and run every time up. The Bambino did it with a smile and not a single malicious intent. In contrast, Cobb, with that steely look and incandescent rage of his, cut the opposition to pieces inch by agonizing inch; and that, for Cobb, was the very essence of the competition. For Ruth, the ball game was often a mere prelude to another glorious night on the town.

In 1923 Babe Ruth put together one of the greatest single seasons on record. Harry Heilmann won the batting crown with an astronomical .403, but that was only 10 percentage points better than Ruth's career high .393, and it deprived him of Triple Crown honors. The first of his 41 homers helped inaugurate the Yankees' new stadium, and on May 30 he came up with a moon shot at Griffith Stadium off Sir Walter in a 6 to 4 Yankee victory. The 1923 and 1924 Ruth-Johnson comparisons:

Babe Ruth, 1923:

Hitting Statistics:	B.A, .393; OB%, .545; SA, .764.
League-leading numbers:	Runs, 151; RBI, 131; BB, 177; Batting Runs, 116; Fielding Runs, 16; **TPI, 10.8.**

Ruth vs. Johnson:	3 for 7, .429 B.A. in 4 games.
Best gm, Ruth vs. W.J:	May 30, New York 6, Washington 4; Ruth homered in first off Johnson.
Johnson vs. New York:	4 games, Won 2, Lost 1, 1 No Decision.
Outstanding Feat:	Led Yanks to Pennant and World Series titles and was selected the AL's MVP.

Walter Johnson, 1924[16]:

Overall record:	Won 23, Lost 7; W%, .767.
League-leading numbers:	Shutouts, 6; Strikeouts, 158; Ratio, 10.4; ERA, 2.72; Opp. B.A, .224; Opp. OB%, .284; **TPI, 4.7**.
Ruth vs. Johnson:	7 for 13, .538 B.A. in 5 games.
Best game, Johnson vs. NY:	Johnson's 3 to 1 victory put Washington in first place on August 28.
Outstanding Feat:	Led Senators to 1924 World Championship; 13 game winning streak; Selected AL MVP.

Three decades down the line there would be another threesome that had pitchers and hitters running for cover. Perhaps not quite as overpowering as the illustrious Johnson-Cobb-Ruth triumvirate brought together here, they are, nonetheless, among Cooperstown's elite. Their names: Warren Spahn, Stan Musial and Willie Mays. Their heroics await examination in the Warren Spahn chapter.

Walter Johnson versus Edward Victor "Knuckles" Cicotte (1884–1969)

He threw, and what's more important, he could control every trick pitch in the book. He was an intelligent, rubber-armed pitcher who, except for the tragedy of the 1919 World Series, might conceivably have gone on to complete a career of Hall of Fame caliber. Detroiter Eddie Cicotte, quite probably baseball's first master of the knuckleball, just got better and better as the years moved on. He was still a 20-game winner in his last season, a season that came to an abrupt end for Eddie and the other seven-men-out on September 29, 1919. Although many claim that the end of Cicotte's line was near anyway, that seems less than likely for a pitcher who kept himself in good shape, worked efficiently and hurled with little effort. But there were to be no more "Cicotte-versus" pairings after the Kenesaw Landis edict that banned the Black Sox from further major league competition. Among the many and bitter consequences of the Black Sox episode, one of them is the loss of focus and emphasis on the pitching artistry, as well as achievements of the stocky righthander they called Knuckles. Just to nudge the tip of the iceberg, here are a few of his accomplishments:

- Won 28 in 1917 (plus a World Series victory), and 29 in 1919, both league-leading figures.
- Had a career TPI total of 25.4 and a number 63 ranking all time among major league pitchers.
- Cicotte was an excellent fielding pitcher, twice racking up 7s in Pitcher's Defense (in 1913 and 1914).
- Eddie's career 2.38 ERA ranks 15th all time, his 10.5 Ratio ranks 40th, and two other category rankings in Hits per Game and Pitching Runs rank in the top 100.
- During the 1917 season Knuckles threw seven shutouts, pitched 346.2 innings, permitted only a .248 Opponents' On Base Percentage, and contributed a miserly 1.53 ERA to the White Sox' pennant-winner.

Those are some of the reasons Eddie Cicotte has been selected as worthy of comparison with Hall of Famers and their record against Walter Johnson. Two others, Carl Mays and Urban Shocker, complete the Johnson non–Hall of Fame roster. Because of his early major league debut date, September 3, 1905, with his hometown Tigers, Eddie Cicotte's pitching log against Sir Walter is the first of the three under review.

Johnson and Cicotte appeared against one another nine times between 1908 and 1919.

The Johnson-Cicotte Log:

Jun 23, 1908	Boston 3, Washington 2	Cicotte WP, Johnson LP
Apr 24, 1912	Washington 5, Boston 2	Johnson WP, Cicotte LP
Jul 13, 1912	Washington 4, Chicago 2	Johnson WP, Cicotte LP
May 27, 1917	Chicago 4, Washington 1	Cicotte WP, Johnson LP
May 27, 1919	Chicago 4, Washington 3	Cicotte WP, Johnson LP

Washington beat Chicago on August 5, 1912, in 10 innings. Starter Cicotte was relieved and received a no-decision. Johnson picked up the victory in relief.

On July 21, 1913, Johnson was the winning pitcher as the Senators beat Chicago 2 to 1. Reb Russell started and was the loser, pitching three innings before giving way to Joey Benz and then Cicotte in relief.

Cicotte was the starting pitcher on August 31, 1914, and Mellie Wolfgang the reliever and winner in a 4 to 3, 10-inning victory over the Senators. Jim Shaw was the starter, relieved by LP Johnson in the 8th.

On September 20, 1914, Washington beat Chicago 3 to 1 in the first game of a doubleheader. Jack Bentley started this game and was the WP, with Johnson, as a reliever, picking up the Save. Cicotte, with a CG, was LP.

The results: Johnson won four of the nine games while losing three and garnering one Save. Cicotte's record was 3 and 4.

The historical record often appears merciless and unforgiving as it bares the wrongs of the past. But though its truth dare not be altered, neither ought

Control, junk and knuckles. That's what Eddie Cicotte used to baffle the hitters.

we forget the merits of past achievements. In Eddie Cicotte's case, there were many, and the many were a good stretch beyond "merely good."

Walter Johnson versus Herbert Jefferis Pennock (1894–1948), "The Knight of Kennett Square"
Pennock was elected to the Baseball Hall of Fame in 1948

Names like Whitey Ford, Billy Pierce, Eddie Plank and Tommy John come to mind when the subject of "slick lefties" comes up. These were the fellows of the lefthanded pitching fraternity who made a handsome living at the edges of the strike zone, nibbling away at the hitter's weaknesses while rarely if ever resorting to the power and thunder of a Randy Johnson or a Lefty Grove. Add one other name to that list: Herb Pennock.

Dubbed the "Knight of Kennett Square" because he moved in company a cut or two beyond baseball's upper crust, and with it all, loved the fox hunt and the thoroughbreds that were part of the social whirl in his hometown, Kennett Square, Pennsylvania, Herb Pennock nonetheless was hooked on baseball. He pursued it with a passion and wound up on the roster of the Mackmen in nearby Philadelphia, where he began, but did not complete, a 22 year sojourn through the AL, serving up a delicate mixture of sharply

The first of a long line of classy southpaws, and perhaps one of the best of them — Herb Pennock.

breaking curves, shoots, drops, and tantalizing "fastballs" that often wound up in the gloves of his outfielders. And he was nobody's fool out there, logging just about every at bat of his opposing hitters, and calling on his treasury of hitters' weaknesses each time they headed to the plate. For all of that, and with his pinpoint control, there were some predictable career numbers, including top 100 rankings among pitchers in Wins Above Team, winning percentage, complete games and shutouts.

Walter Johnson and Herb Pennock appeared as pitchers in the same game 11 times, stretching over a period of 13 seasons. Their last appearance in the same game occurred in 1927, and on that special occasion, more later.

The 11 matchups between Pennock and Johnson produced a remarkable series of games, all the more noteworthy because of the relief pitching of the two hurlers than the usual complete game heroics one would expect between two Hall of Famers. There were but three occasions when a decision marked the completion of a game by both Sir Walter and the Squire, and in each of those games Pennock was the winner. In their rather unusual series of games the final record read: Pennock, five wins, no losses and five no-decisions. One game, played on May 8, 1914, wound up in a 9 to 9 tie. Johnson won but twice, lost four times and registered a no-decision four times, plus that 9 to 9 tie.

During the 1924 season, famous for its Washington world's championship, and during which the Big Train logged 23 wins against but 7 defeats, Herb Pennock turned in the sparkler of the entire Johnson-Pennock series, a 2 to 0 sevenhitter on July 5. The two had saved the best for last inasmuch as this particular game wrote fini to the series. Single runs in the first and sixth frames were all the Yankees could muster, but they were enough to produce one of the Squire's 21 Ws that season. There was only one strikeout in the game, and it wasn't registered by Herb Pennock.

As to that 12th "mystery game" on September 30, 1927, baseball cognoscenti will recognize that date as the day the Babe hit number 60. Beyond that earth-shaking event, one might also note that Walter Johnson appeared as a pinch hitter for pitcher Tom Zachary, who gave up Ruth's record-setting blast. Big Barney came on as a pinch hitter in the ninth inning, facing Herb Pennock, who had relieved winner George Pipgras in the seventh inning. Pennock didn't strike out anyone that day either — and that necessarily included Walter J.

The Johnson-Pennock Log:

Jun 28, 1912	Philadelphia 5, Washington 4 Pennock WP, Johnson LP
	10 innings; both Pennock and Johnson relieved in this game.
May 16, 1913	Washington 9, Philadelphia 2 Johnson WP
	Joe Bush started this game (LP), Pennock relieved.

May 8, 1914	9 to 9 tie game. A ninth inning triple play prevented the A's from winning this game. Pennock and Johnson relieved.	
Sep 30, 1914	Philadelphia 3, Washington 2 Pennock WP Johnson (ND) relieved Jim Shaw (LP).	
May 30, 1917	Boston 3, Washington 2 Bader (WP) started for Boston, Pennock relieved. Johnson (ND) relieved Shaw (LP).	
Apr 15, 1920	Boston 7, Washington 6	Johnson LP
	Allan Russell (WP) started this game, Pennock relieved.	
May 6, 1922	Boston 1, Washington 0	Pennock WP
	Tom Zachary (LP) started for Washington, Johnson relieved.	
May 30, 1922	Washington 7, Boston 4	Pennock LP
	Tom Phillips (WP) and Johnson both relieved Tom Zachary.	
Apr 22, 1923	Washington 4, New York 3	Johnson WP
	Pennock (ND) relieved Bob Shawkey (LP) in this game.	
May 30, 1923	New York 6, Washington 4	Pennock WP, Johnson LP
Jul 5, 1924	New York 2, Washington 0	Pennock WP, Johnson LP

Walter Johnson versus Stan Coveleski (Kowalewski) (1889–1994)

Coveleski was elected to the Baseball Hall of Fame in 1969

Connie Mack's Athletics were elbowed aside by the Boston Red Sox in the 1912 pennant race, momentarily interrupting their domination of the AL. This came despite a star-studded lineup that included a pitching staff of Jack Coombs, Chief Bender, Eddie Plank and three promising first-year men, each of whom debuted before the season ended. Herb Pennock (1 and 2 in 1912) was the first of the three to debut, and "Bullet Joe" Bush started a game on September 30 in his major league inaugural. The third of this precocious trio was a young lad whose previous occupation — beginning at age 12 — was coal miner. Coming from a family of gifted athletes, young Stan impressed his Pennsylvanian neighbors with his pitching and ultimately wound up in the Mack camp, debuting on September 10 with an eye-popping three-hit shutout. Before the three recruits had finished their careers, they had amassed a total of 652 victories, logging 53 seasons in the Bigs between them. Ironically, none of the three hit it big for Connie Mack. Since Coveleski couldn't crack Mack's ace starting rotation, he was sent to the minors. That was a blessing in disguise.

Stan Coveleski spent the next three seasons in the minors, where he picked up the pitch that brought him back to the Show. That pitch was the spitball, the delivery that was the rage during the deadball era. The spitter, a tough pitch to control, became the out-pitch in his arsenal of breaking balls. With it he became a steady winner for the team that plucked him out of the minors, the Cleveland Indians, with whom he spent nine seasons (1916 to 1924), putting up 172 Ws, including four consecutive 20-win seasons and three World Series victories in the 1920 world's championship won by the Speaker-led Indians.

Some of Coveleski's more arresting career numbers include 2.3 base on balls per nine innings pitched, which also indicates his superb mastery of the strike zone; 38 shutouts (number 53 on the honors list); and a lifetime ERA of 2.89 (top 100, all time). In 1917, his first big season, he limited opposing hitters to 6.09 hits per game while permitting the league's hitters only a .194 batting average. The soft-spoken Coveleski, often referred to as "the Silent Pole," who later was a teammate of Walter Johnson's, found that when he was weighed in the balance, he was not found wanting, earning a Hall of Fame berth in 1969.

As for the Johnson-Coveleski matchups, there was far less success for the spitballer from Shamokin, Pennsylvania, when opposing Johnson than when he faced the rest of the AL pitchers. Only once in head-to-head competition did Stan Coveleski beat Johnson, and they met no less than 12 times. But the victory was a big one, as the Indians walloped the Nationals 14 to 1, with Coveleski in command all the way. That day, August 3, 1919, Walter just didn't have it and was routed in the first inning in what proved to be his only whipping at the hands of Coveleski. Note that after the first Washington victory over Cleveland, in which both Johnson (WP) and Coveleski (LP) relieved in a wild, 11 to 9 game, the losing team in these contests scored no more than two runs ten

Spitballer Stan Coveleski won 20 five times and was elected to the Hall of Fame in 1969.

times. Here is the game-by-game breakdown of those interesting Coveleski-Johnson matchups.

The Johnson-Coveleski Log:

Date	Score	Decision
Aug 27, 1917	Washington 11, Cleveland 9	Johnson WP, Coveleski LP

Johnson and Coveleski both appeared as relievers in this game. There were 12 stolen bases, including a run-scoring triple steal.

Jun 3, 1918	Washington 3, Cleveland 2	Johnson WP, Coveleski LP

Walter Johnson relieved Yancy "Doc" Ayres, pitching the ninth inning for the victory.

Aug 15, 1919	Washington 3, Cleveland 2	Johnson WP, Coveleski LP

Both pitchers received decisions as relief pitchers.

May 11, 1921	Cleveland 14, Washington 1	Coveleski WP, Johnson LP
Aug 4, 1921	Washington 3, Cleveland 1	Johnson WP, Coveleski LP
Sep 18, 1921	Washington 4, Cleveland 1	Johnson WP, Coveleski LP
Aug 20, 1922	Cleveland 2, Washington 0	Boone WP, Johnson LP

The rookie, James Boone, dubbed (as might be expected) "Dan'l," shut down the Nats 2 to 0 in twelve innings and won his own game with a single that beat the veteran mound master, Johnson. It was one of those rare occasions, reminiscent of the Alexander over Young one-hitter in 1911, where the old warrior was bested by the youngster.

Jun 18, 1923	Washington 4, Cleveland 3	Johnson WP, Coveleski LP
Jul 22, 1923	Washington 3, Cleveland 1	Johnson WP, Coveleski LP
Aug 9, 1923	Washington 2, Cleveland 1	Johnson WP, Coveleski LP
Jul 15, 1924	Washington 4, Cleveland 2	Johnson WP, Coveleski LP

Cleveland beat Washington 4 to 0 on August 3, 1919. Walter Johnson relieved Jim Shaw (LP). Coveleski (WP) threw a 5-hit shutout.

On August 5, 1923, both Johnson and Coveleski started, but were relieved by Paul Zahniser (WP) and Guy "the Alabama Blossom" Morton (LP) as the Senators beat the Indians 6 to 5.

Walter Johnson versus Urban "Red" Faber (1888–1976)
Faber was elected to the Baseball Hall of Fame in 1964

Aside from the fact that Red Faber and Walter Johnson pitched for some absolutely horrific ball clubs, the two Hall of Famers didn't have much in common beyond knowing that each time out there would be the strong likelihood of losing unless they would somehow manage to silence enemy bats.

Faber, whose entire career was spent with the Chicago White Sox, nonetheless managed to register four 20-game seasons, over 250 career wins (top 50 all time), and a career Clutch Pitching Index of 106, tying him for 51st place in that category with other notables like Rube Waddell and Tommy John. Red's record is, of course, not nearly as majestic as the Big Train's, but then, whose is?

Faber and Teddy Lyons formed a White Sox tandem that pitched together for the Comiskeymen through Chicago's "Dark Ages" following the Black Sox saga (Faber was on hand before that sordid chapter, there during it, and survived as one of the truly *White* Sox after it), which extended into the 1930s. They were together for 11 seasons, both of them accumulating over 4,000 innings to rank 33 and 34 on the all time list. Those combined 8,000-plus innings, often frustrating beyond imagination, represented the kind of

Urban "Red" Faber toiled so well and selflessly for many a loser at Comiskey Park that he was selected for Hall of Fame honors.

"working conditions" Walter Johnson could empathize with. And Sir Walter was there until 1927 to share some of those innings with both Faber and Lyons.

The first time Faber received a starting assignment against Johnson, the Chisox spitballer was into the latter stages of his rookie season, but Faber didn't pitch like a rookie, beating Johnson 2 to 1 on August 9, 1914, in a magnificently pitched game at Chicago. It took until the 11th inning, when Buck Weaver opened the frame with a single, followed by a sacrifice and another single, this time by Eddie Collins, followed finally by Ray Schalk's short fly ball to right and a Weaver dash to home plate, to win the game. It was one of five Faber victories over Johnson, while Johnson was victorious eight times. Each of the Faber-Johnson face-offs resulted in a decision until the last meeting between the two, a 6 to 5 victory in one of Walter J's last career appearances, on September 11, 1927. In that game both Faber and Ted Lyons appeared in relief roles, as did Johnson, the winning decision going to Hod Lisenbee and the losing decision to Lyons.

No AL ball club escaped a Walter Johnson 1 to 0 afternoon. Red Faber and his White Sox teammates were handed theirs when on June 18, 1922, the Senators eked a run home in the bottom of the ninth that came about under circumstances all too familiar to Red Faber. Sam Rice, who was on third, was able to score the game's only run because Earl Sheely dropped Frank Brower's sky high flyball.

Nor did the Pale Hose escape a Johnson one-hitter. Red Faber was in on that one, too, when on August 10, 1917, Big Barney whitewashed the Sox 4 to 0. That day Famer Ray Schalk, Faber's batterymate for many seasons, was the only Chicagoan to register a base hit. Johnson, on the other hand, was the whole show for the Nationals. Two doubles on a three-for-three day, a run scored, and that one-hitter polished off the Sox in an hour and 45 minutes flat.

Red Faber, Ted Lyons and Luke Appling, a sort of patriarchal White Sox trinity, each of whom was a 20-year man with the Pale Hose, were something special in Chicago's south side baseball history. They had to be. And each found his way to Cooperstown despite — or perhaps because of — their long (or should one say long-suffering?) service to the Sox.

The Johnson-Faber Log:

Aug 9, 1914	Chicago 2, Washington 1	Faber WP, Johnson LP
Sep 21, 1914	Washington 6, Chicago 1	Johnson WP, Faber LP
Aug 4, 1916	Chicago 3, Washington 2	Faber WP, Johnson LP
Aug 6, 1916	Washington 2, Chicago 1	Johnson WP, Faber LP
	Both Faber and Johnson were relief pitchers of record in this 10-inning game.	

July 18, 1917	Chicago 3, Washington 2	Faber WP, Johnson LP
Aug 10, 1917	Washington 4, Chicago 0	Johnson WP, Faber LP
Sep 27, 1917	Washington 5, Chicago 4	Johnson WP, Faber LP

Johnson relieved George Dumont in the 6th inning of this game and the Senators went on to win it, Johnson picking up the victory.

Jun 21, 1919	Washington 6, Chicago 3	Johnson WP, Faber LP
May 20, 1920	Chicago 13, Washington 5	Faber WP, Johnson LP

Chicago scored eight runs off reliever Johnson (LP) in the 16th inning.

On July 1, 1920, Walter Johnson threw his only no-hitter, against the Boston Red Sox. Already ailing with a sore arm, he was nonetheless invincible, though he was the beneficiary of a sparkling defensive gem by Joe Judge to get the last out of the 1 to 0 victory.

Jul 17, 1920	Chicago 4, Washington 1	Faber WP, Johnson LP

Resting ten days after his no-hitter, Johnson took on Cleveland and was defeated. His next start was against the White Sox and Red Faber, which resulted in a good outing but a losing score in a game that went into the ninth inning tied at one apiece. The Sox broke it open when Johnson, in pain and weakened, surrendered three runs.

Jun 18, 1922	Washington 1, Chicago 0	Johnson WP, Faber LP
Jul 29, 1925	Washington 8, Chicago 6	Johnson WP, Faber LP
Sep 11, 1927	Washington 6, Chicago 5	

Johnson relieved Hod Lisenbee (WP). Both Faber and Lyons (LP) came on in relief in this game.

Walter Johnson versus George Herman "Babe" Ruth (1895–1948)

Ruth was elected to the Baseball Hall of Fame in 1936

Had he never made the switch from pitcher to outfielder, Babe Ruth would nonetheless have been enshrined in baseball's Hall of Fame. Perhaps he would not have been a member of the elite inaugural class of 1936, but the selection would have been made, no doubt sooner than later. By the time the switch was made permanent with the Yankees in 1920, he had already put together an 89 and 46 record for the Boston Red Sox, adding five more Yankee victories on the mound as his New York career rolled on. His .671 winning percentage was garnished by a spotless world series record, 3 and 0, accompanied by that streak of 29⅔ scoreless innings over the course of his two Red Sox world series in 1916 and 1918.

Of all the players Walter Johnson faced, none, not one of them, was as tough on him as the Babe. And Ruth, who hit a lifetime .324 against Barney, touching him up for 10 four-baggers, didn't confine his relentless attack on Johnson's welfare to the batter's box. Between 1915 and 1918, the primetime of Ruth's pitching career, the two met nine times, and the Bambino polished off the Big Train six times, three of which were 1 to 0 embarrassments for baseball's number one pitcher and all time 1-to-0 master.

How did Ruth do it? The Ruth pitching formula was a mix of breaking pitches, better than average pop and movement on his heater, off-speed pitches, a tight rein on the strike zone, and one intangible. Any pitcher with intentions of beating Babe Ruth would have to match his intensity and competitive fire, something that fueled his entire career — but was never as evident as in a grueling pitcher's duel. It was a factor seldom mentioned and virtually lost as his parade of home runs and incredible hitting unfolded through the 1920s and '30s. But it was at the base of his success as baseball's premier southpaw during the late 1910s. A glance at

The multi-talented Ruth. This fellow might easily have been a Hall of Famer even if he had finished his career as a pitcher.

the record below gives an indication as to the domination of this extraordinary baseball player over baseball's most dominating pitcher.

The Johnson-Ruth Log:

Aug 14, 1915	Boston 4, Washington 3	Ruth WP, Johnson LP
Apr 17, 1916	Boston 5, Washington 1	Ruth WP, Johnson LP
Jun 6, 1916	Boston 1, Washington 0	Ruth WP, Johnson LP
Aug 15, 1916	Boston 1, Washington 0	Ruth WP, Johnson LP
Sep 9, 1916	Boston 2, Washington 1	Ruth WP, Johnson LP
Sep 12, 1916	Washington 4, Boston 3	Johnson WP, Ruth LP
May 7, 1917	Boston 1, Washington 0	Ruth WP, Johnson LP
Oct 2, 1917	Washington 6, Boston 0	Johnson WP, Ruth LP
May 9, 1918	Washington 4, Boston 3	Johnson WP, Ruth LP

The August 15, 1916, and May 9, 1918, games went extra innings, the 1916 game becoming a 13-inning affair, and the 1918 game (the last between the two) going 10 innings. Despite losing to Johnson in their last meeting, Ruth managed to rough up Senator pitching with a five-for-five day. The box score of that game follows:

At Washington, May 9, 1918

Boston	AB	R	H	PO	Washington	AB	R	H	PO
Hooper, rf	4	1	1	2	Shotton, rf	3	0	0	4
Shean, 2b	4	0	1	4	Lavan, ss	5	0	0	2
Strunk, cf	5	0	0	6	Milan, cf	5	0	2	1
Ruth (LP)	5	1	5	1	Shanks, lf	5	1	1	1
McInnis, 3b	3	0	0	0	Judge, 1b	5	0	2	15
Whiteman, lf	2	0	1	4	Morgan, 2b	2	1	0	2
Scott, ss	4	0	0	1	Foster, 3b	4	1	2	1
Hoblitzel, 1b	3	0	1	10	Casey, c	4	1	3	3
Agnew, c	4	0	0	1	Ainsmith, c	0	0	0	0
Schang, c	0	1	0	0	Ayers, p	3	0	1	0
					Johnson (WP)	0	0	0	0
Totals	34	3	9	29*	Totals	36	4	11	30

Line Score:	Boston	100	000	011	0	3-9-1
	Washington	000	000	201	1	4-11-2

2BH	Ruth 3, Hooper	LOB	Boston 6, Washington 8	DP: Boston 1
3BH	Ruth	K	Ayers 4, Ruth 1	Washington 1

With respect to those Hall of Fame claims, a few numbers: First, from the career record book, note that Ruth's 2.28 ERA ranks right up there in a tie for the 10th spot. 7.18 hits per game ties Ruth with Bob Turley in 11th place, and his opponents' batting average, at .221, is low enough to net a 12th

---

* Two out when winning run scored.

place in the all time rankings. During his best single season, 1916, Babe crafted nine shutouts (29th place all time) during a season in which opposing hitters could muster but 6.4 hits per game against him. There is ample indication in these numbers to suggest that, had he continued apace, and allowing for an end-of-career tail-off, he might well have wound up with between 275 and 300 wins, if not more, an ERA of no more than 2.75 and, who knows, Ruth being Ruth, a no-hitter or two thrown in for good measure.

But the final word on the Walter Johnson–Babe Ruth story is not about the ball diamond. It has to do with the genuine respect they had for one another. That was evidenced in the calls they made on one another during the more difficult times when illness slowed them down, or, in the final years of their lives, when it became apparent that their days had been numbered. These two great baseball players were, when the real struggle was upon them, great human beings who had found it within themselves to share the cup of human kindness and compassion. That, too, is a mark of Hall of Fame champions.

Walter Johnson versus Carl William "Sub" Mays (1891–1970)

Submarineball pitcher Carl Mays was a supremely gifted and versatile ball player. He not only pitched well, but was an exceptional fielder. And he could hit. Consequently, he was used both as a relief pitcher (he was credited with 31 career Saves and often used in relief roles) and a pinch hitter. A career record of 208 wins, 31 shutouts and 217 pitching runs (each is a top 100 stat, all time) mark him as an upper echelon pitcher.

But the rose had thorns. However resolute and unflinching he may have been, he was also a testy fellow, described at one time as having the "disposition of someone with a permanent toothache." His insistence on owning the inside of the plate was bound to bring with it more than the usual number of hit batsmen, which, naturally, didn't help matters any. But for that, compounded by the unfortunate and tragic Ray Chapman death resulting from one of his inside pitches, there might have been enough votes, some day, to crown his numbers with a Cooperstown plaque. That would never be, however, even if he had won 308 instead of 208.

During his rookie season, Carl Mays started only six times, but two of those starts were against Walter Johnson, resulting in a no-decision and a loss on June 23, 1915, when Sir Walter fired a 5 to 0 whitewashing at the Red Sox, scattering seven hits. Out of over 125 innings pitched by Mays that season, most were out of the pen, including a July 6th appearance in a game in which Boston beat the Big Train 4 to 1. During the remainder of his years with Boston, Mays matured into a topflight hurler, winning two games in

Submarineballer Carl Mays. On merit, his plaque should be on the wall at Cooperstown.

the 1918 world series against the Cubs, beating them twice by 2 to 1 scores. But by mid-season in 1919 Sub had worn out his welcome in Boston and was moved on to New York in a stormy deal that wound up in the league's front office. In their *Biographical History of Baseball*, Don Dewey and Nick Acocella explain it thusly:

A two-time 20-game winner with the Red Sox by 1919, Mays stalked off the mound at Chicago's Comiskey Park after working only two innings of a July 13 game. Accepting the pitcher's claims of an injury and personal problems, Boston owner Harry Frazee saw no reason not to trade him to the pennant-contending Yankees soon afterward; AL president Ban Johnson took exception, however, claiming that the league could not allow a player to be rewarded for such a tantrum. The ensuing fracas saw lawsuits flying back and forth, three clubowners threatening to jump to the National League, and the other five magnates caving in to their blackmail. With Johnson humbled and his power seriously curtailed, Mays went on to win 26 games for New York in 1920 and another (league-leading) 27 the following year.

The next season Babe Ruth followed Carl Mays to New York, and the two, with the help of still other former Red Sox players (numbering nearly enough to form a team by themselves, and including, among others, pitchers Ernie Shore, Bullet Joe Bush and Herb Pennock, plus position players like Duffy Lewis, Joe Dugan, Wally Schang and Everett Scott), put the Yankee Express on the pennant trail. Regularly. As fast and as predictably as the 20th Century Limited.

Carl Mays won his first encounter as a Yankee with Walter Johnson in a thrilling 14-inning game on August 29, 1919, which featured seven double plays, some outstanding defensive acrobatics and one boo-boo that cost the Senators the ball game. That came with two out in the 14th when, with two runners on, second baseman Bucky Harris and outfielders Sam Rice and Clyde Milan converged on a Duffy Lewis Texas Leaguer, unable to make up their minds as to who should catch it. The Alphonse and Gaston routine enabled Lewis' pop fly to drop, scoring Wally Pipp. Both Johnson and Mays went the route in a game that sent a huge New York throng home happy.

Mays and Johnson met four more times (Mays won two of those matchups, received a no-decision in another, and Johnson bested Mays in a 1921 slug-a-thon) before the submariner was moved on from New York to Cincinnati in 1924, the year that Washington won the pennant and the Yankees, who lost out to Johnson's Senators, could have used the 20 Ws Mays posted for the Reds. Such are the vagaries of major league baseball.

As for Carl Mays, there were five more seasons in the NL before his swan song for John McGraw in 1929, a 7 and 2 effort that closed out the record on one of baseball's most controversial, albeit talented, players. There would be more as the years rolled on, the most recent being Albert Belle. Only one, however, Carl Mays, changed baseball forever with the one pitch that caused the ruling mandating a new ball when the ball in play was dirty or darkened.

The Johnson-Mays Log:

Date	Result	Decisions
Apr 19, 1915	Washington 4, Boston 2	Johnson WP

Mays (SP) left after six innings with an injured ankle.
Collins (LP) relieved Mays, injured sliding into home plate.

Date	Result	Decisions
Jun 23, 1915	Washington 5, Boston 0	Johnson WP, Mays LP
Jul 6, 1915	Boston 4, Washington 1	Mays WP, Johnson LP
Jun 28, 1916	Washington 6, Boston 2	Johnson WP

Mays (ND), relieved Shore (LP) Johnson (HPB), by Mays

Date	Result	Decisions
Sep 12, 1916	Washington 4, Boston 3	Johnson WP

Babe Ruth (SP), Mays (RP), and Shore (LP) pitched for Boston.

Date	Result	Decisions
Jun 26, 1917	Washington 3, Boston 2	Johnson WP, Mays LP

Johnson's hit singled in the winning run in the 9th inning.

Date	Result	Decisions
May 1, 1918	Washington 5, Boston 0	Johnson WP, Mays LP
Apr 28, 1919	Boston 6, Washington 5	Mays WP, Johnson LP
Aug 29, 1919	New York 5, Washington 4	Mays WP, Johnson LP
May 10, 1920	New York 5, Washington 3	Johnson LP

Jack Quinn (SP) was the winner. Mays (RP) finished the game.

Date	Result	Decisions
Apr 25, 1921	Washington 5, New York 3	Johnson WP, Mays LP

Ruth hit one of his 10 career HRs off Johnson in this game.

Date	Result	Decisions
Jun 1, 1921	Washington 8, New York 7	Johnson WP, Mays LP
Sep 8, 1922	New York 8, Washington 1	Mays WP, Johnson LP

Walter Johnson versus Clarence Arthur "Dazzy" Vance (1891–1961)
Vance was elected to the Baseball Hall of Fame in 1955

It would have been a very interesting matchup, Vance against Johnson. Two flamethrowers mixing it up with one laser shot after another. But though the fellow they called "the Orient Express" (though more commonly known as Dazzy) received his first call for duty at Forbes Field in Pittsburgh (and saw a few more outings at Highland Park with the Yankees in 1915 and again in 1918), his ultimate destiny was the NL, where, starting at the advanced baseball age of 31, he proceeded to burn up the league during the sizzling '20s. He turned out to be Brooklyn's answer to the speed kings of the AL.

And so there were no Johnson-Vance afternoons that might have given fans a chance to make some head-to-head comparisons. There was a ball player, however, who didn't hesitate to comment on the two. Babe Ruth had this to say:

> Honestly, I don't think there is any comparison between the two. Johnson was so much better when he was running on top form, that to compare him to any other speed ball pitcher would be like comparing Ty Cobb to a rookie...What makes Vance a fine pitcher is his wildness. That might sound funny, but a fastball pitcher has to be a little wild to be good...If Vance, who is slower than Johnson, wasn't a little wild he would be a sucker for left-handers and an easy mark for righthanders. The difference between Johnson and Vance is this: Johnson is poison to any ball club. Vance is not hard for any team that likes fastball pitchers, such as the Yankees and Giants. I think that right now, with Johnson slowing up a lot, he is every bit as good a pitcher as Vance. In fact, I think he's better.[17]

What a matchup it would have been! Dazzy Vance, pictured here, vs. Walter Johnson when both were in their prime.

Although the Big Train and the Orient Express didn't meet head on, there will be an opportunity to size up manager Wilbert Robinson's interesting lefthander momentarily when his encounters with Pete Alexander come up for review. Stay tuned.

Walter Johnson versus Urban Shocker (Urbain Jacques Shockor) (1892–1928)

A significant number of premier ball players passed away in the prime of their lives. The list of Hall of Famers includes several who would no doubt have played on had their untimely deaths not brought their stellar careers to a sudden halt. Ed Delahanty, Addie Joss and Ross Youngs were three. Others who did not achieve Hall of Fame notoriety but were great players nonetheless include Thurman Munson, Ken Hubbs, Harry Agganis, Charles "Chick" Stahl, Ray Chapman and Lyman Bostock. There are more, but among the many the name of Urban Shocker must be included. Shocker, who was one of 17 spitball pitchers "grandfathered" at the time of the moistened pitch's banishment so that he, and the others, might continue using it until their careers were finished, voluntarily retired after appearing in a two-inning stint early in the 1928 season. In September of that same year he succumbed to complications from an enlarged heart and pneumonia. He had known about his heart disease several seasons before his death but kept on courageously, doing what he loved to do, without creating a stir or saying a word. As a result, his retirement, and then his death, which came shortly before his 36th birthday, sent a shockwave through the baseball world.

In *The Ballplayers*, edited by Mike Shatzkin, baseball historian Adie Suehsdorf penned this about the Browns and Yankees righthander:

> Shocker was an intense, unsmiling fellow, a studious pitcher widely admired for an artful delivery and a profound knowledge of hitters. He allowed almost exactly a hit per inning, yet, as his ERA shows, not many runs. He was stingy with walks, averaging one every four innings. A serious professional, he was known as an excellent fielder and capable hitter, perhaps too serious to have a nickname [p. 997].

And, it must be added, Urban Shocker was not about to be taken down any primrose pathways. He was involved in challenging baseball's reserve system in 1923, an uphill fight for any individual up against the moguls and owners of the game's most precious and indispensable commodity, the players themselves. In a case that had the game's board rooms buzzing, Shocker stood his ground until persuaded, somewhat against his own better judgment, to drop his charges in favor of a settlement in the form of a substantial

An accomplished hurler and a stickler for control, Urban Shocker was the wheelhorse of those great Brownie teams of the '20s.

salary hike and one last season with friend and manager George Sisler before being traded back to the Yankees, whence he originally came, courtesy of one of manager Miller Huggins' very rare mistakes in judgment about a player's potential.

There were 11 Shocker-Johnson confrontations, most of them of the nip-and-tuck variety, with Shocker getting the better of it at 6 and 2, and three no-decisions. Walter Johnson was not quite as fortunate, posting a 2 and 5 record with four no-decisions. One of the more significant meetings was the very first, which was Urban Shocker's debut as a major league pitcher on April 24, 1916, in an 8 to 2 Washington victory over the Yankees in which the rookie was used as a reliever behind loser Bob Shawkey. Not every pitcher can say that his debut was made in a Walter Johnson game!

After that inaugural meeting, it took until 1925 for Sir Walter to beat Shocker, and that game probably had the wee Huggins, a mite of a manager but a cagey one, wondering why he had Shocker brought back to New York. To open Washington's season, with president Coolidge on hand for first-ball ceremonies, Johnson proceeded to do his specialty, holding the Yanks to a single run as the Senators romped in a 10 to 1 victory at Shocker's expense. It was, however, Big Barney's last victory over Urban Shocker, inasmuch as the New Yorkers took two behind Shocker, 19 and 11 that summer, en route to their 1926 pennant.

The last game of the Johnson-Shocker series was played on the first of July in 1926 as the first game of a doubleheader. The Yankees took that one with a ninth inning tally, which marked the sixth time that a game involving the two was won in the last inning whether ninth, or later.

The Johnson-Shocker Log:

Apr 24, 1916   Washington 8, New York 2   Johnson WP

Shawkey (LP) was followed by relievers Nick Cullop and Shocker. Johnson tripled off Shocker in this game.

Jun 12, 1918   Washington 8, St. Louis 6 Shocker LP
Johnson pinch hit and doubled, then pitched the 9th inning to save the game for Stan Rees, who won his only ML victory in his only ML appearance.

Jul 31, 1919   St. Louis 3, Washington 2   Shocker WP, Johnson LP

Aug 25, 1919   St. Louis 4, Washington 3   Shocker WP
Johnson (ND) relieved loser Jim Shaw.

May 8, 1922   St. Louis 6, Washington 5   Shocker WP, Johnson LP
Johnson relieved Mogridge (SP) in the 9th inning.

Aug 6, 1922   St. Louis 8, Washington 4   Shocker WP, Johnson LP
May 20, 1923   St. Louis 9, Washington 8
Shocker (ND) started this game against Tom Zachary (ND), who was relieved by Mogridge (LP) and Johnson (ND). St. Louis' Wayne "Rasty" Wright was a reliever and WP in this 10-inning game at St. Louis.

The world championship Senator pitching staff (1924), L to R, standing: Tom Zachary, Walter Johnson, George Mogridge, "Firpo" Marberry. Kneeling: "Curly" Ogden, Paul Zahniser, "By" Speece and "Oyster Joe" Martina.

Sep 20, 1924 St. Louis 15, Washington 14
Shocker and Johnson were the game's starters but received no-decisions. Johnson, looking for his 13th straight win, left the game after the first inning. Elam Vangilder was the winner for St. Louis, and Fred "Firpo" Marberry was the losing pitcher.

Apr 22, 1925 Washington 10, St. Louis 1   Johnson WP, Shocker LP

Apr 20, 1926 New York 18, Washington 5   Shocker WP, Johnson LP
Johnson was shelled in the third inning. The Yanks pounded Washington pitching for 22 hits.

Jul 1, 1926 New York 3, Washington 2   Shocker WP, Johnson LP

Walter Johnson versus Waite Charles "Schoolboy" Hoyt (1899–1984)

Hoyt was elected to the Baseball Hall of Fame in 1969

He was known as a money pitcher, Miller Huggins' go-to guy when his Yankees were playing for the big stakes. During the 1920s the multi-talented Waite Hoyt flourished like few others, with New York's heavy lumber behind him and those monstrous Yankee crowds cheering him on. And he reveled in every last minute of it — from the season's opener through world series time, that special showcase for Ruth and Hoyt and their pals almost every season. He proceeded from "the Schoolboy" to "the Man on the Mound" without a hitch, turning in a 155 and 96 record between 1921 and 1929 while winning pennant clinchers and world series ball games that set the Yankees apart from everything else on the planet. It was Waite Hoyt who was the leader of the mound corps, the brainy wheelhorse the Hugmen counted on, a sort of Yankee Walter Johnson.

But Waite Hoyt was no Walter Johnson. There was no second Walter Johnson, for that matter. And the very first time the two met, on a sunny day in June of 1922, Mr. Johnson, Esq., taught the Yankees' budding star a thing or two about the fine points of winning — without a Ruth or a Meusel or a team full of pinstriped stars from New York. The box score of that pitching duel follows:

At Washington, June 28, 1922

New York	AB	R	H	PO	Washington	AB	R	H	PO
Witt, cf	4	0	1	0	Judge, 1b	3	0	1	10
McNally, 3b	4	0	1	0	Peckinpaugh, ss	3	0	0	0
Ruth, lf	4	0	2	3	Rice, cf	4	0	0	2
Meusel, rf	4	0	0	3	Shanks, 3b	4	1	1	1
Pipp, 1b	4	0	1	11	Brower, rf	3	0	0	0

Hall of Famer, broadcaster, baseball personality Waite Hoyt, ace of those great Yankee teams of the '20s.

Ward, 2b	4	0	0	3	Harris, 2b	2	0	0	4
Scott, ss	3	0	2	0	Smith, lf	3	0	2	0
Hofmann, c	3	0	0	4	Picinich, c	2	0	0	10
Hoyt (LP)	3	0	0	1	Johnson (WP)	3	0	0	0
Totals	33	0	7	25*	Totals	27	1	4	27

* One out when winning run scored.

Line Score:	New York	000	000	000	0–7–0
	Washington	000	000	001	1–4–0

2BH	Smith 2, Scott	BB	Hoyt 4, Johnson 0
3BH	Pipp	K	Hoyt 4, Johnson 9
SH	Brower	HPB	Harris (by Hoyt)
LOB	New York 6, Washington 8	Umpires	Moriarty and Nallin
BB	Hoyt 4, Johnson 0	Time	1:48

The *New York Times* led off its coverage of the game this way:

> The aged Walter Johnson dusted off his pitching arm here this afternoon and led his Washington teammates to a 1 to 0 victory over the Yankees. With Waite Hoyt doing the pitching for the American League champions, the game devolved itself into one of the prettiest pitching duels of the season at the local [Washington] emporium, for it was not until after one man had been retired in the last of the ninth inning that the Senators were able to bat the run over the plate that gave them the game.
>
> It was the third consecutive shutout that Johnson has pitched and it was the 97th time he has plastered the whitewash brush on his opponents in his big league career. As time is measured in baseball Walter Johnson is getting well along. But in spite of the fact that he has depended upon speed in most of his sojourn under the big tent his arm this season is showing no ill effects. He is able to burn them over the plate with just as much of a smoke screen as ever, a fact to which the Yankees will readily attest.

However well Hoyt pitched that day, and he allowed but four Senator safeties, he was nonetheless out-dueled by the old master and gave up a last-inning single to Howie Shanks, followed by a sacrifice and a one-out double by Earl "Sheriff" Smith that gave Barney the squeaker over his younger adversary.

But there were other Johnson encounters with the brash "Brooklyn Schoolboy." And as time went on, the talent of New York's ace of the '20s began to make itself felt. After losing two of his first three games with Walter Johnson, Waite Hoyt took the measure of the big fellow, who was closing out his Hall of Fame–bound career, by winning the last three engagements in their six game series.

The Johnson-Hoyt Log:

Jun 28, 1922	Washington 1, New York 0	Johnson WP, Hoyt LP
Apr 22, 1923	Washington 4, New York 3	Johnson WP
	Bob Shawkey (LP) was relieved by Pennock and Hoyt.	
May 1, 1924	Washington 3, New York 2	Johnson WP, Hoyt LP
May 29, 1924	New York 7, Washington 4	Hoyt WP

	Jack Russell (LP), relieved starter Johnson in the first game of a doubleheader.	
Jun 2, 1926	New York 5, Washington 4	Hoyt WP, Johnson LP
Aug 13, 1926	New York 7, Washington 5	Hoyt WP, Johnson LP
	Two Lou Gehrig homers helped beat Washington as Walter Johnson left after the fifth inning.	

An insightful look into the most famous of all Yankee teams, entitled *The Wonder Team: The True Story of the Incomparable 1927 New York Yankees,* features this salute to Waite Hoyt by the able baseball historian Leo Trachtenberg:

> Hoyt was elected to the Baseball Hall of Fame in 1969, an honor he well deserved. When he died on August 25, 1984, at the age of 84, the old Schoolboy took with him a fund of baseball memories that were irreplaceable. A witty and engaging man, Waite Hoyt was a link with the days when the Yankees moved into the modern era and began their extraordinary string of pennants and World Championships. A premier pitcher, a survivor of a lively, optimistic time in American history, Waite Hoyt was special as a player, and as a pioneering baseball broadcaster [p. 105].

Walter Johnson versus Theodore Amar "Ted" Lyons (1900–1986)

Lyons was elected to the Baseball Hall of Fame in 1955

Over the course of more than 1200 games in a season in each league, there are bound to be many that fall into the bizarre or odd-ball category. The White Sox had more than their share, and Ted Lyons, the gifted Baylor alum who went right from the campus to the majors, could have told about many that cost him a ball game here and there. One of those happened in the nation's capitol during Walter Johnson's "last stand" in the 1927 season. In one of his very last major league appearances, on September 11, Johnson crossed swords with Lyons in a 12-inning match that was finally won by Washington when the stands had almost been emptied by Senator fans who thought the game had been won before the run scored that actually won the game. This is what happened: Joe Judge opened the bottom of the 12th with a triple. John "Stuffy" Stewart, Senator reserve infielder, was sent in to run for Judge. Then a fly ball produced what everyone thought was the winning run. Ted Lyons didn't think so. He appealed to umpire George Hildebrand that Stewart left third base before the ball was caught, and signaled to shortstop Ray "Flash" Flaskamper (only the White Sox could have a Flaskamper, a one-year, 26-game player, on their roster) to touch third base for the putout.

Chicago's South Side fixture for better than 20 years, Ted Lyons, whose no-hitter beat Boston, 6 to 0, on August 21, 1926.

Umpire Hildebrand upheld Lyons' protest and the game went on, two out, almost empty stands, and Ozzie Bluege up.

Bluege promptly doubled. That brought up Jackie Hayes, a rookie shortstop who got into only 10 ball games in 1927, who singled home the streaking Bluege with the winning run to snatch victory from the jaws of what might easily have been a defeat, and hand Ted Lyons one of his 230 major league losses. There would be more such shenanigans during the many years (1923–1942 and 1946) Ted Lyons pitched for the Pale Hose, but there would also be 260 victories along the way, enough to put the likeable knuckleballer into the Hall of Fame with the class of 1955. Some of his other credentials include top 50 rankings in Complete Games (356), Pitching Runs (313), Wins Above Team (36.2), and a single season Clutch Pitching Index of 130.9 (exceptionally high) in 1942.

The Johnson-Lyons matchups, two in 1924 and two more in 1927, all resulted in Washington victories, although the Big Train and Lyons appeared in but one game in which both were principal figures. Lyons went on to become one of Chicago's most popular ball players, a Johnson-like figure whose team never did rise above the third-place mark during a career that stretched into the post–World War II season of 1946, when, at age 45, he won his last game.

The Johnson-Lyons Log:

Jul 24, 1924   Washington 7, Chicago 5
Walter Johnson and Ted Lyons appeared in this game as relief pitchers (ND). The winning pitcher was Allan Russell (not to be confused with the 1933 Senators' star reliever, Jack Russell). Diminutive Mike Cvengros was the loser.

Sep 22, 1924   Washington 8, Chicago 3   Johnson WP
The Nationals' 6-run sixth inning blew this game wide open.

Jul 17, 1927	Johnson went all the way for the win, and Lyons relieved starter Cvengros, who was charged with the defeat. Washington 7, Chicago 4 Johnson WP, Lyons LP
Sep 11, 1927	Washington 6, Chicago 5 Ted Lyons, who relieved starter Red Faber, was charged with the defeat. Hod Lisenbee, Senator starter, was credited with the victory, and reliever Johnson got the Save.

Walter Johnson versus Charley "Red" Ruffing (1904–1986)

Ruffing was elected to the Baseball Hall of Fame in 1967

SENATORS WIN RAGGED AFFAIR AT GRIFFITH STADIUM, 10–8

Boston	100	050	002	8–12–2
Washington	703	000	00x	10–13–3

The recap might have looked like this:

Washington, May 6, 1925. The Washington Senators bested the Boston Red Sox 10 to 8 today, capitalizing on an opening-round, seven-run outburst to give Walter Johnson another victory over Boston's struggling Bosox. The Nats chased starter Howard Ehmke in the first inning when they batted around and piled up an almost insurmountable lead. Boston came within shouting distance, nudging home five in the fifth stanza. However, the defending world champions were far enough ahead so that neither manager Bucky Harris nor the veteran Johnson gave any thought to bringing on Washington's crack relief corps. Rookie Charley Ruffing was the brightest spot in an otherwise dreary Boston nine, working several innings of solid relief. The box score:

Washington	AB	R	H	PO	Boston	AB	R	H	PO
Leibold, cf	4	1	2	2	E. Williams, lf-cf	4	1	1	3
Harris, 2b	4	0	1	1	Wambsganss, 2b	4	2	2	4
Rice, cf	5	1	2	4	Flagstead, cf	2	0	1	1
Goslin, lf	4	1	0	3	Carlyle, lf	2	0	1	0
Judge, 1b	4	0	1	6	Boone, rf	5	1	2	1
Bluege, 3b	3	2	2	3	Todt, 1b	4	1	2	5
Peckinpaugh, ss	1	2	1	2	Prothro, 3b	4	0	1	2
Adams, ss	2	0	0	0	Connolly, ss	4	1	0	2
Ruel, c	2	2	2	3	Picinich, c	5	1	2	5
Tate, c	2	0	2	3	Ehmke (LP)	0	0	0	0
Johnson (WP)	3	0	1	0	Quinn, p	1	0	0	0
					Ruffing, p	2	1	0	0

					Lucey, p	0	0	0	0
					Vache, ph	1	0	0	0
					J. Heving, ph	1	0	0	0
Totals	34	10	13	27	Totals	39	8	12	24

He started out a loser with some woebegone Red Sox teams but ended up a World Series world-beater who went on to the Hall: Charlie "Red" Ruffing.

Boston's glory days were a distant memory by the time a sturdy young lad named Charles Herbert Ruffing checked into Fenway Park for his big league debut on May 31, 1924. That season the Bosox at least finished a notch above the AL's basement. They soon corrected that with a string of six straight eighth place finishes before surfacing in the sixth slot at the end of the 1931 season. During all six of those bargain basement years, akin to a Baseball Captivity in Babylon, Charley Ruffing was a member of one of the most woeful collection of major league pitchers in the game's storied history. He wasn't the worst of the lot, but he had much to learn, and his record for those years, 39 and 96, showed it. But he did learn what it means to persevere.

There was something about this fellow, as gritty and inwardly tough as they came, that had more than one front office looking at him during those frightful years when playing Boston was a 4th of July celebration with all the fireworks. In New York the Colonel, Mr. Jacob Rupert, always on the hunt for superior talent, took a wary look northward, and when manager Bob Shawkey told him, "Get that fella up there in Boston — we can make a pitcher out of him," Rupert made his move. The rest is some kinda history!

During the next 15 seasons he proceeded to win 231 games for the pinstripers, becoming one of those classy, pace-setting professionals the franchise featured from decade to decade as it ran roughshod over the rest of the league. The move from the basement to the penthouse stirred within him such gratitude that the rest of his career became a pilgrimage whose final destination was the Hall of Fame. Is that an American Pitcher's Turnabout or what?!

The Washington-Boston game (above) was the only Ruffing-Johnson encounter in the scorebooks, despite the two legends spending some four seasons toiling concurrently (the great Johnson on the windup trail, and the emerging star in the beginning stages of his illustrious career). And lest someone might be tempted to think that "Big Red" would never have accomplished the miracle turnaround had he not had the famous pinstripes behind him, with all that meant, it should be noted that many another, with equal opportunity, never quite got it done the way Ruffing did. Note, too, that he is only one of four (Lefty Gomez, Whitey Ford and Catfish Hunter are the other three) long-term Yankees who came to the club after 1930 and eventually wound up in the Hall. Not too bad for a coal miner's son who lost the toes on his left foot as a teen-aged miner, played out a good deal of his career in pain, and spent the first seven-plus seasons in the dank basement of the American League.

Walter Johnson versus Robert Moses "Lefty" Grove (1900–1975)

Grove was elected to the Baseball Hall of Fame in 1947

Lefty Grove could throw his Special Delivery with the mach-one speed of the Concorde. Westbrook Pegler, whose analogy suited Grove's era, proffered that the lean southpaw could throw a lamb chop past a wolf. On the other hand, Babe Ruth, according to Stan Baumgartner in a 1948 *Sporting News* article, said that Grove "didn't have a curve and all you had to do was stand up and let him hit your bat. Grove was easy to follow all the way and he supplied the power, too." The rest of the American league hitters didn't quite see it that way. Laconic Charlie Gehringer, who wasn't exactly an automatic out, had this to say: "Grove's fastball...carried a little but never did anything tricky. But it was so fast that by the time you'd made up your mind whether it would be a strike or a ball, it just wasn't there anymore."

But Lefty Grove's heater wasn't faster than Walter Johnson's. Even during Johnson's final seasons, when he encountered Grove as a young stud throwing sizzling shots at his Senators, Johnson's fast one got there quicker than the time it took for Cool Papa Bell to get into his bunk before the lights went out. And, unbelievably, it was still that quick several years after his retirement, if only for a limited number of pitches. Indeed, baseball's number one flamethrower was number one with lasers. However, it is also true that a Grove or a Feller or a Randy Johnson or a Clemens fastball was just a mite slower, and when a ball reaches the plate in that kind of a whoooosh, that mile per hour or two difference will still flash past the hitter in a whirlwind.

Swoooosh. A strand of white. Another K. He was the last of Connie Mack's super, superstars: Robert Moses "Lefty" Grove.

There's more to pitching, of course, than raw speed. Johnson knew that and Grove soon learned it. When speed becomes part of an arsenal — that's when the hitters are in serious trouble. For Lefty Grove it took a little while, but it came. That's when the fellow who turned out to be the game's greatest left-hander began his run on the record book. More on that just ahead.

Lefty Grove had a thing about Walter Johnson, who was the idol of his teen years. When it came to pitchers, thought the youngster, there was only one, and his name was Walter Johnson. He was the only one worth seeing, and that's what young Robert did when there was enough cash on hand to get a roundtrip ticket from his home in Lonaconing, Maryland, over to Washington, a three hour trip. That "star-worship" puts their first encounter into a little different perspective.

When the time finally came, after six minor league seasons, it was no doubt far from what Grove might have imagined it would be. He opened the 1925 season for Connie Mack in a nightmarish debut, followed that up with more wild pitches in Boston, and lost to Washington, with his hero looking on, before being used in relief in a Senator game in which Walter Johnson did not pitch. The Johnson matchup had to come sooner or later, and on May 27th the two hooked up at Shibe Park, appearing in the same game, though not against one another. Johnson, with relief help from Vean Gregg and Firpo Marberry, outlasted the A's in a 10 to 9 shootout that caused Connie Mack to bring on his $106,000 prize in a relief role for the 6,7 and 8 innings. Grove fanned three during his brief outing, and at least wasn't the loser — this time. Johnson had already been lifted with two out in the sixth stanza. The head to head was soon to come, however, taking place on June

26, again in Philadelphia, with both Grove and Johnson going the route in a 5 to 3 Senator victory. The die had been cast. Two more engagements, both of them resulting in Johnson conquests and Grove losses, finished that chapter in Lefty Grove's career. His 1925 season, unlike that of his idol's, which brought a second straight pennant to Washington and another 20-game season, wound up on the dull side of a 10 and 12 record. It was the only time in his illustrious career that Mack's swifty dipped under the 500 mark. But beyond that, it was a brutal, bloody, season-long seminar in Major League 101, a course that pulled no punches in exposing rookies to the wiles and ways of major league warfare.

Though there would be no more encounters for Lefty of the Walter Johnson kind after the great Senator's final season in 1927, there were challenges aplenty just around the bend, and by 1928 he would be ready to start his incredible run of 152 wins (against only 41 losses) between 1928 and 1933, his last season under Mack's tutelage. Even before winding up in Boston in 1934, the word greatest was regularly used in describing his pitching. Mack's Lightning Rod, as he was often called, was measured for a prominent place at Cooperstown already at that point, and he still had over 100 wins to earn before hitting the magic number, 300. No one, anywhere, doubted that he would get it.

The Johnson-Grove Log:

May 27, 1925	Washington 10, Philadelphia 9	Johnson WP
	William "Slim" Harris was the loser in this game. Grove pitched three innings of relief (ND).	
Jun 26, 1925	Washington 5, Philadelphia 3	Johnson WP, Grove LP
Sep 7, 1925	Washington 2, Philadelphia 1	Johnson WP, Grove LP
Apr 23, 1926	Washington 9, Philadelphia 5	Johnson WP, Grove LP
	Grove was removed in the first inning under a four-run Senator barrage.	

The Big Train: More Than Master Craftsman

On April 14, 1926, Walter Johnson reached back for something special, enabling him to out-duel Eddie Rommel in a 15-inning season opener against Philadelphia, 1 to 0. This was the game he tabbed as his pitching *tour de force*. The master craftsman defied his 39 years and a powerful Athletics lineup as he worked his way through one frame after another until the Senators were able, finally, to push across the winning run. It was the seventh time he had blanked an opening day opponent and the 38th 1-to-0 victory of his career. Both are, and will remain, the standard for eons to come. Both are hallmarks of olympian superiority, and that is what baseball's pantheon is all about. Sir Walter set the kind of records that make the Hall of Fame what it is. And Walter Johnson, pitching legend, solid citizen, gentleman farmer — all of these and more — is one of the very few among the growing list of Famers whose record not only as a pitcher par excellence, but as an exceptional human being, makes the Hall a national shrine celebrating extraordinary achievement and remarkable athletic artistry. It is the Johnsons and the Mathewsons, the Ruths and the Aarons, and among those who will follow, Cal Ripken, Jr., and Greg Maddux, who set those orbital standards, standing above even their Hall of Fame "peers" as *primus inter pares*, first among equals.

4. PETE ALEXANDER

Major League Career Totals:	Won	Lost	Pct.
Philadelphia, Chicago, St. Louis (NL)	373	206	.648

Alexander was elected to the Baseball Hall of Fame in 1938

One of the most significant events in Grover "Pete" Alexander's life did not take place on a baseball diamond. What occurred during World War I, when Alexander and his comrades in arms were subjected to the cannonading of Germany's Big Berthas, however, might well have been one of those signal events. Those days and nights in the trenches, dug into the French soil, filled with earth- and soul-shattering noise, left a mark that was seared into the depths of every soldier's being. Alexander was no exception, and though he survived the combat intact, at least physically, the din of those horrors was in his ears until the day he died. In his *Baseball America*, historian Don Honig explains an incident that hints at the devastation Alexander's experience in the military had on the legendary righthander's psyche.

> A dozen years later [after the war] Alexander was sitting on the bench during spring training. "Some kids up in the grandstand started shooting off fireworks," teammate Bill Hallahan recalled. "A few of the guys gave a little start with each burst. But Alex never budged. He just sat there stiff as a board, teeth clenched, fists doubled over so tight his knuckles were white, staring off into space like he was hypnotized. When finally somebody came and chased the kids off and the noise stopped, he turned and looked at me with a sad little smile" [p. 93].

Until the war came along, Ol' Low and Away, as he was often called, had sailed through seven seasons of superlative pitching for the Phils (he logged a 2 and 1 record with the Cubs, to whom he had been traded for the 1918 season, before his service call-up), winning 190 ball games, with a strike-out-to-walks ratio of 2.75 and a 2.16 ERA. He was clearly on the way to Mathewson-like numbers, and was, as a matter of fact, called "The Second Mathewson" by more than a few knowledgeable sportswriters.

In order to reach the numbers that almost doubled his pre-war victories, it took Pete another dozen seasons (not counting 1918 and 1930, seasons in which he registered only three decisions). Amazingly, his pitching, always a thing of finely-tempered perfection, did suffer not significantly during those latter years. And that, precisely, is the wonder of Grover Alexander's artistry. The epilepsy and subsequent bouts with "Ole Debel Alky," which grew increasingly debilitating as the years progressed, might have taken some of the zip off the fast one, but even through the mists and fog of his most hung-over days, he managed to find the edges of the strike zone, working with customary economy and deadly curveballs that dropped ever so sharply off the edges of the plate. That he achieved what he did is one of baseball's major miracles, especially surviving the big sticks of the '20s with three more 20-game seasons, the last of which came at age 40. For the record, here is a sampling of Pete's more noteworthy accomplishments:

- 16 Shutouts in 1916, highest single-season total in the 20th century (and tied for first place, all time).
- 90 career Shutouts, second only to Walter Johnson.
- 1,000 Fielding Average in 1919.
- 373 career wins, tied with Mathewson for third, all time.
- 345.2 career Wins Above League, number four all time.
- 5,190 career Innings Pitched, number 10 all time.
- 1.22 ERA in 1915, number 11 all time.
- 64.8 TPI, third all time, through the 20th century.

"Ol' Low and Away," Peter Alexander.

Considered in company

with nine Hall of Famers and four other hurlers whose career numbers command respect, this review of the lanky Nebraskan's accomplishments underscores the lofty claims made on his behalf. His illustrious career touched those of Cy Young, an ancient warrior by the time Pete encountered him, and whose major league years extended all the way back to the 1890s; Three Finger Brown; Dazzy Vance; and Carl Hubbell, who threw his last pitch in 1943, positioning "Alexander the Great" in the middle of more than a half-century of the game's history. During one of those years, 1938, Grover Cleveland Alexander received baseball's most distinguished honor, a plaque symbolizing his election to the Hall of Fame.

This is the list of pitchers with whom Alexander is matched:

Name/HOF/Year	Debut/Career Years	TPI/All Time Pitcher Ranking
Cy Young/1937	Aug 6, 1890/1890–1911	78.0/2
Christy Mathewson/1936	Jul 17, 1900/1900–1916	62.9/4
Mordecai Brown/1949	Apr 19, 1903/1903–1916	35.3/23
Charles "Babe" Adams	Apr 18, 1906/1906–1926	15.2/156
Rube Marquard/1971	Sep 25, 1908/1908–1925	-2.3/NR
Eppa Rixey/1963	Jun 21, 1912/1912–1933	26.6/57
Wilbur Cooper	Aug 29, 1912/1912–1926	20.0/102
Dolf Luque	May 20, 1914/1914–1935	26.8/54
Dazzy Vance/1955	Apr 16, 1915/1915–1935	27.4/49
Burleigh Grimes/1964	Sep 10, 1916/1916–1934	23.7/74
Jesse Haines/1970	Jul 20, 1918/1918–1937	6.8/NR
Freddie Fitzsimmons	Aug 12, 1925/1925–1943	22.9/77
Carl Hubbell/1947	Jul 26, 1928/1928–1943	41.1/14

Pete Alexander versus Denton True "Cy" Young (1867–1955)

Young was elected to the Baseball Hall of Fame in 1937

The one and only Pete Alexander–Cy Young matchup, previously covered, was sufficient to link Philadelphia's incomparable Hall of Famer with the "old days," establishing a tie with baseball history that ran a thread of continuity between those earlier days, when the mound hadn't yet been extended to its present 60'6", and the mid-century years of the 20th century, when night baseball, better equipment, and countless numbers of refinements in the game itself emerged, with ever "newer and more improved" ball games, ball players and ball parks that captured an enthusiastic following. It was a half century of spellbinding excitement that positioned the national pastime among the foundation pieces of America's distinctive culture.

One strand in that thread of continuity was great pitching. From Cy Young to Carl Hubbell, the last of the Famers who dueled Pete Alexander, there was still the wonderment and often mesmerizing effect of a pitching masterpiece, put together pitch by pitch, inning by inning, that resulted in an afternoon to remember. Young and Hubbell, among others in the baker's dozen assembled here who matched pitches with "Ol' Low and Away," were capable of consistently putting together those kinds of peerless performances. One of those was the 1 to 0 piece of pitching artistry that Young, the grand old warrior en route to baseball's ultimate honors, and Alexander, the youngster waiting to prove himself in the Main Arena, crafted at Boston's old South End Grounds on September 7, 1911. There had to be a winner, and he was "the young stud from Nebraska." There really wasn't a loser.

Pete Alexander versus Christy Mathewson and Mordecai "Three Finger" Brown

These distinguished Famers (Mathewson, Hall of Fame in 1936, and Brown, 1949), reviewed in the Mathewson chapter, appeared against Pete Alexander during his first several seasons in the majors. In sum, there were 12 matchups, four of them involving Cub mainstay Three Finger Brown. The eight Mathewson-Alexander faceoffs, commencing in the 1911 pennant race, resulted in a four and two record for Alexander, with two no-decisions, while Matty won but three while dropping five. Despite his red-hot rookie season in 1911, Alex and his Phils had to settle for a fourth place finish in a pennant race spearheaded by the Giants and their ace, Mathewson, who that year recorded his ninth consecutive 20-game season while leading the McGrawmen to league honors as they displaced the defending champion Chicago aggregation, led by the veteran Brown. The three fingered Cub stalwart had logged another 21 conquests during 1911, encountering the Phils' young phenom twice, both encounters resulting in Brown victories.

Mordecai Brown and Pete Alexander met two more times before Chicago's hero (Brown's last appearance against Alexander was in 1913, where he spent the season with former Cub teammates Johnny Kling and Joe Tinker in a Cincinnati uniform) moved on to the Federal League, the games coming in 1912, when the Phillies beat him 7 to 5, and in 1913, when he went down to a 3 to 2 defeat in the ninth inning. The final Alexander-Brown reading favored neither, each of them splitting the four decisions.

In Cy Young (reviewed earlier), Walter Johnson (American League titan), Pete Alexander, Three Finger Brown and Christy Mathewson we have five of the deadball era's elite moundsmen, each of whom contributed gargantuan numbers to the record book, each a Hall of Famer beyond dispute, and each with a distinctive style that marked them as one-of-a-kind. Compare the selected career numbers of these pitching greats against five better-than-average hurlers during the deadball era, listed alphabetically, in the following chart (minimum of 10 seasons):

	Yrs	W-L	SH	ERA	OBA	K	TPI	Rank*
Alexander, G.	20	373–208	90	2.56	.250	2198	64.6	3
Brown, M.	14	239–130	55	2.06	.233	1375	35.5	23
Howell, H.	13	131–146	20	2.74	.252	986	16.6	144
Johnson, W.	21	417–179	110	2.17	.227	3509	91.4	1
Leifeld, A.	12	124–97	32	2.47	.248	616	11.3	231
Mathewson, C.	17	373–188	79	2.13	.236	2507	62.9	4
Mullin, G.	14	228–196	35	2.82	.255	1482	14.5	168
Sallee, H.	14	174–143	25	2.56	.258	836	9.8	270
White, G.	13	189–156	45	2.39	.242	1384	20.1	101
Young, D.	22	511–216	76	2.63	.252	2803	78.0	2

The five pitchers above who are paired in this sampling with Alexander, Brown, Johnson, Mathewson and Young pale by comparison, despite their own not inconsiderable achievements. They were accomplished major leaguers, but the gulf between them is sufficient to fix a line of demarcation between the many good ones and the miniscule .05 percent of them all who earned a plaque at Cooperstown.

Pete Alexander versus Charles "Babe" Adams (1882–1968)

The top five winners in the NL during Pete Alexander's record-breaking rookie season in 1911 included two Giants (Mathewson won 26 and Marquard 24), Alexander (with his pace-setting 28), Hickory Bob Harmon (who won 23), and 29-year-old Babe Adams (with 22). Adams was no stranger to baseball fame. His first brush with major league stardom came with a three-victory outing in the Pirates' conquest of the Cobb-led Tigers in the 1909 World Series. But in 1911 he turned in his first big season, with 293.1 innings of stellar pitching, and posting league-leading numbers in Opponents' On Base Percentage (.271) and Ratio (9.3), while anchoring the Pirate staff with a 22 and 12 record. Further, he issued only 42 free passes, amounting to 1.29 walks per nine innings pitched, the kind of figure that would ultimately put him in the top ten, all time, if he could sustain it throughout his career. He did. In a 19 year sojourn in the Bigs, Babe Adams wound up exactly at the 1.29 mark, good for a 10th place ranking since 1876, and second behind teammate Deacon Phillippe for 20th century excellence.

*TPI ratings and overall pitcher ranking taken from *TBE*, 2001.

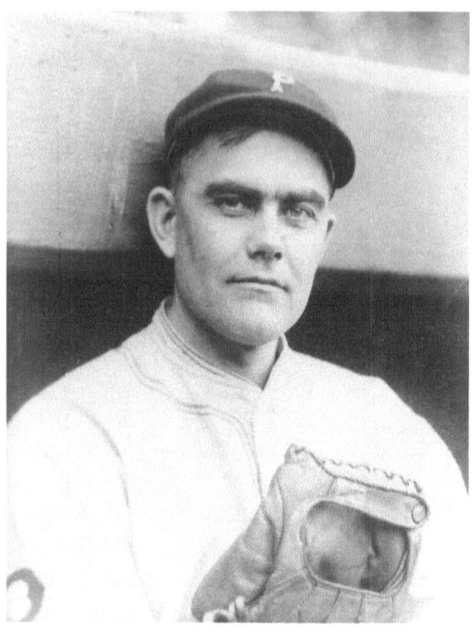

This "Babe" sparked the Pirates to the 1909 world's championship by winning three of the Pirates' four victories over the Cobb-led Tigers.

Without blinding speed, and with just an average breaking ball, Adams relied on speed changes and meticulous control to get by. A final 194–140 record suggests strongly that he did. Adams, the first of baseball's many "Babes," enjoyed his best "no-walks" season in 1920, when, in 263 innings of work, he walked only 18 batters, an almost nonexistent 0.616 per nine innings pitched. During that season a league leading eight shutouts provided almost half of his 17 wins. Tight control paid off for a very average Pittsburgh nine that just managed to stay above .500 with 79 victories and a fourth place finish.

One other "no walks" note: on May 17, 1914, Adams took on Rube Marquard, and though he lost to the Giants, he didn't walk a single batter in the 21-inning duel. That was, and will remain, a major league record for a long, long time to come.

At a career 1.65 walks per game, Grover Cleveland Alexander wasn't far enough behind Babe Adams' 1.29 to make too much difference. During the eight afternoons they met head to head, Pirate and Philly hitters (later, Cubs and Cardinals hitters when Alex moved on to Chicago and then St. Louis) knew they were going to have to hit their way on base. Here is the rundown on the eight game series between Pete Alexander and Babe Adams:

The Alexander-Adams Log:

Jul 26, 1913	Philadelphia 8, Pittsburgh 2	Alexander WP, Adams LP
Aug 5, 1915	Pittsburgh 1, Philadelphia 0	Adams WP, Alexander LP
Jul 26, 1916	Philadelphia 7, Pittsburgh 1	Alexander WP, Adams LP
Jun 26, 1921*	Pittsburgh 11, Chicago 3	Adams WP, Alexander LP
Apr 26, 1922	Chicago 4, Pittsburgh 3	Alexander WP, Adams LP

* In this game the Pirates doubled two Cub runners trapped between second and third, the double play going 6–2–5–1–2.

On August 16, 1912, the first matchup produced a 5 to 3 win for Philadelphia, with Alexander the winning pitcher. Adams relieved (ND).

Alexander relieved in a 3 to 0 Adams three-hitter on July 9, 1915. Brennan was the LP.

Starter Alexander went only 4.1 innings on May 29, 1923, and was the loser as the Pirates beat the Cubs 7 to 6 behind George Boehler. Adams started for the Pirates but lasted only three innings (ND).

In the Alexander-Adams series, Pete won 4 and lost 3 and had one no-decision. Adams won 3, lost 3, and had two no-decisions.

Pete Alexander versus Richard "Rube" Marquard (1889–1980)

Marquard was elected to the Baseball Hall of Fame in 1971

By the year 2000 the Hall of Fame's Veterans Committee had enshrined 93 ball players, the same number as had been selected by the Baseball Writer's Association. 1971 was Rube Marquard's big year. His class consisted of seven former greats, including Dave Bancroft, Jake Beckley, Chick Hafey, Harry Hooper, Joe Kelley, Marquard and Satchel Paige, the first player to be elected from Negro League Baseball. None was cast in the mold of a Ruth or a Johnson or a Spahn or an Alexander, save perhaps the gifted Paige, yet each was deemed worthy of Cooperstown honors, exceeding that imaginary level of "minimal achievement" for enshrinement.

That is not meant to disparage any one of them. In Rube Marquard's case, for example, there was a whirlwind New York Giant stint between 1911 and 1913 that included his famous 19-game winning streak and a three-year, 73 and 28 record that no doubt fueled Hall of Fame interest in his Cooperstown credentials. The handsome switch-hitting southpaw finally hit it big in 1911, helping Big Six Mathewson and his Giant teammates to the first of three successive league titles. That 1911 season will also be recognized among knowledgeable fans as the Great Alexander's smashing major league debut year. It also became the first of a dozen seasons during which the two encountered one another. During that time the two moundsmen, miles apart in personality and pitching style, had at it on 19 different occasions, Marquard emerging with a 7 and 4 record that included seven No Decisions and one tie. That gave him the upper hand over Alexander, who logged a sub-par 6 and 9 reading. There were also three No Decisions and a 1 to 1 tie at the Polo Grounds in 1915. The record:

The Alexander-Marquard Log:

Aug 14, 1911   New York 3, Philadelphia 2   Marquard WP, Alexander LP

Apr 24, 1912	New York 11, Philadelphia 4	Marquard WP, Alexander LP
May 30, 1912	New York 2, Philadelphia 1	Marquard WP, Alexander LP
May 5, 1913	Philadelphia 6, New York 3	Alexander WP, Marquard LP
Jul 1, 1913	New York 10, Philadelphia 0	Marquard WP, Alexander LP
Apr 14, 1914	Philadelphia 10, New York 1	Alexander WP, Marquard LP
Sep 12, 1914	Philadelphia 1, New York 0	Alexander WP, Marquard LP
Sep 30, 1916	Brooklyn 6, Philadelphia 3	Marquard WP, Alexander LP
Jun 21, 1917	Brooklyn 4, Philadelphia 2	Marquard WP, Alexander LP
Oct 1, 1921	Cincinnati 5, Chicago 3	Marquard WP, Alexander LP

In the second of three 1912 matchups, Alex went the route to beat New York 8 to 6 on May 3. Starter and loser Red Ames was relieved by Hooks Wiltse, Mathewson and Marquard (ND).

New York won a squeaker 7 to 6 on May 29, 1913. Alexander started, with ND, and Marquard relieved (ND). Tesreau won the game in relief.

On June 22, 1915, at the Polo Grounds the Phils and Giants battled to a 1–1 tie. The game was called because of both rain and darkness. Alex held the Giants hitless after the first inning.

Shortly after having been picked up by Brooklyn, Marquard (ND) relieved Larry Cheney (WP) to protect a 6 to 3 Brooklyn victory. Alexander went all the way, absorbing the defeat on September 6, 1915.

On October 6, 1915, Marquard (ND) started in a 9 to 6 loss to the Phils. Alex (ND) relieved starter Erskine Mayer (WP).

Now with Chicago, Alexander (ND) relieved Phil Douglas (WP) on May 18, 1919. Marquard's complete game effort was to no avail in this 3 to 2 loss.

In another ND for Marquard, Pete Alexander beat Boston 7 to 2 on July 7, 1922. Frank "Bullet" Miller (LP) was relieved by Marquard (ND).

Rube Marquard started against loser Alexander on August 15, 1923, at Boston, but gave way to reliever Dana Filligim (WP). Alexander turned in a complete game in the 3 to 2 Chicago loss.

On June 14, 1925, Alexander and Marquard met for the last time, with Alex going the route in a 7 to 3 win over Boston. Marquard (ND) was one of two relievers for loser Kyle Graham.

The 1914 season was the kind that the also-rans dream about. It was the year that Boston made the move from the basement to the penthouse in the National League, and it was done at the expense of a New York ball club that wasn't really out of it until the last weeks of the season. One of the games that enabled the Battling Braves to maintain their newly acquired lead was an Alexander *meisterwerk* authored on September 12th when he subdued Rube Marquard and the Giants 1 to 0 with a classy four-hitter. It was one of 90 shutout efforts over the course of his heralded 20-year career, a number that was exceeded only by Walter Johnson's 110. His effort that day resulted in another of his 17, 1 to 0 victories. The list of 1 to 0 winners who have won at least 10 such masterpieces is 25 names long. Here are the top twelve:

1)	Walter Johnson	38	7)	Ed Walsh	13
2)	Grover Alexander	17	8)	Guy White	13
3)	Bert Blyleven	15	9)	Cy Young	13
4)	Christy Mathewson	14	10)	Steve Carlton	12
5)	Dean Chance	13	11)	Stan Coveleski	12
6)	Eddie Plank	13	12)	Gaylord Perry	12

In 1915, when Ol' Low and Away posted a career low 1.22 ERA, he won 12 of his 31 victories via the shutout route (he upped that number to a major league record of 16 the next season). On July 5 of that year he beat the Giants on a one-hitter, one of four that summer, and in no less than 16 of his games that season held his opponents to four hits or less. By that time the rush to Cooperstown was on. Around both leagues they knew that the dark-visaged, sad-faced control artist was a force of immense proportions.

Rube Marquard also made it to baseball's Valhalla. The trip was made on the Broadway Limited, bright lights blazing. For Pete Alexander the trip was less spectacular, but the stars shone brightly above on his awesome career.

Pete Alexander versus Eppa Rixey (1891–1963)
Rixey was elected to the Baseball Hall of Fame in 1963

There was only one Lefty Grove, he of the inflammatory temperament who was not above tearing apart locker rooms after losing ball games. Singlehanded. But there was one who went before, another lefty, long and lanky, fiercely competitive, and, despite his charm and otherwise impeccable social graces, equally volatile and just as dangerous around a locker room after dropping a tough one. His name was Eppa Rixey, one time road-roomie of Pete Alexander, whom he followed into the majors in 1912 just a year after Alexander's first tour of the Big Circuit.

In a 21-year career Rixey amassed 266 victories, just slightly more than the 251 losses he endured while fronting for some mediocre ball clubs in Philadelphia and Cincinnati. Three decades after his last pitch he was selected for Hall of Fame honors by the Veterans Committee, suggesting that there is room at Cooperstown for exceptional pitchers whose lot has been to perform their artistry while patiently putting up with the bobbles, bad throws, lack of clutch hitting and mental lapses that were no doubt at the root of many of his embarrassments. The tall Virginian's career 26.6 TPI puts him in the 57th spot among pitchers, a sabermetric endorsement of sorts for his enshrinement, placing him ahead of Robin Roberts, Rube Waddell, Dizzy Dean and Lefty Gomez on the all time honors list.

On May 24, 1920, the two former roomies crossed paths for the first time after both had served overseas in the U.S. military during the summer of 1918. By 1920 Alexander, now wearing a Chicago uniform, was back in stride, and that season was the scourge of the Senior Circuit, with league-leading figures in wins (27, plus 5 Saves), strikeouts (173), ERA (1.91) and a whopping 363 innings pitched, as he registered the last of his monster years for the fifth place Cubs. On that fine day in May, Pete Alexander won his ninth straight ball game at the expense of Rixey's Phils. The score was 6 to 0 in a game that Rixey kept reasonably close. But the Cubs staged two three-run rallies and were not about to go down to the Phillies, not with old Pete pitching. He allowed only one runner to reach second, Bevo LeBourveau, who had doubled and was promptly wiped out in a double play when third baseman Charlie Deal speared a liner and doubled LeBourveau. One wonders what the visitor's locker room at Wrigley Field must have looked like after Mr. Rixey left it that day.

It took him three seasons, but Eppa Rixey caught up with Alexander on September 12, 1923, when the southpaw, now with Cincinnati, spaced seven hits in a masterfully pitched shutout over the Cubs, 4 to 0. It didn't even the count on whitewashings in the Rixey-Alexander series of 17 games between 1920 and 1928 (that count was 2 to 1 among Alex' eight victories over the Reds), but it probably provided the balm for the numerous disappointments Eppa suffered at the Hands of Ol' Pete. The series record follows:

The Alexander-Rixey Log:

May 24, 1920	Chicago 6, Philadelphia 0	Alexander WP, Rixey LP
Jun 8, 1920	Philadelphia 5, Chicago 3	Rixey WP, Alexander LP
Jul 21, 1920	Philadelphia 6, Chicago 1	Rixey WP, Alexander LP
Jul 25, 1920	Chicago 5, Philadelphia 2	Alexander WP, Rixey LP
Aug 3, 1920	Chicago 3, Philadelphia 1	Alexander WP, Rixey LP
Sep 2, 1921	Chicago 7, Philadelphia 0	Alexander WP, Rixey LP
Apr 12, 1922	Chicago 7, Cincinnati 3	Alexander WP, Rixey LP
Sep 12, 1923	Cincinnati 4, Chicago 0	Rixey WP, Alexander LP
Sep 9, 1924	Chicago 4, Cincinnati 3	Alexander WP, Rixey LP
Apr 28, 1925	Cincinnati 9, Chicago 3	Rixey WP, Alexander LP
Jul 24, 1927	Cincinnati 9, St. Louis 4	Rixey WP, Alexander LP
Apr 24, 1928	St. Louis 7, Cincinnati 2	Alexander WP, Rixey LP

Virgil "Chief" Cheeves (ND) was the starting pitcher in the September 17, 1920, victory of the Cubs over the Phils. He was relieved by Abraham Lincoln "Sweetbreads" Bailey, who picked up his only win of the 1920 season. Alexander relieved Bailey and notched one of his five 1920 Saves. Rixey sustained the 3 to 1 loss.

May 28, 1922: Alexander (ND) relieved Cheeves (WP), who had started. Dolf Luque started in the 8 to 7 Chicago victory and was the loser. He was relieved by Rixey (ND).

Tony Kaufmann was the starter and winner on June 4, 1923, when the Cubs beat the Reds 8 to 7. He had relief help from Alexander, who picked up the Save. Rixey was the starter and loser for the Reds.

July 2, 1923: Cincinnati 8, Chicago 7. Rixey pitched a complete game to win it. Alexander started (ND), and was relieved by Nick Dumovich (LP) and Chief Cheeves (ND).

In an 11-inning game Cincinnati beat the Cardinals on September 3, 1928. Rixey (ND) started this game, and was relieved by Ray Kolp (ND) and the winning pitcher, Ken Ash. Sylvester Johnson started for St. Louis, and was relieved by "Wee Willie" Sherdel (LP) and Alexander (ND), who finished up in the Red's 6 to 5 victory.

In the 17 Alexander-Rixey matchups, Alexander Won 7, Lost 5, and had No Decisions in 5 games, including 2 Saves. Rixey Won 6, Lost 10 and received 1 No Decision.

Pete Alexander versus Arley Wilbur Cooper (1892–1973)

Sinkerballer Wilbur Cooper was a Pirate mainstay for 13 seasons before winding up in Chicago in 1925. There he found himself on the same pitching staff with Tony Kaufmann, John "Sheriff" Blake, Guy Bush, a promising young righthander, and an old antagonist, Pete Alexander. It just so happened that the 1925 Cubs, who labored under no less than three managers, staggered to a last place finish, fighting to the very end with equally inept Brooklyn and Philadelphia clubs for sixth, seventh and eighth. (That race-within-a-race for "bottom of the league honors" was won by the Cubs, incidentally.) As luck would (or would not) have it, Cooper's old team, the Pirates, that season won both the NL crown and the World Series. Imagine what was going through old Wilbur's mind at World Series time that fall.

In the Pittsburgh years that preceded Cooper's waning 1925 and 1926 seasons, the compact, ox-strong lefty had accounted for some 202 Pirate conquests, the most in Pittsburgh's history. There had been four 20-game seasons, another two 19-gamers, and nine straight years with wins in double figures. During those salad days he teamed with Babe Adams to form a one-two pitching punch that saw the Corsairs through some lean, as well as fair-to-middling, years. However, none matched the glory days of the earlier deadball era seasons, when speed, timely hitting and pitching depth made the Pirates annual contenders. The final Cooper ledger was, nonetheless, dotted with strong numbers that positioned him among the top 100 hurlers, all time, in Wins, Complete Games, Shutouts, Innings Pitched and ERA. Further, the man hit like the regulars and fielded his position superbly. He was, all things considered, one of the outstanding pitchers of his era.

One of the more interesting bits of baseball trivia comes from the year that "Coop" and Alexander faced each other twice—1920. That season

A 15-year major leaguer, Wilbur Cooper was a four-time 20-game winner for the Pirates (1912–24).

Cooper started two triple plays against Philadelphia, one on July 7 and another on August 21. On both occasions Cooper caught a Mack Wheat pop up, wheeled and assisted in the second leg of the triple-killing, catching Phillie runners off base. Wheat was the brother of Hall of Famer Zack, both of them playing for the Dodgers between 1915 and 1919 as teammates. The younger of the brothers, Mack, finished his career as a backup catcher with the Phillies in 1919 and 1920.

There were six Cooper-Alexander encounters, and it was not until the last one, on June 22, 1922, that "Coop" managed to win one. Prior to that 8 to 6 victory over the Cubs, the best he could come up with was a No Decision in 1920 and four losses, three of them in extra innings, dating back to August 20, 1915, the Phils' pennant season, when their Alexander-led forces bested Cooper's Pirates 4 to 3 in 11 innings in their initial matchup.

The Alexander-Cooper Log:

Sep 13, 1915	Philadelphia 4, Pittsburgh 2	Alexander WP, Cooper LP
	Alexander and Cooper pitched complete, 13-inning games.	
Aug 18, 1917	Philadelphia 3, Pittsburgh 2	Alexander WP, Cooper LP
	A 14-inning game, both pitchers went the route.	
Apr 28, 1920	Chicago 11, Pittsburgh 1	Alexander WP, Cooper LP
Jun 22, 1922	Pittsburgh 8, Chicago 6	Cooper WP, Alexander LP

Eppa Rixey started against Cooper (LP) on August 20, 1915. Alexander pitched the last four innings in relief and was the winning pitcher in an 11-inning game won by the Phillies, 4 to 3.

Cooper relieved starter Hal Carlson (WP) on June 27, 1920, as the Pirates defeated the Cubs 8 to 3. Alexander was the losing pitcher.

In the six-game series between the two, Alexander won 4 and lost 2, and Cooper won 1, lost 4, and received one No Decision.

Pete Alexander versus Adolfo Domingo "Dolf" Luque "The Pride of Havana" (1890–1957)

Ten days deep into his 20-year major league career, Dolf Luque ran headlong into Grover Alexander as the two of them matched pitches, if ever so briefly, in a 10-inning Braves win over the Phils on May 30, 1914, in the afternoon portion of a Memorial Day twinbill. Alex, who went the route, was the loser, and Luque, who entered the game as a reliever, pitched ⅔ of an inning, giving way to relief pitcher Gene Cocreham, the eventual winner. "The Pride of Havana" appeared in two more games for Boston's Miracle Braves in 1915, and then was shipped off to the minors, not to resurface in a major league uniform until 1918. By this time the miracles had ended in Boston, but were about to begin in Cincinnati, where the small but sturdy right-hander, his pitching repertoire complete, was ready to post the first of his 194 big time wins.

Dolf Luque struck gold once again with the 1919 Reds, who upended the heavily favored and tainted Sox team that became known as the Black Sox. Twice he had entered the Bigs and both times landed on a World Series winner in the early stages of his stay. This time, however, there would be no more seasoning. In his

"The Pride of Havana," Dolf Luque, had one of the sharpest breaking pitches in the game during his 20 year career.

first two seasons with Cincinnati he turned in 16 wins against only 6 losses. He was on his way.

By 1923 Dolf, his mound partner Eppa Rixey, and a solid Cincinnati ball club were ready to make a serious run at McGraw's Giants for the pennant. Though they fell four games short of the big prize, the Reds turned in 91 victories and a strong, second place finish in the NL. In what turned out to be his career year, Señor Luque posted 27 wins, leading the league, along with leading figures in most of the other major pitching stats. Whereas the league ERA was a bloated 4.00, his list-topping ERA was 1.91, and he also led both leagues with six shutouts.

When it came to shutouts, however, the Old Alexander still had a lesson or two up his sleeve, even for the gifted Cuban, as Alex beat the Reds at Wrigley Field, 2 to 0, in a sparkling three hitter, giving up but one free pass and whiffing six. The box score of this brilliantly pitched game:

At Chicago, June 24, 1923

Cincinnati	AB	H	PO	A	Chicago	AB	H	PO	A
Burns, rf	5	1	1	0	Statz, cf	4	2	3	0
Daubert, 1b	4	0	7	3	Holocher, ss	2	0	2	5
Bohne, ss	4	0	5	2	Grantham, 2b	2	0	0	5
Roush, cf	4	0	1	0	O'Farrel, c	3	2	5	0
Duncan, lf	4	0	1	1	Friberg, 3b	3	1	0	1
Pinelli, 3b	3	0	2	1	Miller, lf	4	1	2	0
Fonseca, 2b	3	1	3	3	Heathcote, cf	3	0	1	0
Hargrave, c	2	0	2	1	Elliott, 1b	4	0	13	1
Wingo, c	1	0	1	1	Alexander, (WP)	2	2	1	2
Luque, (LP)	2	0	1	2					
Harper, ph	1	1	0	0					
Keck, p	0	0	0	1					
Totals	29	3	24	15	Totals	29	8	27	14
Line Score	Cincinnati	000		000		000		0–3–0	
	Chicago	000		011		00x		2–8–1	

2BH: Alexander, Harper; SB: Grantham; DP: Fonseca and Daubert, Duncan, Fonseca and Bohne; BB: Luque 6; Keck 0; Alexander 1; K: Luque 3; Keck 0; Alexander 6.

The victory was one of Alexander's 22, and the shutout one of three that year, as the 36-year-old veteran posted the eighth of his nine 20-game seasons. For Luque, the defeat was one of but eight in 1923, and it marked the second time old Alex had whitewashed the Reds behind Luque.

Between them, the Latino Luque and his mound compadre Eppa Rixey served up enough pepper and salsa to keep the NL hopping. Rixey, as previously noted, was a fiery competitor, and the hot-tempered Luque, for example, responded on one sultry summer day to some less than flattering comments from the Brooklyn dugout by steaming into the Dodgers' dugout and popping Casey Stengel on the nose. But it should be noted further that, aside from their fiery temperaments, the Luque and Rixey tandem won 197 ball games for the Reds during the 1920s as they kept the Reds in contention, in so far as that was possible, almost by themselves. That compares very favorably with the Pirates' Adams-Cooper duo, the other two non–Famers in the Alexander matchups, who were winners of 216 games over a similar nine year span between 1912 and 1920.

The Alexander-Luque Log:

Jul 1, 1920	Chicago 1, Cincinnati 0	Alexander WP, Luque LP
	Dolf Luque gave up only 4 hits, giving way to Hod Eller (ND). The winning run was scored in the first inning.	
Jun 1, 1922	Cincinnati 6, Chicago 1	Luque WP, Alexander LP
Jun 24, 1923	Chicago 2, Cincinnati 0	Alexander WP, Luque LP
Sep 1, 1923	Cincinnati 4, Chicago 3	Luque WP, Alexander LP
	The Cubs scored a pair of ninth-inning runs before Luque closed out his 4 to 3 victory over Alexander.	
Apr 24, 1925	Chicago 5, Cincinnati 1	Alexander WP, Luque LP
Sep 5, 1926	St. Louis 7, Cincinnati 3	Alexander WP, Luque LP

On May 30, 1914, Dolf Luque (ND), in his second major league game, relieved starter Dick Crutcher. Alexander (LP) pitched a complete game, losing by a 3 to 2 count.

The Cubs beat the Reds on May 28, 1922, by the score of 8 to 7. Both Alexander (ND) and Luque (LP) started but were relieved. The winning Cub pitcher was reliever Virgil "Chief" Cheeves.

Pete Alexander versus Clarence Arthur "Dazzy" Vance (1891–1961)

Vance was elected to the Hall of Fame in 1955

When, in 1922 at the age of 31, Dazzy Vance finally came to the Big Tent to stay, a cagey old veteran took notice of the long-armed, flame-throwing Dodger hurler, commenting, "That fellow Vance has more stuff on the ball than any other pitcher in the league." The veteran's name? Pete Alexander, no less. And for the next decade Dazzy dazzled the league with suffocating smoke, dancing curve balls and a string of strikeout titles that stretched to seven straight. Ol' Pete was right. And Clarence Arthur Vance turned out to be the dominant National League pitcher of the roaring, soaring '20s.

Regarding that fastball Vance threw: It was one of the quickest to home plate in the game's history. Feller? The Johnsons, Walter and Randy? Amos Rusie? Lefty Grove? Clemens? If they got it to the catcher's mitt any faster, it wasn't fast enough to make any appreciable difference. All of these fellows could bring it. And so could Dazzy. Between 1918 and 1935, when National Leaguers were piling up base hits like John D. piled up greenbacks, only three times did any pitcher have the gall to strike out 200 or more batters in a season. The three pitchers were Vance, Vance and Vance. It gives an indication of just how often hitters like Hornsby, Klein, Hack Wilson, Paul Waner, Bill Terry, et al. shattered the air looking for a ball that was already in the catcher's mitt. At 39, with those Dodgers of Daffiness fame, there was still enough steam in the old K-Machine to nail 173 hitters during a 17 and 15 season in 1930 when the NL's bash boys went absolutely berserk. Dazzy's ERA that season was an in-your-face 2.61, while league pitchers staggered to the end of the year with an average ERA of 4.97. The old Dazzler's 1930 season, by the way, merited the closer scrutiny of Joe Cardello, who penned these lines for the *Baseball Research Journal:*

> From April 25 to June 26 Vance started thirteen games, completed nine of them, and compiled an ERA of 1.68. If you exclude his one poor performance in this stretch — when he yielded seven runs in six innings on June 6 — his ERA is an astounding 1.16. Considering that the ERA for all National League pitchers in 1930 was an astronomical 4.97, Vance's ERA for these two months looks more like Bob Gibson in 1968 — the "Year of the Pitcher" — than anything you'd expect in the Big Bang Era of 1930 [*BRJ*, 1996, No. 25, p. 127].

Cardello wound up his article with this provocative comparison of the Lefty Grove 1930, 28 and 5 masterpiece and Vance's superb effort:

	Grove	Vance
Opp. BA	.247	.246
Opp. OB%	.284	.284
ERA	2.54	2.61
H/9 inn.	8.44	8.39
K/9 inn.	6.46	6.02
Shutouts	2	4
Starter Runs	68.3	68.0
W-L	28–5	17–15
Age	29	39

About the only edge Lefty sported over elder statesman Vance, save his splashy W-L record, was 10 years (it is worth noting that Vance was pitching for a fourth place ball club and Grove for the bone-crushing Athletics, that season's World Champions), and that makes the Dazzler's record all the more dazzling.

And to complete the Vance ledger: on September 8, 1925, Dazzy one-hit the Phillies. Five days later he topped that with a no-hitter, beating the NL's cellar dwellers by nine runs. The score was ten to one. One? Remember, dear reader, he was pitching for the Dodgers, who managed to fumble home a Philadelphia run in the second inning.

As for the Alexander-Vance matchups, far too few in number for avid baseball buffs to bite into, there were three Alexander wins and but one Vance conquest that came during the Dazzler's 22 and 9 season in 1925, when he beat the Cubs at Ebbets Field, 4 to 2.

The Alexander-Vance Log:

May 13, 1923	Chicago 5, Brooklyn 2	Alexander WP, Vance LP
	The Cubs erupted for five runs in the fifth inning. At the completion of this game Alex had logged 51 consecutive innings without issuing a free pass.	
Jul 9, 1925	Brooklyn 4, Chicago 2	Vance WP, Alexander LP
Sep 10, 1927	St. Louis 5, Brooklyn 2	Alexander WP, Vance LP
May 8, 1928	St. Louis 4, Brooklyn 2	Alexander WP, Vance LP
	The win pushed Alexander's record to 3 and 2 in his last good season (in 1928 he won 16 and lost 9), pitching 18 complete games in 244 innings. In the May 6 victory he gave up one earned run and spaced eight hits in a complete game effort.	

Pete Alexander versus Burleigh "Ol' Stubblebeard" Grimes (1893–1985)

Grimes was elected to the Baseball Hall of Fame in 1964

On April 12, 1928, the Pittsburgh Pirates became Pete Alexander's 90th shutout victim at Sportsman's Park, St. Louis. The losing pitcher in the second game of that season was Burleigh Grimes, by this time into his 13th major league campaign and back in the uniform he first wore in his 1916 debut. "Boily," as the Flatbush faithful used to call him during his eight-season sojourn with the Dodgers, would go on to an outstanding year, with 25 victories in 330.2 innings pitched, 28 complete games and four Shutouts, all league-leading numbers. But every one of his 14 losses got his cork. He was that way — begrudging, combative, crotchety and downright mean about his pitching. The last of the grandfathered spitballers, he was as tough a competitor as ever took the hill. But he did respect the good ones, including Alexander, who was among the few he would pay to see pitch. In fact, about

Old Alex he said, "If anybody was ever a better pitcher than that guy, I wouldn't know what his name was. It was a pleasure just to watch him work, even though he was beating your brains out most of the time."

That's what was going on even in the waning, less robust years of Alex' oft-troubled but consistently stellar career. Case in point: that 5-zip afternoon in St. Louis. The whitewash edged his career total to 90, a record for NL pitchers, and second only to Walter Johnson's 110. This one was another of those games that teased his opponents just enough to think they might be able to push a run or two across and beat him, only to find that the old master, full of spring's supple strength and perhaps a nip or two, was minded to have things his own way. That meant that seven bingles, none of them for extra bases, would be rationed so as not to get home plate messed up. And so the Pirates—and disgruntled "Old Stubblebeard"—took their whipping. Here is that historic box score:

At St. Louis, April 12, 1928

Pittsburgh	AB	R	H	PO	St. Louis	AB	R	H	PO
Waner, cf	4	0	1	2	Douthit, cf	4	1	2	5
Adams, 2b	4	0	0	1	Holm, 3b	4	1	2	1
P. Waner, rf	3	0	1	2	Frisch, 2b	3	1	2	2
Wright, ss	4	0	0	1	Bottomley, 1b	4	0	0	15
Traynor, 3b	4	0	1	0	Hafey, rf	4	0	1	0
Grantham, 1b	4	0	1	12	Roettger, lf	4	0	1	0
Barnhart, lf	4	0	1	3	Thevenow, ss	3	1	1	1
Gooch, c	3	0	0	3	O'Farrell, c	4	0	0	3
Grimes (LP)	3	0	2	0	Alexander (WP)	4	1	1	0
Totals	33	0	7	24	Totals	34	5	10	27

Line Score:	Pittsburgh	000	000	000	0–7–1
	St. Louis	120	020	00x	5–10–0

2BH, Douthit, Roettger; 3BH, Holm; SB, Barnhart; DP: Alexander, Thevenow and Bottomley; BB: Alexander 1, Grimes 1; K: Alexander 3, Grimes 2; Umpires: McCormick, Magee and Klem.

Of the 12 pitchers arrayed against Alexander in this review, five were subjected to shutout losses. Rube Marquard (10 to 0 on July 1, 1913), Babe Adams (1 to 0 on August 15, 1915), *Burleigh Grimes* (3 to 0 on July 26, 1921), and Eppa Rixey (4 to 0 on September 12, 1923) were the four who returned the favor. The list of Alexander's whitewashing victims follows:

Date	Shutout Score	Losing Pitcher
Sep 12, 1914	1 to 0	Marquard (LP)
Sep 2, 1915	2 to 0	Mathewson (LP)

Sep 1, 1917	5 to 0	Marquard (LP)
May 24, 1920	6 to 0	Rixey (LP)
Jul 1, 1920	1 to 0	Luque (LP)
Aug 28, 1920	1 to 0	Grimes (LP)
Jul 26, 1921	3 to 0	Grimes (LP)
Sep 2, 1921	7 to 0	Rixey (LP)
Jun 24, 1923	2 to 0	Luque (LP)
Aug 27, 1926	3 to 0	Grimes (LP)
Apr 12, 1928	5 to 0	Grimes (LP)

Of those who were active in Alexander's mind-bending 1916 season, during which he sliced through NL hitters to ring up a record-setting 16 Shutouts (which will endure in perpetuity), only Babe Adams and Rube Marquard squared off against the Whitewash Wizard, and both escaped unscathed in the Shutout Department, though he beat the Pirates and Adams 7 to 1 on July 26.

In January of 1927 Burleigh Grimes was one of five players involved in a three-cornered trade between the Dodgers, the Phillies and the Giants, moving him from Flatbush to the Polo Grounds, where he provided substantial support for McGraw & Co. as the Giants battled both the Cardinals and the Pirates for the NL pennant. The race went right on down to the season's final days before the Pirates won the pennant. That season the 34-year-old battler should have won 20 but had to settle for 19. On one of the two or three occasions a win eluded him, he was lifted for reliever Dutch Henry after matching his favorite nemesis, Old Pete, pitch for pitch through nine innings and a 2 to 2 tie. Two innings later the Giants came up with the winning run, beating Alex 3 to 2, even though it cost Big Burleigh what might well have been the sixth 20-game season of his career.

Just before Spring Training in 1928, John McGraw made another of his personnel blunders that weakened his pitching staff beyond hope of winning the pennant he almost captured in 1927 by trading Old Stubblebeard to Pittsburgh for Vic Aldridge. In 1928 Grimes won a career high 25 (Aldridge won but four that season) for the Pirates, more than enough to put the team he left into the World Series. How much more Grimes could have done beyond winning 13 straight and posting a fine 19 and 8 for the fading Giants' major domo in 1927 to suggest he was worth keeping around stretches imagination beyond reality. But on opening day old Burleigh was wearing a Pirates uniform, ready willing and able to get after the league once more — especially the Giants. Anyway, it turned out to be "just another" of the many stops he made (the only NL teams Grimes missed were the Reds and the Phillies) along his circuitous route to Cooperstown. The final leg of that journey was made in 1964 when he was enshrined in the Hall of Fame.

The Alexander-Grimes Log:

Jun 2, 1917	Philadelphia 9, Pittsburgh 1	Alexander WP, Grimes LP
Aug 9, 1920	Brooklyn 6, Chicago 5	Grimes WP, Alexander LP
	Grimes hurled 7⅓ innings, with relief help from Al Mamaux, who got the Save.	
Aug 28, 1920	Chicago 1, Brooklyn 0	Alexander WP, Grimes LP
	There were no extra base hits among 13 safeties in this game, which featured sensational fielding by the Cubs' shortstop, Zeb Terry.	
Jul 26, 1921	Brooklyn 3, Chicago 0	Grimes WP, Alexander LP
	A sparkling Grimes 5-hitter evened the shutout score in the Alexander-Grimes series — momentarily.	
Jun 13, 1922	Chicago 8, Brooklyn 3	Alexander WP, Grimes LP
May 10, 1924	Chicago 7, Brooklyn 5	Alexander WP, Grimes LP
Jun 11, 1924	Chicago 7, Brooklyn 2	Alexander WP, Grimes LP
	In this early season battle for second place, Gabby Hartnett homered to pace the Chicago victory.	
Aug 7, 1926	St. Louis 3, Brooklyn 0	Alexander WP, Grimes LP
	Alex walked no one and gave up only four hits in blanking the Dodgers. The victory enabled the Cardinals to sweep the five-game series.	
Apr 12, 1928	St. Louis 5, Pittsburgh 0	Alexander WP, Grimes LP
	This was Alexander's final shutout, an NL record-setting number 90.	

On July 16, 1926, Brooklyn beat St. Louis, 8 to 7. Neither Grimes nor Alexander were pitchers of record, the win going to Douglas "Buzz" McWeeney, while Herman "Hi" Bell picked up the loss in relief.

New York beat St. Louis 3 to 2 in 11 innings on May 12, 1927. Grimes started and pitched nine innings (ND), and Dutch Henry received credit for the victory. Alexander pitched a complete game in sustaining the loss.

Burleigh Grimes and Pete Alexander pitched in the same game on August 31, 1928, but not against each other, Alexander having left in the fifth inning, with Grimes entering the game in relief in the ninth inning to pick up the Save. Ray Kremer was Pittsburgh's winning pitcher, and Alexander got the loss. The final score was 6 to 5.

Pete Alexander versus Jesse J. "Pop" Haines (1893–1978)
Haines was elected to the Baseball Hall of Fame in 1970

Jesse Haines debuted with the Cincinnati Reds on July 20, 1918, with a five inning stint during which he gave up one run and one free pass, whiffed two, singled in his only official plate appearance, and otherwise came through what is usually a ball player's nightmare in fine fettle. But it wasn't good enough to convince the Reds to keep him, so he was released and ultimately wound up with Kansas City of the American Association for the 1919 season, where he led the team to a second place finish with a 21 and 5 record. That attracted attention, and before too long the St. Louis Cardinals came calling.

As a 27-year-old rookie in 1920, Jesse Haines went to work, piling up 301.2 innings and a 13 and 20 record with a commendable 2.98 ERA. And he came to stay. There would be no more trips back to the minors or around the league for a uniform change for the rugged 190-pound hurler. St. Louis became his home and there he stayed through 18 seasons, piling up 210 victories, a number surpassed by only one Cardinal hurler, the legendary Bob Gibson.

Among the high spots along the baseball path that wound up at Cooperstown with his 1970 enshrinement, there were three 20-game seasons and four trips to baseball's showcase extraordinaire, the World Series. It was in the 1926 Series gala that he capped a 13 and 4 season with three memorable appearances that, in the long run, probably paved the way to the Hall of Fame for the gritty knuckleballer. Following a relief appearance in game one, manager Rogers Hornsby tabbed Haines for game three, which followed Grover Alexander's 6 to 2 conquest of the Yankees in New York. And Haines came through with a beauty, shutting down the vaunted Gotham artillery on five hits, while beating up on Yankee pitching with a single and a two-run, four-base shot that subdued New York 4 to 0. When it came down to the final and deciding game of the Series at Yankee Stadium, Hornsby once again entrusted the 34-year-old righthander with the starting assignment. This time he battled through pain and Yankee Stadium hysteria to keep the Cards in the game through 6⅔ tense innings before giving way to — who else? — ol' Pete. The stage had been set for one of the most dramatic moments in World Series history, and the well-known Alexander vs. Lazzeri drama unfolded, the Cardinals winning 3 to 2, having carved out one of baseball's more riveting chapters in championship play.

Thus were the two elder statesmen linked in baseball history — the one, Haines, well into the spot-pitching and relieving phase of his career, and the other, Alexander, on the sunset side of a glorious career made even more glamorous by his 1926 histrionics. The Haines-Alexander story began some years earlier, however, when the two first met in Chicago on May 5, 1920. On that day Jess battled the Cubs and erstwhile Federal League sensation Claude Hendrix to a 4 to 4 tie through eight innings. For the Cards' ninth, Cub manager Fred Mitchell called on Alexander, who sent them into the bottom of the ninth without scoring. The run the Cubs scored in the bottom of the ninth won the game and gave Alex his third win of the season. Haines lost the heartbreaker.

But if that one was tough to lose, the next time the two squared off was, by far, even more disheartening — at least for Jess Haines. On October 1, in a game that wound up the 1920 season for both Haines and Alexander, the Cubs and Cardinals fought through 17 innings before the Cubs broke through with the winning tally in the bottom of the 17th. Both went the route at Wrigley Field that day in one of the more remarkable games of the 1920 season. The box score:

At Chicago, October 1, 1920

St. Louis	AB	R	H	PO	Chicago	AB	R	H	PO
Mueller, rf, lf	7	0	3	3	Twombly, rf	7	1	1	1
Janvrin, 1b	7	1	2	17	Terry, ss	7	0	1	5
Stock, 3b	8	1	3	1	Barber, lf	6	0	1	3
Hornsby, 2b	8	0	4	1	Merkle, 1b	5	1	2	21
McHenry, lf	2	0	0	1	Paskert, cf	7	0	1	5
Schultz, lf, rf	5	0	0	4	O'Farrell, c	6	0	0	12
Lavan, ss	8	0	2	3	Deal, 3b	6	0	1	1
Heathcote, cf	6	0	0	8	Marriott, 2b	4	1	2	3
Dillhoefer, c	6	0	1	11	Alexander, p	6	0	1	0
Haines, p	7	0	1	0					
Totals	64	2	16	49*	Totals	54	3	10	51

Line Score:								
St. Louis	100	000	010	000	000	00	2–16–1
Chicago	010	010	000	000	000	01	3–10–3

2BH: Merkle, Marriott, Hornsby; SB: Janvrin, Merkle, Hornsby, Marriott; SH: Janvrin, Heathcote; DP: Lavan, Hornsby and Janvrin, 2; LOB: St. Louis 16, Chicago 6; BB: Alexander 3, Haines 3; K: Alexander 8, Haines 8; Umpires: McCormick and Quigley; Time: 2:45.

The victory was Alexander's 27th in the year that marked the advent of the "Big Stick" in major league baseball. Pete chose that year to record his last sub-2.00 ERA reading (at 1.91), pitch 363.1 innings, complete 33 games and earn a league-high 7.1 TPI for the season, tops for pitchers in both leagues. Haines, meanwhile, led the league in Appearances with 47, threw four Shutouts among his 13 wins, worked a career high 301.2 innings, had a 2.98 ERA, and a low 2.39 BB/9 Innings Pitched, just a trifle under his 2.44 career average.

The long road ahead of Jess Haines filled a Cardinal career that included a no-hitter on July 17, 1924, against Boston's Braves and, on down toward the end, the elder statesman's title of "Pop," a nickname used in respect not only because of his advancing baseball years, but of his professional and give-

---

*One out when winning run was scored.

Jess Haines was a big winner for the Cardinals during the '20s.

it-your-best approach to the game. He might have lost a few heartbreakers here and there, but he was a Cardinal winner, just the same.

The Alexander-Haines Log:

May 20, 1920	Chicago 5, St. Louis 4	Alexander WP, Haines LP
Oct 1, 1920	Chicago 3, St. Louis 2	Alexander WP, Haines LP
Jul 1, 1921	Chicago 8, St. Louis 6	Alexander WP, Haines LP

Jun 24, 1922   Chicago 10, St. Louis 9   Alexander WP, Haines LP
Aug 14, 1922   Chicago 8, St. Louis 6   Alexander WP, Haines LP
May 3, 1923   St. Louis 3, Chicago 2   Haines WP, Alexander LP
Apr 16, 1924   Chicago 13, St. Louis 4   Alexander WP, Haines LP

On May 7, 1930, in one of the last appearances of his career, Grover Alexander started against Jess Haines, lasted only ⅓ of an inning, and was removed in a game St. Louis won 16 to 11, which set an extra base hit record since broken. Although Haines started the game (ND), he was also taken out. The victory went to reliever Jim Lindsey, and Alexander received the loss, the last decision of his career.

Pete Alexander versus Frederick L. "Fat Freddie" Fitzsimmons (1901–1979)

After nearly a dozen years as one of New York's most popular Giants, manager Bill Terry shipped Freddie Fitzsimmons off to Brooklyn, of all places. The date Giant fans never let Terry forget was June 11, 1937. To lose Fitzsimmons was bad enough, but the new Giant, Tom "Rattlesnake" Baker, not only had a nickname that conjured lethal consequences, he had the snake-bitten misfortune of being a promising young hurler whose arm went bad on him. The upshot of "Memphis Bill's" worst trade — ever — was that Fitzsimmons moved on to Brooklyn and came back to haunt the Giants seven more years, a couple of which were absolute gems (16 and 2 with a league-leading winning percentage of .889 in 1940 didn't make Terry's life any easier), while the Giants got one win out of the Baker arm in 1937 and cut him loose in 1938.

Chunky enough to be nailed with the "Fat Freddie" sobriquet, the agile Hoosier not only threw knuckle and curveball bafflers at NL hitters, but fielded his position with the best in the business. And he hit well enough to put a little punch into the bottom of the batting order. All things considered, not a bad package. Of course, that was enough to make Freddie one of the top pitchers of

One of John McGraw's last top pitchers, agile Freddie Fitzsimmons also hit and fielded well.

his era, as he recorded 217 major league wins despite a number of serious injuries over the course of his 19-year career. His numbers added up to a 22.9 career TPI, positioning him at the number 77 spot on the all time pitcher's list, ahead of Famers Vic Willis, Rube Marquard and Don Sutton, among others. Even tough he pitched in only two games against Grover Alexander, he earned the right to appear on the honors list of moundsmen who opposed "Old Low and Away," just the same.

The Alexander-Fitzsimmons Log:

Jun 18, 1927   St. Louis 6, New York 4   Alexander WP, Fitzsimmons LP

On May 5, 1929, Alexander and Fitzsimmons both started but did not complete the game. St. Louis beat New York 9 to 7 as "Wee Willie Sherdel" came on to win the game in relief. The loser was reliever Joe Genewich.

Pete Alexander versus Carl "The Meal Ticket" Hubbell (1903–1988)

Hubbell was elected to the Baseball Hall of Fame in 1947

A lot has been written about Carl Hubbell, and that is as it should be. One of the more prestigious names to line the walls of the Hall of Fame, "King Carl" (another, and more regal, nickname) was the last of John McGraw's super pitching acquisitions, and in a 16-year career that extended into the second global war, he polished off more than 250 opponents, ended up with a 2.98 ERA, outshone the cream of 1934's AL All-Stars with those improbable five consecutive Ks (each went down on his patented screwball), hurled a no-hitter against the Pirates in 1929, bagged MVP honors in 1936, and won no less than 24 straight times through the end of the 1936 season and into May of 1937. And if those aren't enough HOF credentials, there are more. Many more. Sorting through the pile of achievements takes a while, but here are a few more that went into the record book. Consider first his 1 to 0, 18-inning complete game victory over the Cardinals on July 2, 1933, a game that is regarded as one of the great pitching masterpieces in baseball history; or a one-hit effort against Brooklyn at Ebbets Field on Memorial Day 1940, when he beat Dem Bums in what he considered to be the best game he ever pitched. On that occasion Brooklyn managed to get only three balls out of the infield, as Hubbell, with amazing control, pinpointed every one of his 89 pitches. Consider also that in 1933, the year "King Carl" mustered a league leading 23 wins in leading the Giants to the world's championship, he ran a streak of 46⅓ scoreless innings and then reeled off 20 straight World Series innings without giving up an earned run.

That scratches enough of the surface to remind one and all that Carl

Carl Hubbell was "The Meal Ticket." His screwball was next to unhittable, and his pitching savvy took Bill Terry's Giants to the pennant.

Hubbell was an imposing force during an era marked not by an abundant supply of dominating pitchers, but by serious slugging and lopsided scoring orgies. Frankie Frisch summed it up from a player's vantage point in his comment about "the Meal Ticket" after that electrifying 1934 All-Star game performance: "I could play second base 15 more years behind this guy. He doesn't need any help."

An aging Pete Alexander encountered Carl Hubbell in the full bloom of youthful vigor. Six feet tall and a wiry, supple 175 pounds, he was in full command of an assortment of pitches — none better, or more ballyhooed, than the reverse curve that was known as his screwball. During those final Alexander years the ancient warrior was somewhat over-matched by the young southpaw who was on his way to years that were reminiscent of 1915 and 1920 in Pete's glittering career. The fates had ordered, however, that in those latter days the youngster should overtake and carry on for the elder statesman he opposed during their six engagements. Nonetheless, in one of those, during the last days of his career, Ol' Low and Away put together a strong effort that recalled an Alexander of a former day, with a strong six-inning showing on April 20, 1930. Though King Carl won, the game had all the makings for Pete's 374th triumph, which would have put him a notch above Christy Mathewson's 373. But it wasn't to be, and the final accounting went down as a 2 to 1 victory for Carl Hubbell. The six-game series is recounted below.

The Alexander-Hubbell Log:

Aug 18, 1928   New York 3, St. Louis 2   Hubbell WP, Alexander LP
Alexander went into the ninth inning of this game with the score tied 2 to 2. Mel Ott drove home the winning run after Alex thought he had whiffed Ott. Hubbell was in danger only in the third frame, when Alexander doubled and then came home on Ernie Orsatti's home run for the league leaders.

Sep 20, 1928	New York 7, St. Louis 4	Hubbell WP, Alexander LP
Apr 20, 1930	New York 2, Philadelphia 1	Hubbell WP, Alexander LP

The Giants beat the Cardinals 9 to 5 on August 17, 1929. Joe Genewich, in relief of Carl Hubbell, was the winning pitcher. Alexander (LP) was chased after three innings, relieved by Hal Goldsmith.

On April 26, 1930, Alexander appeared as a relief pitcher (ND) in Philadelphia's loss to St. Louis, 7 to 5. Carl Hubbell was the winning pitcher and Les Sweetland was the Phils' losing pitcher.

May 23, 1930, was Alexander's next to last appearance in the major leagues, in a relief appearance (ND) in a game won by Philadelphia, 9 to 8. Hubbell, who went the route, was the losing pitcher. Alexander pitched ⅓ of an inning, relieved, in turn, by Phil Collins, the winning pitcher.

On May 28, 1930, at Boston, Pete Alexander appeared in his last game, again in relief (of starter Phil Collins), finishing up the last two innings in a 5 to 1 loss to the Braves, whose "Socks" Siebold went the distance for the victory. Less than a week later, on June 3, Alexander was released by the Phillies.

Atop Mount Olympus

Through the twentieth century the top four pitchers in the history of the game were Cy Young, Christy Mathewson, Walter Johnson and Pete Alexander. Any questions? Remarkably, their careers overlapped so as to forge a link between the onset and concluding years of the three NL worthies during the first three decades of the 1900s, while the AL's greatest hurler, Walter Johnson, spanned the other three between 1907 and 1927.

Each of these legends was inducted into the Hall of Fame within the first three years of enshrinements, among the first eight players to be so honored. The four finished in 1–2–3–4 order in pitching victories, Wins Above Team and Total Pitching Index numbers. Each is listed several times among the top five in most of the major career pitching categories, and in the top 20 in a number of single season listings. That should do for top drawer evidence. There is, of course, the record book to consult for the rest of the story. Here is a more intriguing question, however. How do these titans compare against one another? In the following comparison chart, note that among the nine "vital statistics" there is a column for OB% (Opponents' On Base Percentage) and for the number of bases on balls issued per game, or 9 innings (BB/9 IP). Further, there are two sets of numbers for Cy Young — his career numbers, and then the statistics for his 1900-and-forward years, because his career began in 1890. The 1900 numbers align him with the other three, each of whom pitched exclusively in the twentieth century. Finally, TPI-AV represents the pitcher's Total Pitching Index average per season for the number of seasons he pitched.

Yrs		W-L	W%	IP	ERA	OB%	K	BB/9 IP	TPI-AV
Young, Career	22	511–316	.618	7356.0	2.63	.287	2803	1.49	3.55
Young, 1900>	12	244–165	.597	3631.2	2.42	.277	1678	1.38	2.63
Mathewson	17	373–188	.665	4788.2	2.13	.273	2507	1.60	3.70
Johnson	21	417–279	.599	5914.1	2.17	.279	3509	2.07	4.35
Alexander	20	373–208	.642	5190.0	2.56	.288	2198	1.65	3.23

In terms of sheer critical mass, we are unlikely to see these numbers soon again, however refined the game becomes; and numbers in certain categories, such as strikeouts per nine innings pitched, which will probably continue to improve, distance themselves beyond the efforts of those who pitched between 1900 and 1930. That said, those numbers above, just a sampling of the surpassing excellence of these mighty Famers, will keep the 21st century's hurlers busy.

And as to Old Low and Away the sum of his efforts against the baker's dozen assembled for review during his 20-year career is as follows:

	W	L	ND	T
Vs. C. Mathewson (6.53)*	4	2	2	0
Vs. C. Hubbell (4.50)	0	4	2	0
Vs. C. Young (4.15)	1	0	0	0
Vs. M. Brown (4.03)	2	2	0	0
Vs. B. Grimes (3.93)	7	4	1	0
Vs. D. Vance (3.69)	3	1	0	0
Vs. A. Luque (3.15)	4	3	1	0
Vs. E. Rixey (2.88)	7	5	5	0
Vs. W. Cooper (2.63)	4	2	0	0
Vs. B. Adams (2.63)	4	3	1	0
Vs. F. Fitzsimmons (2.40)	1	0	1	0
Vs. J. Haines (1.43)	6	2	0	0
Vs. R. Marquard (1.29)	6	9	3	1
Totals	49	37	16	1

But that is a lesser, albeit significant slice of a professional pitcher's life. At a deeper and personal level, there is, beyond these and the other numbers that have been entered into the record books, a more poignant story to tell.

Considering his weaknesses, both physical (epilepsy) and emotional, which brought an increasingly more serious involvement with drugs as his career wore on, Pete Alexander's odyssey from Galesburg, Illinois, where he began his professional career in 1907, to Boston, where his final two major

---

*Numbers in parenthesis represent the pitcher's best eight seasons, Total Pitching Index average.

league innings became history on May 28, 1930, and subsequently on to Cooperstown in 1938, is something just short of miraculous. Perhaps miracles were involved, at that. There was certainly nothing commonplace about the way he summoned the strength, cunning, artistry and baseball know-how from the depths of his persona, where he harbored at one and the same time both the frightening demons that drove him relentlessly from one debilitating downfall to another, and the drive to toil on in the game he loved. That the final record should show such commanding superiority over the individuals and teams he bested is all the more convincing, with respect not only to his final resting place in baseball's Valhalla, but to the numbers and deeds that put him there. They have become a unique part of baseball's treasured annals.

5. LEFTY GROVE

Major League Career Totals	Won	Lost	Pct.
Philadelphia, Boston (AL)	300	141	.680

Grove was elected to the Baseball Hall of Fame in 1947

Competitive fire, burning with white-hot intensity, is that very special and very extraordinary feature of the superstar's persona. For some, like Cy Young or Walter Johnson or Jimmie Foxx, the fire was under control, a part, however necessary, of a more placid, pleasant personality. But make no mistake, it was there just the same. For others, like Ty Cobb or Wes Ferrell or Roger Clemens, the fire raging within blazed with such ferocity that more often than not it laid waste everything it touched. Robert Moses Grove was one of those. Pulling on a pair of spikes was all it took to stoke the fires that lit up the 60'6" distance between himself and "the enemy"—that is, anybody with the audacity to show up in the batter's box with a stick in his hands.

Lefty Grove arrived on the American League scene in 1925, left it behind in 1941, and in between lit enough fires around the league to drive players, coaches, managers, umpires and his own skipper, the saintly Connie Mack, to cover. And when in 1934 he was joined in Boston by Wes Ferrell, who was cast in the same smoldering mold, the two took turns dismantling batting orders, ball clubs and locker rooms, no doubt giving Joe Cronin pause as he contemplated the managerial post that went with his trade from Washington to the Red Sox for the 1935 season. But during the course of a Hall of Fame career that started with league-leading numbers in strikeouts (116 in 1925), picked up steam during the late '20s, and wound up with 300 wins, a .680 career winning percentage (5th high through the 20th century), 595 Pitching Wins (3rd), an .886 single season winning percentage based on his 31 and

Mr. Intensity, Lefty Grove.

4 record in 1931 (which ranks 7th all time), and numerous other starlit numbers, accolades and awards, those gigantic tirades and ferocious outbursts were matched by equally towering accomplishments, earmarking the dour Mr. Grove as one of the game's all time pitching greats.

It took Grove two and one-half seasons to bring his blinding speed and himself under control, to get the feel of the game at the major league level, and to acquire the wherewithal it took to win in big numbers. During his first three seasons his record was an ordinary 43 and 38. Subtract those numbers from his final 300–141 totals and his winning percentage zooms to .714 (257 wins and 103 losses), which would be the only .700-plus career winning percentage in the game's history. But once he found the range, that howitzer hanging from his left shoulder bombarded a league full of sluggers — the Gehrigs, Averills, Greenbergs, Ruths and Goslins — into submission often enough to run up an incredible string of seven 20-win seasons, winning 172 times while dropping but 54 (that's winning at a .761 clip — even better than the .714 cited above) between 1927 and 1933, during the Athletic three-straight pennant years.

TBE (p. 2317, 2001 edition) lists the top ten pitchers according to TPI (Total Pitcher Index) through the 20th century as follows:

1)	Walter Johnson	91.4
2)	Cy Young	78.0
3)	Grover Alexander	64.6
4)	Christy Mathewson	62.9
5)	Greg Maddux	60.0
6)	***Lefty Grove***	59.7
7)	Roger Clemens	57.5
8)	Kid Nichols	57.5
9)	Warren Spahn	50.2
10)	Tom Seaver	48.7

With a 5.5 TPI-2000 season, Greg Maddux edged into fifth place ahead of Lefty Grove by .3 of one victory beyond a league-average pitcher. Maddux' career total will be sufficient to challenge the number two position of Cy Young, barring unforeseen problems as his career winds down, as will Roger Clemens' final total. As the 20th century closed out, however, Grove, along with Young, Johnson, Mathewson and Alexander, all of whom were active between 1900 and 1930 (Kid Nichols, the sixth, whose career closed out in 1906, is in the same position as Maddux and Clemens with respect to the timing of his career as it bridged two centuries) represent the best the game had to offer.

In Lefty Grove, then, we have the game's greatest lefthander, according to the Total Pitcher Index, established at the outset as the prime ranking tool in establishing the list of pitchers considered in this account of master craftsmen of the pitching arts. Warren Spahn, rated some 9.5 victories less than Grove, despite being the winningest portsider in the game's annals, ranks, therefore, behind the game's best "Lefthanded Rapid Robert." ("Rapid Robert" Feller's profile is part of the Grove story.) And to tie them all together, it should be noted that Warren Spahn's ML career began the season after Lefty Grove retired, in 1941.

Another significant ranking tool, employing sabermetric math and terminology, was developed by Tony Blengino[18], whose work first appeared in the 1990s under the title *Dominant Pitchers*, and computed rankings for pitchers in two principal listings, a Career Value and a Peak Seasons Value, as follows:

Pitcher	Career TPI	Career Value	Peak Seasons Value	Blengino Comment
Johnson, W.	91.4 (#1)	#1	#5	Best Pitcher All Time
Young, Cy	78.0 (#2)	#16	#6	Not as dominant as Grove but ranks with Mathewson
Alexander	64.6 (#3)	#14	#21	Career Win % exceeded his teams by 10 %, #1 all time
Mathewson	62.9 (#4)	#5	#4	Just behind Grove/Johnson
Maddux	60.0 (#5)	NL*	NL*	Will rank in top 3–8[†]
Grove	59.7 (#6)	#4	#3	Greatest lefty
Clemens	57.5 (#7)	#17[†]	#12[†]	Will rank in top 3–8[†]
Spahn	50.2 (#9)	NL*	NL*	#62 in "Pittsburgh Consensus"[‡]
Seaver	48.7 (#10)	#8	#10	Upper echelon HOF choice

The listings that appear at this point serve as a review of the status and esteem accorded the several master craftsmen considered thus far, as well as establishing Lefty Grove's prominence among the most dominant pitchers, and certainly *the* most dominant among southpaws, in the annals of major league baseball. Following is one more list, with your permission, of the Hall of Famers and other great hurlers Grove pitched against in his career:

Name/HOF/Year	Debut/Career Years	TPI/All Time Pitcher Ranking
Albert "Chief" Bender (1953)	Apr 20, 1903/1903–1925	14.4/170
Walter Johnson (1936)	Aug 2, 1907/1907–1927	91.4/1

---

*Maddux and Clemens were affected by the date of listing (1995) and would rank higher with a more recent reading of their careers. It is difficult to understand why Spahn was not a part of this listing, although he was rated number 62 on the all time listing for position players and pitchers (see below, Pittsburgh Consensus).

[†]Maddux/Clemens estimations are the author's.

[‡] The "Pittsburgh Consensus" was a ranking of player prominence, all time, done by several SABR members, including Benson and Blengino, at the Society for American Baseball Research (SABR) convention in 1994.

Herb Pennock (1948)	May 14, 1912/1912–1934	6.8/NR
Stan Coveleski (1969)	Sep 10, 1912/1912–1928	27.0/52
Urban "Red" Faber (1964)	Apr 17, 1914/1914–1933	27.2/51
Burleigh Grimes (1964)	Sep 10, 1916/1916–1934	23.7/74
Waite Hoyt (1969)	Jul 24, 1918/1918–1938	15.1/158
Ted Lyons (1955)	Jul 2, 1923/1923–1946	37.1/21
Charles "Red" Ruffing (1967)	May 31, 1924/1924–1947	28.0/47
Wes Ferrell	Sep 9, 1927/1927–1941	30.5/36
Mel Harder	Apr 24, 1928/1928–1947	19.4/109
Vernon "Lefty" Gomez (1972)	Apr 29, 1930/1930–1943	19.9/104
Tommy Bridges	Aug 13, 1930/1930–1946	28.0/47
Bob Feller (1962)	Jul 19, 1936/1936–1956	30.2/37
Early Wynn (1972)	Sep 13, 1939/1939–1963	17.1/136
Hal Newhouser (1992)	Sep 19, 1939/1939–1955	39.3/17

Lefty Grove versus Albert "Chief" Bender (1884–1954)
Bender was elected to the Baseball Hall of Fame in 1953

Lefty Grove versus Walter Johnson (1887–1946)
Johnson was elected to the Baseball Hall of Fame in 1936

Lefty Grove versus Early "Gus" Wynn (1920–1999)
Wynn was elected to the Baseball Hall of Fame in 1972

The trio of moundsmen assembled in this initial Lefty Grove profile represents a six-decade timeframe, a longer span of time than any of the other pitching greats considered in this review. It begins with Chief Bender's 1903 debut and ends with Early Wynn's last major league season in 1963. The third, Walter Johnson, the only one who actually matched pitches with Grove, was active during the first three seasons of Lefty's career, 1925 to 1927, and in terms of sequence, is the first pitcher to be considered among the pitching greats Lefty Grove faced because of his August 2, 1907, debut.

Bender, who came out of retirement to pitch one inning of relief for Eddie Collins' 1925 White Sox, and Early Wynn, who pitched briefly for the Senators in 1939 and 1941 callups before beginning his career in earnest in 1942, were active, if only briefly, during Grove's first and last big league campaigns. Consequently, Bender, Johnson and Wynn, a sort of alpha and omega of pitching generations, introduce us to the Lefty Grove saga at Hall of Fame levels of pitching artistry, however disparate in style, temperament and achievement they might have been.

The first of these, Chief Bender, barely qualifies for consideration because his one inning relief stint at Boston on July 21, 1925, was the only time he was called on as a White Sox pitcher that year. Because of that one inning, during which he was touched for a four-bagger, by the way, he merited active status and one year's service during Grove's first major league season. And if ever one inning of baseball received more colorful coverage than that given by the *Chicago Tribune*'s Irving Vaughn, it must certainly merit a special inscription in the famed newspaper's archives somewhere. In his colorful style, Mr. Vaughn, writing without the constraints of contemporary sensitivities, had this to say about the Chief's work at Fenway Park back in 1925:

> In the ninth, after a pinch hitter had removed Connally [Chicago pitcher George "Sarge" Connally], the second White Sox pitcher, Bender, who before the game had been transferred to the active list, was ushered to the slab midst loud shouting from the multitude. The old redskin, who hadn't hurled anything but minor league ball for about the last seven years, started by passing Flagstead, but then set down the next two batters. That brought up the mischievous Carlyle, who showed no respect for the old master by spanking the pill so hard that it landed in the top row of the right field bleachers [*Chicago Tribune*, July 22, 1925, p. 17, Sports].

Shown here in a White Sox uniform, "Burly Early" Wynn was also a part of those great Cleveland pitching staffs of the 1950s.

The Chief did dispose of the next hitter, Phil Todt, but the damage had been done, and Eddie Collins left well enough alone, returning Bender to his coaching duties for the remainder of the season.

As for Early Wynn, his first appearance in the majors came during the 1939 season, when he was called up from Washington's minor league affiliate at Charlotte during the 1939 season for his September 13 debut and some 20 innings of work. Two years later, in 1941, Lefty Grove's last year, he got into another five ball games, adding three wins against a single loss to the Senators' record during the last weeks of the season.

Wynn, a fiery competitor known as "Gloomy Gus," "Gus," or "Burly Early," toiled long and hard for some weak Washington teams before moving on to Cleveland and then Chicago's White Sox, where he won well over 200 games. His quest for number 300, much like Grove's, was more of a dogged, last-ditch attempt to enter that charmed circle than it was an artistic success. The Big One, Number 300, finally came July 13, 1963, against the Kansas City Athletics. Though his five-inning stint *just* qualified for a victory that day, he got it done just the same, putting him at the same 300 level as the great Grove.

The third of the pitching triumvirate under review at this point is Walter Johnson, who, as Lefty Grove's rookie season got underway in 1925, was entering his 19th major league campaign. By this time he was the grand old warrior of the Senators, and he would once again be expected to do the heavy lifting for Washington as the team set about defending its world championship. That he had turned 37 shortly after the 1924 World Series victory made no difference either to his opponents around the league or, for that matter, to his trusty right arm, still capable of whizzing his fast one past the hitters at speeds of up to 100 m.p.h. But as far as a championship repeat was concerned, that might prove to be problematical, inasmuch as Ty Cobb's hard-hitting Tigers, George Sisler's Brownies and the resurgent Athletics, with a budding cast of fencebusters, had, along with New York's perennial powerhouse, designs on the AL crown. It was the Philadelphia club, however, that was recognized as the most serious contender of the lot, and a pitching staff of Eddie Rommel, Rube Walberg, William Jennings Bryan Harriss (better known as Slim), and Connie Mack's $100,600 acquisition from Baltimore, Lefty Grove, well supported by Al Simmons, Bing Miller, Mickey Cochrane and the muscular youngster, Jimmie Foxx, seemed ready and able to give the Senators a stiff battle for the AL crown.

By the time it was all over, however, it was Washington that bested all comers to take a second straight pennant. Babe Ruth's tummy ache, a wilting A's pitching staff, and the fizzled threats of St. Louis and Detroit were all left in the wake of another Johnson, 20 game–season and a determined band of Senators who knew how to win. En route, the old master held a few tutoring sessions, several of which involved Lefty Grove.

Grove and Johnson crossed swords three times during the 1925 season and again in 1926.[19] Twice in '25, and in their final meeting in '26, the youngster was set down by the one baseball player he idolized during his youth, now his "schoolmaster," the venerable Johnson. The first time the two met, Grove was used by Mack in relief of Slim Harriss, who took the Washington defeat, 10 to 9, in a game in which Sir Walter gamefully went the route, hanging on to a one-run victory. The best of the Johnson-Grove matchups occurred on September 7, 1925, a tense, 2 to 1 affair that the Senators needed to maintain a bulge over the Athletics as the race entered its final stages. On that late summer day in Philadelphia the two speed merchants traded howitzer shots, Washington emerging victorious as Big Barney shut down the A's without a run until the ninth, when Bing Miller singled home the Athletics' first baseman, Red Holt. The box score of the game at Shibe Park follows:

At Philadelphia, September 7, 1925

Washington	AB	R	H	PO	Philadelphia	AB	R	H	PO
McNeely, cf	5	0	0	3	Bishop, 2b	4	0	1	3
S. Harris, 2b	2	0	1	1	Cochrane, c	4	0	1	2
Rice, rf	5	0	2	8	Lamar, lf	4	0	1	2
Goslin, lf	5	0	1	2	Simmons, cf	4	0	1	4
J. Harris, 1b	4	1	1	8	Holt, 1b	4	1	0	11
Bluege, 3b	4	0	1	2	Hale, 3b	4	0	1	0
Peckinpaugh, ss	4	0	1	2	Miller, rf	4	0	1	2
Ruel, c	3	0	0	1	Galloway, ss	3	0	0	2
Johnson, (WP)	4	1	3	0	Grove, (LP)	2	0	1	1
					Baumgartner, p	0	0	0	0
					French, ph	1	0	1	0
					Poole, ph	1	0	1	0
Totals	36	2	10	27	Totals	35	1	9	27
Line Score:	Washington		000	010	010	2–10–0			
	Philadelphia		000	000	001	1–9–0			

2BH, Cochrane, Peckinpaugh; Home Run, J. Harris; LOB, Washington 11, Philadelphia 7; DP, Holt unassisted; BB: Grove 3, Johnson 0; K, Grove 2, Johnson 1; Hit by Pitcher, S. Harris by Baumgartner; IP, Grove 8, Baumgartner 1, Johnson 9; Umpires, Nallin, Geisel, Evans and Hildebrand; Time of Game, 2:05.

Lefty Grove versus Herb Pennock (1894–1948)
Pennock was elected to the Baseball Hall of Fame in 1948

The year 2001 marked the 130th consecutive season of organized professional baseball. During that time Walter Johnson and Lefty Grove have been recognized as the greatest righthanded and lefthanded pitchers in the game's history. Over another century it might well be that others will have replaced them; improbable as that may seem at this point in time, the possibility certainly does exist. However, even should that happen, the names of Johnson and Grove will forever be etched in gold among those designated as the greatest pitchers of all time.

Though they might not have been aware of it at the time, six[20] hurlers, who would later be selected for Hall of Fame honors, were among those who dueled these two mound monarchs. Five of them were Stan Coveleski, Red Faber, Ted Lyons, Red Ruffing and Waite Hoyt. The sixth was Herb Pennock, the accomplished Knight of Kennett Square, a stylish lefty not in the same class with the game's incomparable dominators, but a meticulous workman with impeccable control of the strike zone and an encyclopedic knowledge of the hitters he faced during a highly successful, 22-year career in the Big Show.

Mound Maestro Herb Pennock was always tough for Grove to beat.

Against the two master moundsmen Herb Pennock was more than mildly successful. His record against Sir Walter was five wins, but a single loss, four No Decisions and one tie. Against Lefty Grove he was victorious three times, lost three, and registered two No Decisions. The overall win-loss record in 19 matchups stands at 8–4–6(ND), and one tie over a period of time extending from June 28, 1912, when, as a rookie, Pennock took on Walter Johnson and beat him in the tenth inning, 5 to 4, to August 3, 1933, some twenty seasons later, when he pitched in relief of Johnny Allen in one of those games noted for its significance as a "streak-game." In this one, Lefty Grove shut out the Yanks 7 to 0, embarrassing them with their first shutout in 308 games (dating back to August 2, 1931).

The Grove-Pennock Log:

July 4, 1925	New York 1, Philadelphia 0	Pennock WP, Grove LP
June 25, 1927	Philadelphia 7, New York 6	Grove WP, Pennock LP
Apr 11, 1928	New York 8, Philadelphia 3	Pennock WP, Grove LP
June 21, 1929	Philadelphia 11, New York 1	Grove WP, Pennock LP

Wilcy Moore (LP) started for New York on September 3, 1927, and was relieved by Pennock as the A's beat the Yanks 1 to 0 on a 4-hitter by Grove (WP).

The Yankees beat the Athletics 7 to 4 on September 27, 1927, behind Pennock (WP), who received relief help from Wilcy Moore. Jack Quinn was charged with the loss. Grove pitched in relief (ND).

Howard Ehmke was the winning pitcher on June 29, 1928, with Grove (ND) in relief. Pennock went all the way and sustained the 6 to 4 loss.

On August 3, 1933, the A's shut out the Yankees 7 to 0, as Grove pitched a 5-hitter. Pennock (ND) appeared in relief of Johnny Allen, who was charged with the Yankee loss.

On June 25, 1925, Lefty Grove posted his fourth straight victory, turning around an up-and-down season while beginning to pay the kind of dividends Connie Mack was looking for from his high-priced phenom. At 7 and 4, Grove next took on Walter Johnson, and the old master bested him in a 5 to 3 outing that Goose Goslin put away with a 3-run dinger. The ancient tactician then rested his lean lefty for better than a week, scheduling him next for the Yankees' Fourth of July doubleheader. Miller Huggins countered with a lean lefty of his own, Herb Pennock, by this time a canny 13-year veteran in the midst of the very best campaign of his career, despite winding up with a 16–17 record. During 1925 the Knight led the league in innings pitched (with 277), a fine 11.0 Ratio, a .303 opponents' on base percentage, and 44 pitching runs. It was his second consecutive 3.8 TPI season, a career high. And on July 4 he celebrated the nation's birthday with one of the two or three finest games of his career, shutting down Grove and the Mackmen for 15 innings in a 1 to 0 spine-tingler that spilled across several pages of celebration in the *New York Times*. On this occasion it was savvy that won out over speed, and though Grove was great, Pennock was simply super. The box score follows.

At Philadelphia, July 4, 1925

New York	AB	R	H	PO	Philadelphia	AB	R	H	PO
Dugan, 3b	7	0	1	1	Dykes, 2b	6	0	2	7
Combs, cf	7	0	2	4	Hale, 3b	5	0	0	0
Ruth, rf	5	0	2	6	Lamar, lf	5	0	0	0
Witt, pr	0	0	0	0	Simmons, cf	5	0	1	3
Veach, rf	1	1	1	0	Miller, rf	5	0	0	3

Meusel, lf	5	0	2	3	Perkins, c	5	0	0	12
Gehrig, 1b	5	0	1	18	Poole, 1b	5	0	1	16
Bengough, c	3	0	1	3	Galloway, ss	5	0	0	3
O'Neill, c	3	0	1	4	Grove (LP)	5	0	0	0
E. Johnson, 2b	3	0	1	2	Wanninger, ss	4	0	1	2
Pennock, (WP)	3	0	0	1	Ward, 2b	5	0	1	2
Shanks, ph	1	0	0	0	Paschal, ph	1	0	0	0
Totals	53	1	15	45		46	0	4	44*

Line Score: New York   000 000 000 000 000 01 1–14–0
             Philadelphia 000 000 000 000 000 00 0–4–0

2BH: Meusel; 3BH: Dykes; SB: Ward; DP: Grove, Dykes and Poole; Galloway and Poole; BB: Grove 5, Pennock 0; K: Grove 10, Pennock 5; Wild Pitch, Grove; Umpires: Moriarty, Owens and McGowan; Time of Game: 2:50; Attendance: 50,100.

The *New York Times*' sports scribe Jim Harrison made these interesting comments about the two lefties in his account of the game:

> ...Herb Pennock, the svelte and satiny southpaw, pitched what was undoubtedly the finest game of a long and honorable career. Over the grueling stretch of fifteen innings he allowed only four hits, one of these a misjudged fly. Only eighteen batters toed the pan in the first six innings, and only twenty-one hiked plateward in the last seven frames. In only two of the fifteen rounds did more than three Quaker hitters appear in the batting stall.

> ...Groves,[†] not nearly as steady and finished a workman, nevertheless showed an amazing ability for climbing out of deep holes. In six different innings the Yanks had the tall lefthander on the run, but he side-stepped every punch but the closing one. He filled the bases with nobody out in the thirteenth, but set down the next three Yankees without the semblance of trouble.

These perceptive remarks not only give an insight into the thrilling game witnessed by the holiday throng, but provide a sportswriter's look at the unfinished, though highly gifted rookie who matched pitches and wits with the finely honed, veteran portsider Herb Pennock. Another intensely involved onlooker that day, Grove's wife Ethel, took note of the lanky lefty who beat her husband, remarking later in Lefty's career that from that 1 to 0 game forward she was always apprehensive about an afternoon that pitted Pennock versus Grove.

---

* Two out when winning run scored.

[†]The Groves surname is given detailed attention in Jim Kaplan's fine work on Lefty Grove entitled *Lefty Grove: American Original*. (Published by the Society for American baseball Research, Cleveland, Ohio, 2000.) By 1926 the press, and Lefty himself, had begun to use the G-r-o-v-e spelling, although manager Connie Mack referred to him as Mr. Groves throughout his life.

Herb Pennock finished his Hall of Fame career in Boston with the 1934 Red Sox, as a teammate of Lefty's, where he made a few token appearances, finishing out with a 2 and 0 record while helping along the younger pitchers in a coaching capacity for manager Bucky Harris. It's reasonable to assume that their 1925 duel at Yankee Stadium came up for discussion, as well as Grove's 7 to 0 whitewash of the Yanks on August 3, 1933 (Pennock was a reliever in that game). Lefty wouldn't have let that slip by, now, would he?!

Lefty Grove versus Stan Coveleski

Stanislaus Kowalewski was his original name. He was a Polish lad who knew the hardships of a coal miner's life from personal experience. But he also knew the joys of baseball, and his brothers (one of whom, Harry Frank, was three years older than Stan and enjoyed three successive twenty-game seasons with the Tigers), along with an understanding dad, encouraged him as he moved toward full maturity. And the young lad, who ultimately changed his name to Stanley Coveleski, had enough on the ball to attract the attention of baseball scouts in Pennsylvania. Signed by his hometown Shamokin team in 1908, he advanced to the Tri-State League, where he led the league in wins and helped his Lancaster Red Roses ball club win the 1909 Tri-State League pennant.

The Coveleski odyssey finally wound up in Philadelphia, where Connie Mack gave him 21 innings of work at the end of the 1912 season (he was credited with two wins and a single loss) before shipping him back to the minors. The next time Coveleski surfaced it was in Cleveland, where he would put together a 9-season stretch that put 172 wins into the record book. During that time he logged four consecutive 20-win seasons, the most spectacular of which came in 1920, when he posted a 24 and 14 record for the world champion Indians of Tris Speaker. His 5.9 TPI led the league, and three victories over Brooklyn in the world series were fashioned on the strength of a brilliant 0.67 ERA.

A December 1924 trade moved him to Washington, where, with Walter Johnson and Company, he played on another world's series team, the 1925 Senators. That season, an artistic success by any standard, he led the league in winning percentage, at .800, crafted on a sterling 20 and 5 record. It was also the season that the veteran spitballer encountered the league's latest phenom, the Athletics' blazing fireballer, Lefty Grove.

As Stan Coveleski neared the end of his career in the 1925 and '26 seasons, he was matched with Grove on three occasions. The first was on May 26, 1925, when the old master took the rookie to camp, disposing of him by an 11 to 2 margin in a game in which Mr. Mack removed Grove after five innings. Lefty's next outing wasn't much better, losing to Washington in a

17 to 12 slugfest. The third time was "three and out" in an 8 to 6 contest that earned neither hurler a decision. It was the last Coveleski-Grove confrontation.

The Grove-Coveleski Log:

May 26, 1925   Washington 11, Philadelphia 2   Coveleski WP, Grove LP

On May 25, 1926, Washington beat the A's 17 to 12. Grove was the starting and losing pitcher, and reliever Willard "Bill" Morrell was credited with the victory. Coveleski was also used in relief by the Senators (ND).

Philadelphia lost to Washington on June 25, 1926. Both Coveleski and Grove were relievers in that game (ND). Warren "Curly" Ogden received the win and Eddie Rommel was the losing pitcher for the Mackmen in the 8 to 6, 10-inning game.

In 1928 Stan Coveleski signed on with the New York Yankees after having been released by the Senators the previous June. With the Yanks he won another five games before retiring with a career 215–141 record. Coveleski was one of a half-dozen Hall of Famers who pitched against Walter Johnson, as well as dueling with Lefty Grove. Soft-spoken and hard-working to the end, he was a credit to the game and a worthy Hall of Famer.

Lefty Grove versus Urban "Red" Faber (1888–1976)
Faber was elected to the Baseball Hall of Fame in 1964

In *The Players of Cooperstown: Baseball's Hall of Fame*,[21] this very interesting conjecture about Red Faber is found on page 150:

> In 1919, when the Sox again claimed the American League title [following their 1917 world's championship], they were so heavily favored over the Reds in the World Series that little concern was felt in Chicago when it was announced that an ankle injury would force Faber to miss the occasion. In retrospect, though, Faber's disability may have changed the course of baseball history. Had Red been healthy enough to take his regular turn on the mound, there may well have never been a Black Sox scandal. Faber in 1919 was just reaching his peak and would go on to win 20 or more games in each of the next three seasons.

He was a good one, all right, was Red Faber. But not too many know about the White Sox' spitballing ace who toiled for so many years in the obscurity of the American League's second division. However, the Hall of Fame Veterans Committee concluded that Old Red was not to be forgotten or forsaken by the national pastime, and in 1964 brought him into the select fold, along with another of the Comiskey cast, Luke Appling, who that year won his plaque via election by the BBWAA. They joined Ted Lyons, another of those 20-year White Sox ancients, who took up residence at the Hall some years earlier in 1955.

By 1925, the year of Lefty Grove's entry into the majors, Faber had already logged 174 of his 253 lifetime conquests, had been a Pale Hose bellwether for better than a decade, and had been a part of Chicago's quartet of 1920, 20-game winners, the first major league pitching staff[22] to boast such a foursome. That 1920 staff included Dickie Kerr, Eddie Cicotte and Claude Williams.

Between 1925 and 1933, Faber's final year, nine eventful seasons went into the record books, providing no less than 17 opportunities for Lefty and Red to trade strikes. Among them, several stand out, including a 1 to 0 thriller that Lefty Grove lost in the bottom of the 9th inning in 1926 on a squeeze bunt by Ray Schalk that assuredly brought down the wrath of Grove on Comiskey Park's visitors locker room; a taut struggle Grove won by a 2 to 0 count in 1928 on a two-hitter; and an August 19, 1931, 4 to 2 clash in Chicago on a day Lefty hiked his record to 25 and 2, while recording his 16th straight victory. The box scores of the 1926 and 1931 games follow.

Red Faber only beat Lefty Grove once, but that one was a beauty, a six-hit shutout in Chicago on June 8, 1926. He used to remind Grove with "One to nuttin'!"

At Chicago, June 8, 1926

Philadelphia	AB	R	H	PO	Chicago	AB	R	H	PO
Bishop, 2b	2	0	1	1	Mostil, cf	3	0	2	3
Cochrane, c	4	0	1	1	Hunnefield, ss	4	0	1	4
Lamar, lf	4	0	1	1	Collins, 2b	3	0	0	1
Simmons, cf	4	0	1	4	Sheely, 1b	4	0	0	12

Poole, 1b	4	0	0	9	Falk, lf	4	1	1	2
Dykes, 3b	4	0	2	1	Barrett, rf	4	0	1	1
French, rf	3	0	0	4	Kamm, 3b	2	0	1	0
Galloway, ss	3	0	0	3	Schalk, c	4	0	1	4
Grove (LP)	3	0	0	0	Faber (WP)	2	0	0	1
Totals	31	0	6	24*	Totals	30	1	7	27

Line Score:	Philadelphia	000	000	000	0-6-0
	Chicago	000	000	001	1-7-0

2BH: Bishop, Dykes; DP: Sheely, Hunnefield and Sheely; Bishop Galloway and Poole; Kamm, Hunnefield and Sheely; BB: Grove 5, Faber 2; K: Grove 1, Faber 4; Umpires: Ormsby, Moriarty and Dineen.

At Chicago, August 19, 1931

Philadelphia	AB	R	H	PO	Chicago	AB	R	H	PO
Bishop, 2b	4	0	0	6	Blue, 1b	4	0	0	8
Cramer, cf	5	0	2	0	Sullivan, 3b	4	0	0	1
Cochrane, c	4	0	0	7	Reynolds, cf	4	1	3	1
J.W. Moore, lf	5	0	0	2	Fonseca, lf	4	1	2	2
Foxx, 1b	4	1	2	6	Fothergill, rf	4	0	1	3
Miller, rf	5	1	2	3	Watwood, ph	0	0	0	0
McNair, 2b	5	2	4	0	Kerr, 2b	3	0	0	4
Williams, ss	3	0	1	3	Appling, ph	1	0	0	0
Grove (WP)	4	0	0	0	Cissell, ss	4	0	0	3
					Grube, c	4	0	1	5
					Faber, (LP)	2	0	0	0
					Jeffries, ph	1	0	0	0
					J.S. Moore, p	0	0	0	0
Totals	39	4	12	27	Totals	33	2	7	27

Line Score:	Philadelphia	021	000	010	4-12-1
	Chicago	000	000	002	2-7-3

2BH: Fonseca; 3BH: Reynolds; BB: Faber 2, Grove 0; K: Faber 3, Grove 5; Hit by Pitcher: by Faber 1; Hits off Faber: 12 in 8 innings, 0 off Moore; ER: Grove 0, Faber 1; Umpires: Geisel, Ormsby and Hildebrand.

During the last three to four seasons that Red Faber was with the White Sox, his pitching role changed to that of a spot-starter and relief pitcher, thus accounting for the number of No Decisions (eight) he recorded in the 17 appearances he and Grove logged. Lefty, of course, kept right on in his career-long dual capacity as starter and reliever (or closer). In addition to his ace-of-the-staff status, it is interesting to note that bossman Mack had no qualms about calling him from the pen on any given day. That accounts for, among

*None out when winning run scored.

other things, 55 career Saves and regular relief appearances, even into the Boston phase of his career. It should also be said that Lefty, well aware that the Ws were piling up, never turned down an opportunity to do a late-innings stint that might add to his growing list of victories.

The Grove-Faber Log:

May 11, 1926	Philadelphia 6, Chicago 2	Grove WP, Faber LP
Jun 8, 1926	Chicago 1, Philadelphia 0	Faber WP, Grove LP
May 19, 1928	Philadelphia 2, Chicago 0	Grove WP, Faber LP
Jun 23, 1930	Philadelphia 2, Chicago 1	Grove WP, Faber LP
Aug 19, 1931	Philadelphia 4, Chicago 2	Grove WP, Faber LP
Sep 18, 1931	Philadelphia 3, Chicago 1	Grove WP, Faber LP

The first duel between Faber and Grove took place on August 21, 1925. The White Sox won the game 8 to 2, Faber (WP) beat Eddie Rommel (LP). Grove (ND) appeared in relief of Rommel.

Faber (LP) and Grove (ND) squared off on July 10, 1926, in a slugfest in which both starters were chased. Joe Pate, undefeated in 1926 (9–0), won the game in relief.

Rube Walberg (WP) and Tommy Thomas (LP) started the July 15, 1927, game, a wild and wooly affair won by the A's 13 to 10. Both Grove and Faber relieved (ND).

Grove was charged with an 11-inning loss (7 to 6 on June 10, 1930) as a reliever for Jack Quinn. Red Faber was the Sox' starter (ND) and Hal McKain (LP) relieved Faber for Chicago.

In a 12–inning game Grove was charged with a 7 to 5 defeat, having relieved starter Roy Mahaffey, on June 5, 1931. Faber started (ND), but the win went to reliever Hal McKain.

On June 19, 1931, Lefty went all the way (WP) to beat Pat Caraway (LP) 10 to 4. Faber (ND) relieved Caraway.

Both Grove (ND) and Faber (ND) relieved in a game won by the A's 6 to 5 on June 21, 1931. George Earnshaw won it, and Johnny Moore was the losing pitcher.

Grove (ND) and Faber (ND) pitched in relief on July 8, 1932. The A's beat the Sox 6 to 4, with George Earnshaw (WP) and Sad Sam Jones (LP) the pitchers of record.

Grove (ND) started on August 20, 1932. Ted Lyons was the loser in a 14 to 8 Chicago loss. Faber relieved (ND), and Lew Krausse, Sr., was the winning pitcher. Milt Gaston (ND) started for Chicago.

In Chicago's 100th loss of the 1932 season (September 19), Grove won on September 19 by a 9 to 6 margin. Phil Gallivan (LP) started for Chicago and Faber (ND) appeared as a reliever.

In the last victory of his career, Red Faber won in relief over the A's 9 to 8 on August 27, 1933. Whitlow Wyatt (ND) started that game against Grove (ND). Jim Peterson lost the game in relief.

Lefty Grove versus Burleigh Grimes (1893–1985)
Grimes was elected to the Baseball Hall of Fame in 1964

On his way to the Hall of Fame, Burleigh Grimes found the time to wear the uniforms of seven different teams, winding up his 19-year career as a New York Yankee. His 1 and 2 record with the Bronx Bombers in 1934 was fashioned in a relief role, and it was in that capacity that he dueled with Lefty Grove in a July 3 game won by the Red Sox before a packed house at Yankee Stadium. They got their money's worth that day in a slam-bang affair that ended up 10 to 9 in 11 innings of see-saw ball featuring Hall of Fame batteries (seven Famers were in the game that day) consisting of Grove and Rick Ferrell of the Bosox, and Bill Dickey with starting hurler Red Ruffing and the grizzled reliever Grimes. Beyond that, seven taters, including one by Lou Gehrig, were lofted into the Yankee stands.

The last of the grandfathered spitballers, "Boily," as Brooklynites called him during his salad days with the Robins, and Grove were called into action in stanzas six, seven and eight in their only regular season confrontation. Rube Walberg, who finished up for the Mackmen, was the winner, and Joe McCarthy's ace fireman, Johnny Murphy, who relieved Grimes, was knicked for the loss.

Both Lefty Grove and Burleigh Grimes were in the midst of trying times during the 1934 season. For Grove it was a time of transition from blazing his way through the league with one cannon shot after another to finessing his way under the constraints of a dead arm and advancing age. But while Lefty overcame his problems, ultimately recording 105 wins for Tom Yawkey and his Carmine during his Boston stay, thus enabling him to top out at the magic 300 number, for Burleigh Grimes, the gritty battler, the end had come. Yankee Stadium turned out to be his last port of call.

Lefty Grove versus Waite "Schoolboy" Hoyt (1899–1984)
Hoyt was elected to the Baseball Hall of Fame in 1969

Lefty Grove's first major league victory came at the expense of New York's Yanks on May 5, 1925. His appearance that day marked the fifth time Connie Mack called on his heralded rookie that season, each time in relief, and the win evened his record at 1–1. Grove came into the game in the fifth frame following starter Stan Baumgartner and Rube Walberg, was dented for a go-ahead run during his stay and then became the beneficiary of some timely hitting as the A's went ahead, finally winning the tilt by an 8 to 7 score. In four innings of work (Lefty was lifted for a ninth inning stint by reliable Eddie Rommel, who earned the Save), the young fireballer walked four, gave up four hits and hit catcher Steve O'Neill, as well as coughing up a wild pitch — hardly an impressive performance, but apparently enough to win the first of his 300 victories. Al Simmons, who, along with Jimmie Foxx, was responsible for many a Grove conquest during his Philadelphia career, was the chief thorn in the Yanks' side that day, his seventh inning homer providing a lead for Grove that was cemented with a final two-run uprising in the top of the ninth.

Bob Shawkey, Miller Huggins' starter in that historic game, was lifted in favor of the erstwhile "Schoolboy," Waite Hoyt, in the fourth inning, who worked into the ninth inning, when Sad Sam Jones, who was charged with the loss, and finally Ray Francis, finished the ragged contest. The Hoyt-Grove engagement that day would be the only 1925 matchup in what eventuated in a subpar year for the Brooklyn-born Yankee favorite. But Waite Hoyt's time was coming. He warmed up for his best major league season, 1927, with a 16 and 12 mark in 1926, one of his dozen losses that season coming at the hands of Grove on June 28, when he was manhandled by the Athletics, 7 to 1. In a special in the *New York Times*, James B. Harrison had this to say about Mack's improving Lefty:

> You can't hit what you can't see and the Yanks brought a lot of bad eyesight with them to Philadelphia today. The left-handed dips and bends of Lefty Grove were practically invincible to the naked eye. He struck out ten of the hated visitors and held them to seven widely dispersed hits, and the Athletics won, 7 to 1.
>
> Grove, they say, is the best southpaw since Rube Waddell and the Yanks are ready to swear out a deposition to that effect. His fast ball came up hopping like a kangaroo, his curve had the blind staggers; it whirled and sagged and took unique angles and his control was so perfect that he tossed no more than two bad balls to any batter...
>
> Waite Hoyt was not so good. Five innings did for the merry mortician of Flatbush. Herb McQuaid pitched two innings and E. Garland Braxton one, but six of the seven runs came during the Hoyt administration.

What a difference a year makes! While there was still a great deal of polishing to do before the budding star was to shine brightly in the baseball firmament, it was obvious by this time that the American League would have its hands full with Lonaconing, Pennsylvania's, lustrous one, Robert Moses Grove.

And with respect to Waite Hoyt, let it be duly noted that his tussles with the two legends produced a 4 and 5 record, with six No Decisions and a tie, in logging a 3–2–1ND record against Walter Johnson and a 1–3–5ND–1 Tie record against Grove.

The Grove-Hoyt Log:

Jun 28, 1926   Philadelphia 7, New York 1   Grove WP, Hoyt LP

Apr 12, 1927	New York 8, Philadelphia 3	Hoyt WP, Grove LP
Jul 20, 1930	Philadelphia 5, Detroit 3	Grove WP, Hoyt LP
Aug 20, 1930	Philadelphia 10, Detroit 6	Grove WP, Hoyt LP

On April 15, 1927, the Yanks and A's played to a 9–9 tie. Grove (ND) and Hoyt (ND) pitched in relief.

In the following contests either Hoyt or Grove, or both, were involved in No Decision games:

May 5, 1915 (Phl 8, NY 7), Grove WP, Hoyt ND
May 24, 1928 (NY 9, Phl 7), Hoyt ND, Grove LP
May 22, 1930 (NY 20, Phl 13), Hoyt ND, Grove ND
Jul 22, 1930 (Det 6, Phl 5), Hoyt ND, Grove LP
Jun 27, 1931 (Phl 9, Det 5), Grove WP, Hoyt ND

In one of those twists of good fortune some (but not many) ball players are favored with, Waite Hoyt wound up the American League phase of his career in Philadelphia. Connie Mack, seeking another experienced winner, took Hoyt off the waiver line when Detroit saw fit to dismiss him. He might not have been able to help a foundering Tiger ensemble, but the Athletics, with power and their ace southpaw, Grove, who headed up a bevy of flame-throwing righthanders, found in the Schoolboy just what they needed to round out their pennant quest in 1931. His 10 and 5 helped the cause considerably, helping the A's to their third straight AL crown.

After Moose Earnshaw blanked the Cardinals in game four of the 1931 World Series, evening things at 2 and 2, Mack called on Hoyt in game number five. Alas, he was driven from the mound after a two-run sixth, and Wild Bill Hallahan went on to beat the Mackmen 5 to 1, as the Cardinals moved on to win the championship in St. Louis in the seventh game of the grueling chase for baseball's blue ribbon.

But the old gayblade wasn't finished quite yet, signing on in the NL to pitch for another seven seasons, the best of which was a 15 and 6 effort for the Pirates during the very season, 1934, that Lefty Grove spent with his new ball club, the Red Sox, nursing his ailing wing along until a second wind also brought him back from the ranks of the almost-retired. Both of them were on the far side of their careers, but neither lost the determination or savvy that ultimately commanded the respect of the Hall's Veterans Committee, which brought the Schoolboy on for a permanent engagement at Cooperstown in 1969 to join Lefty, already in residence since 1947.

Lefty Grove versus Ted Lyons (1900–1986)
Lyons was elected to the Baseball Hall of Fame in 1955

The 1999 *TBE* (p. 172) carried these lines in its tribute to Ted Lyons among its sketches of the top 400 ball players of all time:

5. Lefty Grove

...Fans in other cities celebrated pennants; in Chicago they celebrated Ted Lyons. Possibly the most popular player ever to take the mound in the Windy City, he earned fans' devotion with his upbeat personality, indomitable spirit, and by being one of the greatest pitchers of all time.

One of the few Hall of Famers who never played an inning of minor league ball, Lyons pitched for the first time in the first big league ball park he ever saw, Sportsman's Park, St. Louis, on July 2, 1923. He was still throwing his assortment of breaking pitches in 1946, the year he came back to Chicago after a three-year hitch with the Marines, part of it in the South Pacific arena of World War II action, when he was tapped for managerial duties. That ended a 21-year career so distinguished that it was deemed worthy of the Hall in 1955. Through it all he maintained the same unflappable, "nice-guy" demeanor that earned *TBE's* accolade cited above.

Those who might question his status among "the greatest" are asked to check his record, made against a background of mediocre Chicago ball clubs whose maddening habit it was to boot ground balls at just the wrong time, misjudge fly balls that ushered in costly runs, and find their way into the darker regions of the AL standings. Despite that, he won more than he lost, logging a respectable 260–230 record in the final counting. It has often been said in connection with this accomplished hurler that, had he pitched for better ball clubs, he would certainly have won more than 300. No matter. He took the hand he was dealt, played it, and made his way to Cooperstown just the same.

Lyons, often a tough-luck pitcher, had very little luck with Mack's A's and hardly any at all with Lefty Grove. Genial Ted only won seven times in their 21-game series.

Ted Lyons was another of those Famers who faced both Grove and Walter Johnson. As fate would have it, in fact, he had the dubious privilege of losing to both of them in successive starts, the first against Lefty on July 13, 1927, and the second on July 17, against Big Barney. In four Johnson matchups Lyons was winless, recording a loss and three No Decisions in relief roles while Johnson won two, recorded a Save in another, and received one No Decision. Those four encounters were far fewer than the 21 in which Lyons and Grove participated. The complete record follows:

The Grove-Lyons Log:

Jun 15, 1927	Chicago 6, Philadelphia 4	Lyons WP, Grove LP
Jul 13, 1927	Philadelphia 7, Chicago 5	Grove WP, Lyons LP
Aug 22, 1929	Chicago 4, Philadelphia 3	Lyons WP, Grove LP
Jun 3, 1931	Philadelphia 2, Chicago 1	Grove WP, Lyons LP
Jul 9, 1932	Chicago 7, Philadelphia 0	Lyons WP, Grove LP
Aug 7, 1932	Chicago 3, Philadelphia 1	Lyons WP, Grove LP
Jul 10, 1933	Philadelphia 3, Chicago 2	Grove WP, Lyons LP
Jul 31, 1936	Boston 7, Chicago 3	Grove WP, Lyons LP
Aug 7, 1937	Boston 5, Chicago 4	Grove WP, Lyons LP
Jun 18, 1938	Boston 4, Chicago 3	Grove WP, Lyons LP
Jun 11, 1939	Chicago 7, Boston 5	Lyons WP, Grove LP
Jun 16, 1940	Boston 4, Chicago 3	Grove WP, Lyons LP
Jun 8, 1941	Boston 5, Chicago 3	Grove WP, Lyons LP

The Lyons-Grove series started on July 12, 1926, when Ted Lyons beat the Red Sox 8 to 6. Jack Quinn was the loser, and Grove pitched in relief.

On September 15, 1927, Grove picked up a Save and Quinn the victory. Lyons was the loser as the Athletics won 5 to 4.

Howard Ehmke was Mack's starter and loser on August 25, 1928, when the Sox beat the A's 9 to 3. Lyons was the winner and Grove recorded a No Decision in relief.

In the September 11, 1929, game, Lefty Grove was shelled for four runs in the first inning of a game won by the A's, 7 to 4. The A's responded with seven of their own in the bottom of the first, and from that point on Grove's reliever, Bill Shore, blanked the Sox, and Sox reliever Hal McKain returned the favor, shutting out the Mackmen the rest of the way. Shore was the winner and Lyons, who gave up five tallies, was the loser.

Chicago beat Philadelphia 6 to 5 on June 7, 1930. Grove started, but reliever Eddie Rommel was charged with the loss. Lyons came on in relief of Frank "Dutch" Henry, the winner, to record a Save. Henry lost 17 games in 1930 and was victorious only twice. This game was one of his two shining moments that season.

Although Grove started on July 16, 1930, he was not credited with a victory in a lopsided game won by the A's 14 to 7. Shore picked up the win in a come-from-behind Philadelphia victory. Lyons was charged with the defeat.

On August 20, 1932, both Red Faber and Ted Lyons pitched in relief of starter Milt

Gaston. Lew Krausse, Sr., was the winning pitcher in relief of starter Grove in the A's' 14 to 8 win. Lyons was charged with the loss.

In the last Grove-Lyons engagement of the series, Boston beat Chicago 8 to 6 on June 15, 1941. Although Grove started, he did not get the win. That went to reliever Mike Ryba. Ted Lyons went all the way, sustaining the loss.

In the 21 game series between them, Lyons and Grove had the following records:

	W	L	ND	S
Grove	9	5	6	1
Lyons	7	13	0	1

An interesting note about the last eight games in the series: During those eight contests, played between July 10, 1933, and June 15, 1941, four went extra innings and two more, on August 7, 1937, and June 11, 1939, were won in the bottom of the ninth. Four times the margin of victory was one run, and in another three games the outcome was decided by a two-run margin. Small wonder that the Grove-Lyons matchup packed the house, as the crowd of 36,859 at Comiskey Park did on June 8, 1941, when Lefty won his 297th in a 10-inning thriller, 5 to 3.

On August 14, 1929, a Jimmie Foxx smash sent Grove and the A's home a winner over Cleveland in a 17-inning marathon in which Lefty went all the way. It was his longest major league ball game. But he paid for it during his next two outings. Just four days later he lost to St. Louis, and then Ted Lyons and Co., with a little help from Ol' Sol, who dished up an oppressively hot and humid day, took him on in an August 22 tilt at Comiskey Park. Mose, as Grove was usually called by his teammates, entered the game with an 18 and 3 record, and left it 18 and 4 when the Sox mustered the winning tally with one out in the bottom of the ninth. One shudders to think what things looked like in the A's club house, or how many uniform jerseys he shredded beyond his own. The Sox tried hard to give Lefty number 19 by putting three infield errors to work in the eighth, but Mr. Steely-Nerves buckled down and put out a three-run Athletics rally, then won it in the ninth. Such was life on Chicago's South Side during the prime of Theodore Lyons. Nothing quite certain until the very last out had been laid to rest!

Lefty Grove versus Charles "Red" Ruffing (1905–1986)
Ruffing was elected to the Baseball Hall of Fame in 1967

Lefty Grove and Red Ruffing, two of the AL's glittering stars of the late twenties through the early forties, dueled one another 23 times, sometimes as relievers but much more often as starters, especially on days when their owners and managers wanted sellout crowds, or, more directly, when the must-games were on the line. This was particularly true during the thirties, when Grove and Co., first for Philadelphia, and later for Boston, were in search of pennant spoils that were usually under tight New York surveillance.

Among those 23 confrontations were six Ruffing victories, as compared to ten for Grove. On 15 occasions neither pitcher was charged with a loss or a victory, with seven No Decisions going to Grove and eight to Ruffing. Among the 14 losses were five charged to Grove and nine to Ruffing. In a series that tipped favorably to Ol' Mose, there was nonetheless a stretch of five straight victories at Boston's expense, featuring three consecutive Ruffing shutouts that rang down the curtain on their 16 years of hurling warfare. If he hadn't been exactly overwhelming before, at least Big Red left it all behind in a blaze of convincing superiority.

The first of six blankings that dotted this distinguished series of games came on September 7, 1928, when Grove threw a four-hitter at Boston's Red Sox in a 1 to 0 white-knuckle special. Big Red, the Carmine's burly righthander (who that season would make his way through a nightmarish 10 and 25 reading), held the Athletics to six hits himself that day, but lost the game in the sixth stanza in a game that snuffed potential rallies with five twin killings, 11 Grove whiffs and brilliant fielding by both clubs. The box score follows.

September 7, 1928 at Fenway Park

Philadelphia	AB	R	H	PO	Boston	AB	R	H	PO
Bishop, 2b	3	1	2	0	Rothrock, rf	4	0	1	3
Haas, cf	4	0	1	1	Myer, 3b	4	0	1	2
Cochrane, c	4	0	1	11	Rogell, ss	3	0	0	1
Simmons, lf	4	0	0	3	Berry, ph	1	0	0	0
Foxx, 1b	4	0	0	7	Flagstead, cf	3	0	1	2
Miller, rf	4	0	1	0	Todt, 1b	3	0	0	8
Dykes, 3b	3	0	0	0	Williams, lf	3	0	0	3
Boley, ss	3	0	1	5	Regan, 2b	2	0	0	6
Grove, (WP)	3	0	0	0	Hofmann, c	3	0	0	1
					Ruffing, (LP)	3	0	1	1
Totals	32	1	6	27	Totals	29	0	4	27

Line Score:	Philadelphia	000	001	000	1–6–2
	Boston	000	000	000	0–4–1

2BH: Boley, Miller; DP: Foxx unassisted; Bishop, Boley and Foxx; Todt and Rogell; Hofmann, Regan and Todt; Ruffing and Myer; BB: Ruffing 1, Grove 1; K: Grove 11, Ruffing 1.

Though they lost—as usual—the Bosox that day put together one of their best games of the summer. It was Charley Ruffing's fate to be the chief victim of both circumstances and his woefully inept teammates to lose a baleful of ball games in Boston, and this one was to be no exception.

For Red Ruffing there was, however, light at the end of the tunnel, a light that shone all the way from New York. And when the beam, directed by Bob Shawkey, Colonel Jake Rupert's 1930 field boss, hit Ruffing, it signaled the end of his Boston miseries. The pinstripes he donned soon turned things around in a career that saw him move from his former pitching regimen to one ordered by the old Yankee slabmeister, Shawkey. The key difference in the Boston and New York pitching mechanics Ruffing employed was the use of his entire body in tossing a baseball, as differentiated from an almost total reliance on his strong right arm to do his pitching. Shawkey, like his own former mentor, Albert "Chief" Bender, tutored his new pitcher in the art of body control and power in pitching. In 1930 Red Ruffing went from 0 and 3 in Boston to 15 and 5 in New York, with some assistance from his newfound pinstriped friends. More importantly, however, Shawkey's message got through, and though the Yankee mentor was unceremoniously dumped at the end of the 1930 season in one of the zaniest and most unfair changes in Yankee history, he did manage to present the Yanks with a pennant ticket that lasted through the rest of Red Ruffing's Yankee career.

Before leaving Boston, however, Big Red did manage to get the Red Sox out far enough ahead in a 10 to 0 plaster job on the A's on September 29, 1929, so that the Bosox could leave the mop-up to the bullpen while Red rested contentedly on the bench as his colleagues bombed Lefty Grove. The joy in Puritan Land registered all the way down the East Coast!

Among the last four of the six whitewash masterpieces referred to above was a 2-hit gem fired by Lefty at the Yanks in a winning 8 to 0 embarrassment of the Bronx Bombers on April 17, 1936. That came during a season in which the Yankees swept aside all comers to regain the AL crown that had eluded them since the last of the "Ruthian" pennants in 1932. Later that summer Ruffing was to even the 1936 count with a 4 to 2 conquest, his 15th, in a 20 and 12 season. By that time the team of Ruffing, from the starboard side, and "the Gay Castillian," Lefty Gomez, from the portside, were in control of the race to the flag. They then went on to beat their crosstown rivals from Coogan's Bluff for the first of their four-straight world's championships.

The final chapter in the Grove-Ruffing series was written on May 30, 1940. By then the two old warhorses (Lefty was 40 and Big Red 36), eyeing one another warily, as always, had been through 22 confrontations. And that final meeting was a real rouser. Played before the third largest crowd in Yankee Stadium history, the Yankees disposed of the Yawkeymen 4 to 0, who got to Ruffing for only two singles, while knicking the Old Master, by this time in hot pursuit of number 300, for a three-run second inning that proved to be more than enough to win.

On July 11, 1939, the All-Star game was played at Yankee Stadium in the midst of Red Ruffing's best major league campaign. He was the starting pitcher for the AL. Lou Gehrig, incapacitated and retired, was named the Honorary Captain for the Junior Circuit winners that day; and another elder

A Red Ruffing–Lefty Grove matchup was usually a sell-out. They met 23 times between 1925 and 1940.

statesman, Lefty Grove, was selected to the All-Star roster, his last such honor in a season during which he was to lose but four times and lead his league in Winning Percentage. During 1939 Ruffing's 21 and 7 paced one of the strongest Yankee lineups ever assembled. His five shutouts led the league, as did the Yankee defense and a power-laden offense, even without "Capt. Lou." But pitching was the pivotal factor as the Yanks romped home 15 games ahead of Lefty Grove's Bosox. An interesting sidenote: 1939 was the season Ted Williams debuted, and he did so behind Lefty Grove on April 20 in the Yankee Stadium season opener. His first major league hit, a double, went into the record books that day. The pitcher he doubled against? Red Ruffing, who started the season with a 2 to 0 victory. The loser? Lefty Grove. Even in his sunset years, it usually took a pitching masterpiece the likes of Ruffing's shutout to beat him.

The Grove-Ruffing Log:

July 4, 1927	Philadelphia 10, Boston 2	Grove WP, Ruffing LP
Sep 1, 1928	Philadelphia 14, Boston 2	Grove WP, Ruffing LP
Sep 7, 1928	Philadelphia 1, Boston 0	Grove WP, Ruffing LP
Aug 31, 1929	Philadelphia 9, Boston 4	Grove WP, Ruffing LP
Sep 29, 1929	Boston 10, Philadelphia 0	Ruffing WP, Grove LP
May 25, 1931	Philadelphia 5, New York 4	Grove WP, Ruffing LP
Jul 4, 1935	Boston 4, New York 3	Grove WP, Ruffing LP
Apr 17, 1936	Boston 8, New York 0	Grove WP, Ruffing LP
Aug 4, 1936	New York 4, Boston 2	Ruffing WP, Grove LP
May 30, 1938	New York 10, Boston 0	Ruffing WP, Grove LP
Apr 20, 1939	New York 2, Boston 0	Ruffing WP, Grove LP
May 30, 1940	New York 4, Boston 0	Ruffing WP, Grove LP

In the initial Grove-Ruffing matchup on June 1, 1925, the Red Sox beat Philadelphia 5 to 3. Ruffing (WP) went all the way. Grove (ND) relieved Rube Walberg (LP).

On June 2, 1926, Jack Quinn (WP) started against Ruffing (LP) and was relieved by Grove (ND) in a game the A's won 5 to 1.

Tony Welzer, born in Germany, was the reliever and winner for the Red Sox on July 1, 1926, as the Bosox beat the A's 10 to 5. Both Grove and Ruffing were relievers (ND). Rube Walberg was the loser.

In a 5 to 4 game won by the Athletics on July 4, 1928, Ruffing (LP) and Grove (Save) were both used as relievers. Eddie Rommel was WP.

In 1928 Lefty Grove twice fanned three consecutive batters on nine pitches, striking out the side, first on August 23 in the second inning and then on September 27 in the seventh inning.

Neither starter Red Ruffing nor reliever Bob Grove were pitchers of decision in a 9 to 8 Athletics win over Boston on April 15, 1932. Merritt "Sugar" Cain was the winner and George Pipgras the loser.

Red Ruffing (ND) started and Walter Brown (LP) finished in a 16 inning game won by the A's, 8 to 7. Lefty Grove, who pitched the last seven innings, was the winner on June 1, 1932.

On June 4, 1932, the Mackmen beat the Bosox 10 to 7. Grove (WP) went all the way. Ruffing (ND) relieved Walter Brown (LP).

On June 10, 1933, Grove pitched a complete game (WP), beating the Yanks 9 to 5. Ruffing (ND) relieved Russ Van Atta, New York's losing pitcher.

New York lost to Philadelphia, 11 to 9, on August 12, 1933. Ruffing and Grove both started. Reliever Walberg was the winner, and Johnny Murphy, who relieved Ruffing, was the loser.

Boston beat New York in an 11-inning game, 10 to 9, on July 3, 1934. Rube Walberg (WP) and J. Murphy (LP) both relieved in this game, as did Lefty Grove (ND). Red Ruffing (ND) was New York's starting pitcher.

On August 11, 1937, New York beat Boston, 8 to 5, in 14 innings. Reliever J. Murphy was the winner, and reliever John "Black Jack" Wilson was the loser. Grove (ND) and Ruffing (ND) were the starters.

Lefty Grove versus Wesley Cheek "Wes" Ferrell (1908–1976)

Out there on the mound he was as mean and tough and cussed ornery as they came, in a class by himself as one of baseball's most angry and combative ball players. He lost 128 major league ball games and hated every last loss, every last out that humiliated him. But he also won 193 times. And despite a monumental temper that matched Lefty Grove's, his career bordered on Hall of Fame caliber — if not worthy of the Hall. In fact, a case could be made that this colorful fellow, Wes Ferrell, does belong in baseball's Valhalla. More on that just ahead.

The reason Wes Ferrell appears here is, of course, because of his skirmishes with Robert Moses Grove. They were highly productive — for Lefty Grove. Truth be told, it would have been much better had Mr. Ferrell, the country squire from North Carolina, never been paired with his temperamental counterpart in a ball game. They faced each other 11 times, and Lefty won nine while Ferrell lost eight. Grove only lost once and Ferrell only won once. Twice Ferrell was credited with No Decisions. That is about the most lopsided series in the entire Grove saga. That it should happen to a quality star such as Wes Ferrell is one of baseball's mysteries, but that's the way it turned out.

And yet, years later, here is what Wes Ferrell had to say about Lefty Grove.

> He was my idol. Lefty Grove. Fastest pitcher I ever saw. The Greatest. Why, I wasn't good enough to carry his glove across the field. Dizzy Dean was great, and so was Koufax. And Bob Feller was fast, of course. Bob had spectacular

stuff. Didn't have to fool around on the corners; just get it over the plate. *But Grove was faster.* He'd just throw that ball in there, and you'd wonder where it went to. It would just *zing*! and disappear. You can believe he was fast because that's all he threw. He'd just keep fogging them in there. He didn't start throwing breaking stuff until late in his career.[23]

Part of what was probably the most famous brother team as battery mates in the game's history, Wes finally got to pitch to his older brother, Rick, when he was traded to Boston in 1934. That trade united him not only with his brother, but with none other than his old tormentor, Grove. For almost four seasons the two hotheaded aces led the league in a variety of stats, and in bats broken over dugout railings and kicked water buckets. They gave their Bosox teammates, who stifled chuckles in self defense over their antics, 100 victories between Ferrell's May 25, 1934, arrival and June 10, 1937, when he was traded, along with brother Rick, to Washington for Bobo Newsom and Ben Chapman. Along the way, the two of them gave Boston and the rest of the AL all they could handle, even though both, ironically, had to convert to finesse pitching after arm troubles had rendered their fast ones less than terrifying.

As for Lefty's domination over Ferrell, here is the game-by-game log:

Jul 1, 1931	Philadelphia 4, Cleveland 3	Grove WP, Ferrell LP
Jul 25, 1931	Philadelphia 6, Cleveland 3	Grove WP, Ferrell LP
Aug 15, 1931	Philadelphia 4, Cleveland 3	Grove WP, Ferrell LP
May 5, 1932	Philadelphia 15, Cleveland 3	Grove WP, Ferrell LP
Aug 17, 1932	Philadelphia 11, Cleveland 0	Grove WP, Ferrell LP
May 12, 1933	Philadelphia 7, Cleveland 3	Grove WP, Ferrell LP
Aug 15, 1933	Philadelphia 8, Cleveland 7	Grove WP, Ferrell LP
Aug 15, 1937	Washington 8, Boston 3	Ferrell WP, Grove LP
Sep 6, 1937	Boston 6, Washington 2	Grove WP, Ferrell LP

On May 11, 1929, Ferrell and Grove appeared in the same game for the first time. Philadelphia won behind Grove, beating John "Jovo" Miljus, 4 to 2. Wes Ferrell appeared as a reliever (ND).

Ferrell started the May 17, 1931, game (ND), won by Philadelphia 15 to 10. Grove (ND) relieved in this game. Pete Jablonowski, who later changed his name to Pete Appleton, was the loser.

On July 21, 1935, Lefty Grove beat Tommy Bridges at Fenway Park, 7 to 6, thanks to a Wes Ferrell pinch home run that plated three runs after Grove had lost his lead because of a three run ninth that almost made the Tigers a winner. That made Ferrell a winner in a Grove game!

The record shows that Lefty Grove had all the better of it when it came to pitching against Wes Ferrell. The Ferrell record, compiled across a span of 15 seasons, is nonetheless worthy of Cooperstown consideration, causing more than one knowledgeable observer to wonder why the Shrine has no Wes Ferrell plaque mounted alongside brother Rick's. One of those, Bill James,[24] made this pithy and insinuating statement in his *Politics of Glory*:

> His [Wes Ferrell's] career won-loss record (195–128) was better than those of twelve starting pitchers[25] who are in the Hall of Fame. He was the best-hitting pitcher of all time. The Hall of Fame has certainly elected worse players.
>
> His brother, for example [p. 331].

For those interested, here is a comparison of the Ferrell numbers with others whose win numbers are in the same 190 range (** indicates Hall of Famer, PR indicates Pitching Runs, and SH indicates Shutouts in the chart below):

Player/ML Yrs.	W-L-W%	IP	SH	PR	BA	ERA	TPI
Bucky Walters, 1934–50	198–160, .553	3104.2	42	152	.243	3.30	29.0

The best brother-battery in the history of the game, temperamental Wes Ferrell and his brother Rick, a Hall of Famer.

**Dazzy Vance, 1915–1935	197–140, .585	2966.2	29	281	.150	3.24	27.4
**Ed Walsh, 1904–1917	195–126, .607	2964.1	57	310	.194	1.82	44.9
Tommy Bridges, 1930–1946	194–138, .584	2826.1	33	256	.180	3.57	28.0
Dolf Luque, 1914–1935	194–179, .520	3220.1	26	245	.227	3.24	26.8
Dwight Gooden, 1984–2000	194–112, .634	2800.2	24	140	.196	3.51	17.7
Wes Ferrell, 1927–1941	*193–128, .601*	*2623.0*	*17*	*147*	*.280*	*4.04*	*30.5*
**Rube Waddell, 1897–1910	193–143, .574	2961.1	50	240	.161	2.16	24.4
Dutch Leonard, 1933–1953	191–181, .513	3218.0	30	267	.168	3.25	26.7
Doc White, 1901–1913	189–156, .548	3041.0	45	134	.217	2.39	20.1
**Lefty Gomez, 1930–1943	189–102, .649	2503.0	28	322	.147	3.34	19.9
Deacon Phillippe, 1899–1911	189–109, .634	2607.0	27	153	.189	2.59	15.1

Lefty Grove versus Melvin Leroy "Mel" Harder (1909–)

Mel Harder was good enough as a teenager to make the Cleveland pitching staff, appearing in 23 games in 1928, with an 0–2 record. In 1947, when he finally called it a career, he was still in Cleveland, one of but a half dozen 20-year men not fortunate enough to have played on a pennant winner. During the year he made his rookie rounds, he debuted on April 24, and two weeks later he was put into a game with the Athletics on a day the A's pulverized the Indians 12 to 5. The winning pitcher? Lefty Grove. It was the first of 18 meetings between two of the AL's top pitchers of the 1930s.

Mel Harder continued in his relief role in games with Lefty Grove right on through a June 10, 1932, appearance. By that time there had been five encounters and the Indians hadn't won any of them, but Harder wasn't charged with a loss in any of them, either. That was soon to come, however. And it was to be a bitter one.

On July 31, 1932, 81,179 Clevelanders made their way through the brand new turnstiles of Municipal Stadium on the Lake Erie waterfront to cheer their Indians as they took on Lefty Grove and his Athletics in the immense baseball arena's inaugural game. Grove, the old heartbreaker, not about to be upstaged by such an auspicious event, threw a dazzler at the Indians, a four-hit blanking that trashed an equally superb performance by Mel Harder, the unfortunate loser in a 1 to 0 game that might have been played during the salad days of the deadball era.

Harder's next starting assignment against Lefty came the next summer on a September day in Philadelphia. What happened was similar to what transpired on July 25, 1941, when Harder and Grove matched breaking balls for the last time. On that historic day during the year of DiMaggio's 56 straight, Williams' .406 and Pearl Harbor, as baseball buffs everywhere recall, Ol' Mose won his 300th in a game that once again showcased his fierce determination and perseverance. There, too, was a Jimmie Foxx home run that provided the punch in a 10 to 6 conquest over Joe Krakauskas, the starter and loser. Mel Harder was also a part of that day as a reliever for Krakauskas.

So too, on September 6, 1933, a younger Mose won his 20th game, and Jimmy Foxx slashed one of Harder's better curve balls into the stands at Shibe Park to ice a 5 to 4 victory for the Athletics. Mel had run into a combination that had been terrorizing the AL for years, first at Philadelphia and then later in Yawkeeland. It seems they treated everybody alike. Lousy.

As overwhelming as Lefty was in the Grove-Harder series, winning 11 and dropping but a pair of games (there were three No Decisions and two Saves to round out the record), he didn't quite have things entirely his own way. As a matter of fact, he ran squarely into the teeth of a stiff Harder gale on June 16, 1935, when the Indians ace disposed of the Red Sox 4 to 0 at the Forest City. A scratch single by Bing Miller in the second inning was the only hit the Carmine could muster in a game that brought Harder as close to no-hit land as he was ever to come. That win upped his record to 9 and 3, as "Wimpy," as his teammates called him, moved a step closer to the second of his two 20-game seasons with a 22–12 record. They were part of a distinguished career in which he logged 223 major league victories that etched his name among the top 75 winners in the history of the game.

Wes Ferrell, Mel Harder and Tommy Bridges, whose matchups with Grove follow Harder's, are the three non–Famers included in the Grove profile. Each of the three has something unique to offer. From time to time there have been those among baseball's cognoscenti who have wondered whether they weren't as Cooperstown-worthy as some of the others already honored. Mel Harder, for example, registered a career TPI of 19.4, to rank 109th on the all time list. Those Famers who followed him in the list include:

	TPI	W-L	PR	ERA
Mel Harder	19.4	223–186	190	3.80
Joe McGinnity	18.8	246–142	186	2.66
Early Wynn	17.1	300–244	170	3.54
Chief Bender	14.4	212–127	101	2.46
Don Sutton	13.2	324–256	263	3.26
Jack Chesbro	10.9	198–132	58	2.68
Herb Pennock	6.8	241–162	150	3.60
Jess Haines	6.8	210–158	114	3.64
Rube Marquard	–2.3	201–177	58	3.08

New Hall of Fame election rubrics were sanctioned in 2001. They call for a wider range of voters in a more liberalized scheme of screening and voting for the game's candidates. Perhaps that will prove to be the opening that will pave the way for the Harders, Santos, Ferrells and Blylevens. As the game approaches the 16,000 mark of players who have been part of the major league's history, there remain less than 5 percent of its total membership who have been honored with plaques. That percentage seems restrictive enough to make membership a distinctive honor that separates the many great players from the superstars whose portfolio of qualifications legitimately underscores their selection. Is Mel Harder one of those? The vote from this corner is — not quite, and yet, no less qualified than some of the pitchers listed above.

Mel Harder, an astute developer of Cleveland pitchers, faced Grove 13 times in his lifelong Indians career.

The Grove-Harder Log:

Jul 31, 1932	Philadelphia 1, Cleveland 0	Grove WP, Harder LP
Sep 6, 1933	Philadelphia 5, Cleveland 2	Grove WP, Harder LP
May 23, 1934	Boston 7, Cleveland 5	Grove WP, Harder LP
Jun 16, 1935	Cleveland 4, Boston 0	Harder WP, Grove LP
Jun 26, 1935	Cleveland 8, Boston 7	Harder WP, Grove LP
Sep 1, 1936	Boston 4, Cleveland 1	Grove WP, Harder LP
Aug 3, 1937	Boston 13, Cleveland 2	Grove WP, Harder LP
Jun 9, 1938	Boston 8, Cleveland 0	Grove WP, Harder LP

Lefty Grove beat the Indians 12 to 5 on June 15, 1928. Garland Buckeye was charged with the defeat. Mel Harder was a reliever (ND).

Mel Harder (ND) relieved starter Ken Holloway (LP) in a game won by Grove on May 9, 1930, 9 to 4.

On September 13, 1930, the A's beat the Indians 9 to 2. Both Grove and Harder appeared in the game as relievers (ND). George Earnshaw was the winner, and starter Willis Hudlin was the loser.

The Indians lost to the A's on May 16, 1931, 12 to 5. Grove (WP) went the route. Tommy Thomas (LP) and Harder (ND) both relieved.

On June 10, 1932, Cleveland lost to the A's, 10 to 7. Rube Walberg was the starter and winner, with relief from Grove (ND). Willis Hudlin was the Cleveland loser. Mel Harder (ND) pitched in relief.

The A's beat the Indians 7 to 2 on May 20, 1933. Sugar Cain was the winner and Grove (ND) relieved him. Harder (ND) relieved loser Willis Hudlin.

Philadelphia beat Cleveland on September 9, 1933, by the score of 5 to 3. Roy Mahaffey (WP) started for the A's and Grove (Save) relieved. Starter Clint Brown of the Indians was charged with the defeat. Mel Harder pitched three innings of relief (ND).

On May 7, 1940, Cleveland starter Mike Naymick (LP) was relieved by Harder (ND). Grove went all the way to record the 6 to 4 win.

Cleveland beat Boston 9 to 6 on July 20, 1940, as Mel Harder went the route. Grove (ND) started and was relieved by Earl Johnson (LP).

Al Milnar was charged with Cleveland's 10 to 6 loss on July 25, 1940, as Lefty Grove won his 300th ball game. Mel Harder (ND) relieved starter Joe Krakauskas (ND), coming on in the fourth inning with none out and two on. 16,000 attended this game, including 6,000 Ladies Day fans. Ted Williams' two-run homer off Mel Harder tied the game in the fifth inning, and the Bosox went on to win it with a four-run outburst in the bottom of the eighth.

Lefty Grove versus Vernon Louis "Lefty" Gomez (1908–1989)

Gomez was elected to the Baseball Hall of Fame in 1972

The Hall of Fame welcomed eight baseball heroes in 1972. It was a duke's mixture of seven former players and an executive, Will Harridge, the former president of the American League. Among the players were Sandy Koufax, Early Wynn, Ross Youngs and two of the Negro Leagues' stellar stars, Josh Gibson and Buck Leonard. The list also included two Yankees, catcher Yogi Berra and "the Gay Castillian," Lefty Gomez, a.k.a. "Goofy." What a pair! The hallowed halls of Cooperstown would never be the same once these two were let loose inside baseball's august shrine.

Gomez stories, like those of the legendary Yogi-man, fill encyclopedias, and their one-liners will forever be a part of baseball lore. One of those stories involves Joe McCarthy, the Yankees' Hall of Fame manager during the height of El Goofo's career. Gomez was seated near Marse Joe during a Yankee game, taking a peek now and then out of the corner of his eye to see whether he could pick up the signs McCarthy was giving. Along about the fifth inning McCarthy, without batting an eye or even looking in his direction, said, "Gomez, just pay attention to the ball game. You'll never pick up my signs, anyway."

But McCarthy knew just how good Gomez was and patiently overlooked the talented portsider's wisecracks and antics. Blazing fast and insistent on owning the inside of the strike zone, he followed Lefty Grove as the AL's next Triple Crown winner with two of his own in 1934 and 1937. And beyond his AL conquests he inflicted enduring pain on NL pennant winners, never losing a game in world series competition, and

"El Goofo," Lefty Gomez, Yankee prankster and *bon vivant*, was all business when it came to squaring off against Grove. The two Famers pitched before sellouts each time they met.

winning three out of four All-Star game decisions in the 1930s.

During those dreary Depression years the two Lefties were indeed bright spots for sports fans. An ironic twist of baseball fate placed those two superb hurlers side by side, both lefthanded, both of them big winners, and both Cooperstown bound. Between 1930 and 1940 the two mustered 374 wins, as against 174 losses, for an awesome .682 winning percentage, divided, incidentally, with a nod in Lefty Grove's direction. So one might suspect that the Grove-Gomez log would be most interesting. And through 15 matchups it was.

The 15 engagements produced more wins for Gomez than Grove (7 to 5), two shutouts (both by the Castillian), and Lefty Grove's 295th victory in the last Gomez-Grove meeting of the series (an 8 to 4 Boston win on May 12, 1941). The nail-biter in the series was a 2 to 1 Yankee victory made possible by a towering DiMaggio blast leading off the last of the eighth inning at Yankee Stadium in 1939. One other game of interest occurred on April 15, 1932, when the Athletics beat the Bronx Bombers in the last of the ninth, 9 to 8, as Al Simmons singled and then went to third on a wild pitch by losing pitcher George Pipgras, who then gave up a sacrifice fly to Jimmy Dykes that allowed Simmons to score the winning run. In that game 10 future Hall of Fame players were on display: Simmons, Cochrane, Foxx and Grove for the A's, and Yankees Lazzeri, Ruth, Gehrig, Dickey, Ruffing and Gomez.

The Grove-Gomez Log:

Aug 29, 1931	Philadelphia 7, New York 4	Grove WP, Gomez LP
Apr 20, 1932	New York 8, Philadelphia 3	Gomez WP, Grove LP
Sep 27, 1933	New York 7, Philadelphia 0	Gomez WP, Grove LP
Sep 25, 1937	New York 5, Boston 2	Gomez WP, Grove LP
Apr 28, 1938	Boston 6, New York 1	Grove WP, Gomez LP
Jul 10, 1938	Boston 6, New York 4	Grove WP, Gomez LP
Jul 2, 1939	Boston 7, New York 3	Grove WP, Gomez LP
Sep 6, 1939	New York 2, Boston 1	Gomez WP, Grove LP
May 12, 1941	Boston 8, New York 4	Grove WP, Gomez LP

On April 15, 1932, Philadelphia beat New York 9 to 8. Both Grove and Gomez were used as relievers in this game. The winning pitcher was Merritt Cain, and the loser was George Pipgras.

Lefty Gomez beat the Athletics 5 to 4 on June 2, 1933. The A's started Roy Mahaffey (LP) and Grove relieved (ND).

The Athletics beat the Yanks 11 to 9 in a wild one on August 12, 1933. Grove, the starter, and reliever Gomez were not the pitchers of record. Red Ruffing (ND) started for New York, but the loss was charged to Walter "Jumbo" Brown. Rube Walberg was the winner.

On April 19, 1938, Lefty Gomez was the winner as the Yanks beat the Athletics 5 to 3. Grove started (ND) but the loss was charged to Charlie "Broadway" Wagner.

The Yanks blanked the A's behind Gomez' 5-hitter, 4 to 0, on September 8, 1938. Lefty Grove (ND) relieved starter Bill Harris, who was charged with the loss.

Reliever Emerson Dickman earned the victory in a 4 to 3 Boston win over New York on July 9, 1939. Starting pitchers Grove and Gomez (ND), were relieved by Monte Pearson of the Yanks (LP) and Emerson Dickman of the Red Sox (WP).

Lefty Grove versus Thomas Jefferson Davis "Tommy" Bridges (1906–1968)

There is always some "King of the Hill" around as promising rookies are breaking in. In 1930 "the King" was Lefty Grove, and the promising rookie was Tommy Bridges, who later became one of baseball's premier curveball pitchers. First, with respect to "the King:" In 1930 he won the first of his two Triple Crowns, with 28 wins, 209 Ks and a 2.54 ERA. It was his fourth straight 20-win season (there would be three to follow), and produced league leading figures in Saves (9), W% (.848), Opponents' BA (.247), Ratio (10.5) and Pitching Runs (68). Lefty's 2.54 ERA was crafted against a background of outrageous slugging in both leagues that summer as the AL hit at .288 and its pitchers recorded a flabby 4.65 ERA. That 1930 season, coupled with Grove's 1931 log, would have been enough right there to send him off to Cooperstown.

Connie Mack packed his "Mr. Grove" off to Boston for a bundle of Boston owner Tom Yawkee's greenbacks. Mack remained solvent, but Yawkee gained the greatest lefty in the game's history.

And what about the promising rookie? He did what promising rookies often do, pitch in a few games here and there, post a modest win-loss record, and leave enough of an indication that he would soon be ready for bigger things. One of those indications of future greatness came in his August 13, 1930, debut. Entering his first game as a relief pitcher, he looked up to find none other than Babe Ruth staring him in the face, coaxed him into a ground out, and then fanned another one-and-only, Lou Gehrig. Auspicious indeed!

A week later it was Bridges' lot, or honor, or misfortune, or just plain bad luck (any of the four would be appropriate) to run into Lefty Grove at Shibe Park on a day when the Mackmen were enjoying themselves at the expense of the Tigers in a game they won by a 10 to 6 margin. The rookie was once again called out of the pen by manager Bucky Harris and promptly tagged for three runs, no doubt the A's' crude way of welcoming a newcomer to the Bigs. But the youngster settled down and came out of the rest of his three-inning stint in fairly decent shape. Veteran Waite Hoyt was charged with the loss in that one, but Tommy, left to his own starting assignments against Grove, would find out—time and again—just how Hoyt felt in a game against Ol' Mose.

In those Grove-Bridges engagements, a dozen in all, the lean Tiger ace won but two, lost six and escaped on four other occasions with No Decisions. On the other hand, the Grove log read seven wins, two losses and three No Decisions. As with Wes Ferrell and Mel Harder, the other two non–Famers in the Grove profile, Bridges, as good as he was, found the old southpaw a tough nut to crack. He did, however have the last word.

On August 2, 1941, Tommy came in to relieve Paul Trout, the Dizzy One, who some years later teamed with Hal Newhouser as they led the Tigers to a 1945 world's championship. On this particular day, Lefty, who was facing his favorite AL patsies, found them particularly feisty, as they nailed him for four markers their first crack out of the Fenway Park dugout. But the Bosox caught up and Lefty hung on to record his last complete game. However, it was to no avail. Instead, it was Tommy Bridges who emerged victorious, clinging stubbornly to a 6–5 lead that made him a winner in Grove's first start after his festive 300th win on July 25 against Cleveland.

The Bridges record, logged in its entirety as a Detroit Tiger, shows 194 wins and a lifetime .584 winning record, including three straight 20-win seasons, four world series victories, an All-Star game victory in 1939, and a "perfect" one-hitter against the Washington Senators in 1932. On the numbers charts for pitchers he ranks in the top 100 in Shutouts, Pitching Runs, Pitching Wins and Wins Above League. Those are the marks of a highly successful twirler. Not in the Grove class (very few are) to be sure, but good enough to best all but 46 of the game's best pitchers on the all time TPI list.

One of the all time great curveball pitchers, the Tigers' Tommy Bridges.

The Grove-Bridges Log:

Jul 21, 1935	Boston 7, Detroit 6	Grove WP, Bridges LP
Jul 25, 1936	Boston 18, Detroit 3	Grove WP, Bridges LP
Aug 27, 1936	Detroit 4, Boston 2	Bridges WP, Grove LP
Jul 21, 1937	Boston 10, Detroit 3	Grove WP, Bridges LP
May 21, 1938	Boston 8, Detroit 3	Grove WP, Bridges LP
May 21, 1939	Boston 8, Detroit 3	Grove WP, Bridges LP
Aug 27, 1941	Detroit 6, Boston 5	Bridges WP, Grove LP

The Grove-Bridges series began with a 10–6 Philadelphia victory on August 20, 1930, a week following Tommy Bridges' ML debut against the New York Yankees. Waite Hoyt was the starter and losing pitcher for Detroit. Bridges relieved (ND). The win was Lefty Grove's seventh in a row, and upped his record to 21 and 4.

Isidore Goldstein (LP), a one-year career man with the Tigers (W3, L2), born in Odessa, Russia, was the starting pitcher and Bridges (ND) relieved in this 8 to 1 game on June 13, 1932. Lefty Grove (WP) pitched a complete game for the A's.

On July 28, 1932, Detroit beat Philadelphia 4 to 2. Bridges (ND) started and Vic Sorrell picked up the win in relief. Kim McKeithan was charged with the loss. Grove (ND) pitched in a relief role.

Boston beat Detroit in 10 innings, 6 to 5, on July 30, 1937. Bridges started against Grove. Neither was the pitcher of record. Reliever Jack Wilson was the winner, and George "Slick" Coffman, Detroit reliever, was charged with the loss.

In a 10-inning game, Boston beat Detroit on August 5, 1938, by the score of 9 to 8. Eldon Auker (ND) started for Detroit and was relieved by Bridges (LP). Jim Bagby, Jr. (WP), relieved starter Grove (ND).

Lefty Grove versus Bob Feller (1918–)

Feller was elected to the Baseball Hall of Fame in 1962

Lefty Grove versus Harold "Prince Hal" Newhouser (1921–1998)

Newhouser was elected to the Baseball Hall of Fame in 1992

By the time Bobby Feller and Hal Newhouser came along to make their way in the AL, Lefty Grove was into the smoke-and-mirrors stage of his career, winning games on guile and precision as he slowly but very surely trudged on toward the 300 victory mark. As youngsters, however, Feller, the latest rage among flame-throwing pitchers, and Newhouser, with so much stuff on the ball that he just had to be brought aboard the Tigers' pennant bandwagon in 1940, certainly got Lefty's attention. But after twenty seasons around professional ball players, he no doubt reserved his judgment until he saw for himself whether either or both of them had what it took to make a

Manager Al Lopez stands between Hal Newhouser (left) and Bob Feller, welcoming "Prince Hal" to his pitching staff in 1954.

successful career out of the opportunity they had been handed by Cleveland (in Feller's case) and by Detroit (Newhouser's hometown).

Both Newhouser and Feller showed him plenty. As Ol' Mose headed into retirement, it was evident that only a serious injury would prevent either of them from completing illustrious careers. And by the time America went to war in response to the Pearl Harbor tragedy, Feller, who had already been around six seasons — sporting a 107 and 51 mark, with 1233 whiffs to his credit (7.8 strikeouts per nine innings pitched, which, as this is being written, would still place his name among the top 15 strikeout artists all time), and league-leading marks in almost every major pitching category — was already regarded as a shoo-in for Hall of Fame honors.

For Newhouser, who hit his stride during the war years with phenomenal but down-played stats that weren't taken seriously for years after his retirement because of the stigma of wartime major league ball, the recognition took much longer in coming. Struggling to bring his own temperament and too-fiercely competitive nature under control so that his God-given abilities might be used to greatest advantage, he finally came into his own in 1944 after four less-than-ordinary seasons. And then it came. Big time. He strung together three extraordinary seasons in 1944, '45, and '46, winning 80 times and losing but 27, while posting gargantuan TPI numbers of 6.2, 7.5 and 6.8. Another 20-win season in 1948 raised his career total to four, accounting for almost half of his lifetime victories.

For Bob Feller the call to Cooperstown came in 1962, a scant six years after his last game, when the BBWAA elected him in his first year of eligibility, along with Jackie Robinson. Hal Newhouser, on the other hand, grew old waiting. After hanging up his spikes in 1955, it wasn't until 1992 that Cooperstown beckoned, and then it was via the Veterans Committee in a decision that was unpopular in some quarters even then. There was a collective sigh of relief in Detroit when, finally, the announcement was made. "The Prince" had finally gotten his just due, at least as the Motor City denizens saw it.

The end for both Feller and Newhouser came less than a year apart, and came as both were wearing Cleveland uniforms, Newhouser having been brought over to the Indians for spot-starting and relief duties during Cleveland's title-winning season in 1954. The two old warriors didn't get a chance to do their stuff in the world series, but both closed out the season with superb numbers: Feller at 13 and 3, and Newhouser at 7 and 2, combined for a 20 and 5 record that made a major difference in Cleveland's pennant chase.

The Lefty Grove–Bob Feller–Hal Newhouser competition was limited to four games as the two young hurlers got their careers underway. For Feller there was a 7 to 3 victory over Grove the very first time they met, on June 27, 1938. On that occasion young Bobby raised his record to the 9 and 2 mark in a season that ultimately wound up at 17 and 11. But in 1939 the league's new Whiffmaster found the Red Sox ready and waiting at Fenway on August 1. En route to a 15–4 log that earned winning percentage honors for the season, Mose took the Indians into camp by a 7 to 5 margin. That evened the record between the two at one apiece.

The first Newhouser-Grove face-off took place during the Tigers' run on the pennant in 1940 when they took on the Bosox at Briggs Stadium, August 4. Hal Newhouser was manager Del Baker's starting pitcher that day, and the 19 year old, 9 and 9 on the season, managed but four-plus innings of work as Boston tamed the Tigers 7 to 3. Ol'Mose, who had disposed of the Detroiters 58 times before this ball game, added number 59 against only 16 losses during his career. A Ted Williams triple and a Jimmie Foxx four-bagger led the attack on Newhouser.

The second of their two tilts was played on August 27, 1941, in what proved to be Lefty's last start against the Bengals. But this time neither he nor Newhouser lasted through the first inning in a game won by Detroit, 6 to 3. That day Grove left the game in the first inning, having pulled some rib cage muscles pitching to leadoff hitter Tuck Stainback. So the final Newhouser-Grove tally favored Grove with a 1–0 record to Newhouser's 0–1, each picking up a No Decision.

There are, of course, more interesting stories in the Feller and Newhouser careers to retell. And while their roles in the Lefty Grove story are minor, almost nonexistent, the story is no less compelling than that first and only duel between Cy Young, the grizzled veteran, and Pete Alexander, the bright young rookie. All five of these stellar performers, now a part of baseball's Hall of Fame heritage, helped make the game the spellbinding and enduring American treasure that it is.

The Greatest Lefty

The game's 20 greatest lefthanders are listed below, according to the Total Pitcher Index (TPI), a sabermetric calculation used throughout this review as a comprehensive measurement that states as a numerical value how many victories a pitcher has accumulated beyond those contributed by league-average hurlers either for a single season, or, when added together, for a career. The top three pitchers in the game's history include Walter Johnson (91.4) and Cy Young (78.0), followed by the game's premier southpaw, Lefty Grove, at 59.7. One other sabermetric measurement has been added to the listing below to further underscore Famer Grove's superiority among lefthanders — that of Adjusted Pitching Wins.[26] Here again we find Mr. Grove way out in front of an imposing list of portsiders, besting Carl Hubbell, who places second to Grove, by some 25 Pitching Wins. (The listing is through the 2000 season.)

		Years	TPI	Wins	Adjusted Pitching Wins*
1)	Lefty Grove	17	59.7	300	61.5
2)	Warren Spahn	21	50.2	363	36.7
3)	Carl Hubbell	16	41.4	253	37.3
4)	Hal Newhouser	17	39.3	207	30.7
5)	Whitey Ford	16	39.2	236	35.4
6)	Steve Carlton	24	33.7	329	29.4

*Adjusted Pitching Wins (APW) are calculated by dividing adjusted pitching runs by the number of runs required to create an additional victory over that of the league average. APWs have been normalized to league average and adjusted for the home park factor. A pitcher who has recorded more than five APWs in a single season, as Grove did five times in his career, has had an exceptional year. Only 30 pitchers in the game's history have accumulated more than 30 career APWs. Only seven of them are lefthanders.

7)	Randy Johnson†	13	31.8	179	33.9
8)	Tom Glavine†	14	30.9	208	23.9
9)	Eddie Plank	17	26.9	326	27.7
10)	Tommy John	26	25.6	288	19.5
11)	Harry Brecheen	12	25.0	133	21.2
12)	Rube Waddell	13	24.4	193	26.7
13)	Jimmy Key	15	24.2	186	22.0
14)	Billy Pierce	18	23.9	211	23.9
15)	Jesse Tannehill	15	21.1	197	11.9
16)	Chuck Finley†	15	20.9	181	21.6
17)	Sandy Koufax	12	20.5	165	24.3
18)	Guy "Doc" White	13	20.1	189	13.8
19)	Lefty Gomez	14	19.9	189	23.9
20)	Eddie Lopat	12	19.1	166	18.2

Both the priority order and the names on the list (as well as some names *not* on the list) will surprise many of baseball's numbers-wise fans. Sandy Koufax' ranking at number 17 will draw the ire of many, as will Hal Newhouser's lofty number four spot, and the absence of pitchers like Jim Kaat, whose ranking is number 21, Mel Parnell, Wilbur Wood or Mike Hampton might cause still others to wonder. But one thing is certain: in the final counting, enough of the numbers, no matter their combination or order, find a way to put the fellow with the flaming fast one, Robert Moses Grove, at the head of the list. The full accounting of his distinguished career underscores the numbers, as exemplified by his record against the many illustrious stars in this chapter, from Walter Johnson to Lefty Gomez. The Alexanders, Mathewsons and Groves are the ones who make the Hall.

†Still active.

6. Warren Spahn

Major League Totals	Won	Lost	Pct.
Boston, Milwaukee, New York, San Francisco (NL)	363	245	.597

Spahn was elected to the Baseball Hall of Fame in 1973

Major league baseball clubs went to their 1942 spring training camps under the heavy clouds of World War II. Between "the day that will live in infamy," December 7, 1941, and the reporting date for hundreds of major and minor leaguers readying for another season, a significant number of ball players had already been called up for military service or had enlisted. The global conflict, entering its most devastating years, left its oppressive mark everywhere, as it did in every American household. The Edward Spahn family in Buffalo, New York, was no exception.

The Spahn family, eight in number, had more than a nodding acquaintance with the national pastime. Dad played semi-pro ball, and there was a youngster in the brood, Warren by name, who showed so much promise that by the time he had won his last game as an undefeated junior at South Park High School, he had convinced Braves scout Bill Myer that a signing would soon be in order. What was impressive about the young phenom was not only his explosive speed and his command of the strike zone, but his savvy and intelligence. He could tell you how he pitched to every hitter down to the last pitch he threw.

The Braves lost no time in getting the southpaw's signature on a contract and assigned him to their Bradford, Pennsylvania, farm club after his 1940 high school graduation.

By 1942, as America girded for war, Warren Spahn was ready for a look with the big club, debuting with a pair of appearances in relief, the first on

April 19 against the Giants, and the second a day later against Brooklyn, hurling ⅔ of an inning the first time out and three frames against the Dodgers. Then it was back for a full season with the Hartford Bees before two more September appearances. Shortly thereafter he received a different kind of call, this one from Uncle Sam, and a new uniform, which he wore with distinction during a three year hitch that took him overseas and into heavy action. He came out of it with a Purple Heart and Bronze Star, steeled in the ultimate arena of warfare, a determined and focused young man who was ready to return to the Big Show. After what he had been through, the challenges ahead would never seem too big or too difficult for him to handle.

Spahnie's return to the game he loved was marked, from day one in the Braves' 1946 training camp, with the characteristics that had been forged on the anvil of minor league baseball and his wartime experience: steely determination, awesome concentration (it was said of him that when he was ready to pitch, a train could have roared through the infield behind him and he never would have known it), a thinking man's approach to the game, and a variety of pitches and speeds, all of which were under his tight control. That combination of skills and mental toughness saw him through 5,243.2 innings of major league pitching (the eighth highest total all time), more victories than any lefthander in the game's history (363), and a place of honor in the Hall of Fame (1973).

In this collection of the game's greatest moundsmen, Warren Spahn leads off the second half of the 20th century, weaving a thread of continuity with those who have gone before, beginning with Cy Young and continuing on through Lefty Grove, who threw his last pitches in 1941. Each of Spahn's predecessors, who have been celebrated in previous chapters, was a 300 game winner, and on August 11, 1961, Spahn joined the even dozen who had gone before with a 2 to 1 victory over the Cubs.

Warren Spahn, a consummate craftsman, was baseball's winningest lefty.

The continuity, along with this additional insight, was explored in Roger Kahn's *The Head Game*[26]:

> Until Spahn won his three hundredth game, in 1961, the idea of winning three hundred had become dubious. Up to that moment in Milwaukee County Stadium twelve men had won three hundred major league games, but just six — Cy Young, Mathewson, Eddie Plank, Walter Johnson, Grover Cleveland Alexander, and Lefty Grove — pitched in the twentieth century. Grove won his three hundredth and last game in 1941. That, some concluded, was that. The three hundred game winner, like the legal spitter and the New Deal, was history.

Well, not quite. In 1942 Warren Spahn came along and, after time out for World War II, proceeded to pile up the numbers that led to August 11, 1961. Beyond Milwaukee's ace, however, there came another seven who notched 300 before the 20th century breathed its last. And as for continuity, Milwaukee's great portsider picked up where Grove left off. The exploration of that lively and colorful sojourn lies directly ahead.

Eleven Hall of Famers and three other great hurlers in the list below were active at some time during Warren Spahn's career:

Name/HOF Election	Debut/Career Years	TPI/All Time Pitching Rating
*Carl Hubbell, 1947	Jul 26, 1928/1928–1943	41.4/14
Murry Dickson	Sep 30, 1939/1939–1959	19.5/105
Harry Brecheen	Apr 22, 1940/1940–1953	25.0/66
Robin Roberts 1976	Jun 18, 1948/1948–1966	25.9/59
Don Newcombe	Jun 20, 1949/1949–1960	18.4/119
Sandy Koufax 1972	Jun 24, 1955/1955–1966	20.5/96
Jim Bunning 1996	Jul 20, 1966/1966–1971	13.4/193
Don Drysdale 1984	Apr 17, 1956/1956–1969	34.6/26
Bob Gibson 1981	Apr 15, 1959/1959–1975	43.7/13
Juan Marichal 1983	Jul 19, 1960/1960–1975	29.5/39
*Gaylord Perry 1991	Apr 14, 1962/1962–1983	34.9/24
*Phil Niekro 1997	Apr 15, 1964/1964–1987	33.8/27
*Steve Carlton 1994	Apr 12, 1965/1965–1988	33.7/28
*Ferguson Jenkins 1991	Sep 10, 1965/1965–1983	29.8/38

Warren Spahn versus Carl "The Mealticket" or "King Carl" Hubbell (1903–1988)

Hubbell was elected to the Baseball Hall of Fame in 1947

Carl Hubbell, like his contemporary, Lefty Grove, was one of the game's

---

* Active during Spahn's career but did not appear against him.

premier lefthanders. His election to the Hall of Fame in 1947, four scant seasons after his final campaign, came at the very first opportunity the BBWAA had to acknowledge his stellar career, a telltale indication of his stature among the game's elite. Like Grove in the AL, Hubbell was the NL's link between baseball's earlier days (his duels with Pete Alexander were detailed in the Alexander profile) and the second half of the 20th century. As such, it seems appropriate to begin the Warren Spahn story with the master of the screwball, the great New York Giant they called the Mealticket. Spahnie's career, in turn, spans the 1942–1965 era.

Four of the hurlers on the Spahn honor list were active during his career but did not pitch against him. One of them was Carl Hubbell. Nonetheless, if a doubleheader in which both Spahn and Hubbell appeared can suffice at least partially to satisfy the profile requirement, there is a date in baseball history that will fill the bill. That date, marked by extraordinary events, was September 26, 1942.

It was a day that was noteworthy if for no other reason than that two of the game's most impressive Hall of Famers were on display in a twinbill at the Polo Grounds, though it must be admitted that the Braves' young southpaw, Warren Spahn, in his very first major league starting assignment, would have to prove his worth in the years to come. The other southpaw, King Carl Hubbell, in his penultimate season, had already earned his Cooperstown credentials as he took the hill against the visiting Bostons in the doubleheader opener.

In the twinbill curtain raiser the Mealticket hung on long enough, aided by Johnny Mize and Mel Ott circuit smashes, to subdue the Braves 6 to 4. It was Hubbell's 249th major league victory, with the last four to follow during his last season, 1943.

The extraordinary feature of the day occurred during the nightcap in a game that found the Braves losing 5 to 2 as Spahnie took his warmups for the last of the eighth inning. At that point the stands emptied, inexplicably, as

Carl Hubbell.

204 What Makes an Elite Pitcher?

hundreds of youngsters scrambled over the playing field, totally out of control and no doubt driven by youthful exuberance. And, despite the best efforts of the Polo Grounds' ushers and guards, who tried frantically to restore order, the riot roared on. The game had to be called and, under league rules, Boston was declared a 9–0 forfeit winner. That didn't mean that, even though Spahn was the pitcher for the winning team, he would also be declared the winning pitcher of his first major league start. League rules specified that there were to be no pitchers of record, even though all the hitting and pitching records of the day would count. That also meant, incidentally, that Spahn's third inning single would count, ultimately adding to the 363 hits he made during his career, a number that matched — exactly — his 363 victories.

There would be no more Spahn starts until 1946. Uncle Sam saw to that. One wonders how many times during his service hitch Warren Spahn's mind drifted back to that late September afternoon at the Polo Grounds, recalling what had to be one of the more bizarre days of his career. But such was the start of one of the game's masters, even as another was making his way to the end of the line, in the midst of that worldwide conflagration known as World War II. The doubleheader box score follows:

Forfeit Gives Braves a Split at the Polo Grounds
September 25, 1942, Game 1

Boston	AB	R	H	PO	New York	AB	R	H	PO
Holmes, cf	4	1	1	2	Bartell, ss	5	0	1	0
Roberge, 2b	4	0	0	2	Witek, 2b	4	0	0	0
Fernandez, lf	4	0	1	2	Ott, rf	2	4	2	1
Lombardi, c	4	1	2	3	Mize, 1b	4	2	4	15
McElyea, pr	0	0	0	0	Young, cf	2	0	1	2
Klutz, c	0	0	0	2	Maynard, lf	4	0	2	2
Ross, rf	4	0	0	1	S. Gordon, 2b	4	0	0	1
West, 1b	4	0	1	11	Mancuso, c	3	0	0	6
Wietelmann, ss	3	1	1	1	**Hubbell (WP)**	4	0	0	0
Gremp, ph	1	0	0	0					
Donovan (LP)	1	1	1	0					
Sain, p	1	0	0	0					
Totals	34	4	8	24	Totals	32	6	10	27

Line Score: Boston   003 001 000   4–8–0
             New York   201 020 01x   6–10–0

September 25, 1942, Game 2

Boston	AB	R	H	PO	New York	AB	R	H	PO
Holmes, rf	3	1	1	0	Bartell, ss	3	1	1	2
Roberge, 2b	4	0	1	3	Witek, 2b	3	2	1	1
P. Waner, rf	4	0	1	3	Maynard, rf	3	1	2	3

Fernandez, rf	4	0	1	1	Mize, 1b	4	0	1	12
West, 1b	2	0	0	7	Young, cf	4	0	1	4
Klutz, c	3	0	0	4	Barna, lf	4	0	1	1
Detweiler, 3b	3	0	0	1	S. Gordon, 2b	2	1	1	0
Wietelmann, ss	3	0	0	2	Fox, c	2	0	0	1
Spahn, p (ND)	3	1	1	0	Carpenter, p (ND)	2	0	1	0
Totals	29	2	6	21*	Totals	27	5	10	24

Line Score	Boston	001	000	01	4–8–0
	New York	200	100	2	5–10–0

Warren Spahn versus Murry Monroe Dickson (1916–1989)

Kenny Boyer, Cardinal third-baseman who roomed with Murry Dickson, claimed that he drank coffee all day long and ate once a week. Those in baseball who knew him, knew that the only thing he did during the rest of the week was pitch. The little righthander from Tracy, Missouri, had a half dozen pitches, a sneaky fast heater and a passion to play. And he had something in common with a great many fine ball players who put in productive major league careers across a span of more seasons than their native abilities really should have allowed: Dickson, among those, was a survivor.

Murry Dickson's first survival test was to get through Branch Rickey's far-flung minor league empire, where he toiled with who knows how many St. Louis Cardinal wannabes. The difference between Dickson and 97 percent of the others was that he kept at it like a feisty fox terrier until he wrangled a chance to show his stuff for the big team in late 1939 and again in 1940. But manager Ray Blades and his staff didn't see enough to persuade them that Dickson belonged. Undaunted, Dickson went back to the minors, paced the Columbus Red Birds to the American Association championship in 1941 with 21 wins, wound up on the Cardinal

Winner in double figures a dozen times, Murry Dickson gave it all he had in a 16-year career.

*Game forfeited (9–0) to Boston after 8½ innings played.

varsity squad for the 1943 season, and that year recorded his first six of 172 career wins. By this time he was going on 26, and, like many another service-eligible ball player, found out that Uncle Sam needed him more than the Cardinals, interrupting his career for the next two years.

Finally, in 1946, Murry Dickson set sail in earnest on his career, back just in time to celebrate his 30th birthday with the pennant-winning Cardinals, who went on to win the World Series on the back of Enos Slaughter's "mad dash" to victory in game seven of that exciting series. And who was the starting pitcher in that historic game? It was Mr. Dickson, who got two-deep into the eighth inning before being relieved by Harry Brecheen, the ultimate victor. That's just about the sum and substance of Dickson's career: very good, but rarely in the spotlight as "the Big Winner." Not many remember that Dickson's winning percentage of .714, based on his 15 and 6 won-loss record, was the NL's best for 1946. His 2.88 ERA that year was a career low and ranked right up there among the league leaders.

It was in 1947 that Murry Dickson and Warren Spahn got together for the first of their 16 duels (making Dickson the most frequently matched pitcher against Spahnie among those reviewed in his profile). Their May 4 engagement wound up in a 4 to 3 victory for Spahn, who pitched just a shade better than Dickson, giving up but four hits before leaving in favor of reliever Andy Karl. Later that summer Spahnie threw a shutout at Dickson and his Cardinals, the first of two in the series. The second came in the opening game of a May 6, 1951, doubleheader at Boston, when Spahn blanked the Pirates (who had picked up Dickson in a 1949 trade) by a 6 to 0 score. Spahn picked the right game to pitch, because in the second of the two tilts Cliff Chambers dished up a no-hitter to beat the Braves 3-zip as the Pirate lefty got out of one jam after another, issuing eight free passes while striking out four.

Although the series record read Spahn, nine wins, five losses and two No Decision, and Dickson, five victories against eight losses and three No Decisions, Dickson pitched well throughout and turned in an outstanding game for the Phillies on June 24, 1954, when he shut down the big Milwaukee Brewer bats of Hank Aaron and Eddie Mathews to beat the Brewers 2 to 1 in a game that Spahn entered in the ninth frame, relieving for Gene Conley, the tall and lean Braves righthander. Rather than Spahn earning a Save that day, the Phils promptly hung a two-spot on Spahnie, scoring two to overcome a 1–0, Brewer lead. The 2 to 1 victory was characteristic of Dickson's career. Hang on. Survive, right on down to the 11th hour.

Murry Dickson's NL career was divided among three teams, most of it with the Cards, along with a five year hitch in Pittsburgh where he won 20 in 1951 and lost 21 in 1952, and a three year stay in Philadelphia with Robin Roberts & Co. in 1954, '55 and '56. He finished his career in the AL with

Kansas City and New York, enabling him to get into another world series in 1958 (used as a reliever by Casey Stengel in games two and four). It was in the fourth game of the series that he confronted Warren Spahn once more, closing out the game with a run-less ninth inning in a game in which Spahnie stifled the Yankees with two hits in a 2 to 0 masterpiece. But Dickson picked up the winner's share in the series as the Yanks beat Spahn's Braves in seven games. That might well have been Murry Dickson's "balm in Milwaukee" after his many heartbreaks in the NL.

It came just in time. Dickson pitched his final major league innings in Kansas City, close to his hometown just up the road, with a 2 and 1 encore in 1959. The fellow Joe Garagiola called "Edison" because of his creative approach to pitching, featuring so many different pitches and speeds that catchers didn't have enough fingers for signals, had finally used them all up, and at 43 he reluctantly retired. He had dueled with a number of future Hall of Famers, one of them Warren Spahn during his great Milwaukee years, had his share of success, and settled down to more than the meal a week Kenny Boyer allotted him during the early days of his career. In Missouri you have to show 'em, and Missouri's own Murry Dickson was one of those. He had to be shown he didn't belong and doggone if he didn't stick — for almost 20 years of big league class.

The Spahn-Dickson Log:

May 4, 1947	Boston 4, St. Louis 3	Spahn WP, Dickson LP
Jul 16, 1947	Boston 3, St. Louis 0	Spahn WP, Dickson LP
Sep 18, 1947	Boston 6, St. Louis 2	Spahn WP, Dickson LP
May 9, 1948	St. Louis 6, Boston 4	Dickson WP, Spahn LP
May 21, 1949	Boston 8, Pittsburgh 2	Spahn WP, Dickson LP
May 2, 1950	Pittsburgh 6, Boston 1	Dickson WP, Spahn LP
Jul 18, 1950	Boston 11, Pittsburgh 2	Spahn WP, Dickson LP
May 6, 1951	Boston 6, Pittsburgh 0	Spahn WP, Dickson LP
Jul 28, 1951	Pittsburgh 8, Boston 4	Dickson WP, Spahn LP
Jul 25, 1952	Pittsburgh 3, Boston 2	Dickson WP, Spahn LP
May 19, 1954	Milwaukee 6, Philadelphia 2	Spahn WP, Dickson LP
Jun 13, 1954	Milwaukee 9, Philadelphia 5	Spahn WP, Dickson LP
Sep 12, 1954	Philadelphia 5, Milwaukee 2	Dickson WP, Spahn LP

Alpha Brazle (LP) relieved Dickson (ND) in a game won by Boston, 9 to 6. Warren Spahn pitched a complete game to get the win against St. Louis on June 24, 1947.

Rip Sewell, the famous Ephus Ball pitcher, relieved Dickson (ND), who had started on June 15, 1949, and got credit for the Pirates' 8 to 7 win over Spahn's Braves. Spahnie had started (ND) against Pittsburgh's Bill "Bugs" Werle (ND). Reliever Vic Lombardi was tagged with the loss.

On June 27, 1954, the Phillies beat the Braves 2 to 1. Dickson started that game (ND), but reliever Steve Ridzik picked up the win. Gene Conley started for the Braves, gave way to Spahn after the eighth inning, and Spahn received the loss.

Warren Spahn versus Harry "the Cat" Brecheen (1914–)

Spahn and Brecheen in NL Heartbreaker at
Wrigley Field, Chicago, July 8, 1947

American League	000	001	100	2-8-0
National League	000	100	000	1-5-1

Americans	AB	R	H	PO	Nationals	AB	R	H	PO
Kell (Det), 3b	4	0	0	0	H. Walker (Pit), cf	2	0	0	1
Johnson (NY), 3b	0	0	0	0	Pafko (Chi), cf	2	0	1	2
Lewis (Wash), rf	2	0	0	1	F. Walker (Brk), rf	2	0	0	1
Appling (Chi), ph	1	1	1	0	Marshall (NY), rf	1	0	0	3
Henrich (NY), rf	1	0	0	3	W. Cooper (NY), c	3	0	0	6
Williams (Bos), lf	4	0	2	3	Edwards (Brk), c	0	0	0	2
J. DiMaggio (NY), cf	3	0	1	1	Cavaretta (Chi), 1b	1	0	0	1
Boudreau (Clv), ss	4	0	1	4	Mize (NY), 1b	3	1	2	8
McQuinn (NY), 1b	4	0	0	9	Masi (Bos), c	0	0	0	0
Gordon (NY), 2b	2	0	1	0	Slaughter (StL), lf	3	0	0	1
Doerr (Bos), 2b	2	1	1	0	Gustine (Pit), 3b	2	0	0	0
Rosar (Phil), c	4	0	0	6	Kurowski (StL), 3b	2	0	0	0
Newhouser (Det), p	1	0	0	0	Marion (StL), ss	2	0	1	0
Shea (NY), (WP)	1	0	0	0	Reese (Brk), ss	1	0	0	0
Soence (Wash), ph	1	0	1	0	Verban (StL), 2b	2	0	0	0
Masterson (Wash), p	0	0	0	0	Stanky (Brk), 2b	2	0	0	2
Page (NY), p	0	0	0	0	Blackwell (Cin), p	0	0	0	0
					Haas (Cin), ph	1	0	1	0
					Brecheen (StL), p	1	0	0	0
					Sain (Bos), (LP)	0	0	0	0
					Musial (StL), ph	1	0	0	0
					Spahn (Bos), p	0	0	0	0
					Rowe (Phil), ph	1	0	0	0
Totals	34	2	8	27	Totals	32	1	5	27

2BH: Williams, Gordon; Home Run: Mize; SB, Doerr; DP: Reese, Stanky and Mize; Wild Pitch: Blackwell; Passed Ball: W. Cooper; LOB: Americans 6, Nationals 8; Strike Outs: Newhouser and Page 0, Sain and Spahn 1, Brecheen and Shea 2; Blackwell 4; BB: Newhouser, Blackwell, Brecheen, Sain 0; Spahn, Masterson, Page 1; Shea 2; Umpires: Boyer and Passarella (AL), Conlan and Henline (NL); Time: 2:19; Attendance: 41,123.

Warren Spahn and Harry Brecheen were on the same side in one of the more dramatic All-Star games on record. Though knicked for the run that tied the game, "the Cat," Harry Brecheen, delivered three creditable innings for his manager, Eddie Dyer, and for a National League contingent that found itself next to helpless in the face of four Junior Circuit hurlers, led by Frank "Spec" Shea, the game's first rookie winner, except for a home run shot by Johnny Mize halfway up into the right field stands. Spahn's partner, Johnny Sain, gave up the run that proved to be the winner on a Stan Spence single that scored Bobby Doerr in the top of the seventh. Spahnie finished up with two near-flawless innings, but the NL stars couldn't solve Joe Page's offerings in relief of the Senators' Walt Masterson and went down to their 10th defeat in 14 games.

Who was this fellow they called "the Cat"? Harry Brecheen was a tough little customer who stuck with it tenaciously through a dozen major league campaigns of top drawer pitching. His hero was Carl Hubbell, and the two had a thing or two in common. They were both lefties, both featured the screwball, both fielded their position (Brecheen with cat-like quickness) like shortstops, both pitched in baseball's glossy showcase, the world series, and both used their brains as much as their arms on the mound. King Carl, of course, wound up in the Hall, and though Harry Brecheen hasn't, and probably never will, his career rank, up there at number 66 with a lifetime 25.0 TPI, is better than a number of the Hall's more famous pitchers, suggesting the closer look accorded here in the Warren Spahn collection of noteworthy competitors. Brecheen also happens to be the first moundsman Spahn met among the 14 worthies assembled, including 11 from the Hall, plus Murry Dickson, Don Newcombe and one of Eddie Dyer's favorite ball players, Brecheen. That initial confrontation took place on July 27, 1946, before 33,732 Braves fans, and was won by Boston, 5 to 2, in the first of their five series matchups. In the four that followed, the two lefties split at two and two.

The Spahn-Brecheen Log:

Jul 27, 1946	Boston 5, St. Louis 2	Spahn WP, Brecheen LP
May 21, 1948	Boston 3, St. Louis 1	Spahn WP, Brecheen LP
Aug 1, 1949	Boston 8, St. Louis 1	Spahn WP, Brecheen LP
Jun 10, 1951	St. Louis 5, Boston 4	Brecheen WP, Spahn LP
Jun 22, 1952	St. Louis 8, Boston 1	Brecheen WP, Spahn LP

One of Harry Brecheen's losses during his best major league season, 1948, came at the hands of Spahn, who bested him in a tight, 3 to 1 game at Boston. On a rainy night in Beantown, Brecheen went six innings, giving up four hits and allowing two of the Braves' three runs, all of them unearned, incidentally. The only Cardinal tally came on a Musial four-bagger, ruining Spahnie's shutout bid in the eighth stanza. Spahn's old tormentor, "the Man," waited just a little too long to help "the Cat" along.

Brecheen recovered from that loss, moving on to a 20 and 7 season with league leading numbers in shutouts (seven), an ERA at 2.24, strikeouts (149), a very low 9.4 ratio, and a .265 opponents' on-base percentage. His 5.3 TPI that year was topped only by 24-game winner Johnny Sain's 5.4 during a season that brought "Spahn and Sain and pray for rain" to the baseball lexicon.

By 1948 Harry Brecheen was already in his mid–30s, having had a late

"The Cat," Harry Brecheen, was a smart lefty who beat his opponents with his brains and an assortment of pitches that consistently hit the black edges of home plate.

start with the Cardinals. During the late 1930s Max Lanier, Al Brazle, Ernie White, Preacher Roe and Brecheen, all portsiders (and each with big years either for the Cardinals at some time during the '40s, or, in Roe's case, with those "Boys of Summer Dodgers" during the 1950s), competed for the one or two starting lefty slots on the pitching staff. Manager Eddie Dyer had a soft spot in his heart for the little battler from Broken Bow, Oklahoma, who had pitched for him in 1938 when, with Houston, he fashioned an 18 and 4 record with four shutouts. Dyer saw to it that when he picked up the managerial reins in 1946, Brecheen was a part of the Cardinals' starting rotation. "The Cat" gave Dyer no reason to regret it.

The most famous Brecheen scenario took place in the 1946 world series when he came on in the eighth inning to win the series-winning game with two innings of relief for Murry Dickson, who had started. With the win, he became the first lefthander to win three world series games. There would have been no world series heroics, however, without his victory over Brooklyn at Ebbets Field in the second game of a best-two-of-three series in the 1946 pennant playoffs. In this one he preserved Dickson's win with ⅔ of an inning of relief in the ninth, striking out both Eddie Stanky and Howie Schultz to end the game that sent the Cardinals to the world series. Coincidentally, the Dickson-Brecheen tandem appears one-two in the Spahn profile.

For those who might not have noticed: Harry Brecheen *does* hold one major league record that will be tough to beat. He owns the number one spot among pitchers with 30 or more innings in world series play, having left behind an 0.83 ERA. Surprising? Now then, who is the runner-up? Babe Ruth, with his 0.87. Equally surprising!

A Spahn Special: Spahnie, the Man and the Say Hey Kid

On July 11, 1961, Danny Murtaugh, manager of the NL All-Star team, named 40year-old Warren Spahn to start against Whitey Ford at Candlestick Park in San Francisco in the 29th renewal of baseball's summer classic. Spahn, in the midst of his eleventh, 20-game season, responded with three perfect innings that got the Senior Circuit off to a good start in a game that wound up going ten innings before the Murtaugh charges beat Casey Stengel's crew 5 to 4. Two NL mainstays backed up Spahnie. Stan the Man Musial, veteran Cardinal superstar, and mercurial Willie Mays, the Say Hey Kid, were in the lineup to help pack the offensive punch that complimented those crisp, razor sharp offerings of the amazing Brewer southpaw who, like Ol' Man River, just kept rolling along.

The 1961 contest marked the fourth time this peerless threesome had appeared together as teammates in an All-Star game — the first in 1954, followed by games in 1956 and 1958. The last time at least two of them were together as teammates occurred during the final days of Spahnie's career with the San Francisco Giants. On one of the more memorable occasions during the Old Master's last trip around the Senior Circuit, he beat his former teammate Bob Buhl, then with the Chicago Cubs, on September 12, 1965, at "the Stick" for his 363rd and final major league conquest. Backed by the irrepressible Mays, Spahnie threw a complete game at the Cubbies, beating them 9 to 2. The only runs scored by the Cubs came on homers by first baseman Johnny Boccabella. There was one other tater in that ball game. Guess who? Right — Say Hey hit a two-run shot that put the game out of reach for the Bruins, at least on that day and with Warren Spahn on the hill. The box score follows.

Spahn Wins No. 363 at San Francisco, September 12, 1965

Chicago	AB	R	H	BI	San Francisco	AB	R	H	BI
Young, cf	4	0	0	0	Schofield, ss	5	1	2	0
Abernathy, p	0	0	0	0	Alou, J, rf	5	1	2	2
Beckert, 2b	4	0	0	0	Henderson, pr, cf	0	1	0	0
Williams, B, rf	4	0	1	0	Mays, cf	5	1	1	2
Santo, 3b	4	0	1	0	Alou, M, rf	0	0	0	0
Boccabella, 1b	4	2	2	2	McCovey, 1b	2	2	0	0
Browne, B, lf	2	0	0	0	Burda, 1b	0	0	0	0
Hoeft, p	0	0	0	0	Hart, 3b	5	0	2	1
Campbell, R, ph	1	0	0	0	Davenport, 3b	0	0	0	0
McDaniel, L, p	0	0	0	0	Gabrielson, lf	3	1	1	0
Landrum, cf	0	0	0	0	Haller, c	2	0	0	0
Banks, ph	1	0	0	0	Lanier, H, 2b	4	1	2	2
Krug, c	3	0	0	0	Spahn (WP)	3	1	1	1
Stewart, ss	4	0	2	0					

Musial (.314) and Mays (.322) hit Spahnie better than most, but it was always a down-on-the-mat at bat when Spahn was pitching.

Buhl, (LP)	1	0	0	0						
Kuenn, ph, lf	2	0	1	0						
Totals	34	2	7	2	Totals			34	9	11	8
Line score:	Chicago				010	000	001	2–7–3		
	San Francisco				022	001	04x	9–11–0		

2BH: Lanier 2, Kuenn, Alou, J; HR: Boccabella 2, Mays; SF: Spahn; LOB: Chicago

7, San Francisco 8; K: Buhl and Spahn 4, Hoeft and McDaniel 1, Abernathy 0; BB: Buhl 5, Spahn 2, Hoeft and McDaniel 1, Abernathy 0; Wild Pitch: Buhl; Time: 2:05; Attendance: 41,070.

But this Spahn Special is not really about teammates. Instead, as in the matchups featuring Walter Johnson, Babe Ruth and Ty Cobb, this one pits the two greatest NL players of the Spahn era, Musial and Mays, against Spahn. First, then, to review some of the pertinent career numbers logged by Musial (15th highest TPR rating) and Mays (3rd, all time):

	Yrs/GP	Hits	HR	RBI/gm	OPS*	RP†	BA	TPR
Stan Musial	22/3026	3630/4	475/20	.645/91	977/11	3425/5	.331/28	71.4
Willie Mays	22/2992	3283/10	660/3	.636/23	944/23	3305/5	.302/NR	95.9

Numbers behind slash marks (above) indicate all time ranking positions. NR: that particular number or average is not among the top 100 rated.

Stan Musial and Warren Spahn competed against one another across a span of 18 eventful seasons (1946–1963) in one of the more celebrated matchups in the annals of the game. Subject of numerous articles and comparative statistics, the two waged friendly war — always with great respect and admiration for each other's superb talent and productivity — and always in the upper stratum of baseball competition.

Shortly before the end of his career, Spahn discussed his years of friendly rivalry with St. Louis' all time favorite with sports scribe Joe Reichler. Let Reichler tell it:

> I'll show you how much respect I had for Musial as a hitter. He was the only batter I intentionally walked with the bases loaded. There were two out and the count on Musial went to three and two. I wasn't going to give him anything good. The next pitch was well outside, and he walked, forcing in a run. We won the game 2 to 1. If I'd given Musial a good pitch, we'd probably have lost...
>
> You know what made Musial better than the rest? Desire and concentration. He never ceased to amaze me. I never did discover a weakness in his batting style. He had the most unorthodox stance I ever saw, but I can't recall one instance when he hit the ball without getting the fat part of the bat on it.[27]

---

*OPS (batter's On Base percentage, plus SA) is calculated by adding On Base Percentage and Slugging Average, and indicates the level of the batter's skill in getting on base and in producing runs. The sum is known as Production. Babe Ruth is the all time leader in this category, with a record of 1164, some 200 points higher than Musial and Mays.

†RP (Runs Produced) is calculated by adding a batter's RBI and Runs Scored, and subtracting from the sum his home runs. Ty Cobb was instrumental in producing more runs than any player in the game's history (4067). Musial ranks 5th and Mays 9th in this category.

The numbers above, merely scratching the surface of Musial's prodigious output over 22 seasons of big league ball, are not nearly as impressive as the Man himself. Self-effacing and team-oriented, he played more than 3000 ball games and nailed opposing pitchers for a base hit per game-plus. "Stosh," as he was often called, rewrote the Cardinals' record book, and put his name on the major leagues' all time list somewhere among the top five in nine major hitting departments, most notably at number two in extra base hits and in total bases, and at number three in runs created and in doubles.

Against the game's winningest lefthander he hit .314, 70 points higher than the other NL hitters averaged. But there were those days when Spahn had the better of it, enough O-fers to remind Number Six that as good as he was, the fellow out there on the hill was a craftsman of exceptional ability who could send the best of them back to the bench, including Musial, mumbling to himself about whatever happened to that famous Spahn screwball between the mound and the plate. Reflecting on some of those tough at bats he suffered on Spahn's better days, the Man said, "[Spahn was] the best pitcher and one of the great athletes of my era. Spahnie knew everything about his profession, and he was smart enough to change before he had to. In the early years he had the good high fast ball, a nice change, terrific control inside the strike zone, but only a fair curve. A lot of pitchers would have stayed where they were. Not Spahn. He began tinkering with a screwball, and as the fast ball began to go, he'd come at you with the screwjie." Those are the adjustments of a smart cookie. That's what made Spahn, Spahn.

The end of the line came for Stan Musial in 1963, and on September 13 of that year he took that strange, peek-a-boo stance of his against Spahn for the last time. On his last time up against Spahnie he did the very same thing he did in his first appearance against him back in June of 1946. He doubled. As some wag put it, "He sure didn't improve much!"

Several days later the Man wound up his career with a day St. Louisans never forgot. On that day he did what he could do best. He had two farewell bingos to give the fans a memory or two before lapping the park and saying adieu.

And then there was the Say Hey Kid. A headache if ever you saw one — both with a club in his hands and out there in the outfield. And that is to say nothing about the things that happened when he got on base. Here was a ball player who could beat you — regularly — in a hundred different ways. His name was Willie Mays and he roamed the fields of green for 22 seasons, the same number as Stan Musial. During 12½ of those seasons he matched wits with Warren Spahn, and during the latter part of Spahn's last year, he made those signature basket-catches behind him.

One of the more interesting quotes about Wondrous Willie came from Warren Spahn: "He [Mays] was something like 0 for 21 the first time I saw him. His first major league hit was a home run off me — and I'll never forgive myself. We might have gotten rid of Willie forever if I'd only struck him out."

Spahn didn't, of course, and the rest became one of the most enchanting chapters in baseball's history book. From 1951 to 1965, with time out for military service in 1953, Mays and Spahn found the time to chase each other from ball park to ball park, coast to coast, etching memories of unbelievable baseball mastery into the minds of fans and writers and their contemporaries whenever they met. They were the kind of players who caused seasoned veterans to drop everything in pre-game drills just to get a glimpse of their magic at work. And when the game started the fun *really* began.

One of those days when Willie had himself nine innings of fun came on April 30, 1961, a day when Mays even outdid the Mays of incredible achievements. To put that day in perspective, it might be well to note that only two days before he had been collared, as Spahn, in a masterful display of pitching artistry, no-hit the Giants in a tense 1 to 0 shutout, disposing of Willie with what Spahnie felt was uncommon ease, causing him to remark that he could tell something was bothering Willie. "He even looked as though he was having trouble holding up the bat," said Spahn. As a matter of fact, Mays did. He had been having digestive and stomach problems, and even though he played through his discomfort, he was definitely not up to par. Nor was he any better the morning of April 30. In fact, his roomie, Willie McCovey, and Giants trainer Dr. Bowman had all they could do to get Willie into uniform, something Mays insisted on because, after all, there was a game to play.

Willie Mays felt a little better — fast — after his first time up. A home run off Milwaukee's Bob Buhl would have that kind of effect. Warming to the task, things just got better and better as the Say Hey Kid kept right on jerking one after another out of County Stadium until the number got up to four, tying the major league mark. His last two cannon shots passed the 450 foot mark as they settled into the far reaches of Milwaukee's outfield stands. Of the 660 dingers he hit in his electrifying career, those four not only topped them all, they were just what the doctor ordered.

Warren Spahn faced the Giants 73 times between Willie Mays' arrival on the big league scene in 1951 and 1965, Spahnie's last year. During that time the Say Hey Kid logged 258 at bats and 83 base hits (his .322 average is very close to Musial's .314 against Spahn), 21 of which found the seats, including one of the most dramatic of his career. That one came in the 16th inning of one of the great pitching duels in the game's annals, matching the 42-year-old Spahn against Juan Marichal,[28] who, at 25, was into the fourth season of what would turn out to be a Hall of Fame career. In the bottom half of the 16th, Willie was the Giants' leadoff hitter, and he put the ball and the game out of reach with a shot that topped off Marichal's shutout, 1 to 0.

At San Francisco, July 2, 1963

Milwaukee	AB	R	H	BI	San Francisco	AB	R	H	BI
Maye, lf	6	0	0	0	Kuenn, 3b	7	0	1	0
Bolling, 2b	7	0	2	0	Mays, cf	6	1	1	1
Aaron, rf	6	0	0	0	McCovey, lf	6	0	1	0
Mathews, 3b	2	0	0	0	F. Alou, rf	6	0	1	0
Menke, 3b	5	0	2	0	Cepeda, 1b	6	0	2	0
Larker, 1b	5	0	0	0	Bailey, c	6	0	1	0
Jones, cf	5	0	1	0	Pagan, ss	2	0	0	0
Dillard, ph, cf	1	0	0	0	Davenport, ph	1	0	0	0
Crandall, c	6	0	2	0	Bowman, ss	3	0	2	0
McMillan, ss	6	0	0	0	Hiller, 2b	6	0	0	0
Spahn, (LP)	6	0	1	0	Marichal, (WP)	6	0	0	0
Totals	55	0	8	0	Totals	55	1	9	1

Line Score								
Milwaukee	000	000	000	000	000	0	0–8–1
San Francisco	000	000	000	000	000	1	1–9–1

2BH: Spahn, Kuenn; HR: Mays; SB: Cepeda, Maye, Menke; LOB: Milwaukee 11; San Francisco 9; K: Spahn 2, Marichal 10: BB: Spahn 1 Marichal 4; Umpires: Burkhart, Pelekoudas, Walsh, Conlan; Time: 4:10; Att: 15,921.

Mays wasn't quite as fortunate in Spahn's first 1961 effort against the San Franciscans. Just as the season was getting into full swing, Spahnie followed his September 16, 1960, no-hitter with another, this one at Milwaukee, in a taut, 1 to 0 thriller that was over, for all practical purposes, in the first inning, when Hank Aaron drove home Milt Bolling with the only run of the game.

Mays, including all of his Giant teammates, went for the collar that raw evening in Milwaukee, as Spahn posted his 290th victory and 52nd shutout, increasing the major league shutout record for lefthanders.

At Milwaukee, April 28, 1961

San Francisco	AB	R	H	BI	Milwaukee	AB	R	H	B
Hiller, 2b	2	0	0	0	McMillan, ss	3	0	0	0
Kuenn, 3b	3	0	0	0	Bolling, 2b	3	1	2	0
Mays, cf	3	0	0	0	Mathews, 3b	3	0	0	0
McCovey, 1b	2	0	0	0	Aaron, cf	3	0	1	1
Cepeda, lf	3	0	0	0	Roach, lf	4	0	1	0
F. Alou, rf	3	0	0	0	Spangler, lf	0	0	0	0
Bailey, c	3	0	0	0	Adcock, 1b	3	0	1	0
Pagan, ss	2	0	0	0	Lau, c	2	0	0	0
M. Alou, ph	1	0	0	0	DeMerit, rf	4	0	0	0
S, Jones (LP)	2	0	0	0	Spahn (WP)	4	0	0	0
Amalfitano, ph	1	0	0	0					
Totals	25	0	0	0	Totals	29	1	5	1

Line Score	San Francisco	000	000	000	0–0–1
	Milwaukee	100	000	000	1–5–0

HPB: Bolling by Jones; DP: Spahn, McMillan and Adcock, 2; SH: McMillan; LOB: Milwaukee 11, San Francisco 5; K: Jones 9, Spahn 5; BB: Jones 5, Spahn 2; Umpires: Donatelli, Burkhart, Pelekoudas, Forman, Conlan; Time: 2:16; Att: 8,518.

In 1998 *The Sporting News* came out with *Baseball's Greatest Players*, a book, said *TSN*, that celebrated the 20th century's best. Written by Ron Smith, the book also featured an Introduction by the Say Hey Kid himself. Smith and his *TSN* friends took on the daunting challenge of ranking the top 100 players, including Negro League players, in its all time, all star cast. Willie Mays took second place in the prestigious top-3 ranking spots, right behind Babe Ruth and ahead of Ty Cobb. Not too far behind was Stan the Man, who rounded out the top ten players in the game's history through 1998. Warren Spahn was rated the top lefty in the number 21 spot overall, the fifth best pitcher overall behind Mathewson (rated 7th), Alexander (12), Cy Young (14) and Satch Paige (19). The Premier Lefthanders list below presents both *TSN* ratings and *TBE*'s sabermetric ratings for all pitchers, including starters and relievers. You will want to compare these with your own list of baseball's top portsiders. The legend for the list follows:

SNRO   *Sporting News* Rank Overall
SLHR   *TSN* Lefthanded Pitchers Rank
TBTPI   *Total Baseball Encyclopedia*'s Total Pitcher Index rating
TBLR   *TBE*'s Lefthanded Pitchers Rank

Premier Lefthanders

	SNRO	**SLHR**	**TBTPI**	**TBLR***
Spahn	21	1	50.2	2
Grove	23	2	59.7	1
Koufax	26	3	20.5	20
Carlton	30	4	33.7	6
Hubbell	45	5	41.1	3
Ford	52	6	39.2	5
Plank	68	7	26.9	10
Gomez	73	8	19.9	24

Not bad at all...Having Mays, Musial and Spahn on the same ball diamond at the same time was one of those rare treats that fans treasured for a lifetime. These three titans followed in the footsteps of Walter Johnson, Babe

---

* Hal Newhouser (TBE number 4, 39.3 career TPI), Randy Johnson (31.8/7), Tom Glavine (8/30.9) and John Franco (29.5/9) are the lefthanders who complete *TBE*'s top 10 through the 2000 season.

Ruth and Ty Cobb, and added to the legacy left behind for a later day when Greg Maddux, Jeff Bagwell and Barry Bonds took up the cudgel of excellence for their own generation.

Warren Spahn versus Robin Evan Roberts (1926–)
Roberts was elected to the Baseball Hall of Fame in 1976

A 17-year-old rookie sensation, much in demand because he could throw baseballs at breathtaking speeds, was called on by the Illinois State Amateur Baseball Association to throw out the first ball at its 1936 state baseball championships. His name was Bobby Feller, who that summer debuted with 62 innings of work for the Cleveland Indians, striking out 76 while winning five and losing three. The young man was the talk of the baseball world. Not much older than the youngsters playing in the Association's championship game, he was an ideal choice for first ball honors.

That day Robin Roberts was Johnny-on-the-Spot, getting Feller to sign the ceremonial ball. Only ten, he had already been touched by fate on a course that would ultimately lead to the very same Hall of Fame that would honor Rapid Robert with a plaque in 1962. Some years later Robin Roberts helped the Hall of Fame celebrate America's bicentennial year with his own induction into the Hall. 40 years after that championship day in Illinois the cycle had come full circle for Springfield, Illinois', most famous baseball player.

Robin Roberts made his way through 19 seasons of distinguished hurling, guided by advice that has been indispensable to those in some of the other professions: Location, Location, Location. For Roberts, that's what pitching was all about. Emphasizing rigorous control of the strike zone, he threw pitch after pitch, strike after strike, exactly where he wanted to, winding up with a lifetime mark of 1.7 walks per game. Only 27 pitchers in the history of the game were better than that, and 15 of those pitched in the 1876 to 1892 era.

There wasn't anything fancy about the Roberts approach to the game, and hitters knew what to expect. The trick was doing something about it. His KISS pitching principle (Keep It Simple, Stupid) guided him through six straight 20-game seasons, five straight 300-plus Innings-Pitched seasons and five straight years during which he led the league in complete games. That kind of productive durability put some persuasive credentials into his Cooperstown portfolio.

During his National League years (he spent from 1962 to 1965 with Baltimore in the AL), some of his sternest competition came from the Dodgers' pitching staffs of the 50s, principally Don Newcombe, Don Drysdale and Sandy Koufax; Murry Dickson, later a teammate; Sal Maglie, Joey Jay, Harvey

Haddix and Bob Friend. Another was Warren Spahn, whom Roberts met on 11 different occasions. Those Spahn-Roberts confrontations are worthy of further examination.

Among them were two Spahn shutouts in consecutive skirmishes during the 1949 season, Roberts' 24th shutout on April 29, 1954, a sparkling one-hitter that led the Phils to a 4 to 0 victory, and a 5 to 3 Roberts victory in 1957 that broke a seven-game losing streak starting on June 6 and running an eight week stretch during a trying 22-loss season. The 11 Spahn-Roberts engagements produced an 8 and 3 record for Spahnie, as compared to three wins against six losses and two No Decisions recorded by the Phils' ace righthander.

Sorting through the years Roberts and Spahn spent together in the NL, 15 all told, there is one game the two shared as teammates worth recalling. On July 14, 1953, Robin Roberts started for the NL All-Stars at Crosley Field in Cincinnati, pitched three scoreless innings while fanning two and giving up but a single hit, and was followed by the game's winner, Warren Spahn, who took the mound for the Nationals during the fourth and fifth frames, putting up two more AL goose-eggs, and, because the NL pushed two across during his turn that day, receiving credit for the NL's 5 to 1 victory. On that day two tough competitors, neither of whom gave an inch to any ball club, joined in common cause to lay the ground work for a solid Senior Circuit victory.

20th All-Star Game at Cincinnati, July 14, 1953

AL All-Stars	AB	R	H	PO	NL All-Stars	AB	R	H	PO
Goodman, 2b	2	0	0	1	Reese, ss	4	0	2	1
Fox, 2b	1	0	0	1	Hamner, ss	0	0	0	0
Vernon, 1b	3	0	0	6	Schoendienst, 2b	3	0	0	0
Fain, 1b	1	1	1	1	Williams, 3b	0	0	0	2
Bauer, rf	2	0	0	3	Musial, lf	4	0	2	3
Mize, ph	1	0	1	0	Kluszewski, 1b	3	0	1	5
Mantle, cf	2	0	0	0	Hodges, pr, 1b	3	0	1	5
Hunter, pr	0	0	0	0	Campanella, c	4	1	1	6
Doby, cf	1	0	0	1	Mathews, 3b	3	1	0	0
Rosen, 3b	4	0	0	2	Bell, cf	3	0	0	4
Zernial, lf	2	0	1	1	Snider, ph, cf	0	1	0	1
Minoso, lf	2	0	2	0	Slaughter, rf	3	2	2	4
Berra, c	4	0	0	4	**Roberts, p**	0	0	0	0
Carrasquel, ss	2	0	0	2	Kiner, ph	0	0	0	0
Kell, ph	1	0	0	0	**Spahn (WP)**	0	0	0	0
Rizzuto, ss	0	0	0	0	J. Robinson, ph	1	0	0	0
Pierce, p	1	0	0	0	Dickson, p	1	0	1	0
Reynolds (LP)	0	0	0	0	Simmons, p	0	0	0	0
Kuenn, ph	1	0	0	0	Ashburn, ph	1	0	1	0

Garcia, p	0	0	0	1					
E. Robinson, ph	1	0	0	0					
Paige, p	0	0	0	0					
Totals	31	1	5	24	Totals	32	5	10	27
Line Score	Americans		000		000	001	1–5–0		
	Nationals		000		020	12x	5–10–0		

2BH: Reese; SB: Slaughter; LOB: Americans 6, Nationals 7; HBP: Mathews by Reynolds; DP: Carrasquel and Vernon; K: Roberts, Spahm and Garcia 2; Pierce and Simmons 1; Reynolds, Paige and Dickson 0; BB: Roberts, Spahn, Simmons, Reynolds, Garcia and Paige 1 each; Pierce and Dickson 0. Managers: Stengel, AL; Dressen, NL; Umpires: Conlan, Donatelli, Engeln, Stevens, McKinley and Napp; Time: 2:19; Attendance: 30,846.

Some years later, during his retirement, Robin Roberts was asked the usual questions about big thrills during his career. Beside the most obvious to baseball buffs, that 1950, 10-inning, pennant-winning victory over the Dodgers that made him the Phils' first 20-game winner in 35 years, Roberts singled out the 1953 All-Star game. Why? Because it was a day that Mickey Mantle was asked to bunt — and with the wind blowing out at Crosley Field! Mantle succeeded in his mission, but the concession was all the sweeter because of the deference accorded the Phillies' fastballer. Winning that game surely had something to do with it, as well.

The Spahn-Roberts Log:

Sep 10, 1948	Boston 13*, Philadelphia 2	Spahn WP, Roberts LP
Apr 27, 1949	Boston 2, Philadelphia 0	Spahn WP, Roberts LP
Sep 10, 1949	Boston 1, Philadelphia 0	Spahn WP, Roberts LP
Apr 29, 1954	Philadelphia 4, Boston 0	Roberts WP, Spahn LP
Aug 24, 1956	Milwaukee 6, Philadelphia 1	Spahn WP, Roberts LP
May 7, 1957	Philadelphia 8, Milwaukee 4	Roberts WP, Spahn LP
Jul 25, 1957	Philadelphia 5, Milwaukee 3	Roberts WP, Spahn LP
Aug 25, 1957	Milwaukee 7, Philadelphia 3	Spahn WP, Roberts LP
Aug 28, 1961	Milwaukee 7, Philadelphia 1	Spahn WP, Roberts LP

On May 27, 1952, Robin Roberts went eight innings (ND) in a 12 inning game won by Milwaukee, 4 to 2. It was the first time that season that Roberts failed to go the route. His record at that point was 7 and 1. Spahn pitched a complete game and was the winner.

In another 12-inning game, on September 13, 1956, Spahn again went the route to pick up his 17th win. The losing pitcher was Curt Simmons, who relieved Roberts (ND) in the 11th stanza.

---

*In the first Spahn-Roberts matchup everyone in the Boston lineup had at least one hit, and Spahn had two, a double and the first of his 35 career home runs.

Warren Spahn versus Donald "Newk" Newcombe (1926–)

There were a number of ball players who burned up the league as rookies and wound up with Rookie of the Year laurels. Nomar Garciaparra in 1997, Dick Allen in 1964, Fernando Valenzuela in 1981, and Mike Piazza in 1993 are numbered among them. And don't forget Big Newk. Though he started the 1949 season in Montreal, the strapping flamethrower had been called up to the Dodgers already before June and had been given his first starting assignment by manager Burt Shotton on May 30. He sunk his teeth into that opportunity with a 3 to 0 shutout, the first of a league-leading five that summer. A scant six weeks later he found himself on the mound facing the AL's best in the All-Star game that was played in his own back yard, Ebbets Field.[29] A few months later he was at it again, this time in baseball's glitter-match, the World Series, that season showcasing New York's Yanks and Brooklyn's beloved Bums. And when the BBWAA got around to selecting the Rookie of the Year, they selected Donald Newcombe. The Dodger ace followed his auspicious start with 19 and 11, and 20 and 9, records for a three-year reading of 56 and 28, winning two out of every three decisions as the Dodgers

Don Newcombe, the big Dodger with the intimidating fastball, pictured here with Roy Campanella; Larry Doby, the first black ALer; and the fabled Jackie Robinson.

became the Boys of Summer, winning the pennant twice and finishing second twice between 1949 and 1952.

There was more World Series fun to come, only Big Newk was not to be a part of it, spending the next two seasons in military service during the Korean conflict. By the time he got back it was 1954, and it took the whole season to get the big fellow back on track, which certainly had something to do with the Giants winning the pennant.

Newcombe first encountered Warren Spahn on August 12, 1950. For Newk, it wasn't a very good way to start what turned out to be a limited number of engagements (four) over the decade they made the NL circuit together. The 1950 matchup resulted in a 10 to 2 plastering of the Dodgers in a game marred by seven Brooklyn errors and other lapses reminiscent of former years at Ebbets Field. The Braves that day worked over Newcombe for nine hits and seven runs in five innings of work. But on at least one count the huge Flatbush fireballer looked like the Newk Dodger fans knew. That was at the plate, where his single was one of the six hits his team managed against Spahn.

That raises an interesting point concerning Newcombe and Spahn, both of whom were, for pitchers, superior hitters. Spahn, whose tenure doubled Newcombe's, enjoyed his best hitting season in 1958 with a .333 (36 for 108), and he hit his 31st career four-bagger in 1961, a top career mark in ML history. But he wasn't the threat at the plate that Newcombe was. Very few were. Big Newk hit over the .300 mark five of his 10 seasons in the Bigs, reaching career highs of .359 in 1955 and .361 in 1958. With only 10 seasons of ML play, he ranks 12th in Pitcher Batting Runs, with 79, right at eight per season, the highest number for pitchers per year in the 20th century except for Babe Ruth, who accounted for 12.8 in the six years of his abbreviated pitching career.

Don Newcombe's relatively short career, reaching its zenith in 1956, when he became the first pitcher to win Cy Young and MVP awards in the same year, was cut short by his inability and disinclination to deal with his alcoholism. But though it humiliated him and drove him out of the game he dearly loved, he did eventually come to grips with it, much to his credit, and today stands ready to counsel those likewise afflicted. In the long run, that's a more significant accomplishment than major league awards or a place of honor at Cooperstown.

Neither the careers of Newcombe or Spahn, nor the season's outcome of their teams, were affected by a number of do-or-die career confrontations (as, for example, was the case with Spahn and Roberts or Gibson, Mathewson and Mordecai Brown, and Tom Seaver and Steve Carlton). There were, after all, but four, and at no time during the two 1950 meetings, or in 1958, or in 1960, when Newk was wobbling toward the end of his career with

Cincinnati, was there a game with the pennant on the line. The final tally on the Newcombe-Spahn series reflected as much. Spahnie won one, lost one and registered two No Decisions. Newk's record was 0–2–2.

The Spahn-Newcombe Log:

Aug 12, 1950   Boston 10, Brooklyn 2   Spahn WP, Newcombe LP

On September 27, 1950, Brooklyn beat Boston 9 to 6, as the Dodgers scored four in the bottom of the seventh. Newcombe (ND) started against Spahn (ND), but the pitchers of decision were Dan Bankhead, who won it, and Bobby Hogue, who lost it.

Jimmy Dykes debuted as manager of the Cincinnati Reds on August 14, 1958. That day he started Newcombe (LP), who went the distance in a 3 to 0 Redleg loss. Joey Jay (WP), who surrendered but one hit, a single to Jerry Lynch, was relieved by Warren Spahn (ND) in the ninth.

Cincinnati beat Milwaukee 6 to 5 on July 9, 1960, in a ten-inning game won by a pinch single off reliever Spahn (LP) that scored Frank Robinson. Newcombe started the game (ND), but the win went to reliever Bob Grim, who came on in the seventh inning.

Warren Spahn versus Sanford "Sandy" Koufax (1935–)
Koufax was elected to the Baseball Hall of Fame in 1972

Warren Spahn versus Don Drysdale (1936–1993)
Drysdale was elected to the Baseball Hall of Fame in 1984

Many who watched the 2001 World Series, which showcased Curt Schilling and Cy Young Award winner Randy Johnson, the season's most dominating mound duo, were reminded of former pitching pairs who led their teams to pennants and World Series victories. From among the best of those pairs the 20th century has to offer, five are presented below.

Of special interest, especially in this particular profile, is the work of Sandy Koufax and Don Drysdale. Their five best consecutive seasons with the Dodgers compares favorably with the others, among whom will be found nine Hall of Famers and four who are individually profiled in matchups against the Mound Maestros assembled in this review.

The Legend:

P	Pennants the pitching duo helped win together.
CY	Cy Young Awards between the two pitchers. Note: Hypothetical Cy Young Awards (*) per Bill Deane's *TBE* listing, 2001 ed, pp. 208.
5TPI	Each pitcher's cumulative TPI ratings for the seasons listed.

	Yrs	W-L	W%	P	CY	5TPI	5TPIAve.
C. Mathewson	1903–07	104–58	.707	2	4*	21.9	4.38
J. McGinnity	1903–07	132–73	.644	2	4*	9.2	1.84
R. Lemon	1952–56	104–57	.646	1	1*	18.7	3.74
E. Wynn	1952–56	100–55	.645	1	1*	14.1	2.82
S. Koufax	1962–66	111–34	.766	3	4	21.0	4.30
D. Drysdale	1962–66	98–70	.583	3	4	16.0	3.20
J. Marichal	1966–70	98–46	.681	0	0	14.9	2.98
G. Perry	1966–70	96–66	.593	0	0	14.0	2.80
J. Palmer	1969–73	99–42	.702	3	1	16.7	3.34
D. McNally	1969–73	95–55	.633	3	1	6.5	1.30

Warren Spahn squared off against the Koufax-Drysdale combination 15 times between 1957 and his final year, 1965. During that time Koufax was victorious four times, lost two and recorded three No Decisions. Don Drysdale was pitted against Spahnie six times, winning two, losing three, and logging one No Decision. Spahn himself won two from each of the Dodger heroes, lost four times to Koufax, and twice to Drysdale. The complete record follows:

The Spahn-Koufax-Drysdale Log:

Jul 30, 1958	Milwaukee 4, Los Angeles 3	Spahn WP, Koufax LP
Jun 17, 1959	Los Angeles 10, Milwaukee 2	Koufax WP, Spahn LP
Sep 2, 1961	Milwaukee 4, Los Angeles 0	Spahn WP, Koufax LP
Sep 15, 1961	Los Angeles 11, Milwaukee 2	Koufax WP, Spahn LP
Jun 13, 1962	Los Angeles 2, Milwaukee 1	Koufax WP, Spahn LP
May 30, 1963	Milwaukee 7, Los Angeles 4	Spahn WP, Drysdale LP
Jun 28, 1963	Milwaukee 1, Los Angeles 0	Spahn WP, Drysdale LP
Jun 16, 1964	Los Angeles 5, Milwaukee 1	Drysdale WP, Spahn LP
Jun 11, 1965	Los Angeles 2, New York 1	Drysdale WP, Spahn LP
Jun 20, 1965	Los Angeles 2, New York 1	Koufax WP, Spahn LP

The Spahn-Koufax-Drysdale series began in Brooklyn on August 4, 1957, w h e n the Braves beat the Dodgers 9 to 7 in a game won by Bob Buhl. Sal Maglie lost the game in relief. Koufax pitched one inning in relief, and Spahn (ND), who started, was relieved by Buhl.

Los Angeles beat Milwaukee in 16 innings, 7 to 6, on August 18, 1959. Don Drysdale started for the Dodgers (ND). Larry Sherry, LA's relief ace, was the winner, and Warren Spahn, who finished up for the Braves, was charged with the defeat.

In a 12-inning game, LA beat Milwaukee 6 to 5 on September 29, 1959. Neither of the starters, Spahn or Koufax, were around at the finish. Reliever Stan Williams was the winner and Bob Rush the loser.

On June 24, 1960, Drysdale (LP) started for LA against Spahn (ND), who was relieved by Bob Buhl (WP). Milwaukee won 4 to 2.

Bob Buhl (WP) finished for Spahn as the Braves beat the Dodgers 8 to 7 in 11 innings on July 30, 1960. Koufax started (ND) for LA, and Larry Sherry was the losing pitcher.

Twin Trouble: Don Drysdale (left) and Sandy Koufax.

One of the innumerable Yogi Berra one-liners put Sandy Koufax' last few seasons into sharp perspective. When asked during the 1963 World Series how Koufax could have won as many as he did during a brilliant 25 and 5 campaign, the Yogiman replied, "I don't see how he *lost* five games during the season." And the way Sanford Koufax pitched between 1962 and 1966, raising his Total Pitching Index each season from 1.6 to 6.0 before retiring, while lowering his career ERA to 2.76, was a persuasive argument for his 1972 selection for Hall of Fame honors. This fellow was nothing less than otherworldly during the five year span that brought to a close a career still in its orbital ascendancy, but ended, alas, when, at 30, he retired because of the developing and potentially crippling arthritis in his pitching arm. It brought an abrupt halt to a career marked liberally with one outstanding effort after another, to whit: no-hitters during each of the 1962 to '66 seasons; 382, 1965 strikeouts; two straight shutout victories over Minnesota in the 1965 World Series, during which he gave up seven hits all told; and an 18-K game against the Cubs on April 24, 1962, which signaled the beginning of his stretch of utter dominance over NL hitters. Three pitching triple crowns, an MVP and a threesome of Cy Young awards, in that same awesome 1962–66 span, were followed by his election to the Hall as the youngest player ever ushered into those august surroundings.

Three Koufax-Spahn matchups stand out as afternoons (and evenings) of awesome pitching achievement. They include a 4 to 0 Spahn whitewashing of the Dodgers on September 2, 1961, when the Braves' ace recorded his 17th career win against the Bums at Milwaukee's County Stadium; and two, 2 to 1 Koufax victories, one on June 13, 1962, when Sandy smacked his first ML home run and picked up his ninth win in 11 tries in Milwaukee, and the other a gem of an outing which matched Koufax with the ancient mariner, by then well on his way to his 45th birthday. It was a game that featured the mature, salty offerings of the old master, and the younger, polished flamethrower who gave Spahn's Mets but one hit. That hit represented the total offensive output in a 2 to 1 nail-biter won in the sixth frame on a pair of Dodger runs. The Met's hit was a Jim Hickman fourbagger that put the Mets ahead momentarily. That game was the last great Spahn effort as his career gradually wound down to its 1965 ending.

The other half of the Dodgers' explosive pitching tandem was one of the great intimidators of the '50s and '60s. Don Drysdale, a big, brawny power pitcher cut in the Bob Gibson–Early Wynn mold, was a pitcher who never lost a game — at least not in his own mind. He was out there to get rid of you, whatever that took, and his canon shots to home plate, often dangerously close to the hitter, took their toll on the NL's hitting brigade. During the same Koufax period of dominance, from 1962 to '66, the "Big D" picked up a 1962 Cy Young Award for his 25 and 9 season. In 1965 he recorded another 20-win season and completed his fourth straight 300 innings-pitched campaign.

Between the two of them, Drysdale and Koufax accounted for 209 out of 473 Dodger victories from 1962 to '66, nearly half of the team's total. In 1968, during "the Year of the Pitcher," by then the remaining stalwart of the onetime, one-two LA punch, Drysdale set a new record for consecutive scoreless innings (at 58.2) that stood until Dodger Orel Hershiser came along in 1988 to break it. But during the very next season Drysdale's career came to a shuddering halt when he came up with a torn rotator cuff. "Big D" explained things this way: "A torn rotator cuff is cancer for a pitcher. And if a pitcher gets a badly torn one, he has to face the facts: it's all over, baby."

But before it was all over this one was a powerful equalizer. Drysdale was the kind of go-to guy any manager would want to have on his staff. McGraw would have loved this fellow.

Drysdale and Warren Spahn dueled on six different occasions. Another of those 1 to 0 ball games, a delight for those who came to the ball park to see their favorite pitcher mow 'em down, surfaced on June 28, 1963, when Spahn, in the midst of his last 20-game season, took the Dodgers in a shutout that pushed his record to 11 and 3. Drysdale's Dodgers managed but three singles in a game won in the first inning on a Joe Torre sacrifice fly that scored Lee Maye. It was Spahnie's 58th shutout (his career total was 63, an ML record for lefties), and it was his first victory over a Dodger team in its own ball park in 15 seasons.

But Don Drysdale's moment in the sun came soon thereafter. In 1964 he beat Spahn 5 to 1 at Los Angeles, giving up only four hits, and in 1965 he threw another four-hitter, this time at the Mets, beating them 2 to 1. The big fellow won his own game with a towering blast in the eighth inning at Shea Stadium. The win came on June 11, just nine days before the 2 to 1, one-hit Koufax victory at Los Angeles.

It would take a lot of arguing and some tortured statistics to convince knowledgeable baseball fans that there was a better one-two, lefty-righthander pitching tandem over an extended period of time than the Dodgers' Drysdale and Koufax. The contention in this corner is that, with a close-but-not-quite nod in the direction of Rube Waddell and Albert "Chief" Bender (1902 to 1906), Sandy and "Big D" rule the roost.

Warren Spahn versus Jim Bunning (1931–)
Bunning was elected to the Baseball Hall of Fame in 1996

Today he's Senator James Bunning, representing the Commonwealth of Kentucky. But on June 21, 1964, he became the only pitcher in the history of the major leagues to throw a perfect game on Father's Day, when he shut down the New York Mets at Shea Stadium. It was the first perfect game in the NL in some 84 years when, on June 17, 1880, John Montgomery Ward of Providence threw a perfect no-no at the Buffalo Bisons. One of baseball's more intelligent pitchers, a match for the likes of a Tom Seaver or a Warren Spahn, Jim Bunning realized that there was enough zip on his heater to get

It all came together for Jim Bunning on Father's Day, June 21, 1964, when he threw a perfect game against the New York Mets at Shea Stadium.

by in the minors, but not enough to succeed often in the majors. So he made the necessary adjustments in pitches, like adding a crackling slider to his repertoire, studying hitters, and maintaining control of the strike zone, enabling him to rack up 2855 Ks, as compared to only 1000 walks, in a 17 year career.

Over that 17 year span Bunning became the first ML hurler to strike out 1000 hitters in both leagues, to pitch in the All-Star game for both leagues, and the first modern era pitcher to win more than 100 games in both leagues. That was accomplished on behalf of the Tigers in the American League (118–87) and the Phils, Pirates and Dodgers in the NL (106–97). Three seasons stand out during his career: a breakthrough campaign with Detroit in 1957 (20–8, 267.1 innings pitched and 33 pitching runs, both league-leading numbers), and sterling back to back efforts in 1966 and '67 at a time when the Phillies gradually headed south after their heartbreaking 1964 second place finish to the Cardinals in a race that everyone (except the Cardinals, of course) thought the Phils should have won.

Jim Bunning tangled with Warren Spahn on only three occasions, due principally to Bunning's nine-season tenure in the AL. They met for the first time in a 5 to 3 Phils win propelled by Rich Allen's four-master that provided Bunning with his third straight win in the young 1964 season on May Day. It was one of his 19 wins that season, and at that point, in early May, the Phillies already knew that their staff of Chris Short, Dennis Bennett, Art Mahaffey, Ray Culp and the ace of the pitching corps, Bunning, was going to have Philadelphia in the running all the way.

The sparkler among the three Spahn-Bunning tilts came in Spahnie's last season when, on May 5, 1965, Jim Bunning bested him with a 1 to 0 four-hitter at Shea Stadium. It took that kind of an effort to subdue Spahn, in his 21st ML campaign, who also pitched a four hitter. Unfortunately for Spahn, one of those four hits was a home run—and it was hit by James Paul David Bunning, no less. The sixth-inning blow was garnished by Bunning's four whiffs, a solitary free pass, and a flawless game afield. Spahn's figures matched Bunning's, except for the Bunning dinger, a fatal difference. (The box score follows below.) The final faceoff came three weeks later when the Mets, powered by Ed Kranepool's hitting, chased Bunning in the sixth, defeating the Phillies 6 to 2, inching Spahnie one more win closer to his record-setting 363 conquests. That completed the Spahn-Bunning series, with an edge to the tall Phillie righthander at two games to one.

As with George Davis, Nellie Fox, Vic Willis and Richie Ashburn, it took a while to put a bottom line on Bunning's Hall of Fame career. In Senator Jim's case that was tidied up with his 1996 selection for Cooperstown honors.

Philadelphia at Shea Stadium, New York, May 5, 1965

Philadelphia	AB	R	H	BI	New York	AB	R	H	BI
Rojas, cf	4	0	1	0	Klaus, 3b, ss	2	0	0	0
Callison, rf	3	0	0	0	Napoleon, ph	1	0	0	0
Allen, 3b	3	0	1	0	Hunt, 2b	4	0	1	0
Stuart, 1b	4	0	1	0	Lewis, rf	4	0	1	0
Wine, ss	0	0	0	0	Kranepool, 1b	3	0	0	0
Covington, lf	2	0	0	0	Christopher, lf	3	0	1	0
Del Greco, lf	1	0	0	0	Swoboda, cf	3	0	1	0
Taylor, 2b	3	0	0	0	McMillan, ss	2	0	0	0
Triandos, c	3	0	0	0	Gonder, ph, c	1	0	0	0
Amaro, ss, 1b	3	0	0	0	Cannizzaro, c	2	0	0	0
Bunning (WP)	3	1	1	1	Berra, ph	1	0	0	0
					Hickman, 3b	0	0	0	0
					Spahn (LP)	3	0	0	0
Totals	29	1	4	1	Totals	29	0	4	0
Line Score	Philadelphia	000	001	000	1–4–0
	New York	000	000	000	0–4–0

Errors: none; HR: Bunning; LOB: Philadelphia 4, New York 3; SH: Allen; DP: Philadelphia 2, New York 1; BB: Bunning 1, Spahn 1; K: Bunning 4, Spahn 1; HPB: Callison by Spahn; Time: 1:52; Attendance: 14,134.

Warren Spahn versus Pack Robert "Gibby" or "Bob" Gibson (1935–)

Gibson was elected to the Baseball Hall of Fame in 1981

The *real* Bob Gibson appeared during the latter stages of Warren Spahn's career. Up to that time he was growing to full stature as one of baseball's most intimidating and dominating hurlers. Accordingly, the last dozen years of the Cardinals' winningest pitcher will get more detailed scrutiny in the Tom Seaver chapter, which sketches their nine-season rivalry.

Over a span of seven years Spahn and Gibby dueled 10 times, with the following results:

The Spahn-Gibson Log:

Jul 2, 1960	St. Louis 7, Milwaukee 1	Gibson WP, Spahn LP
Sep 12, 1960	Milwaukee 4, St. Louis 2	Spahn WP, Gibson LP
Jun 4, 1961	Milwaukee 7, St. Louis 1	Spahn WP, Gibson LP
Jul 13, 1962	St. Louis 6, Milwaukee 0	Gibson WP, Spahn LP
May 14, 1963	Milwaukee 4, St. Louis 3	Spahn WP, Gibson LP
May 11, 1965	St. Louis 4, New York 3	Gibson WP, Spahn LP

The Spahn-Gibson series began with a 3 to 1 Milwaukee victory in a 10-inning game at St. Louis on August 25, 1959. Don McMahon was the winner in relief of Spahn (8 IP). Gibson started (9.1 IP) and was charged with the loss.

Milwaukee beat St. Louis on May 11, 1960. Spahn (WP) beat Lindy McDaniel, who started for St. Louis. Gibson (ND) appeared as a RP.

On August 3, 1960, the Cards beat the Braves 13 to 8. Neither Spahn (ND) nor Gibson (ND) finished the game. The victory went to reliever Bob Grim of the Cardinals. Joey Jay was charged with the defeat.

In a 10-inning game at Milwaukee, the Braves beat the Cardinals 3 to 2 on July 30, 1961, Spahn earning the win and Anderson the loss in relief of Gibson (9.1 IP, ND). The final tally on the Gibson-Spahn series: Spahn won five, lost three and received two No Decisions; Gibson won three, lost four and was charged with three No Decisions.

During the Spahn years, Bob Gibson put together the first of his many Hall of Fame credentials. In 1962, a far better year than his 15 and 13 record might indicate, he checked in with his first sub-3.00 ERA, logged a league leading five shutouts and was elected to the NL All-Star team for the first time, working two innings for the NL losers (the AL broke through for one of their rare victories during that era) in the second All-Star game on July 30 at Wrigley Field. That summer he threw a three-hit shutout at the Braves on July 13, victimizing Spahn & Co. six-zip, for the third of his five whitewash jobs, helping along his final 2.85 ERA reading, which placed him fifth in a tightly bunched foursome behind Sandy Koufax' 2.54. By the end of the 1962 campaign it was already evident that Bob Gibson would not long tolerate anything less than a first place finish.

The Cardinals almost got the job done behind Gibby's 18 and 9 in 1963, Stan the Man's last season, but wilted just enough down the stretch to lose out to their hated rivals, the Dodgers. In 1964, Musial or no Musial, they brought the NL pennant back to St. Louis and topped it off with a World

Series win over the Yankees, thanks largely to the overpowering work of one Mr. Gibson, who beat the perennial AL champs twice after absorbing a sobering 8 to 3 loss in the second game to Mel Stottlemyre.

By the time Warren Spahn made his farewell trip around the NL circuit in 1965, Bob Gibson was well on his way to super-stardom. The two met for a final tête-à-tête on May 11, 1965, when Gibby bested the Old Master, still a force to be reckoned with, in a tight, 4 to 3 Cardinal victory over the Mets. It was, in its own way, a sort of passing of the guard from one tough customer to another. Spahnie had passed the baton along to worthy hands.

You would want this fellow on the mound when the game for all the chips is played: Bob Gibson.

Warren Spahn versus Juan (Sanchez) "Manito" Marichal (1937–)

Marichal was elected to the Baseball Hall of Fame in 1983

Juan Marichal. Better than Sandy Koufax? And if better than Koufax, the very best during the 1950–70 era? The era had its share of good ones. Whitey Ford, Bob Gibson, Robin Roberts and Mr. Spahn himself were also active during that time, each a force to be reckoned with. According to the Total Pitching Index listing, eight of Marichal's Hall of Fame contemporaries stack up this way:

	Yrs	Career Span	TPI
Warren Spahn	21	1942–1965	50.2
Bob Gibson	17	1959–1975	43.7
Whitey Ford	16	1950–1967	39.2
Bob Lemon	13	1946–1958	38.4

Don Drysdale	14	1956–1969	34.6
Juan Marichal	16	1960–1975	29.5
Robin Roberts	19	1948–1966	25.9
Sandy Koufax	12	1955–1966	20.5
Early Wynn	23	1939–1963	17.1

Varying years of service play into the career index ratings, of course, as do a multiplicity of other factors, but the gist of contention is that the higher the TPI rating, the more valuable the player was to his team. And as for pitchers, that meant more victories for his ball club than league-average hurlers were able to contribute. On that score Juan Marichal comes out ahead of Sandy Koufax by some nine wins, a substantial difference as these things are measured. Does that make him better than Koufax? Don't try to tell that to Sandy's Angelino friends. In LA the Koufax name has no superior. There, the very mention of the name Marichal stirs visceral reaction. But that is another of baseball's twice-told tales. Nor does it settle anything.

Phil Brown took up the Koufax-Marichal comparison in a 1993 *Baseball Research Journal* article entitled *Was Marichal Better Than Koufax?* (pp. 42–43), and came up with a coin-toss to determine which of these great hurlers was better, concluding his article with: "There wasn't a dime's worth of difference between them." That dead-even rating, which may come as a surprise to many, doesn't solve anything, but it does bring Juan Marichal's brilliant career into focus as one that ranks right up there with the very best.

The high-kicking Dominican was, all other arguments aside, one whale of a pitcher, especially between 1962 and '69, when he put 172 Ws into the Giants' victory column, an average of 21.5 per season. During that time he matched Warren Spahn pitch for pitch seven times

Whatever it takes ... Juan Marichal threw every pitch in the book—and well enough to win 20 games six out of seven straight seasons.

and emerged victorious six times, sustaining but a single loss in a series that extended from 1960 to '64. The very last encounter, an 8 to 4 San Francisco victory, was the only one in which the losing team was able to muster more than a couple of runs. That says volumes about what was going on when Marichal tangled with Spahn.

The most spectacular example of their pitching mastery occurred on July 2, 1963, when they dueled with stubborn and relentless tenacity through 15 innings of a scoreless tie that was dramatically broken up by a Willie Mays tater in the bottom of the 16th. Stubborn tenacity? Both Marichal and Spahn were asked repeatedly during the latter stages of the game if they felt they had enough left for another inning. The younger one insisted that he wasn't about to be outlasted by the old man pitching for the Braves, and the elder statesman, by this time 42 and in the midst of what would turn out to be a 23 and 7 season, looked straight ahead, a steely glint in his eye, and remarked to manager Bobby Bragan that the battle with "the youngster" (Marichal) would go on as long as there was one more pitch left in his arm. Spahnie did have one more left, but since Willie Mays wasn't included in those commiserations, he took that one pitch downtown and ended things in Maysian splendor. Of Marichal's 25 wins that year, that one had to be the sweetest.

It seems more than a little strange that in Juan Marichal's three best seasons he never received a single vote for the Cy Young Award. The breakdown:

		W-L	ERA	Ratio	CY Award
1965:	Koufax	26–8	2.04	7.8	Unanimous
	Marichal	22–12	2.13	8.3	no votes
1966:	Koufax	27–9	1.73	8.9	Unanimous
	Marichal	25–6	2.23	7.9	no votes
1969:	Seaver	25–7	2.21	9.6	23/24 votes*
	Marichal	21–11	2.10	9.1	no votes

Did the BBWAA voting members pick the right award winners? Probably, though Marichal has a more convincing case against Seaver than Koufax. Was Koufax worthy of a unanimous award decision in '65 and '66? Probably not, but by that time the Koufax mystique had become such a pervasive phenomenon that there was no way others might even be considered. *Sic transit* awards and voting.

The Spahn-Marichal Log:

| Jul 28, 1960 | San Francisco 3, Milwaukee 2 | Marichal WP, Spahn LP |
| Jun 15, 1961 | San Francisco 11 Milwaukee 2 | Marichal WP, Spahn LP |

---

* In 1969 Phil Niekro received one vote, Seaver the remainder.

Apr 10, 1962	San Francisco 6, Milwaukee 0	Marichal WP, Spahn LP
Jun 24, 1962	San Francisco 3, Milwaukee 1	Marichal WP, Spahn LP
Apr 28, 1963	Milwaukee 3, San Francisco 1	Spahn WP, Marichal LP
Jul 2, 1963	San Francisco 1, Milwaukee 0	Marichal WP, Spahn LP
Apr 14, 1964	San Francisco 8, Milwaukee 4	Marichal WP, Spahn LP

Warren Spahn versus Gaylord Jackson Perry (1938–)
Perry was elected to the Baseball Hall of Fame in 1991

Warren Spahn versus Phillip Henry "Knucks" Niekro (1939–)
Niekro was elected to the Baseball Hall of Fame in 1997

Warren Spahn versus Steven "Lefty" Carlton (1944–)
Carlton was elected to the Baseball Hall of Fame in 1994

Warren Spahn versus Ferguson A. "Fergie" Jenkins (1943–)
Jenkins was elected to the Baseball Hall of Fame in 1991

Four Hall of Famers who toured the ML circuit for an aggregate total of 89 seasons and captured seven Cy Young Awards en route were on hand during the final years of Warren Spahn's career. Though none of them pitched against Spahnie, each debuted shortly before his 1965 retirement, and two of them, Phil Niekro and Gaylord Perry, were teammates of Spahn's briefly in the 1964 and '65 seasons (Niekro in Milwaukee and Perry in San Francisco).

Fergie Jenkins debuted on September 10, 1965, with the Phillies, although his fame as a pitcher will always be associated with Chicago's Cubs. The Phillie hookup, however, links him in a shirttail way with Steve Carlton, whose great Cy Young years were spent in Philadelphia togs. And then there is the Warren Spahn–Bob Buhl–Braves and Cubs relationship. Buhl, in 1965, his last effective year (he finished up with the Phils in '66 and '67), took the hill as a Cub hurler on September 12 against Spahn in what turned out to be the last complete game of Spahn's career. That day Spahnie beat his former teammate 9 to 2 to post his final major league win, number 363. That's an admittedly roundabout way to tie up the kind of convoluted relationships baseball often spawns, but it does connect players and teams in strange ways. There's more...

Earlier that same '65 season, Lew Burdette took on Warren Spahn in an August 31 game. Burdette, at that point in his career wearing a Phils uniform, was another of the 1958–59 Brave stalwarts who spent a part of the 1965 season in Philadelphia (Lefty Carlton broke in on that same staff), and presided over a 2 to 0 whitewashing on August 31, the last defeat Spahn suffered in a shutout ball game. And so Spahn's final 7 and 16 record in 1965 (3 and 4 in San Francisco), and consequently the final reading on his sparkling ML career, also had a number of significant footprints on it belonging to the Cubs, Braves and Phillies.

Gaylord Perry cut his ML teeth in San Francisco's bullpen. He debuted in 1962 but started only 11 times in 44 appearances during his first two seasons, and didn't make it big until 1966, when he was a 20-game winner. During Spahn's last season the lanky spitballer (more on that ahead in the Seaver story) relieved Spahn five times, thus enabling him to say that although he didn't start a game against the great lefty, he at least appeared in the same lineup.

Phil Niekro's career lasted through 24 seasons, chiefly because he threw that most maddening of pitches (for both catchers *and* hitters), the knuckler. Like Perry, he worked out of the bullpen, relieving Spahn twice in his rookie season. The first of these, both in May of 1964, was as a reliever in the sixth and seventh innings of a game won by Jim Bunning, 5 to 3. Later in that same month Niekro appeared again behind Spahn, both of them getting No Decisions for their labors that day in a game the Mets won 4 to 2.

It took a while for both of these fellows to get on-track, but when they did they were on their way to 300 career wins, each with his own specialty pitch. They had one other thing in common. Both had brothers who put up some fancy numbers of their own. The Niekros and Perrys established marks as brothers that will be hard to overcome. The Perry brothers combined for more strikeouts and shutouts than any other set of brothers, and the Niekros (Joe's 22 years of service almost matched Phil's 24) established the standard for victories, 529.

Warren Spahn's career was as long as it was illustrious, and while the three righthanders of this last quartet of Hall of Fame pitchers who pitched during Spahn's career didn't quite attain the stature of the National League's greatest lefthander, they were pitchers a full cut above many of the hurlers whose plaques line the walls at Cooperstown. The remaining member of this quartet, Steve Carlton, ranks among the greatest southpaws of all time. Each of them, far more active during Tom Seaver's career than their nodding acquaintance with Spahnie during his last ML campaign, receive sustained attention in the Seaver chapter just ahead.

Fergie Jenkins, Gaylord Perry, Steve Carlton and Phil Niekro. A manager should be so fortunate as to have such a foursome in his rotation!

"One They're Looking for and One to Cross Them Up"

Sliders, curves, a better than average heater, an occasional screwball, and even a forkball here and there, all thrown at varying speeds, and each

Warren Spahn (left) with Johnny Sain. The two Boston Braves mainstays were master craftsmen.

delivery thrown to the weakness of the hitter — that's what made the Spahn arsenal so devastating. Disrupting the hitter's timing combined with the unexpected: call it the Spahn Formula. Very few before or since could master the art of this master. Christy Mathewson before Spahn, and Greg Maddux after, come to mind. But not many more.

As the years moved along the numbers piled up. No-hitters, a Cy Young Award, *TSN* All-Star team selections, the 1960 Sid Mercer award and the 1961 Lou Gehrig Memorial award were among a multitude of accomplishments and awards that came Spahn's way. He had become the consummate mound craftsman, a pitcher's pitcher who excelled at fielding, hitting, and holding men on base with that exceptional pickoff move of his, and, when the occasion demanded, who had the moxy to survive those two-on-none-out situations with the game up for grabs. Hall of Fame honors were inevitable to everyone except Spahn himself, who never, ever, took anything for granted. They were accorded in Spahnie's first year of Cooperstown eligibility — an ultimate statement about a player's status among the game's greats.

The first of Spahn's pitching teammates to play with him on a pennant winner was Johnny Sain, a successful hurler himself, who studied the game, played it, and coached it as few before or since. He had this to say about pitching:

> A pitcher has to be mature beyond his years. A pitcher is not like any other ball player. The very nature of his job sets him apart. There are only two men on the diamond who cannot lose their composure, who must remain above things. Those are the manager and the pitcher. A batter can kick and scream and fielders can get mad. But when a manager or a pitcher loses his composure, the advantage swings to the other side. Pitching is only partly physical skill. There is so much of it that's psychological. I can't stress enough how important that is.[30]

Sain, whose name was immortalized in baseball lore because it rhymed with rain, as in "Spahn and Sain, then pray for rain," had it right. His career in baseball was a living testimony to the veracity of his philosophy about pitching.

There was another, however, who took that philosophy to another level. His name was Warren Edward Spahn, and he had it down to perfection.

7. TOM SEAVER

Major League Career Totals:	Won	Lost	Pct.
New York, Cincinnati (NL) Chicago, Boston (AL)	311	205	.603

Seaver was elected to the Baseball Hall of Fame in 1992

Tom was indeed terrific. Bill Mazer provides the whys and wherefores:

> A mediocre pitcher can win a spate of games if his team scores enough runs for him. But a superior pitcher is one who wins despite inferior hitting and fielding behind him. Tom Seaver suffered such a fate through many seasons with the Mets. Yet, by the start of the 1977 season Seaver had amassed 182 wins and 107 losses.
>
> From 1967, when Seaver first broke in with the Mets and won the National League's Rookie-of-the-Year award, to the beginning of 1977, the Mets had not quite won 50 percent of their games. However, in that span, Seaver won nearly 65 percent of his decisions.[31]

Seaver was also an exception. Right from the start. He wasn't one of those Al Kaline–like Little League phenoms who started early and kept right at it, moving directly from Baltimore high school diamonds to the Bigs, and ultimately on to the Hall of Fame. Nor did the younger Seaver attract scouting raves. But when he began blowing away a few college ball clubs as one of USC's mound aces, there was enough interest to prompt the Braves to offer him a $40,000 signing bonus. That wasn't exceptional, but what followed was, resulting, finally, in a voiding of the signing contract by Commissioner William Eckert, who subsequently ruled that the rights to the sturdy young flamethrower would go, lottery style, to any team matching or topping the

Braves' $40,000. The Mets, yes, the Mets, that same rag-tag bunch of baseball Huck Finns that finished a woebegone 66 and 95 in 1966, came to the lottery, checkbook in hand, and bet $50,000 they could win it. They did. And Tom Seaver, with only one season of minor league ball behind him, stepped into the major league arena in 1967 to begin his Cooperstown career. The rest was Hall of Fame history, though not all of it (not even the more spectacular part of it, aside from those improbable 1969 pennant winners), was spent in a Mets uniform.

Tom Seaver, the ace of the Miracle Mets.

It has been frequently pointed out that the Terrific One performed his wonders in front of some desultory ball clubs, and that what made him exceptional was his ability to rise above mediocrity, dragging his teammates by the heels to success, if not to heights, despite themselves. Tom Seaver refused to bend to less than superiority, evidenced by a lifetime winning percentage of .601, 106 games over .500, while pitching for teams that were under .500 forty percent of his career. And by the time his last game had been won, a strong 3 to 1 conquest of Minnesota on August 18, 1986, there was already common consent that he would be elected to the Hall in his first year of eligibility. And he was.

The great ones waste little time getting on with the march to fame. Tom Seaver began the march to Cooperstown on April 20, 1967, with a 6 to 1 victory over Curt Simmons and Chicago's Cubs at Shea Stadium. It was the Mets' third win in seven games that season, but their .429 winning percentage at that point was some distance removed from what would turn into a 61 and 101 nightmare. That summer the Mets' stats, compared with Seaver's, looked like this:

	W-L-%	CG	H/G	OBA	Op.OB%	Ratio	FA	ERA
Mets (Tm/Staff)	61–101 (.377)	36	8.6	.253	.323	12.2	.975	3.73
Seaver	16–13 (.552)	18	8.0	.241	.303	11.0	.982	2.76
National League		(Av, 35/tm)	8.5	.249	.312	11.6	.978	3.38

The pattern was set. It made little difference that a team behind him might be less than world beaters. When Tom Terrific took the hill they would play at his level, not theirs. The Seaver compass would be fixed on its own course of excellence, defying inferiority and spurring superiority. The result that first season was a Rookie of the Year award, the Mets' pathetic record not withstanding. And there was much more to come: three Cy Young awards, more than 300 wins, a no-hitter and eight appearances in All-Star games, each with a winning NL squad — plus that miracle season of 1969 when Seaver's 25 and 7 spearheaded a New York pennant that was followed by their World's Championship over a fine Baltimore team.

More than a few of baseball's more astute observers have pointed out that Tom Seaver was the best pitcher to wear a New York uniform (some would suggest that it would not be too improbable to say *any* uniform) since Christy Mathewson. That princely comparison is probably right on the money. There are precious few who may be mentioned in the same breath as the Big Six. The list of qualifiers would have to approach the game, and hitters in particular, with intelligence and precision; their repertoire would include a moving fastball, sharply breaking pitches and controlled change of speeds; they would be agile "fifth-infielders"; they would possess a calculating, dauntless inner fire; and they would find ways and means to adapt to changing circumstances. And after all that, who would qualify? Tom Seaver's name tops this distinguished and very short list. Others who come to mind: recent contemporaries Roger Clemens and Greg Maddux, Bob Gibson, and perhaps Robin Roberts. Among southpaws, Steve Carlton and Lefty Grove would merit consideration. Those who would not — for example, Walter Johnson, Pete Alexander, Whitey Ford and Amos Rusie, all great hurlers in their own right, but with different styles — were almost totally unlike Mathewson or Seaver.

Because Tom Seaver bridged eras featuring pitchers who were expected to finish what they started, and a new age in which terms like Quality Starts, Holds and Saves[32] reflected changes in the responsibilities and expertise of the game's diversified pitching staffs, the number of the pitcher's starting assignments[33], as well as the number of matchups with other starters, gradually diminished. Other changes, such as the number of teams in each league, interleague play, and three and four (sometimes two) game series have also meant fewer matchups between staff aces. Tom Seaver experienced these evolving developments in the game, especially during the second half of his career. Consequently, 19 pitchers, including 11 Hall of Famers, are listed from both leagues (Seaver's AL years were the last three seasons of his career) for Tom Terrific's profile. Presented in chronological order by debut date, the list follows.

Name/HOF/Year	Debut/Career Years	TPI/All Time Pitching Rank
Jim Bunning 1996	Jul 20, 1955/1955–1971	13.4/193
*Don Drysdale 1984	Apr 17, 1956/1956–1969	34.6/26
Bob Gibson 1981	Apr 15, 1959/1959–1975	43.7/13
Juan Marichal 1983	Jul 19, 1960/1960–1975	29.5/39
Gaylord Perry 1991	Apr 14, 1962/1962–1983	34.9/24
Phil Niekro 1997	Apr 15, 1964/1964–1987	33.8/27
Steve Carlton 1994	Apr 12, 1965/1965–1988	33.7/28
Jim Palmer 1990	Apr 17, 1965/1965–1984	34.9/24
Ferguson Jenkins 1991	Sep 10, 1965/1965–1983	29.8/38
Don Sutton 1998	Apr 14, 1966/1966–1988	13.2/198
*Nolan Ryan 1999	Sep 11, 1966/1966–1993	20.7/94
Bert Blyleven	Jun 5, 1970/1970–1992	30.7/35
Rick Reuschel	Jun 19, 1972/1972–1991	24.7/68
Steve Rogers	Jul 18, 1973/1973–1985	15.3/155
Jack Morris	Jul 26, 1977/1977–1994	7.7/NR
Dave Stieb	Jun 29, 1979/1979–1993 and 1998	26.8/54
Frank Viola	Jun 6, 1982/1982–1996	14.7/166
Bret Saberhagen	Apr 4, 1984/1984–	27.7/46
Jimmy Key	Jun 6, 1984/1984–1998	24.2/71

Tom Seaver versus James Paul David "Jim" Bunning (1931–)

Bunning was elected to the Baseball Hall of Fame in 1996

Jim Bunning is one of seven pitchers who were reviewed in the Warren Spahn profile. He appeared against Tom Seaver but once, and ever so briefly, during his second-to-last season major league season. By that time he was a veteran of 15 campaigns, nine of them with the Detroit Tigers. In 1970 he returned to the Phillies after three seasons with the Pirates and Dodgers, winning 10 of his 25 decisions. His Shea Stadium outing on June 19, 1970, against Seaver was, unfortunately, his worst that season.

New York Times scribe Gerry Eskenazi opened up his review of Seaver's 10th win that season with these observations:

> Only an act of God could have stopped the Mets and Tom Seaver last night — and one nearly did. With the New Yorkers trouncing the Philadelphia Phils by 9–0 in the second inning, a heavy downpour halted the game.

---

*Active during Seaver's career but did not appear against him.

> But it was only for 15 minutes. The crowd of 43,866 at Shea Stadium cheered — or was it sighed? — as the tarpaulin was lifted. The Mets went on to a 13–3 rout.
>
> It was Seaver's third consecutive victory, lifting his won-lost mark to 10–5, and he struck out 11 and walked no one. But his mastery of the Phillies ended after holding them scoreless for 38 straight innings...
>
> The biggest bunch [of the Phillies' runs] last night came in the first inning — the Mets scored seven runs, all against Jim Bunning. The lean right-hander, who tomorrow celebrates the sixth anniversary of his perfect game against the Mets, gave up eight hits and 10 New Yorkers faced him in the inning...
>
> In ending Bunning's four-game winning streak with a 15 hit barrage, the Mets also moved to within 3½ games of the Cubs, the National League's Eastern Division leaders.
>
> —*New York Times*, June 20, 1970, pp. 33–34

The greats also have their "lesser endeavors," and this was certainly one of them. The 1970 edition of the Mets hit a not-too-sensational .249 as a team, unsuccessfully defending their miraculous 1969 title. But they put on their hitting shoes that night, touching up Philly pitching for three two-baggers, a triple and two dingers. It was a gala evening for New Yorkers, a sour, let's-get-it-over-with nightmare for Philadelphians.

Jim Bunning, with his crackling slider and edges-of-the-plate control, finished his distinguished career with the Phils in 1971 with 224 lifetime victories and that 1964 Father's Day, perfect game against those same pesky Mets. On that day he also drove in a pair of runs as he became the first pitcher in the game's history to craft a no-hitter in both leagues. His AL meisterwerk came at the expense of the Boston Red Sox on July 20, 1958. Though it took some time coming, he was honored with a Hall of Fame plaque in 1996, affirming a pair of significant modern era firsts: the first to ring up 1000 strikeouts as well as winning 100 games in both major leagues, along with an All-Star game first as a pitcher for teams from both leagues.

Tom Seaver versus Donald Scott "Big D" Drysdale

As Don Drysdale's career was winding down, Tom Seaver's was heating up. The years their careers coincided were 1967–69, commonly known as the Year(s) of the Pitcher, a time when pitching so dominated baseball that baseball's caretakers saw fit to lower the mound, extend the strike zone and make certain that the "little things," like balks, were being called. How much that might have bothered the likes of a Drysdale or a Seaver, if at all, was never really hashed over for publication, but it's a good bet that both of them found a way to live with it without undue stress.

"Big D," Don Drysdale.

Reviewed with Sandy Koufax previously, the Intimidator of the Dodgers' Dynamic Duo, Drysdale, did not go head to head with Tom Terrific, although in 1967 and, in particular, 1968, "Big D" put together the last two good seasons of his career with a '68 log of 14 and 12 and a 2.15 ERA. During the 1967 to '69 seasons, Tom Seaver took on the Dodgers five times, but neither Drysdale nor his sidekick Koufax were around to complicate things for the Mets' ace. By the time another year had gone by, Koufax, whose spikes were already in mothballs, and Drysdale, who would soon be shelving his, were bystanders as Seaver roared through the 1969 NL season with his winningest record (25 and 7).

During the past half century, managers have had far fewer opportunities to match aces during a given series. Days and pitching turns march on, and, as it frequently happens, the aces miss one another or are held back for one good reason or another. In the case of Drysdale and Seaver, that's exactly what happened, much as one might have wished it otherwise. The face-off would have made for an interesting evening.

Tom Seaver versus Pack Robert "Bob" Gibson (1935–)
Gibson was elected to the Baseball Hall of Fame in 1981

There have been pitchers who have crafted better seasons than Bob Gibson's 1968. But not many. In the so-called "Year of the Pitcher," Bob Gibson stood tall, posting miniscule numbers that typified the pitching dominance characteristic of the 1965–70 era. Gibson's record that season, which led to his unanimous selection as the Cy Young award winner, was a thing apart. His 13 shutouts (3rd all time), 1.12 ERA (4th all time) and an almost invisible Opponents' BA of .184 (15th all time) were the pivotal numbers in a 22 and 9 season, all of which causes wonderment at how, indeed, he was victimized with 9 "Ls" that extraordinary season.

As it turned out, one of Gibby's early season victories came within a whisker of winding up in the loss column, when, on May 6, he was entangled in an 11–inning heart-stopper with young Tom Seaver. It was the first of eleven meetings between the two, and the Cardinals finally put the Mets away in that game with a Lou Brock leadoff triple that ultimately became the winning run on Orlando Cepeda's single. Gibson had given up but three hits, all in succession in the fourth stanza, resulting in New York's only run, while stretching his early season record to 3 and 1. The loss was Seaver's second against a single win, though his ERA at that point was 1.58.

As the years moved along, Seaver and Gibson met on ten other occasions, treating baseball buffs to one electrifying evening after another. In ten of the eleven, the losing team mustered but a run or two, four winding up as 2 to 1 ball games. The only exception was an April 26, 1971, game that got away from Gibby and his Cards, 12 to 2. But it was Tom Seaver who emerged top dog in the series, putting together six wins against three losses and a pair of No Decisions. You can imagine how well that set with Mr. Contentious, Bob Gibson.

Baseball has had its share of hard-bitten, fiercely competitive warriors. A die-hard, all-ornery lineup of Hall of Famers who played every game with an artistic paranoia that drove them to superstardom might include Frank Chance at first base, Jackie Robinson at second, Dave Bancroft at short, George Brett at third, Carlton Fisk behind the plate, and an outfield of Enos Slaughter, King Kelly and — who else? — Ty Cobb. The pitcher? Bob Gibson more than fills the bill, shading Famers like Early Wynn, Don Drysdale, Joe McGinnity, Burleigh Grimes and Nolan Ryan for "honors." A ball club like that wouldn't be losing ball games for lack of effort or intensity, and the man on the mound, Mr. Gibson, wouldn't have to be told that it was important to play at 110 percent. For these guys, and Gibson in particular, that was a given.

Tom Seaver found himself embroiled in a typical Gibson outing in the

1973 season opener with Gibson & Co. on April 12, 1973. In the season-opening series at St. Louis, the two were matched and put on a 2 to 1 thriller, as well as dusting one another with beanies that roared over and at batting helmets. In one of Tom Seaver's more celebrated victories he made it a point to stand up to any ideas of intimidation ol' Gibby might have had, rifling a shot or two at Gibson's whiskers in the midst of a rather historic exchange in the sixth frame when Gibson, after ducking a Seaver sizzler, said, "You've got better control than that, Tommy." Seaver fired back: "Remember the one you put under my helmet last year? That was uncalled for, with a man on first and me batting in a bunting situation." The game resumed without further incident, but the point had been made. And Seaver's name had the "W" behind it.

The box score follows:

New York Mets at Busch Stadium, St. Louis, April 12, 1973

New York	AB	R	H	BI	St. Louis	AB	R	H	BI
Harrelson, ss	5	1	2	0	Brock, lf	4	0	0	0
Millan, 2b	3	1	0	0	Sizemore, 2b	3	0	1	0
Milner, 1b	4	0	1	1	J. Cruz, cf	4	1	1	1
Staub, rf	3	0	0	0	Torre, 1b	4	0	1	0
Jones, lf	2	0	0	1	Simmons, c	3	0	1	0
Garrett, 3b	4	0	1	0	Reitz, 3b	4	0	0	0
Chiles, cf	4	0	1	0	Carbo, rf	3	0	0	0
Dyer, c	4	0	0	0	Busse, ss	2	0	0	0
Seaver, (WP)	3	0	1	0	McCarver, ph	1	0	1	0
Hennigan, p	1	0	0	0	Tyson, ss	0	0	0	0
Gibson, (LP)	3	0	0	0					
Totals	33	2	6	2	Totals	31	1	5	1

Line Score:				
New York	200	000	000	2–6–0
St. Louis	000	000	100	1–5–3

2BH: Harrelson, Chiles, Sizemore, Simmons; HR: Jose Cruz; DP: Mets, 1; LOB: Mets 8, St. Louis 5; Sac: Millan; Sac. Fly: Jones; BB: Seaver 2, Hennigan 1, Gibson 2; K: Seaver 7, Hennigan 0, Gibson 7; PB, Simmons; Save: Hennigan; Time: 1:51; Att: 6,356.

The Seaver-Gibson Log:

May 6, 1968	St. Louis 2, New York 1	Gibson WP, Seaver LP
Apr 13, 1969	St. Louis 3, New York 1	Gibson WP, Seaver LP
Apr 19, 1969	New York 2, St. Louis 1	Seaver WP, Gibson LP
Sep 11, 1970	St. Louis 5, New York 2	Gibson WP, Seaver LP
Apr 26, 1971	New York 12, St. Louis 2	Seaver WP, Gibson LP
May 7, 1971	New York 3, St. Louis 1	Seaver WP, Gibson LP
Sep 1, 1971	New York 7, St. Louis 1	Seaver WP, Gibson LP
Apr 12, 1973	New York 2, St. Louis 1	Seaver WP, Gibson LP
Apr 23, 1975	New York 2, St. Louis 1	Seaver WP, Gibson LP

On August 7, 1972, St. Louis beat New York 3 to 2 in 13 innings at St. Louis. Neither Seaver, who pitched through eight innings, nor Gibson, who went 10, were the pitchers of decision. Reliever Tug McGraw was the winner and Diego Segui was the loser.

In a Shea Stadium twinbill, Gibson and Seaver squared off in the opener on April 11, 1974, the game turning on the Cards' two-run eighth, St. Louis beating the Mets 8 to 7. Relievers Mike Garman (WP) and Craig Swan (LP) finished up for Gibson (ND) and Seaver (ND).

Tom Seaver versus Juan Antonio (Sanchez) "Manito" Marichal (1937–)

Marichal was elected to the Baseball Hall of Fame in 1983

"Manito," Juan Marichal

As with other Mound Maestros in this book, Tom Seaver was matched with Hall of Famers who also appeared on the "lineup card" of the other maestros. For example, both Warren Spahn and Seaver had in common at least one faceoff with Jim Bunning, Bob Gibson, Fergie Jenkins and Juan Marichal, whose profile appears after Gibson's by virtue of his July 19, 1960, ML debut. It is interesting to note that by the time the Seavers, Suttons and Blylevens (just three among the many) appeared on the scene, ML baseball had evolved to a point where ball players enjoyed a freedom of movement among franchises that the pioneers of antiquity could only dream about. Consequently, the movement among players from team to team and from league to league increased to a point where by the 1990s it was an annual guessing game as to which player would be moving to which team for the coming season.

Toward the end of his career, Juan Marichal made one of those moves, from the NL's San Francisco Giants over to the AL's Boston Red Sox, where in 1974 he coaxed a 5 and 1 record out of his aging and ailing right arm. Two token appearances a year later with the Los Angeles Dodgers closed out his career in the Senior Circuit.

The Marichal-Seaver matchups, but three in number, are another of those baseball mysteries. Why, between 1967 and 1974, did the two confront one another so rarely? One would expect at least nine or ten games between two such stars, but the Big Pairing just didn't materialize. During those years both hurlers posted better than merely acceptable numbers. Seaver's follow those of Marichal's for the years 1967–1973:

Marichal	Age	W-L	CG	SH	ERA	PR	TPI
1967	29	14–10	18	2	2.76	14	1.6
1968	30	26–9	30	5	2.43	20	2.7
1969	31	21–11	27	8	2.10	50	5.6
1970*	32	12–10	14	1	4.12	-2	-0.7
1971	33	18–11	18	4	2.94	17	1.8
1972	34	6–16	6	0	3.71	-5	-0.4
1973	35	11–15	9	2	3.82	-3	0.5

Seaver	Age	W-L	CG	SH	ERA	PR	TPI
1967	22	16–13	18	2	2.76	17	2.3
1968	23	16–12	14	5	2.20	24	3.0
1969	24	25–7	18	5	2.21	42	5.5
1970	25	18–12	19	2	2.82	40	4.5
1971	26	20–10	21	4	1.76	54	6.6
1972	27	21–12	13	3	2.92	16	2.3
1973	28	19–10	18	3	2.08	51	5.5

For whatever reason(s), baseball's followers had to content themselves with only three matchups between the two Famers. Two of these came in 1968, and the final, during the Dominican's last full NL season, was reported by the *New York Times*' Leonard Koppett, the only sportswriter named to the writers' wing of both the baseball and basketball Hall of Fame.

> San Francisco, August 10, 1973: What would have been a classic confrontation a few years ago — Tom Seaver pitching against Juan Marichal — merely reflected the inexorable march of time tonight as Seaver's New York Mets walloped Marichal's San Francisco Giants, 7–1.
>
> The explanation was simple enough: Seaver, at 28, is in his prime; Marichal, at 34, is past his. When Marichal was 28 he ate Mets for breakfast, so that even now his career won-lost against them is 26–7, including two losses in three decisions this year. But at 34, he already was struggling when Wayne Garrett socked a three-run homer for a 6–0 lead in the fifth in a situation created by a two-out error.

---

* Marichal's subpar 1970 was caused by a severe reaction to a penicillin injection which led to chronic arthritis and severe back pain, nearly ending his career, but he did bounce back in 1971 for another good year before his condition hastened the end of both his effectiveness and career.

That was more than enough for Tom Seaver to improve his '73 log to 14 and 6 before moving on to a final 19 and 10 mark — plus his second of three Cy Young awards.

One of those years Koppett was referring to in his account of Marichal's 7 to 1 loss was 1968. That season he whipped NL ball clubs 26 times, including Seaver (in 5 to 4 and 9 to 5 matchups), and he might well have won a Cy Young award had it not been for an outstanding Bob Gibson effort. Named the Giants' opening day pitcher for 1968, Marichal opposed Seaver at Candlestick Park on April 10, and had a huge hand in helping beat the Mets in a thrilling ninth-inning victory that really should have been won by the New Yorkers.

Neither Marichal nor Seaver was a pitcher of record that day, both having been removed after eight innings of a sharply pitched duel. Then came the ninth, which Seaver entered but didn't survive. He managed to retire dangerous Willie McCovey, who had already nailed him for a seventh-inning roundtripper, on a popup. This came after a Mays single, followed by a passed ball that moved the 37-year-old Giants legend to second, and a Jim Ray Hart single, to make it a 4 to 3 ball game. That brought out Gil Hodges, who, in his baptism of fire as the Mets' new commander, replaced Seaver with reliever Danny Frisella. It wasn't the most propitious choice Mr. Hodges might have made, as Frisella presided over a final two-run foray that snatched victory from the jaws of defeat and got the Giants off to a first place start. Frank Linzy, who pitched a scoreless ninth for the Giants, received credit for the victory which, in all probability, should have been a Marichal loss. But the baseball gods smiled on the Giants and frowned on the Mets that day, and the history book had its entry: San Francisco 5, New York 4. There was no footnote to explain Gil Hodges' confoundment.

Juan Marichal's record against Tom Seaver, singletons in victory (June 15, 1968: 9 to 5) and defeat (August 10, 1973: a 7 to 1 loss), plus one other game that wound up as a No Decision (April 10, 1968), has little, if anything, to say about his Hall of Fame career. That was built on a baffling array of speeds, arm motions and bedeviling pitches that broke over the plate in wholly unpredictable ways. Hitters never quite knew what to expect next from the fellow they called "the Dominican Dandy." Those breaking pitches, incidentally, were not out of the junkyard. Juan Marichal busted that ball over the plate with plenty of mustard on it. The complete package made for total devastation — right from the start. In his debut he blanked the Phils, shutting them down on one hit in a 2 to 0 victory over John Buzhardt on July 19, 1960. From that point on, he added one sterling credential after another in single game, single season and career achievements that convinced the BBWAA to put the Marichal plaque on Cooperstown's walls in 1983. Among those achievements were his 1966, 7.88 Ratio record, 17th best all time; a miserly .230 On Base Percentage, also in 1966, 21st all time; and 10 shutouts in 1965, which tied him for 16th all time. His June 15, 1963, no-hitter against Houston, and that pitching masterpiece won finally in the 16th frame against Warren Spahn (a 1 to 0 victory for Marichal), on July 2, 1963, were still other evidences of a master of pitching arts and sciences at work. Among the Dominican Republic's many gifts to ML baseball, "Manito" Marichal was one of the very best.

Tom Seaver versus Gaylord J. Perry (1938–)

Perry was elected to the Baseball Hall of Fame in 1991

There was never any doubt that Gaylord Perry used a spitter as one of his primary pitching weapons. The trick was to catch him at it. The baseball rule book states in Rule 8.02 that a pitcher is prohibited from either defacing or applying any foreign substance to the ball — and that the umpire is the sole judge as to whether any portion of the rule has been violated. Thus armed, baseball went about its business with finely tuned radar whenever Mr. Perry took the hill. Alas, the number of times he was caught can be counted on one finger.[34] What is the message here? Umpires, managers, coaches, veteran ball players, even knowledgeable spectators, are wise in the ways and wiles of baseball tomfoolery. They know trick pitches when they see them. Or do they? But catching the culprit red-handed, despite all the help from every corner of the ball park, proved to be futile — indeed, frustrating.

While all the hub-bub over his spitter was going on, Gaylord Perry pitched his way into the record book and ultimately into baseball's Valhalla, thumbing his nose at the naysayers all the way. More than 300 wins, a no-hitter against Bob Gibson, Cy Young awards in both leagues, and five 20-game seasons are, after all, hefty evidences of superior accomplishment, spitter or no spitter. And more: in good humor, but with unrepentant, even insolent glee, he authored *Me and the Spitter* at the height of his career, just two seasons after having been awarded his AL Cy in 1972.

Winner of three more lifetime victories than Tom Seaver (314 to 311), Perry dueled Seaver five times but wound up on the losing side of the series, two games to Seaver's three. In each of the five games, Seaver and Perry were the pitchers of decision, the third of the series being the spine-tingler of the set.

On April 14, 1979, on a Spring Training–like day in San Diego, the two aces hooked up in a close, early season game in which the Padres finally prevailed with a ninth inning rally that pushed across the winning run to beat Tom Terrific 3 to 2. The Reds had opened up a two-run lead in the first inning on a Johnny Bench single, but found themselves stymied the rest of the way by Gaylord Perry's mystifying bag of tricks. After the score was tied via a two-run sixth, the game settled down to a string of goose-eggs on the scoreboard until Broderick Perkins singled to open the last of the ninth. There followed a walk to "the Human Rain Delay," Mike Hargrove, and finally a Fernando Gonzalez single that scored the winner for Perry and the Pads. On that day, at least, the Padres, who went on to a miserable 68 and 93 record, played championship baseball behind Perry, who the year before had copped his second Cy Young award with his 1978, 21 and 6 record.

The Seaver-Perry Log:

Jul 27, 1970	New York 5, San Francisco 3	Seaver WP, Perry LP
Aug 12, 1978	San Diego 4, Cincinnati 2	Perry WP, Seaver LP
Apr 14, 1979	San Diego 3, Cincinnati 2	Perry WP, Seaver LP
Aug 12, 1979	Cincinnati 9, San Diego	2 Seaver WP, Perry LP
Sep 27, 1981	Cincinnati 4, Atlanta 2	Seaver WP, Perry LP

Tom Seaver versus Philip Henry "Knucks" Niekro (1939–)

Niekro was elected to the Baseball Hall of Fame in 1997

All right, you trivia pros, who were the NL's first pennant playoff pitchers in the newly formatted playoff scheme for NL and AL pennants in 1969? Hint: one of them pitched in the Bigs for 24 years and never made it to the World Series. Right! The answer is Phil Niekro of the Braves and Tom Seaver of the Mets. They squared off in Atlanta on October 4, 1969, to begin the best-three-of-five series that would determine the NL pennant winner, who would go on to meet the AL winner. And concerning this man Niekro ... quite a story...

But first, another puzzler: how many pure knuckleball pitchers have been elected to the Hall of Fame? Think on that for a bit.

It isn't altogether unfair to liken knuckleball hurlers to Rodney Dangerfield, who, even unto old age, still hadn't gotten any respect. Bill James had quite a bit to say about that in his 2001 *New Bill James Historical Baseball Abstract*.[35] What this shrewd baseball observer has to say is particularly germane in any conversation about Phil Niekro, one of the few pure knucklers in the game's history (pure, meaning that he used his knuckleball pitch better than 80 percent of the time). Now then, what does Mr. James have to say about the subject?

> Did you ever notice that no knuckleball pitcher has ever won the Cy Young award?...
>
> According to the Win Shares system the best pitcher in the American League in 1971, and by a pretty decent margin, was Wilbur Wood. Wood

also had a great year — 334 innings, 22–13 won-lost record, 1.91 ERA — and he did draw one vote in the Cy Yound balloting, but only one. Why wasn't he a larger part of the discussion?

It is the direct and indirect effect of throwing the knuckleball. Looking more carefully at the data, I found that six knuckleball pitchers show up as deserving of the Cy Young Award (actually, three pitchers including Phil Niekro [ed: note that our man Niekro, under discussion in this profile is mentioned] *four times*)...

The *in*direct effects of the knuckleball on Cy Young voting are greater than the direct effects. The indirect effect can be illustrated best by looking at *Phil Niekro, 1978*. Phil Niekro in 1978 went 19–18 for a last-place team, the Atlanta Braves; he pitched 334 innings, which led the National League by 59 innings, struck out 248 men, which was second in the league, and posted a 2.88 ERA despite pitching in what was, at that time, by far the best hitter's park in the National League, the Launching Pad. By the Win Shares method[36] he ranks the best pitcher in the National League by a huge margin, 8.63 Win Shares (about 25 runs). Every other pitcher since the award began who had led by that kind of a margin, anything even close to that, has won the Cy Young Award. Niekro drew no first-place votes, and was seventh in the Cy Young voting.[37]

The contention from Bill James' corner is that the Phil Niekros and Hoyt Wilhelms of the baseball world are vastly underrated in the many rankings and "Greatest" lists that baseball aficionados eagerly devour. The two of them, Niekro and Wilhelm, are, incidentally, the only pure knuckleballers in the Hall. (That answers the question posed above.) With respect to rankings, here is a sampling of Top 100 Pitchers lists:

	Bill James	TBE*	Kelley[†]	TSN[‡]	McCaffrey[§]
Niekro	26	27	59	NR	NR
Wilhelm	27	15	75	NR	in alphabetical listing

Those professional slights notwithstanding, there was room in the Hall of Fame for Phil Niekro and Hoyt Wilhelm after all, and that was what mattered most for both of them. At the end of the day they had beaten rather stiff odds.

---

*Thorn and Palmer, Total Baseball Encyclopedia ratings based on TPR (Total Player Ratings).
 [†]Sabermetrician Brent Kelley's top 100 pitchers listing in his 1988 publication The 100 Greatest Pitchers.
 [‡] From listing in The Sporting News: "Baseball's 100 Greatest Players" lists 27 pitchers among the 100 greatest players.
 [§]E.V. and R.A. McCaffrey poled former ball players in 1986 and in 1987, and published the results under the title Players' Choice. On pp.207–208 they list the greatest 100 players alphabetically.

As things turned out, "Knucks" was the first Famer Tom Seaver encountered. The confrontation took place in Atlanta on May 17, 1967. Seaver, 3 and 1 going into that game, looked like he was on his way to number four until Hank Aaron and Joe Torre, each registering their ninth homers of the young season, did him in. Torre's blast came with the score tied as the ninth inning began. The inning — and the game — was over as quickly as Torre's leadoff shot found its way into the seats. The beneficiary was Niekro, who had entered the fray as a reliever in the eighth. With knuckleballs fluttering, he disposed of the Mets in 1–2–3 order, picking up his first victory of the season. That was the first of their 10 meetings in the NL (both were in the AL between 1984 and '86 but were not booked against one another), and those classic duels between precision power and bobbing, weaving slow stuff produced six Niekro wins against four for Tom Terrific.

Aside from a 9 to 3 licking the Braves took on May 14, 1969, every last one of the remaining matches resulted in one-run or shutout ball games. Among the gems in the series were Niekro's three-hitter, resulting in a 5 to 0 conquest of the Mets on May 21, 1969. Seaver matched that one with a three-hitter of his own, beating the Braves 4 to 0 to chalk up his 20th victory in 1977. But the big fellow went that victory one better in 1979 as he led the Reds to a 2 to 0 win at Cincinnati on April 19 when Ken Griffey, Sr., caught a wayward Niekro flutterball and rifled it into the far reaches of Riverfront Stadium, providing Seaver with the only run he needed. The box score follows:

Atlanta Braves at Cincinnati Reds, April 19, 1979

Atlanta	AB	R	H	PO	Cincinnati	AB	R	H	PO
Royster, 3b	3	0	1	2	Griffey, Sr, rf	4	1	2	1
Hubbard, 2b	4	0	0	1	Concepcion, ss	4	0	1	1
Matthews, rf	3	0	0	3	Morgan, 2b	4	0	0	5
Burroughs, lf	4	0	0	4	Foster, lf	3	1	1	3
Lum, 1b	4	0	0	6	Driessen, 1b	3	0	0	8
Murphy, c	3	0	0	6	Knight, 3b	3	0	1	1
Bonnell, cf	3	0	0	1	Geronimo, cf	2	0	1	2
Frias, ss	2	0	1	1	Correll, c	3	0	0	5
Beale, ph	0	0	0	0	Seaver (WP)	3	0	0	1
Chaney, ss	0	0	0	0	Niekro, (LP)	2	0	0	0
Office, ph	1	0	0	0	Skok, p	0	0	0	0
Totals	29	0	2	24	Totals	29	2	6	27

Line Score: Atlanta   000   000   000   0–2–0
                Cincinnati   000   100   10x   2–6–0

2BH: Frias; HR: Griffey, Foster; SB: Royster; CS: Concepcion; LOB: Atlanta 5, Cincinnati 4; BB: Niekro 1; Int: Geronimo; Skok 0, Seaver 3; K: Niekro 4, Skok 1, Seaver 5; WP: Niekro; Umpires: Treitel, Grooms, Sharkey and L. Harris; Time: 1:58; Att: 16,182.

7. Tom Seaver

Leave it to the Yankees to be involved in benchmark events. It was as a Yankee that Phil Niekro won his 300th game, and it was at Yankee Stadium that Tom Seaver won his 300th — and, as fate would have it, in the very same year. On Phil Rizzuto Day, August 4, 1985, Seaver threw a six-hitter at the Yanks, beating them 4 to 1 in front of 54,032 cheering New Yorkers. Not to be outdone by the 40-year-old Seaver, Phil Niekro, at 46, administered an 8 to 0 blanking of the Blue Jays in Toronto on the last day of the 1985 campaign, October 6, becoming the oldest pitcher to hurl a complete-game shutout. An interesting sidenote: Niekro didn't throw a single knuckler in that game, most likely as an in-your-face gesture, until he nailed the final batter with the last two pitches of that milestone ball game. Yes indeed, they were knuckleballs.

"Tom Terrific."

The Seaver-Niekro Log:

May 17, 1967	Atlanta 4, New York 3	Niekro WP, Seaver LP
May 26, 1968	Atlanta 2, New York 1	Niekro WP, Seaver LP
May 14, 1969	New York 9, Atlanta 3	Seaver WP, Niekro LP
May 21, 1969	New York 5, Atlanta 0	Seaver WP, Niekro LP
Jul 4, 1971	Atlanta 2, New York 0	Niekro WP, Seaver LP
Apr 29, 1976	Atlanta 2, New York 0	Niekro WP, Seaver LP
Jul 4, 1966	Atlanta 5, Cincinnati 4	Niekro WP, Seaver LP
Sep 25, 1977	Cincinnati 4, Atlanta 0	Seaver WP, Niekro LP
Apr 19, 1979	Cincinnati 2, Atlanta 0	Seaver WP, Niekro LP
May 1, 1983	Atlanta 2, New York 1	Niekro WP, Seaver LP

Tom Seaver versus Steve "Lefty" Carlton (1944–)
Carlton was elected to the Baseball Hall of Fame in 1994

The Chicago Cubs opened the 1965 season with staff ace Larry Jackson on the mound opposing Bob Gibson and his defending world champion Cardinals. Though the game ended in a 10 to 10 standoff and could hardly be called an opening day classic, it was significant, at least to the extent that the names of both Gibson and one of the Red Bird relievers, Steve Carlton, appeared in the box score. That day, April 12, marked Carlton's first appearance in a sparkling career that extended through 24 seasons and eventually earned the native Floridian Hall of Fame honors.

Steve Carlton's success and fame as one of the premier left-handed hurlers in baseball rests primarily on the most electrifying slider in the game's history. Thrown from a three-quarter motion, his slider was doubly effective because he could paint the outside edge of the plate with it against lefties and run it in on the hands of the right-handed hitters. To make that work took not only exceptional control, but strength.

Throughout his career Carlton's uncompromising workout regimen never varied. There was no such a thing as a day off. Exercises like pushing his pitching arm into a big bucket of uncooked rice, which he incorporated into his martial arts training program, were part of his running, stretching and modified weights regimen, a routine that made game days seem like a cake walk for him. For Lefty it paid off. The combination of natural talent, outstanding control, command of several pitches, extraordinary strength and intense concentration resulted in four Cy Young awards and a barely believable single-season outing in 1972 during which, among other things, he won 48 percent of his *team's* games, 27 of 56.

Steve Carlton, who dueled Tom Seaver 15 times between 1972 and 1983.

Contemporaries the stature of a Carlton and a

Seaver could be expected to wage baseball warfare often, their managers seeking to trump the opposition's ace card with one of their own. Consequently, the two dueled on no less than 15 occasions between 1972 and 1983.

The Seaver-Carlton Log:

May 21, 1972	New York 4, Philadelphia 3	Seaver WP, Carlton LP
Sep 24, 1972	New York 2, Philadelphia 1	Seaver WP, Carlton LP
Apr 6, 1973	New York 3, Philadelphia 0	Seaver WP, Carlton LP
Jun 21, 1974	New York 3, Philadelphia 1	Seaver WP, Carlton LP
Apr 8, 1975	New York 2, Philadelphia 1	Seaver WP. Carlton LP
Sep 3, 1976	New York 1, Philadelphia 0	Seaver WP, Carlton LP
Aug 26, 1977	Philadelphia 4, Cincinnati 2	Carlton WP, Seaver LP
May 1, 1978	Philadelphia 12, Cincinnati 1	Carlton WP, Seaver LP
May 11, 1978	Philadelphia 4, Cincinnati 1	Carlton WP, Seaver LP
Jul 28, 1978	Cincinnati 2, Philadelphia 1	Seaver WP, Carlton LP
May 10, 1978	Cincinnati 5, Philadelphia 3	Seaver WP, Carlton LP
Aug 18, 1981	Cincinnati 3, Philadelphia 2	Seaver WP, Carlton LP
May 24, 1982	Philadelphia 9, Cincinnati 1	Carlton WP, Seaver LP

With a two-run rally in the bottom of the ninth, the Reds beat the Phillies 3 to 2 on April 8, 1981, in the season opener at Cincinnati. Reliever Tom Hume was the winning pitcher, and Sparky Lyle, in relief of Carlton (ND), was the losing pitcher. Tom Seaver received a ND.

Steve Carlton was the losing pitcher in the 1983 season opener at Shea Stadium, 2 to 0. Doug Sisk was the winning pitcher in relief of Tom Seaver (ND).

Both Seaver and Carlton migrated to the AL, where they were on opposing teams in 1986 when Carlton signed with the White Sox after having been released by the Phillies, but they did not face one another as American Leaguers.

Eleven of the 15 ball games in this series were decided by two runs or less, exactly what might have been expected when pitchers of the Seaver-Carlton caliber crossed swords. On those days managers[38] scratched for what they could get, hoping against hope that a bingle or two might fall in at just the right time.

Steve Carlton was the loser ten times against Seaver (Carlton won only four, with one ND), losing by 1 to 0 and 2 to 0 counts, as well as three 2 to 1 games, all of them reminiscent of those early 1900s pitching masterpieces. Further, the two greats met four times as opposing pitchers in season openers. Mr. Terrific also won that series-within-a-series, 3 to 0 with one ND. His 3 to 0 whitewashing of the Phils on April 6, 1973, was one of two shutouts he fired at Carlton-led teams during their historic series of matches.

Steve Carlton was the Cy Young award winner in 1972 when, pitching for the last-place Phillies, he came up with a 27 and 10 record that defied all baseball logic simply by pitching so brilliantly that even the Phils could win behind him. Notwithstanding, four of his ten losses that marvelous season came at the hands of the Mets, and two of those four were administered by Tom Seaver, one near the beginning of the season in his first encounter with "the Silent Sphinx" (so named because of his aversion to media people), and the other in the 1972 season's finale at Shea Stadium, both one-run losses. In between he ran off a string of 15 straight wins while putting together the makings for a pitcher's Triple Crown. Carlton's 1972 achievement stands as one of the greatest single-season pitching efforts in the game's history.

A decade later fortunes, as so often happens, reversed themselves, not only for the Mets, who finished the 1982 season dead last in the NL East, but for the Reds, for whom Tom Seaver at that point in his career was still pitching. His Reds, with a 61 and 101 record that was as equally wretched as Carlton's '72 Phils (59 and 97), found innumerable ways and means to lose ball games and ruin pitching records. Seaver's suffered accordingly, at 5 and 13. By May 24, when the Reds met the Phils, Tom's not-so-terrific log stood at 1 and 5, and before the day was over it was 1 and 6, pounded into the artificial turf of Riverfront under a 9 to 1 onslaught. With the exception of a single tally in the fourth inning spliced together by two hits, Carlton, on his way to his fifth victory, shut the Reds down on three safties, in command all the way — as he was so often during his last 20-game season, a year spiced with league-leading figures in Ks (286), complete games (19), shutouts (6) and innings pitched (295.2). Lefty's 23 wins that season left him with 285 career victories, and during the next season he would rack up his 300th victory with a 6 to 2 win over the Cardinals — and in St. Louis. The box score of Carlton's 9 to 1 conquest of Seaver and the Reds follows.

Philadelphia at Riverfront Stadium, Cincinnati, May 24, 1982

Philadelphia	AB	R	H	BI	Cincinnati	AB	R	H	BI
Dernier, rf	5	0	3	1	Milner, lf	4	0	1	0
Rose, 1b	4	1	1	1	Trevino, c	4	0	0	0
Unser, 1b	0	0	0	0	Cedeno, cf	3	1	0	0
Schmidt, 3b	4	2	2	1	Driessen, 1b	3	0	3	0
Matthews, lf	3	0	1	0	Concepcion, ss	4	0	0	0
Gross, lf	1	0	0	0	Bench, 3b	2	0	0	0
Diaz, c	5	2	2	3	Householder, rf	3	0	1	1
Brusstar, p	0	0	0	0	Oester, 2b	3	0	0	0
Maddox, cf	5	2	3	0	Seaver, (LP)	1	0	0	0
Trillo, 2b	3	0	0	1	Landestoy, ph	1	0	0	0
Aguayo, 2b	1	0	0	0	Leibrandt, p	0	0	0	0
DeJesus, ss	5	1	2	1	Barranca, ph	1	0	0	0
Carlton (WP)	3	1	2	1	Shirley, p	0	0	0	0
Virgil, ph, c	1	0	0	0					
Totals	40	9	16	9	Totals	29	1	5	1

Line Score:	Philadelphia	032	021	100	9–16–0
	Cincinnati	000	100	000	1–5–0

2BH: Maddox, Schmidt, DeJesus, Rose, Driessen, Milner; HR: Diaz; SB: Dernier, Schmidt, Driessen, Milner; SH: Carlton; DP: Cincinnati 1, Philadelphia 3; K: Carlton 3, Brusstar 0; Seaver 4, Leibrandt 0, Shirley 0; BB: Carlton 3, Brusstar 0, Seaver 4, Leibrandt 0, Shirley 0; WP: Seaver; Umpires: Gregg, Engle, Brocklander and Runge; Time: 2:19; Att: 17,110.

Tom Seaver versus James A. "Jim" Palmer (1945–)

Palmer was elected to the Baseball Hall of Fame in 1990

In the short span of time between 1984 and '86, Tom Seaver's AL sojourn, which closed out his score of years in the Big Time *sans peur et sans reproche*, coincided with contemporaries he had encountered in the NL. However, Don Sutton, who had been with Los Angeles and Houston (1966–82), was the only hurler Tom Terrific had met in the NL and again in the AL during that 1984–86 period. Phil Niekro, Steve Carlton, Nolan Ryan and Bert Blyleven were also on hand at the time, but only Blyleven (Pirates, 1978–80), who was not matched against Seaver during his NL years, came up against him once in 1985 and again in '86.

Seaver's AL years produced encounters with eight of the notables reviewed in his profile. Bret Saberhagen, Jack Morris, Jimmy Key, Frank Viola and Dave Stieb, still to come, complete the list — except for the first Famer he met in the AL. That pitcher was Jim Palmer, who is the man of prime concern at this juncture. There was only one time when he and Tom Seaver were opposing pitchers, and although it was enough to bring two Hall of Famers together in the same game, the occasion was not nearly as festive for Palmer as it might have been at an earlier stage of his career.[39]

Career endings are

Handsome Jim Palmer, who was winding up his career in 1984 as Tom Seaver began his AL career.

rarely pleasant. Most come despite the best of intentions and over protestations that there are still victories and base hits left in those once-magnificent abilities. In 1984 the Orioles took a chance on their aging superstar, Jim Palmer, Baltimore's "Posterboy" hero. He had already entered eight 20-game seasons into the record books, been honored with three Cy Young awards, and become the youngest pitcher to throw a world series shutout when he blanked the Dodgers in Los Angeles on October 6, 1966, in a four-hit masterpiece, among many another noteworthy accomplishments in a distinguished career. Was there enough left after 18 seasons to notch a few more wins in 1984? The answer was not long in coming.

Albert Williams, a journeyman Nicaraguan righthander pitching for Minnesota's Twins, took the measure of Palmer in an early season start on April 8. Then Toronto ace Dave Stieb bested him ten days later to run Big Jim's record to 0 and 2. While he hadn't been blasted, he wasn't impressive enough to raise high hopes, either. But a third start was in order in the early stages of the season, and so on April 23 manager Joe Altobelli wrote Palmer's name into the starting pitcher's slot. His foe that day would be Tom Seaver.

The visiting O's opened at Comiskey Park with a run in the opening stanza on a Cal Ripken double that scored Gary Roenicke, but the Sox, aided by an unearned run, came back to tie it in the bottom of the first. Palmer got by the second, aided by a twinkling, but by the third frame, tell-tale signs that Big Jim was beginning to falter appeared. A Carlton Fisk boomer far into the seats, and the solid crack of White Sox wood on horsehide, told skipper Altobelli that the relief corps would soon get its call. After facing three Oriole hitters in the top of the fourth, Altobelli had seen enough to prompt his first call to the bullpen, and that was all for Jim Palmer on his No Decision outing against Tom Seaver. On the other hand, Seaver, though likewise saddled with a ND, moved on through his first season with the Pale Hose to a workmanlike 15 and 11 record.

One cannot help but wonder what must have been passing through Tom Seaver's mind that day as he watched one of baseball's best take the kind of pounding that had the retirement call written all over it. Not yet that close to the end of the line, Mr. Seaver himself was nonetheless getting up there, and no doubt making mental notes about what he might prefer his own final curtain call look like.

April of 1984 moved on into May, and on the 2nd, Palmer was called out of the bullpen to stay the hand of the Indians, locked in an extra-inning tie with the O's. That night he pitched the last three innings, losing to Cleveland as he surrendered the winning runs in the 16th frame. It wasn't too long after that, on the 22nd of May, that Jim Palmer pulled on his Oriole togs for the last time. He was released the next day after refusing to go on the voluntarily retired list. Like so many great ones before him, they had to peel the uniform off his back before he would call it a career.

But though his career was over, it was a thing of rare beauty that led to his Hall of Fame election as the Orioles greatest pitcher and one of the classic mound craftsmen of the 20th century. Only two other pitchers in AL history had won 20 as often as he did: Walter Johnson (12 times) and Lefty Grove (8, as did Palmer). That's rare company.

Tom Seaver versus Ferguson "Fergie" Jenkins (1943–)
Jenkins was elected to the Baseball Hall of Fame in 1991

In 1969 Tom Seaver won 25 ball games, none more important in the pennant race than his 21st, a 7 to 1 victory over Fergie Jenkins. That one at Shea Stadium on September 9 pulled the Mets to within a half game of the front-running but fading Cubs. The next day they swept a twinbill from the Montreal Expos while Leo Durocher's Bruins lost to the Phillies, and the Miracle Mets moved into the NL penthouse on their way to one of baseball's more celebrated Cinderella stories.

Although Jenkins and Seaver were in the NL together for nine seasons, there were only three matchups, which, given the stature of the two titans, seems strange. Nonetheless, each of the three meetings had its own significance, and each delivered according to the high expectations one might attach to those kinds of encounters. Jenkins, already well on his way to a third straight 20-game season in 1969, had established himself as the bell-cow of the Cubs' pitching staff, and would eventually put his name on the short list of Chicago's greatest pitchers. The younger Seaver, with fewer seasons behind him, was, despite his youth, already drawing comparisons with a young Turk of another era, Christy Mathewson. And, though it took Jenkins longer to get his Cooperstown ticket than it did Seaver, both wound up there just the same.

Fergie Jenkins mastered his craft, every last part and parcel of it. The Canadian hit, fielded and pitched like a Famer. Working in front of some less-than-sensational teams, he suffered the consequences, losing 13 times during his career by 1 to 0 scores, and victimized 45 times by shutout losses. But he also won almost 300 games and was a six-time 20-game winner. The Jenkins record also sported an eye-popping mark of but two walks per nine innings pitched, and better than six whiffs per game. His 10.4 Ratio ranks as number 27 all time. Another of those high IQ hurlers, Jenkins approached hitters and ball clubs not only aware of their strengths and weaknesses, but aware of his own and his teammates', as well. The complete package kept weaker ball clubs in games he pitched, and proved to be a winning formula for teams like the 1967–72 Cubs and the 1975 Texas Rangers, for whom he won a career high 25 games.

As for those two other games involving Jenkins and Seaver: both were masterfully pitched early season victories for Jenkins, as he defeated the Mets 3 to 1 in a ball game in which the Cubs knicked Seaver for home runs in three consecutive innings, one of them by Jenkins himself. That April 25, 1969, victory was matched several seasons later when, on April 17, 1973, Jenkins came close to no-hitting the Mets, shutting them down with an artful two-hitter, 1 to 0. Rick Monday's fourth-inning four-bagger, one of only five hits Seaver permitted, proved to be the winning blow. In that game Jenkins walked one, fanned five and evened his early season record at 1 and 1 as he retired 25 of the last 27 Mets he faced.

The trials and temptations Ferguson Jenkins overcame during and after his career were an important part of his life, and of far more consequence than a ball game won or lost, however much those vicissitudes and tragedies might have affected the record. He faced and overcame them — especially the loss of his first wife in an automobile accident, and that of his daughter and girl friend two years later — much as he did in duels with Tom Seaver and the rest of his mound adversaries, with calm and composure and often in the midst of tumult. That, too, is Hall of Fame–like heroism that earns respect and honor.

Tom Seaver versus Donald Howard "Don" Sutton (1945–)
Sutton was elected to the Baseball Hall of Fame in 1998

The era of the mid '60s to the mid '80s produced a remarkable number of pitchers whose longevity, as well as their productivity, was unusual when considering the changes that rushed more and more hurlers into the game for strategic reasons. Despite that, a choice group of the game's elite piled up big numbers that, for many, led directly to the Hall. Don Sutton, the fourth pitcher in the listing that reviews some of those huge, record-book entries, was one of those active, 4500-inning-plus pitchers. Sutton, who was matched with Tom Seaver in both leagues, endured 23 major league campaigns because, among other reasons that had to due with his capabilities, he was never out of shape. His viewpoint: "I believe the biggest key to any pitcher's success is to treat the ability to pitch as though it were a gift, to treat it with respect and reverence, and to make sure that when you go out there you've got 100 percent of your ability ready to go with you. Don't short-change your body, because it is a gift." Accordingly, Sutton paid the price, and the ultimate dividends were worth it: a spot among the game's elite at Cooperstown.

The following list details some of those out-sized pitching numbers:

Don Sutton, who started 756 ball games (third high all time).

	Yrs-seasons	IP	W-L	PR	WS	C-TPI
Phil Niekro	1964–87/24	5404.1	318–274	196	375	33.8
Nolan Ryan	1966–93/27	5386.0	324–292	217	289	20.7
Gaylord Perry	1962–83/22	5350.1	314–265	315	367	34.9
Don Sutton	1966–88/23	5282.1	324–256	263	318	13.2
Steve Carlton	1965–88/24	5217.1	329–244	240	367	33.7
Tom Seaver	1967–86/20	4782.2	311–205	422	391	48.7

Tommy John	1963–89/26	4710.1	288–231	217	289	25.6
Fergie Jenkins	1965–83/19	4500.2	284–226	161	323	29.8

    PR   Pitching Runs
    WS   Win Shares (Bill James value category)
    C-TPI   Career Total Pitching Index (Sabermetric value category)

Sutton and Seaver, both of whom appear in the workhorse listing above, met a baker's dozen times during their ML travels. Unlike the other pitchers in the Seaver profile, Sutton tangled with Seaver in both leagues, on 11 occasions in the NL and twice with him in the AL, the latter two in rather extraordinary exhibitions reviewed ahead.

Don Sutton's fast ball wasn't among the top-tier heaters, and his breaking pitches weren't as good as those of a Blyleven, a Carlton or a Koufax (whose Cy Young, 1966 season, his last, came during Sutton's rookie year), but Sutton's changeup and his command of the strike zone were right up there among the best in the game. Low Ratio and Walks-per-nine-IPs, both indicators of a pitcher's ability to deal with hitters on their own terms, limiting scoring opportunities and making the hitter put the ball in play, usually on the ground, were hallmarks of a Sutton effort. His career numbers in both, 10.4 in Ratio and 2.29 Walks-per-nine-IPs, rank high on the all time lists.

The very first time Seaver and Sutton dueled the game went through nine innings in a scoreless tie at Los Angeles. The Mets edged a run home in the top of the 10th that went unanswered, and Sutton lost a five-hitter. But Tom Terrific was just that, walking but one, giving up four well-spaced singles and breaking a seven-game Dodger winning streak. That 1968 series inaugural was indicative of what was to come. Eleven of the 13 games, each a low-scoring tilt that might easily have gone one way or another, were decided by two runs or less.

The Seaver-Sutton NL Log:

Jun 10, 1968	New York 1, Los Angeles 0	Seaver WP, Sutton LP
Aug 2, 1968	New York 3, Los Angeles 2	Seaver WP, Sutton LP
Jun 14, 1969	New York 3, Los Angeles 1	Seaver WP, Sutton LP
May 5, 1970	New York 5, Los Angeles 4	Seaver WP, Sutton LP
Jun 14, 1971	Los Angeles 3, New York 2	Sutton WP, Seaver LP
Sep 20, 1978	Cincinnati 4, Los Angeles 3	Seaver WP, Sutton LP
Jul 30, 1979	Cincinnati 2, Los Angeles 0	Seaver WP, Sutton LP
May 8, 1981	Cincinnati 4, Houston 0	Seaver WP, Sutton LP
Aug 15, 1982	Houston 7, Cincinnati 3	Sutton WP, Seaver LP

On July 17, 1970, the Dodgers beat the Mets 1 to 0 in 10 innings. The Mets' Tug McGraw (LP) relieved Seaver (ND), as Sutton got the win on a five-hit shutout.

The Dodgers won a 6 to 4 game on a Von Joshua homer in the ninth. Sutton was the winner and Tom Hume, in relief of Seaver (ND), was the losing pitcher.

The Seaver-Sutton AL Log:

In a game that extended over two days, with 17 innings played on May 8, 1984, Don Sutton was Milwaukee's starting pitcher at Comiskey Park, pitching through seven innings. Five relievers followed Sutton, four pitching through the 17th inning on the 8th. The game was continued on the ninth, with Chuck Porter finishing the last 7.1 innings of the game (LP) that was ended when Harold Baines homered in the White Sox' half of the 25th inning. That made Tom Seaver, who started the 17th against Porter, the winning pitcher. Then he started the regularly scheduled game on May 9 and was the winner in that game, also. Don Sutton, who had given up four hits and no earned runs, received a No Decision.

The California Angels, with Don Sutton pitching, defeated the White Sox in one of Seaver's last games before going to the Red Sox, where he finished his career. The game was played on June 9, 1986, featuring a brilliant Sutton two-hitter, as the Angels won, 3 to 0. Tom Seaver went seven innings, sustaining the loss.

The Sutton-Seaver series, 13 games strong, wound up with Seaver at 8 and 3 with two NDs and Sutton at 5-7-1, and was distinguished by its absence of a single blow-out, with a premium on precision pitching. And if that was the choice of those fans who liked nothing better than a pitcher's duel, they certainly could count on getting their money's worth when these fellows were out there working on the hill against one another.

By way of completing the Sutton-Seaver record, it should be noted that they were teammates, playing in All-Star games in 1973, '75 and '77, with Sutton the winner in the 1977 clash at Yankee Stadium. In each of those ball games the NL took the AL into camp, a pleasant memory for both of the those highly competitive, accomplished hurlers.

Tom Seaver versus Nolan Ryan "The Ryan Express" (1947–)
Ryan was elected to the Baseball Hall of Fame in 1999

There's nothing Lilliputian about the numbers Nolan Ryan put up in a marathon career that wound up after 27 years, the longest on record, spiced with 5714 strikeouts, 100 mph heaters and the number one spot all time for fewest hits per nine innings pitched, 6.56. And we haven't even gotten around to seven no-hitters, the last of which was thrown at the tender age of 43. Despite having lost 292 ball games, third high on that list, the BBWAA found no objection to extending the welcoming carpet at Cooperstown in his first year of eligibility for the Hall in 1999. There also happened to be 324 victories and all those other "little things," like 9.55 strikeouts per game, 5386 innings pitched, 61 shutouts, which tied him with Tom Seaver for the seventh spot on that particular list, and 773 games started, second only to Cy Young's 815.

And then there were the Mets. Ah yes, the fumble-bumble Mets. It was

The Ryan Express.

in New York that the Texan started out his career — one year earlier than Tom Seaver. But between them and another bright and shiny young Met by the name of Jerry Koosman, they soon made believers out of New Yorkers first, and then the rest of the baseball world, however nonplussed it, as well as they, might have been when, in 1969, their team, those same Mets who had lost 101 games in 1967 and another 89 in 1968, turned the world upside down, winning everything in sight, including the world series laurel wreath!

With an opening chapter like that, the careers of Nolan Ryan, Jerry Koosman and Tom Seaver would have to be bestsellers. And indeed they were. Seaver, Koosman and the flame-throwing Ryan logged 66 major league seasons between them, and this wondrous triumvirate of hurlers ran up a total of 855 victories plus enough golden moments to fill up the careers of a host of topflight pitchers.

As so frequently happens, this precocious trio was soon broken up. Nolan Ryan left for the greener pastures of California where, for cowboy Gene Autrey, he toiled for another eight seasons before coming home to his native Texas in 1980 to pitch for the Houston Astros. That gave him his first opportunity to work a ball game against his old colleague, Tom Terrific. Alas, the matchup never took place, and by the time Ryan got back into the AL to finish out his career with the Texas Rangers, Seaver had moved to the higher elevations of the broadcast booth. Consequently, there is no contest extraordinaire between them to grace the record book. There *is* one ball game, however, in which they were reunited as teammates: the 1973 All-Star game played at Kansas City in 1973, when both had a hand in beating the AL, 7 to 1. Some years later, when Ryan was with California and Seaver was putting together a 14 and 2 year with the Reds, they were on opposing All-Star teams, each contributing an inning to the summer gala which was won, again, by the Senior Circuit, 5 to 4.

With the kind of Mach-1 speed that Nolan Ryan brandished right on up to his last game in the Bigs, he devastated hitters in both leagues. He ranks among the top five flamethrowers in the history of the game. There were Amos Rusie, Walter Johnson, that other Johnson, Randy, Lefty Grove and the Ryan Express. And it was the Ryan Express who got there "fustest wid' da mostest!"

Tom Seaver versus Rik Aalbert "Bert" Blyleven (1951–)

Bert Blyleven and Tom Seaver were potential opponents in both leagues but didn't get around to a shootout until July 8, 1984. Prior to that time Bert Blyleven had been in the NL between 1978 and 1980. It was in the AL, when the Dutchman was pitching for Cleveland and Minnesota during Seaver's years in the AL, that they finally met for the first of their three matchups.

The first of these was played in Chicago. Neither made it through the seventh inning of the 1985 tilt, the White Sox prevailing 9 to 8 with a four-run eighth that pinned the loss on rookie reliever Steve Farr and provided Juan Agosto with his second win of the season, also in relief.

On May 7, 1985, this time in Cleveland, Tom Seaver made one of the very few relief appearances of his career, coming on to retire the last two outs in the bottom of the sixth for starter Floyd Bannister. The Sox' relief ace at that time, Bob James, then came in to finish out Bannister's victory, as the Pale Hose beat the Indians 7 to 4. Bert Blyleven started that game, went seven innings, and was charged with the defeat.

The best of the Blyleven-Seaver encounters was the last, played at Comiskey Park on July 19, 1985. In a sparkling exhibition of pitching, the two matched pitches, Blyleven's hooks and Seaver's pot-

Bert Blyleven, who threw that knee-buckling hook.

pourri of power pitches, surrendering but one run between them. That came in the second inning when Carlton Fisk found one of Big Bert's offerings to his liking and spiked it into the seats for what proved to be the winning tally in a 1 to 0 ball game. One mistake, one run, one loss. And while the Sox mustered only four other hits that day, Seaver's Hall of Fame battery mate had given Tom Terrific the wherewithal to beat Cleveland and record his 10th win at that point — and Blyleven's 10th loss. As good as the Indians' ace was, Seaver was better, allowing only four hits, stranding six, walking only one and fanning four. That game was prototypical of many another, matching Seaver against an opponent who pitched well enough to win almost every time out — but not against Tom Terrific, which is precisely why he was the Terrific One.

The Blyleven-Seaver series ended up with no wins, two losses and a No Decision for Blyleven, and one win, no losses and two No Decisions for Seaver.

Since his retirement in 1992 after a 22-year career, Bert Blyleven has stood on the fringes of baseball immortality. It is rather unlikely that he will be elected to the Hall of Fame, and that raises a number of comparison questions, as well as giving pause regarding the whys and wherefores of HOF selections. Much like Ron Santo, Negro Leagues catcher Biz Mackey, Bobby Grich and "Indian Bob" Johnson among position players, and "Bucky" Walters, Lon Warneke, Jim Kaat and "Big Ed" Reulbach among the pitchers, Blyleven's career, though impressive, has not caught the electors' imagination, or at least has failed to garner enough respect among them to cause his admission to baseball's pantheon. And with respect to Bert Blyleven, that is more than a little puzzling.

Possessed of one of the two or three best curve balls in the game's history, Blyleven's name is listed in *TBE*'s number 35 spot among pitchers, a position better than that of no less than 28 Famers. In the James rating system, he ranks at number 39 in Win Shares per season, with 26.36. On that list of the game's 100 best, 17 Famers fall in line behind him. In numerous other rating lists Blyleven's name appears, usually between the number 30 and 75 spot among the game's best moundsmen. Some of his more persuasive numbers grace the major career listings, including 60 shutouts (#9), 685 games started (#8), 301 Wins Above League (#15) and 287 victories (#22). Beyond that, his post-season record in two world series and two league championship series is as outstanding as it is usually overlooked, having won three games in three tries in the LCS setting, while winning three and losing one in his two Fall Classic opportunities.

As with many others reviewed in the Seaver profile, Bert Blyleven found himself involved with Tom Terrific on one other occasion, the 1973 All-Star game at Royals Stadium in Kansas City. That night he was touched up for two NL runs in the third and turned out to be the losing pitcher. Seaver that night hurled a scoreless eighth inning in a game started and won by Rick Wise of the Cardinals. At least in matters Seaver-Blyleven, there isn't much question as to superiority between the two. But with respect to the Hall—?

Tom Seaver versus Rickey Eugene Reuschel (1949–)

On September 5, 1972, Tom Seaver ran headlong into a nasty three-hitter thrown by 22-year-old Rick Reuschel, the burly Cubs pitcher, who slammed the door in the face of the Mets, evening his rookie record at 7 and 7 with a 3-zip victory that knocked off Seaver, who had won 16 as the game commenced. But three singles, one free pass and five Ks—all that and still more accomplished on a night when he was rushed into the game in place of Bill Hands, manager Whitey Lockman's scheduled starter, who was incapacitated by a lingering stone bruise in his pitching hand. The blanking was one of four he authored in a 10-victory freshman campaign, and certainly got Tom Seaver's attention.

That late summer engagement was the first of seven which ultimately led to Reuschel's 2 and 5 record in the series, the other win having been crafted on an August 17, 1978, four-hitter that took the wind out of Cincinnati's sails, 2 to 0, during Tom Terrific's first full season in the Queen City on the Ohio. In the remaining five of this series there were four Seaver conquests and one game in which Reuschel was the loser but Seaver was not the pitcher of decision, the win in that one going to the Mets' reliever, Skip Lockwood.

Rick Reuschel. The first time he squared off with Seaver he threw a 3-zip shutout at Tom Terrific and his Mets.

The Seaver-Reuschel Log:

Sep 5, 1972	Chicago 3, New York 0	Reuschel WP, Seaver LP
Sep 13, 1974	New York 6, Chicago 0	Seaver WP, Reuschel LP
Aug 17, 1978	Chicago 2, Cincinnati 0	Reuschel WP, Seaver LP
Jul 15, 1979	Cincinnati 7, Chicago 1	Seaver WP, Reuschel LP
Sep 5, 1980	Cincinnati 5, Chicago 3	Seaver WP, Reuschel LP
May 19, 1981	Cincinnati 5, Chicago 0	Seaver WP, Reuschel LP

With one out in the 10th inning, the Mets beat the Cubs 3 to 2, on July 3, 1976, reliever Lockwood getting the win in relief of Seaver (ND). Reuschel (LP) went all the way, sustaining his sixth loss.

It is readily evident that there was some pretty classy pitching going on when those two met. We know all about Tom Seaver, but it should be noted that Rick Reuschel was a force to reckon with during his 19-year stay in the Big Show. *Baseball: The Biographical Encyclopedia*[40] has this to say about Reuschel:

> Although he looked more like someone pitching at the annual Fourth of July picnic than a major league hurler, Rick Reuschel was one of baseball's more effective pitchers for nearly 20 years. An intense competitor, Reuschel could field well despite his 6-foot 3-inch, 235-pound frame. He could even run — the climax of the 1986 Pirates highlight film showed Reuschel scoring a winning run from second base with a thunderous slide at home.

Relying on airtight control, a no-windup throw and enough of a variety of fastballs to keep hitters off stride, he worked his way through 3500-plus innings to post double-figure win numbers in 13 of his 19 seasons. He celebrated his 40th summer with a snappy 17 and 8 reading for San Francisco during their pennant-winning 1989 season. Big Rick was one of the outstanding craftsmen of his era, and that is why his series of matches with Tom Seaver appears with those of Famers and other great moundsmen of Seaver's day. During that superb 1989 season of his, Reuschel defeated his former team, the Cubs, in the LCS' series-clinching encounter. Earlier that summer he was the NL's starting pitcher at Anaheim, a game which the AL won with five early inning runs, one of which was a gargantuan circuit clout by Bo Jackson in the first-inning off Reuschel, who left after his first inning start. The 5 to 3 NL loss was pinned on John Smoltz.

One of many brother combos who pitched in the majors, Rick and his brother Paul managed to pull of a first when, on August 21, 1975, they combined on a shutout against the Dodgers. That, along with his 1985 Comeback Player of the Year award and those shutout victories over Tom Seaver, rank as A-number-one achievements in a noteworthy career.

Tom Seaver versus Stephen Douglas "Steve" Rogers (1949–)

While Tom Seaver was assembling all the appropriate pieces of a Cy Young year in 1973, there was another award-winning year in the making north of the border. That was being fashioned by Steve Rogers of the Montreal Expos, whose '73 rookie season was one of the 40 best on record. Debuting in mid–July, the 23-year-old native of the Show-Me state came up to the majors intent on showing the Expos that he had the stuff to make the big team's rotation. That he did — and more. His 10–5 record, featuring a gaudy 1.54 ERA, included two wins over the Seaver-led Mets, one of them against the Terrific One himself. His efforts were rewarded with TSN's Rookie Pitcher of the Year award.

Beyond his natural physical gifts, Steve Rogers was endowed with superior intellect. The latter was never minimized, neither in the classroom, where as a collegian he majored in petroleum engineering at Tulsa University, nor on the diamond, where his 90-plus heater and pitching know-how attracted major league attention.

Any number of great hurlers were successful as pitchers because their approach to the art of pitching was as much cerebral as it was physical. Among them, these names will be familiar: Jim Palmer, Robin Roberts, Tommy John, Eddie Plank, Tim Keefe, Urban Shocker, Greg Maddux and Warren Spahn. Add two more names to that distinguished list: Steve Rogers and Tom Seaver. Mind games, which usually start in the pitcher's box and spread out to the fielders behind the pitcher, the managers, the coaches and the hitters, were their foundation pieces for pitch and location selections, and because the whole of baseball action begins with a pitch, there is no overestimating the mental aspect

Steve Rogers, Montreal ace whose career statistics set the pace for Expo pitchers.

of the decisions and selections a hurler makes. Pitchers like Spahn and Rogers and Seaver gave that aspect of the game much more than "idle thought."

Seven games made up the Seaver-Rogers series, and in the span of ten seasons that lapsed before the last matchup took place in 1982, Steve Rogers emerged victorious four times and Tom Seaver twice. The complete record follows.

The Seaver-Rogers Log:

Sep 8, 1973	Montreal 3, New York 1	Rogers WP, Seaver LP
Aug 8, 1975	New York 7, Montreal 0	Seaver WP, Rogers LP
Apr 9, 1976	New York 3, Montreal 2	Seaver WP, Rogers LP
Sep 29, 1976	Montreal 7, New York 2	Rogers WP, Seaver LP
May 16, 1980	Montreal 2, Cincinnati 1	Rogers WP, Seaver LP

In a 14-inning game finished neither by Seaver (7.1 IP, ND), nor Rogers (6 IP, ND) on July 23, 1978, the Cincinnati Reds beat Montreal 5 to 4. Relievers Manny Sarmiento (WP) and Wayne Twitchell (LP) were the pitchers of decision.

In the last game of the Rogers-Seaver series, played on May 29, 1982, the Expos beat the Reds 4 to 2. Seaver started for the Reds (ND). Reliever Joe Price was charged with the loss. Steve Rogers went all the way to pick up the win.

As Tom Seaver himself once said, "In every game there are only six or seven pitches you make that might have a direct effect on the outcome of the game, and sometimes it comes down to just one. Then, it better be the right one." That was true in a game played in Montreal on May 16, 1980, when a tight ball game had the wheels turning both in the dugout and out there on the mound where Seaver, pitching with all the wit and savvy of a 14-year veteran, was locked in a pitching duel with Steve Rogers. That night Seaver made all the right pitches through six innings of a scoreless duel with the younger Rogers, not permitting a hit. Then in the seventh, Expo outfielder Ellis Valentine singled, and, late-stages of a ball game being what they are, Seaver bore down, measuring each hitter and choosing his spots with extra care. He emerged from that frame unscathed. Meanwhile, Steve Rogers had given up several base hits, but none for extra bases, and no free passes were issued to the Reds. But Rogers was nonetheless touched for a run in the top of the seventh, and the way Tom Terrific was rolling along, that one run looked like it might stand up.

It didn't. The Expos' first hit came in the bottom of the seventh on a Valentine single, and that was, perhaps, the wee small voice whispering that there might be trouble ahead. Some of those crucial seven or eight pitches that mean the difference were used up to get the Expos retired without scoring a run, sending the game to the eighth with the Mets still ahead 1 to 0.

Then it was Steve Rogers' turn, and in the eighth he retired the Mets' first two hitters, only to have Dan Driessen single to center. But Gary Carter erased Driessen with a perfect throw on a steal attempt, and that put an end to whatever thoughts the Mets might have had of adding an insurance run or two.

That brought on the bottom of the eighth, and Seaver went out to "mop up." But that wasn't to be, either, because a Carter single, combined with Warren Cromartie's double and a sacrifice fly by pinch hitter Tom Hutton scored two, and though Seaver finished the inning, he had apparently expended all of those "just right" pitches and lost his second game of the young season. Rogers, on the other hand, won his third, having lost four going into that evening's game and having had the pleasure of out-dueling one of the game's greats.

Steve Rogers finished the 1980 season with 16 wins and a 2.98 ERA, good for fifth best in the NL. During his best year, two seasons later, four of his 19 wins were shutouts, and his 2.40 ERA was the best in the major leagues.

His 12-year career, played entirely in the uniform of the Expos, though but six wins over the .500 mark, provided Montreal with 158 victories, the most ever for an Expo pitcher. And in most of those, pitching in front of some weak Expo clubs, the difference between winning and losing was out there on the mound — between the ears.

Tom Terrific, American Leaguer

Tom Seaver's heart was in New York. Though he had pitched as capably for the Reds as he had for the Mets before going to Cincinnati, he came back to the Big Apple for the 1983 season ready, more than willing, and still quite able to resume his career in front of the fans who had always rated him *numero uno*. The 1983 Mets, however, went through two managers, numerous roster changes and the miseries that go with finishing dead last. It was a repeat of Seaver's 1967 rookie season. That would seriously complicate his artistic accomplishments in the season ahead, but despite pitching on a staff that completed only 18 games all season, along with other subpar numbers, Seaver pitched well, starting 35 times, completing five and blanking two of his opponents among the nine hard-earned victories he was able to cobble together under the prevailing circumstances.

When the 1983 season ended, the front office went to work, and by the time the Mets went to spring training in 1984, the club had been transformed. And to the outright horror of Met fans, Tom Seaver, unprotected in the major league compensation pool after the '83 season, was snapped up by the Chicago White Sox, who were trying to improve their 1983 divisional champions. It wasn't only Met fans who were in shock. Tom Seaver was, in turn, disbelieving that it could ever happen, deeply disturbed by it, and, finally, just plain livid over the sudden change in his career.

Tom Seaver an American Leaguer? That would have been akin to moving Christy Mathewson or Pete Alexander or Carl Hubbell from the NL to some also-ran in "that other" league. But it had happened before, and Tom Seaver determined to make the best of the no-way-out situation. So he packed his bags and headed for Sarasota, Florida, where Chicago's Pale Hose went through their spring training routine in 1984. There he would prepare for the "Coda" of his 20-year career.

The years 1984–86 in the AL turned out to be Tom Seaver's last three under the Big Tent. And they were far from petering-out years. During those seasons he started 33 times in each of his two full Chicago seasons, and another 28 in his curtain-call season, divided between the White Sox and Boston's Red Sox. During that time he added another 38 wins to his 273 NL victories, pushing him over the coveted 300 mark. The most significant of those AL conquests happened, as the baseball gods surely must have willed it, in New York with 54,032 wildly-cheering Gothamites, many of them Met fans, cheering him on to his 300th win. It came on August 4, 1985, and, to the utter delight of the New York Mets, it came at the expense of the hated Yankees.

Five of the better moundsmen during Seaver's mini–AL era have been selected as his competitors for review during that period. They include Jack Morris (July 26, 1977), Dave Stieb (June 29, 1979), Frank Viola (June 6, 1982), Bret Saberhagen (April 4, 1984) and Jimmy Key (June 6, 1984).[41] These pitchers will be reviewed as a group and in chronological order during the 1984–86 seasons.

Carlton Fisk (L), with Tom Seaver, a Hall of Fame battery, the first for the White Sox since the days of Ray Schalk, Red Faber and Ted Lyons.

Tom Seaver: The American League Log

May 14, 1984	Chicago 2, Kansas City 0	Seaver WP, Saberhagen LP
Jul 3, 1984	Chicago 9, Detroit 5	Seaver WP, Morris LP

On August 30, 1984, Toronto beat Chicago 4 to 3. Loser Tom Seaver pitched a complete game, starting against Jim Clancy (ND). Jimmy Key came on in the ninth to get a Save behind winner Jim Gott.

The Twinkies beat the White Sox in 13 innings on September 20, 1984, at Minnesota. Tom Seaver (ND) started against Frank Viola (ND). Relievers Bert Roberge (LP, Chicago) and Joel Davis (WP, Minn.) finished up.

May 20, 1985	Toronto 6, Chicago 1	Key WP, Seaver LP
Jul 10, 1985	Chicago 1, Detroit 0	Seaver WP, Morris LP
Aug 24, 1985	Toronto 6, Chicago	3 Stieb WP, Seaver LP
Sep 3, 1985	Kansas City 3, Chicago 2	Saberhagen WP, Seaver LP
Aug 18, 1986	Boston 3, Minnesota 1	Seaver WP, Viola LP
Sep 19, 1986	Toronto 6, Boston 4	Stieb WP, Seaver LP

In a game played at the Metrodome, the White Sox beat the Twins 4 to 3 on June 25, 1986. Reliever Joel McKeon received credit for the win. Starter Tom Seaver pitched the first five innings (ND), followed by relievers McKeon, Bill Dawley (ND) and Bob James (Sv). Frank Viola, with relief help from Keith Atherton (Sv), was the winning pitcher.

Note: The record above does not include games involving Don Sutton, Jim Palmer and Bert Blyleven, each of whom was reviewed in the NL portion of Tom Seaver's career. In their AL matchups, Seaver beat Palmer in their only game; he won against Sutton (ND) in the record-breaking game of May 8–9, 1984, and lost to Sutton's two-hitter, 3 to 0, on June 9, 1986; and recorded a win, a loss and a ND against Blyleven.

Note also: Roger Clemens, whose rookie season was 1984, was on the Boston roster from 1984 forward, capturing his first Cy Young award in 1986, but did not appear against Tom Seaver. The two were Red Sox teammates during the last weeks of Seaver's career (June 30, 1986, to the end of the season).

Tom Seaver versus Jack Morris (1955–)

The kind of pitcher a manager wants on his staff is the kind of pitcher who will win big ball games. Jack Morris did that. In spades. He brought home three world championships for three different ball clubs during his 16-year career. In his clashes with Tom Seaver he broke even, when on July 10, 1985, he throttled the White Sox, scattering five hits in a 1 to 0, Seaver-like outing. That made up for his only other matchup with Seaver, a messy 9 to 5 loss in which he was shelled in a five-run inning that broke the ball game wide open.

In the 1984 Tiger runaway from the AL, Jack Morris started out with

Jack Morris' 21 and 6 paced the Toronto pitching staff in their 1992 pennant season.

a 10–1 mark as the Bengals roared to an opening 35 and 5 record en route to a world championship that Fall. One of those 10 conquests was a no-hitter against the White Sox on April 7. The very next day another pitcher of no-hit fame took the mound against the Tigers — Tom Seaver. Alas, in his first AL start, the Tigers beat him 7 to 3. There would be no one-upping Jack Morris, at least not on that occasion.

Jack Morris went on to capture the Babe Ruth award for his MVP performance in the 1984 World Series, and added yet another in 1991 when he led the Minnesota Twins to an upset Series championship over the Atlanta Braves. In one of the premier pitching performances in World Series history, he beat the Braves in game seven, 1 to 0, in 10 innings of tense, spine-tingling play. Those were the kind of ball games in which a manager wanted a Jack Morris on the hill. He would see to it that the bullpen phone would never ring. That's what made him MVP.

Tom Seaver versus Dave Stieb (1957–)

On August 24, 1985, Dave Stieb, into a monster season for Toronto during which his 2.48 ERA, Opponents' BA of .213 and 49 Pitching Runs led the AL, locked horns with Tom Seaver. He sailed along without permitting a run — or a hit — until leadoff hitter Rudy Law broke up his no-no and scoreless stint in the bottom of the ninth with a shocker into the Comiskey Park stands. Up came Bryan Little, who tagged Stieb for his only tater of the season, making the score 6 to 2 with no one out. That brought on relievers Gary Lavelle and Tom Henke, who finally got things settled down to preserve Stieb's 6 to 3 victory. Despite the two long shots, it was one of the better Toronto pitching efforts of the season.

The winningest pitcher north of the border, Dave Stieb.

Tom Seaver's major league swan song occurred on September 19, 1986, as he sought to improve his record for the Boston Red Sox at Toronto against Dave Stieb in the second of their two matchups. Stieb, who was finishing out a dissatisfying and unsuccessful season, entered the game with a 5–11 mark, but pulled together enough support and went six innings, long enough to earn his sixth victory. Behind 3 to 2 after four frames, manager Joe McNamara and Tom Seaver agreed it was time to bid farewell, thus bringing an end to one of the finest pitching careers on record.

The box score of that historic game:

Boston at Toronto, September 19, 1986

Boston	AB	R	H	BI	Toronto	AB	R	H	BI
Boggs, 3b	4	1	0	0	Fernandez, ss	4	0	1	1
Barrett, 2b	3	0	2	0	Upshaw, 1b	1	1	0	1
Buckner, 1b	3	1	2	0	Moseby, cf	3	0	0	0
Stapleton, pr,1b	0	0	0	0	Bell, lf	4	1	2	1
Rice, lf	4	0	2	1	Barfield, lf	3	2	1	1
Baylor, dh	4	0	0	0	Whitt, c	3	0	0	0
Evans, rf	4	0	0	0	Leach, dh	4	1	1	1
Armas, cf	4	1	1	0	Gruber, 3b	2	0	1	1
Gedman, c	4	1	2	1	Mulliniks, ph,3b	1	1	0	0
Romero, pr	0	0	0	0	Iorg, 3b	0	0	0	0
Owen, ss	3	0	0	0	Lee, 2b	4	0	1	0
Greenwell, ph	1	0	0	1	Stieb, (WP)	0	0	0	0
Tarver, pr	0	0	0	0	Cerutti, p	0	0	0	0
Seaver, (LP)	0	0	0	0	Henke, p	0	0	0	0
Stewart, p	0	0	0	0					
Lollar, p	0	0	0	0					
Stanley, p	0	0	0	0					
Totals	34	4	9	3	Totals	29	6	7	6

Line Score: Boston   200 000 101 4-9-0
             Toronto   021 003 00x 6-7-1

2BH: Barrett, Barfield; HR: Gedman; SF: Upshaw; SB: Gruber, Upshaw; CS: Barrett; DP: Boston 1, Toronto 1; PB: Wjitt; K: Seaver 1, Stewart 0, Lollar 0, Stanley 5, Stieb 4, Cerutti 0, Henke 1; BB: Seaver 2, Stewart 4, Lollar 0, Stanley 0, Stieb 4, Cerutti 0, Henke 0; WP: Stieb.

Tom Seaver versus Frank Viola (1960–)

Tom Seaver's 311th and final major league win was a flashback to those typical low-scoring, taut pitching duels he had been a part of in his NL days. The vintage savvy and finesse of many years was on display at Minnesota's Metrodome on August 18, 1986, when he beat Frank Viola and the Twins 3 to 2 as the Bosox came from behind with two ninth-inning markers. Viola pitched well that evening, but just as he had been in his score of years on major league mounds, Tom Seaver was a tad better when he had to be. The only run he gave up was a homer off the bat of Roy Smalley, Jr., the 376th four-base blow (there was a grand total of 380) he had surrendered; but, like so many of those that went before, though it may have tied up the game, it didn't unravel his overall performance—another of those characteristic Seaverisms.

1988 AL Cy Young award winner Frank Viola.

Prior to Seaver's Metrodome win, he had dueled with Frank Viola in 1984 in a No Decision effort that Viola's Twins won, 5 to 4. That game was turned over to relievers. Earlier in the 1986 season, while Seaver was still with the White Sox, he received another ND in a game Viola lost by a 4 to 3 score. The final Seaver-Viola tally stood at 1–0–2 for Seaver and 0–2 and 1 for Viola.

Frank Viola was one of the top-drawer lefties of his era, a 1988 Cy Young winner and a World Series winner in two out of the three games he pitched in the Twins' victory over the Cardinals in 1987. A 1990, 20-game winner with the Mets, Seaver's old team, Viola had at least that much in common with Tom Terrific.

Tom Seaver versus Jimmy Key (1961–)

James Edward Key made his AL debut on April 4, 1984, four days before Tom Seaver took on Jack Morris and the Tigers in Seaver's Junior Circuit inaugural. Key spent the 1984 season learning his trade, working out of the bullpen, appearing in 63 innings, with a 4 and 5 record. One of his relief appearances was against the White Sox in an August 30 game at Chicago. That day Key's Blue Jays beat Tom Seaver 4 to 3 with a top-of-the-ninth rally that overcame a 3 to 2 Pale Hose advantage. Key's last-inning mop-up job preserved the Jays' win and earned him one of his 10 saves in his rookie season.

By the 1985 season Jimmy Key was well on his way to becoming the best lefty in Toronto's history. His record that year, as of his second matchup with Tom Seaver on May 20, 1985, was 2 and 2. Toronto's 6 to 1 victory moved the suave southpaw's mark to 3 and 2, at the expense of Seaver before some 45,000 Canadians at Toronto's Skydome. That season Key won 14 and lost but six. There was more and better ahead.

Jimmy Key was a winner. His career 186–117 mark left him with a winning percentage of .614, ranking him among the top 60 hurlers all time. Using one of the 20th century's better curveballs and a sinking fastball, he recorded his winning record, and an outstanding World Series log, to pitch with Cy Young award precision, placing second in the voting for that prestigious award in both 1987 and 1994. And he also had the privilege of pitching against the Terrific One, Tom Seaver.

Jimmy Key, who won the deciding game of the 1996 World Series over Greg Maddux, 3 to 2.

Tom Seaver versus Bret Saberhagen (1964–)

Who knows?! Had it not been for a Mr. Tom Seaver, Bret Saberhagen's rookie season might have been an 11–10 winning year. May 14, 1984, changed that. In Chicago the youngster was taken into camp by the well traveled vet and lost a 2 to 0 ball game, despite pitching well enough to win. But there was this former NL giant out there who gave up only five scattered hits, and he was not to be denied. Seaver went to a 4 and 2 mark, and Saberhagen to 1 and 2. So 1984 ended with 10 wins and 11 losses.

But Bret Saberhagen moved on to make the list of noteworthies arrayed against Tom Seaver. He rang down the curtain on the 20th century with 166 Ws, two Cy Young awards and two Comeback of the Year awards. Though injuries threatened to curtail his career more than once, he has, through super control, a variety of pitches and one of the best pickoff moves in the game, stayed a few steps ahead of the man with the baseball scythe, logging 20-game seasons in 1985 and 1989, and career lows in ERA (2.16) and Ratio (8.7, a top-100 mark) in his 1989, Cy Young season.

Bret Saberhagen, a two-time Cy Young award winner, 1985 and 1989.

It was during his first award-winning season that the second and final Saberhagen-Seaver duel took place. In that one, on September 3, 1985, the youngster got even with the vet, beating him 3 to 2, as the Kansas City Express moved on to its 1985 pennant. Powered by Saberhagen, Brett, Frank White, Charley Leibrandt, Willie Wilson, *et al.*, they won it all that Fall.

Terrific — Just Terrific!

> Not since Babe Ruth created the Yankees image in the 1920s had any single player done so much for, and meant so much to, a big-league franchise.[42]

Name them: The Babe, certainly. Christy Mathewson, of course. Joe DiMaggio and Lou Gehrig, Willie Mays, Mickey Mantle and Tom Seaver. All of them are Toast-of-the-Town, New York names. Magic names, names deserving of a special place among the Special, they're the first among equals among New York's baseball nobility. They're at the core of the "equals" residing in baseball's Valhalla, the Hall of Fame.

Baseball literature is replete with accolades about Tom Seaver, Fresno, California's most famous baseball son. For example, in chronicling baseball's 20th century, David Nemec and Saul Wisnia said that, "For the millions of Mets fans who watched a miracle unfold [ed: in Seaver's career], however, none of it compared to '69 when The Franchise came of age."[43] Almost from the start, Tom Seaver, "the Franchise," began to spiff up the Mets record book, expanding outward into all time record listings, and finally putting it all together in a Hall of Fame career. Rest assured, the references to this man's contribution to 20th century baseball will not soon end. They're going to be talking about him for a long, long time to come.

8. ROGER CLEMENS

Major League Career Totals Through the 2001 Season	Won	Lost	Pct.
Boston, Toronto, New York (AL)	280	145	.659

K-Master Roger Clemens.

The twelve fastest pitchers to home plate are: Roger Clemens, Bob Feller, Lefty Grove, Randy Johnson, Walter Johnson, Sam McDowell, J. R. Richard, Amos Rusie, Nolan Ryan, Dazzy Vance, Rube Waddell, Smokey Joe Williams. *Honorable Mention:* Dizzy Dean, Bob Gibson, Rich "Goose" Gossage, Sandy Koufax, Herb Score.

These are the fellows whose pitches were heard but rarely seen. They threw the kind of pitches that gave the hitter less than three-tenths of a second to make up his mind whether to swing, and if he should swing, where to level his lumber to make contact with that blazing sphere coming at him. Which of those above could complicate a hitter's life the most with the fastest heater of them all is dependent on who makes up the list, but most, if not all of the names on this "Quick List" will appear when the subject is flamethrowers.

William Roger Clemens, poised to cross

the 300-win threshold as this is being written, and a lock for election to the Hall in his first year of eligibility during a record-breaking career based primarily on otherworldly heat, has been enormously successful, from his high school days forward, on something far less sensational but far more essential: control. Hear him out: "Any kid who believes that throwing hard is all he needs to do to be successful on the mound is mistaken. The reason I performed well in high school was because I threw strikes. I've carried that with me throughout my career. You can turn the lights out in a stadium and I can still throw strikes. But I didn't develop velocity until I matured and understood that the power comes from my lower body."

Of course, being able to throw a splitter or a cut-fast ball in the high 90s doesn't hurt, and it has enabled the fiery Clemens to pile up huge numbers as he has made his way to the forefront of most of the significant numbers listings. The critical mass he leaves behind will leave those who follow with a challenge or two. Here is a sampling:

Career Stats (through 2001 season)

Ranking	Category	Stats
4	Pitching Wins	56.6
4	Pitching Runs	552
4	Strikeouts	3717
5	Total Pitching Index	60.1
6	K/game	8.61
14	Wins Above Team	65.6
29	Wins Above League	272.4
27	Opponents' BA	229
27	Hits/game	7.65
28(t)	Shutouts	45

Single Season Stats

12(t)	Winning % (2001)	870
17	Pitching Wins (1997)	7.6
19	Pitching Runs (1997)	74.1
22	Total Pitching Index (1997)	8.0
23	K/9 IP (1998)	10.39

Tack on his two 20-K games, six Cy Young awards and two Pitching Triple Crowns, and the magnitude of Roger Clemens' achievements takes on Bunyanesque proportions. They have caused more than a few well-respected observers to suggest that there is sound reason to put Clemens in the number one spot among pitchers, all time. Along with Greg Maddux, another whose exploits merit top-5 consideration, the Rocket closed out the 20th century by etching his name on the list of all time greats. These two, already living legends, join the other seven mound maestros already profiled as the century's very best.

Roger Clemens' matchup list, as with the list for Greg Maddux (who follows Clemens), consists of many active pitchers and few Hall of Famers. The obvious reason for this is their active status. The choices for the Clemens profile are listed below in a different arrangement than for the seven mound maestros who preceded him.

The Hall of Famers

	CTPI*	TBE Rank[†]	Yrs. Active in AL During Clemens' Career
Jim Palmer (HOF, 1990)[‡]	34.9	27	1984
Phil Niekro (HOF, 1997)	33.8	30	1984–87
Steve Carlton (HOF, 1994)[‡]	33.7	31	1986–88
Nolan Ryan (HOF, 1999)	20.7	96	1984–93
Don Sutton (HOF, 1998)	13.2	198	1984–88

The Clemens Era Top Pitchers

Greg Maddux	64.7	3	2000[§]
Randy Johnson	37.1	21	1989–98
Kevin Brown	35.1	25	1986–95
Pedro Martinez	34.9	26	1998–01
Bert Blyleven	30.7	35	1984–92
Mike Mussina	28.7	45	1991–00
Bret Saberhagen	27.7	49	1984–91, 1997–01
Dave Stieb	26.8	55	1979–93, 1998
Tommy John	25.6	63	1984–89
Jimmy Key	24.2	71	1984–98
Kevin Appier	19.7	100+	1989–00
Chuck Finley	19.3	100+	1986–01
Frank Viola	14.7	100+	1984–89, 1992–96

Please note: Though not chosen to be a part of the Clemens profile, the following pitchers merited consideration: David Cone, Dwight Gooden, Ron Guidry, Charlie Leibrandt, Jack Morris, Andy Pettitte, Kenny Rogers and David Wells.

Clemens and the Famers

Phil Niekro, Don Sutton and Nolan Ryan, a Hall of Fame contingent that graced the early stages of Roger Clemens' career; Steve Carlton, who pitched in the AL but was not matched against Clemens; and Jim Palmer,

---

*CTPI — Career Total Pitching Index.
[†]TBE Rank — *Total Baseball Encyclopedia* ranking based on CTPI at the end of the 2001 season.
[‡] Active during Clemens' career but did not appear against him.
[§]Greg Maddux appeared against Clemens in an Interleague Game.

whose impressive career was in its final days at the time of Clemens' debut,[44] appeared against the Rocket a combined total of six times. The results follow in chronological order:

May 12, 1985	Oakland 5, Boston 3	Sutton WP, Clemens LP
Aug 30, 1986	Boston 7, Cleveland 3	Clemens WP, Niekro LP
May 27, 1987	Boston 1, Cleveland 0	Clemens WP, Niekro, LP
Apr 30, 1989	Texas 2, Boston 1	Ryan WP, Clemens LP
May 5, 1989	Boston 7, Texas 6	Clemens WP, Ryan LP
Sep 7, 1992	Boston 3, Texas 0	Clemens WP, Ryan LP

In three of the games listed above, the venerable aces, Sutton (age 40), Niekro (45) and Ryan (46), gave Boston's ox-strong youngster all he could handle. Sutton's win was at Boston, where the veteran righthander proved to be tough enough in the pinches to get through seven innings (even though Tony Armas knicked him for two roundtrippers), as he won out by a 5 to 3 margin. Phil Niekro's 1 to 0 loss was part of a pitching duel between the old master of the knuckleball and Clemens, on his way to a second straight 20-game season. On September 7, 1992, Ryan locked horns with the Rocket, who gave up but four hits to win his fifth shutout of the season, a league-leading number. Ryan's effort was just as strong, but he weakened just enough in the eighth inning to give up a pair of runs, the first of the game. Another tally in the ninth edged the final score to 3 to 0.

A look at some career numbers might be helpful in putting these six pitchers (the sixth would be Clemens) into perspective as they relate to one another. The first three columns are rankings by *TBE, The Sporting News* (from the 1998 listing of the 100 greatest players, out of which a separate pitcher's list has been drawn), and the Bill James Win Shares listing. The career numbers:

	TBE/TPI*	TSN†	James‡	W-L-Pct.	OBA§	K/Gm#	H/Gm#	ERA
Clemens	60.1	17(3)	333/11	280–145/.659	.229	8.61	7.65	3.10
Palmer	34.9	18(4)	312/17	268–152/.638	.230	5.04	7.63	2.86
Niekro	33.8	NR(5)	374/26	318–274/.537	.247	5.57	8.40	3.35
Carlton	33.7	9(1)	366/15	329–244/.574	.240	7.13	8.06	3.22
Ryan	20.7	14(2)	334/24	324–292/.526	.204	9.55	6.56	3.19
Sutton	13.2	NR(5)	319/31	324–256/.559	.236	6.09	7.99	3.26

*Note that the listing is ordered from highest to lowest career Total Pitching Index ratings through the 2001 season, still the most reliable rating and ranking instrument among the several available as of this writing.

†TSN: The Sporting News 1998 rating of the 100 greatest players. The first number is the rating taken from a listing of pitchers extracted from the list of 100 players. The number in parenthesis indicates the order among the six pitchers above. NR indicates Not Rated in TSN listing.

‡James: Bill James Win Shares statistic, the first number followed by his ranking position among the 100 greatest pitchers.

§OBA: Opponents' Batting Average career statistic.

#K/Gm, H/Gm: Strikeouts and Hits per nine innings pitched.

Analysis: The most obvious position of prominence is Clemens' Total Pitching Index, with an enormous 25.2 lead over is closest rival, Jim Palmer. And that lead will grow as Clemens finishes out his career. His 60.1 Index positions him at number five, all time, behind Johnson (1), Young (2), Greg Maddux, with 64.7 (3), and Alexander (4).

Palmer, Niekro and Carlton, bunched in the TPI mid-30s ratings, are a disparate threesome. Three radically different pitching styles have produced a likewise differing set of career statistics. The three did not, of course, meet Clemens in their prime (Palmer not at all), though in the case of Phil Niekro, knuckleballer supreme, that would not have made a difference in effectiveness. Although Clemens beat him twice, that is no indication of dominance or inferiority over the course of 20-year careers.

Nolan Ryan, whose 6.56 hits allowed per game ranks as number one all time, and who will always be recognized as one of the greatest power pitchers (along with the two Johnsons, Walter and Randy; Feller; Grove; and Clemens himself), shares with Don Sutton the bottom rung of this sextets. The pairing, like the trio above, is a mismatch of styles and talents, and their ranking in this setting is hardly indicative of their place among the full compliment of pitching greats.

A significant number of the pitchers who follow Clemens' Hall of Fame rivals are Cooperstown candidates. The first tier of these pitchers includes Randy Johnson, Greg Maddux and Pedro Martinez. A second tier of hurlers, though not the prohibitive favorites the first three are, include Bert Blyleven, Kevin Brown and Mike Mussina. Finally, Jimmy Key, Bret Saberhagen and Dave Stieb have an outside chance of some day entering the Hall. The first of Clemens' remaining competitors is Greg Maddux, who, like the Rocket, will enter the Hall in his first year of eligibility.

Roger Clemens versus Gregory Alan "Greg" Maddux (1966–)

The Texas Rangers hosted the San Francisco Giants on June 12, 1997, in the first interleague game to get underway during the regular season. After almost a century of play, the two leagues finally agreed to do battle with one another on a limited basis. Three years later, the interleague slate, by now an annual schedule highlight, featured a three-game weekend set at Atlanta between the Yankees and the Braves. In the Saturday game before a capacity throng, with Braves fans looking for revenge after having seen their heroes defeated 5 to 2 in the series opener, managers Bobby Cox and Joe Torre, in his first year as the Yanks' skipper, selected the two best pitchers, bar none, in the second half of the 20th century to square off in what promised to be the kind of duel fans of earlier eras saw when Christy Mathewson met Chief Bender, or when Warren Spahn faced Whitey Ford.

This time the reigning titans of the mound were Clemens and Maddux,

He's headed for the Hall: Greg Maddux.

names synonymous with pitching artistry, success and mature pitching wisdom. The turnstile count was 48,423, to be exact, and it would have doubled had there been room, such was the stir this match caused. But contrary to what might have been expected, the game, however pleasing it may have been to Atlanta's faithful, was something less than a pitcher's duel. Two doubles and a homer off Maddux and Clemens, plus an assortment of walks and singles, pushed across enough runs to chase both of them. Neither was the pitcher of decision in the Braves' 11 to 7 victory. That was left to the relieving corps, as each manager used three hurlers to follow their staff ace. Consequently, they both left the field with an 0–0 record (the two did not pitch against each other in the 1999 World Series) in the only game in which they faced one another. All that aside, the matchup does stir interest — precisely because two future Hall of Famers had the pleasure of mixing it up at least once for the record. The historic box score follows.

New York (AL) at Atlanta (NL), June 3, 2000

New York	AB	R	H	BI	Atlanta	AB	R	H	BI
Knoblauch, 2b	6	2	2	0	Q. Veras, 2b	4	2	2	0
Jeter, ss	4	3	4	1	A. Jones, cf	4	1	0	0

O'Neill, rf	4	1	3	1	C. Jones, 3b	4	2	2	2
Spencer, rf	2	0	0	0	Joyner, 1b	4	1	0	0
B. Williams, cf	5	0	1	1	Galarraga, ph, 1b	1	0	1	1
T. Martinez, 1b	4	0	1	1	Jordan, rf	5	1	2	4
Posada, c	0	0	0	0	Bonilla, lf	4	1	1	0
Turner, c	3	1	2	2	Hubbard, pr, lf	1	1	0	0
Ledee, lf	4	0	0	0	Furcal, ss	3	2	1	0
Jose, ph	1	0	0	0	Lunar, c	2	0	0	1
Brosius, 3b	4	0	0	0	J. Lopez, ph, c	2	0	2	3
Clemens, p	3	0	0	0	G. Maddux, p	2	0	0	0
Grimsley (LP)	0	0	0	0	Remlinger (WP)	0	0	0	0
Stanton, p	0	0	0	0	Lockhart, p	0	0	0	0
Nelson, p	0	0	0	0	R. Sanders, ph	1	0	0	0
Leyritz, ph	0	0	0	0	Seanez p (H)	0	0	0	0
					Weiss, ph	1	0	0	0
					Rocker, p (SV)	0	0	0	0
Totals	40	7	13	6	Totals	38	11	11	11

Line Score:				
New York	211	201	000	7–13–4
Atlanta	113	010	23x	11–11–1

2BH: Knoblauch, B. Williams, Bonilla, J. Lopez (2); Home Runs: Turner, B. Jordan; SB: Knoblauch, Jeter, O'Neill (2), Furcal; HPB: Furcal by Grimsley, Leyritz by Rocker; IBB: Matinez, Lopez; K: Clemens 7, Nelson 1, Maddux 5, Remlinger 1, Rocker 1; BB: Clemens 4, Syanton 1, Nelson 1, Remlinger 1, Rocker 1. Umpires: Gibson, Meriwether, Rippley, Tschida; Time: 3:57; Attendance, 48,423.

Roger Clemens versus Randall D. "Randy" or "The Big Unit" Johnson (1963–)

Safeco Park, Seattle's new baseball arena, was the scene of the 2001 All-Star game. Some of baseball's elder statesmen, looking for the world like youngsters in their prime, played starring roles in the game's annual midseason extravaganza. Roger Clemens, not quite 39, opposed Randy Johnson, approaching his 38th birthday; and Cal Ripken, the game's MVP, making his farewell circuit around the league at 40, figured prominently in the AL's 4 to 1 conquest of the visiting NL'ers. The game marked the sixth appearance for Clemens and the seventh for Johnson, but this one was the first time they started against each other in an All-Star game. Both delivered the expected. Opening the game with two scoreless innings, they breezed through their stints, giving up a single blow between them while fanning four, three of which were penciled into the scorebook by "the Big Unit." In each of their other All-Star games they appeared singly. That made the 2001 game something special for baseball fans in both leagues.

One of the most intimidating power pitchers of his day, and no doubt in the game's history (as well as baseball's tallest player), Randy Johnson used his height and whiplash, sidearm delivery to throw one of the game's meanest, most sharply-breaking heaters, which moved him right on up to the top of baseball's strikeout list. During a 14-year career (through the 2001 season), he has sent 3,412 hitters back to the bench after victimizing them with 100 mph fastballs that actually hiss on their way to home plate. His 11.17 strikeouts per game during that span have been instrumental in chalking up a number seven all time ranking in Opponents' Batting Average (.213).

But those numbers don't tell the whole story. Ask John Kruk, who faced Johnson in the 1993 All-Star game at Camden Yards in Baltimore. Kruk, by no means an automatic out and a career .300-hitter, had the unnerving experience of being exposed to one of Johnson's howitzer shots that "got away," as it crashed into the stands behind home plate after having whizzed past him. Turning the occasion into one of baseball's more playful and lighter moments, Kruk took a little bow toward the mound after a third strike put him out of harm's way. Many accomplished hitters and veterans in both leagues knew exactly what was going through John Kruk's mind.

K-King Randy Johnson.

Any afternoon or evening that would showcase a Clemens-Johnson outing would have to be an experience apart for everyone in the ball park. There were only two, and though they appear as "just another game" over the course of a season or a career, they were attended by capacity crowds each time. That delivers its own message.

In the first of these the Rocket beat the Mariners at Seattle on May 31, 1992, scoring twice in the second frame to take the lead. In the fifth, Mike Greenwell sent a 3–2 pitch back to the mound that careened off Johnson's elbow for a single, forcing "the Big Unit" both to leave the game and take the loss, which eventually became a 7 to 1 victory for the Bosox. A Ken Griffey homer deep into the rightfield seats was the only telling Mariner blow of the day, as Clemens raised his early season record to 8 and 3.

In an early season game, again at Seattle, the next duel took place. This time Randy Johnson shut the Red Sox down on five hits and, in command of the proceedings all the way, beat the Rocket 4 to 2. The only annoyances were single-run taters by "the Hawk," Andre Dawson, and by Scotty Fletcher. The usual number of Ks, nine, were a part of the Johnson portfolio for the evening's work on April 25, 1994.

By 1998 Randy Johnson had moved on to the National League, leaving behind the possibility of more matchups with Clemens, save for interleague or post-season encounters. A July 31 swap with the Mariners brought Johnson to Houston, where he finished out the season with a 10–1 NL mark and an incredible 1.28 ERA. During the next three seasons "the Big Unit," having been picked up by Arizona's Diamondbacks, racked up 57 wins (as against but 22 losses) and three straight 300-plus strikeout years, and, finally, a world's championship in which he was a three-game winner and co–MVP. Standing at the top of his career, he had staked a claim to the Hall. The call will undoubtedly come during his first year of eligibility.

A mighty triumvirate of hurlers paced the major league pitching corps during the 1990s and into the 21st century. Roger Clemens, Greg Maddux and "the Big Unit," Randy Johnson, are the equal of any threesome they followed in one or another of the great eras in baseball history. W. Johnson-Mathewson-Bender, Gibson-Carlton-Seaver, Spahn-Ford-Koufax: each a trio of legendary names. Add the Clemens-Maddux-R. Johnson combination to the glitter, if you please.

Roger Clemens versus James Kevin Brown (1965–)

Kevin Brown shares the spotlight on the Clemens Honor Roll with 13 other moundsmen who have pitched in both leagues. Jim Palmer, Greg Maddux, Mike Mussina, Jimmy Key and Chuck Finley are the remaining pitchers, each of whom has hurled exclusively in one league. The freedom of player movement, one of the characteristic features of the free agency era, has resulted in a miniscule number of players whose major league sojourn will be made with one team; and as the years move on, the 20-year, one-team player will in all likelihood become extinct.

Brown, a ML pitcher for 15 seasons through 2001, is one of those who has worn a number of uniforms while spending his first nine seasons in the AL before moving on to a six year hitch in the Senior Circuit. His productivity in both leagues has ball clubs standing in line each time his contract expires, a telltale commentary about his pitching skills. Doug Myers and

Mark Gola[45] make these insightful comments about the lean and lanky Georgian:

> In his prime and on his game, Kevin Brown is the most difficult pitcher to hit in the major leagues. With perhaps the best combination of movement, location and velocity in recent memory, Brown can be so nasty that he still has hitters messed up three days later.... By keeping the ball down, when Brown does make a mistake it rarely ends up getting taken out of the park.... Because Brown is more likely to coax a ground ball than blow a batter away, and because he pitches to the umpire's strike zone, he works less hard for his outs. Brown's typical inning will last fewer than 14 pitches.

Former All-Star and MVP first baseman Keith Hernandez has observed that what makes the Gerogia Tech alum so effective is his ability to throw his sinker in the low-to-mid 90s, a rare and exceptional tool in his pitching kit. And that's but one of a number of pitches that Brown throws from a variety of deliveries. The variety, complimented by an engineer's grasp of his trade, makes for hitting miseries, and the record book documents his success in recent years. After a break-out, 21 and 11, 1992 season with the Texas Rangers, and his subsequent move to the NL, where he crafted a .630 winning percentage, winning 92 and losing 54 between 1996 and 2001, he has moved into the higher ranges of the career stat lists, and his lifetime 35.1 TPI rating is already well within Hall of Fame territory. He may not make the trip to Cooperstown the first time around, but he is more than likely to get the nod somewhere down the line, particularly if he finishes his career with three or four more solid seasons.

As for challenging Roger Clemens, there was one game, but one only,

A 21-game winner in 1992, Kevin Brown.

that gave Brown the opportunity to upstage Clemens, who, by the time their June 22, 1995, confrontation came around, was just getting into his accustomed pitching rhythm after having begun the season on the DL (April 17–June 2) because of a strained muscle behind his throwing shoulder. Brown, having moved from the Rangers to the Orioles for the '95 season (he was 5–5 entering the game at Baltimore), had lost his previous three games, and Clemens also lost his previous game with Milwaukee to even his record at 1–1. And so the two entered the game even up against the league. But before the evening was over, Kevin Brown stood at 5 and 6, having failed to get through the second inning. The Red Sox pushed across two in that frame and manager Phil Regan pulled Brown in favor of his relievers. Clemens, on the other hand, worked into the seventh, picking up his second win with a fairly creditable (for him) six-hit victory.

Kevin Brown went on to a 10–9 season for the Orioles in 1995, packed his bags, and signed with the fledgling Florida Marlins organization, where he promptly set the NL afire with two seasons that culminated in the Marlins' incredulous capture of the 1997 world's championship over a highly favored Cleveland ball club. It was Brown's fire, team leadership and outstanding pitching in the clutch that was largely responsible for that championship. He may not have been able to beat Clemens, but he *was* indeed a champ, something the Rocket had to wait for until landing in the Big Apple with Joe Torre's Yankees.

Roger Clemens versus Pedro Jamie Martinez (1971–)

In 1997 Pedro Martinez won the National League Cy Young Award. That year he won 17 games for an Expo outfit that wound up six games under the break-even mark. He started off the season with eight straight wins, giving up but eight earned runs. He had spent the previous three seasons in Montreal, each one a winning effort, winding up the three, however, a scant 10 games over .500. With a fastball that seared the strike zone with speeds up to 98 mph, and an effective slider, he was more than earning his keep as one of the more promising young mounsdmen of the Senior Circuit. But like some thunderbolt from above, he exploded into superstardom with his '97 eight-game streak at the start of the season. What made the difference between good and great? As it might have been put during the Clinton years, it's the change-up, stupid!

Ah yes, the change-up. When a pitcher can master the delivery, which requires that he use the same arm speed, making the delivery and rotation of the ball look like a fastball, he has at his disposal the wherewithall to inflict serious harm to the one thing the hitter most relies on: timing his stroke so that he gets the maximum effect out of his swing when he makes contact with the ball. And if, as Warren Spahn and many others have emphasized over the years, the most difficult aspect of hitting is timing, then disturbing the hitter's timing is exactly what great pitchers must do.

By the time the Expos started the '97 season, Pedro Martinez, with help from pitching coach Joe Kerrigan, had the change-up down pat. What looked like another 95 mph sizzler came sauntering to the plate at a mere 80 mph, a devastating change in speed that had the hitters twisted in knots trying to "reload" in time to get at least some wood on the ball. A 1.90 ERA to go along with an Opponents' BA of .184, to put him 13th on the all time single season list (his OBA of .167 in 2000 was so good, it tops the all time list!) that season, says the hitters didn't quite make it.

Pedro Martinez gave up only 5.31 hits per game in 2000, third lowest on record.

In Pedro Martinez, therefore, Roger Clemens would be facing a rival so worthy that to say his competition would be Hall of Fame stuff would be no exaggeration whatsoever. Would that the fates had decreed a 15 to 20 matchup series à la Christy Mathewson vs. Three Finger Brown of an earlier day. Not to be. Through the 2001 season there were but three. And in only one of these, already referred to in the Introduction, was there a clearcut winner, Martinez, in that May 28, 2000, 2 to 0 Boston conquest.

On June 14, 2000, Clemens and Martinez were matched, again at Yankee Stadium before a huge sellout crowd, in another of those Boston–New York white-knucklers. For Roger Clemens the day ended in a hurry. He was lifted after just one inning because of a pull in his groin, after which he was placed on the DL for a 15 day hiatus while recovering. And though Martinez pitched well, his Red Sox teammates could not overcome the relief work of Ramiro Mendoza, Jason Grimsley (the winner), and the incomparable Mariano Rivera, the Yankee Save-Master, who combined to bring the Bronx Bombers home a winner, 2 to 1. The loss went to knuckleballer Tim

Wakefield, who hurled the last two innings. It was during Wakefield's watch that Tino Martinez connected for a game-winning shot that made the difference in the ball game. A Martinez won the ball game, all right, but it was, for Boston fans, the wrong Martinez.

In the final of the three games involving the Dominican, Pedro Martinez, and the Rocket, New York beat Boston at Fenway, 3 to 2, on April 14, 2001. On that occasion both pitchers left the game without a decision, each hurling in outstanding fashion through seven innings before turning the game over to relievers Mike Stanton, who won it for the Yanks, and Steve Schourek, who was the loser. Both pitchers spiffed up their ERAs, but the game didn't help the W-L record, so Clemens closed out at 2 and 0 in what would become an unbelievable 20 and 3 season — and bring on another Cy Young award, Clemens' record-setting sixth.

Barring serious physical problems, it is no stretch to expect this exceptional Latino, Senor Pedro Martinez, to finish up his career in the 50 TPI range or higher before he's thrown his last pitch. That would put him at or near the Gibson-Seaver level. He should wind up among the 25 best all time in the single season or career listings, including ERA, OBA, Ratio, Hits per game (as of the 2000 season he was second to Nolan Ryan at 6.73 hits per game) and Opponents' On-Base Percentage. All of that, and more, suggest Hall of Fame, with or without 300 Ws.

Roger Clemens versus Bert Blyleven (1951–)

Blyleven's 4,970 Innings Pitched ranks 13th among major league hurlers.

Because he spent three seasons with Pittsburgh (1978–80), where he dueled with Tom Seaver, we've already met the tall, slender Dutchman, Bert Blyleven, and his off-the-table hook. And by the time he encountered Roger Clemens he had already spent 15 productive summers in the Bigs.

When Clemens caught up with Blyleven, Bert had just completed a fine 19 and 7 season with Cleveland's Indians that might well have been a 20-gamer had he not suffered a broken bone in his right foot that cost him at least four to five starts during the September stretch run. But 1985 was another story. Cleveland, a franchise not known for its roster and hold-over stability, was in the midst of another squad shuffle, and on August 1 would send Blyleven to Minnesota in a four-for-one swap.

Earlier in that 1985 season Blyleven and Clemens hooked up in an afternoon engagement at cavernous Cleveland Stadium in the first of their two meetings. Blyleven would see what he could do about evening up his 2–3 record at the expense of the Red Sox. Unfortunately, he ran headlong into one of Roger Clemens' better days, a day so good, in fact, that Blyleven's Indians were subjected to a 5 to 0 whitewashing, let down on five harmless singles. The Red Sox, meanwhile, pieced together a two-run third, another run in the fourth inning, and another twosome in the top of the eighth to win handily. The shutout was the budding star's only one that season and the second of his career. The box score follows.

Boston at Cleveland, May 17, 1985

Boston	AB	R	H	BI	Cleveland	AB	R	H	BI
Boggs, 3b	5	0	3	1	Butler, cf	4	0	1	0
Evans, rf	3	0	0	1	Bernazard, 2b	3	0	0	0
Rice, lf	4	0	2	1	Franco, ss	4	0	0	0
Armas, cf	5	0	1	0	Vukovich, rf	4	0	1	0
Easler, dh	5	0	0	0	Jacoby, 3b	3	0	1	0
Buckner, 1b	4	1	1	0	Hargrove, 1b	4	0	2	0
Gedman, c	4	1	1	1	Tabler, dh	3	0	0	0
Barrett, 2b	3	1	1	0	Carter, lf	3	0	0	0
Gutierrez, ss	4	2	2	0	Bando, c	3	0	0	0
Clemens (WP)	0	0	0	0	Blyleven (LP)	0	0	0	0
Totals	37	5	11	4	Totals	31	0	5	0

Line Score:	Boston	002	100	020	5-11-0
	Cleveland	000	000	000	0-5-0

2BH: Buckner, Gedman; SH: Barrett; SF: Rice; SB: Gutierrez; LOB: Boston 9, Cleveland 6; K: Clemens 10, Blyleven 8; BB: Clemens 2, Blyleven 2.

Two years later, almost to the day, this time at the Metrodome, the Red Sox once again took the measure of Blyleven and his Minnesota colleagues, by a 6 to 1 margin. Despite another well pitched game, the Bosox had all they needed after a two-run, first-inning Boggs tater. From that point on Blyleven put the brakes on and the game went scoreless until the ninth, when Boston disposed of Blyleven with four markers that sealed Clemens' victory. The Rocket had extended his goose-egg hurling through 17 straight innings against Blyleve before the Twins finally scored their only run of the game.

The two losses to Roger Clemens were part of Blyleven's 287–250 ML record. The two homeruns were among the 430 he surrendered in a career marked as much by the fourbaseblow as his curveballing artistry. The hanging hook caused its fair share of problems, true enough, but there were enough of those sharpbreaking demons to record 3701 Ks, roughly four to one whiffs over dingers, making him one of the era's great hurlers.

Between June 3, 1998, and June 1, 1999, Roger Clemens won 20 straight ball games, an AL record.

Roger Clemens versus Michael Cole "Mike" Mussina (1968–)

With men on base, Mike Mussina looked as though he really didn't belong in the Big Time. His unique deep bend before delivering the ball no doubt had base runners licking their chops when he first appeared on the Oriole scene in 1991. But that, like much else about the Williamsport, Pennsylvania, hurler, never got in the way of a career that begins to look as though it might bring about an election to the game's Valhalla. After some 11 seasons of high caliber hurling, with 164 wins tucked away by the end of the 2001 season, it was time to take one of the best pitchers of the '90s seriously. Behind him were two 15-K games, a Baltimore-record 218 strikeouts in 1997, and an overall .641 winning percentage which, if it stands up, would rank him up there among the 25 best pitchers — ever. His pivot and move to first base out of a spin move that keeps the runners honest, by the way, has kept him out of trouble with men on base; and, even more importantly, he fills out the fifth infielder role so capably that he has been a four-time Gold Glove winner.

Mike Mussina signed with the Yankees as a free agent after the 2000 season, ending a decade as the Orioles' staff ace. Year in, year out, he had silently piled up quality starts and quality numbers. His 1994 and 1995 seasons had been shining examples of outstanding productivity, leading the league in shutouts while running up a 19 and 9 record for the '95 O's. The year before he only lost five times while winning 16. But his New York signing brought an end to his Baltimore heroics — and it also brought an end to his competition with Roger Clemens, who by this time was in his third year in pinstripes. That put him directly into the glare of the Big Apple's kliegs (as well as one Mr. Steinbrenner's) and away from the relative obscurity and quiet of the Baltimore area. It bothered him not at all.

Capable Mike Mussina, who became a teammate of Roger Clemens in 2001.

What Makes an Elite Pitcher?

As September of 2001 began, Mike Mussina was on the top end of a 13 and 11 record, a mark that might easily have been 16 and 8. But that is not nearly as important as what happened as the Yankees made their way through September en route to their fourth straight AL pennant. Mike Mussina got it all going with a "perfect" one-hitter on September 2, defeating the Red Sox 1 to 0 in one of those pitcher's masterpieces. First, the box score:

New York at Boston, September 2, 2001

New York	AB	R	H	BI	Boston	AB	R	H	BI
Knoblauch, lf	5	0	1	0	Nixon, cf	4	0	0	0
Jeter, ss	4	0	0	0	Lansing, ss	3	0	0	0
Justice, dh	3	0	0	0	Alcantara, lf	3	0	0	0
B. Williams, cf	4	0	0	0	Ramirez, dh	3	0	0	0
Martinez, 1b	3	0	2	0	Bichette, rf	3	0	0	0
Bellinger, pr, 1b	0	1	0	0	Daubach, 1b	3	0	0	0
Posada, c	4	0	1	0	Hillenbrand, 2b	2	0	0	0
O'Neill, rf	3	0	0	0	O'Leary, ph	1	0	0	0
Velarde, 3b	2	0	0	0	Merloni, 2b	3	0	0	0
Johnson, ph	1	0	0	0	Oliver, c	2	0	0	0
Wilson, 3b	1	0	1	1	Everett, ph	1	0	1	0
Soriano, 2b	4	0	1	0	Lewis, pr	0	0	0	0
Mussina (WP)	0	0	0	0	Cone (LP)	0	0	0	0
Lowe, p	0	0	0	0					
Totals	34	1	6	1	Totals	28	0	1	0

Line Score: New York 000 000 001 1-6-0
Boston   000 000 000 0-1-3

2BH: Posada, E. Wilson; SB: Jeter, Soriano; LOB: New York 9, Boston 1; DP: New York 0, Boston 2; K: Mussina 13, Cone 8, Lowe 1; BB: Mussina 0, Cone 3, Lowe 0. Umpires: Fichter, Welke, Hirschbeck and Meriwether. Att: 33, 734. Weather: 65 degrees and clear.

So it was that going into the ninth inning David Cone, no stranger to textbook pitching performances, had held the Yanks scoreless, himself offering up a pretty salty exhibition on a clear late summer evening. But Mike Mussina was so much better that not even one batter reached first base. Perfect.

Then things started to happen. The Yankees got to Cone for a run on substitute Enrique Wilson's double, a blow that drove home pinch-runner Clay Bellinger. It was all they got, but all the Yanks needed. That brought about the bottom of the ninth, an infamous inning as far as no-no's go. This game proved no different. Like many another before him, Mike Mussina erased the first two hitters and then faced pinch-hitter Carl Everett, got two strikes on him, and then winced as Everett drove a rope into left-center for Boston's only hit. Mussina disposed of Trot Nixon on a ground out, but the damage had been done. Just the same, before the season was over, Mussina had tacked on three more wins, hoisting his record as a Yankee to 17 and 11.

With respect to the fellow who became his teammate when he signed with the New Yorkers, there were five occasions on which Mike Mussina matched power pitches with the Rocket. The results follow.

The Clemens-Mussina Log:

Sep 15, 1993	Boston 6, Baltimore 5	Clemens WP, Mussina LP
May 17, 1994	Baltimore 3, Boston 2	Mussina WP, Clemens LP
Aug 12, 1995	Boston 7, Baltimore 0	Clemens WP, Mussina LP
Sep 30, 1999	Baltimore 5, Boston 0	Mussina WP, Clemens LP

The April 15, 1999, game resulted in a 9 to 7 victory for Baltimore. In that game neither Clemens nor Mussina was a pitcher of record, the win going to reliever Art Rhodes. Reliever Mariano Rivera was charged with the loss.

The five-game set featured two shutouts, one by each star. In the 5 to 0 tilt at Camden Yards, Mussina scattered eight hits, fanning 10. While they managed only five hits themselves, the O's bunched a few of them in a three-run third that iced it. That one returned the favor of several seasons before when Clemens had zippered the Orioles at Boston on a six-hitter. That day the Bosox pounded out 15 hits, 11 against Mussina, driving him to cover in a four-run eighth. The Rocket blew his fast one past Oriole hitters for 9 Ks, evening his record at 4 and 4 in a 10 and 5 season during which his innings dropped to 140 under the pressure of arm and shoulder injuries. On those days he felt like the Rocket of old, things like that 5 to 0 victory over Mike Mussina and Co. happened.

For most pitchers the secret to success is location, location, location. For Mike Mussina the secret has been mechanics, mechanics, mechanics. He has been consistent with his mechanics almost beyond imagination. It seems that his several deliveries always come out of the same motion, thrown from the same spot on the pitching slab, and to the same corners of the plate. That has enabled him to stay ahead in the count and to find those spots in the strike zone the hitter is least able to get around on. It's a demanding prescription for pitching success, and few are able to strike a balance between that kind of concentration and launching 95 mph heaters, changeups in the low 80s, and breaking balls the way Mike does.

Heading into his 33rd year as this is being written, it is conceivable that Mike Mussina will add another four to five years of top flight pitching to his record. That would put his career up there with the 40-plus TPI pitchers. They're the ones among the top echelons of the game's great pitchers. Right!

Roger Clemens versus Bret William Saberhagen (1964–)

In five tries through the 2001 season, Bret Saberhagen was unable to find the winning combination in his rivalry with Roger Clemens. Each time his ball club came close, but at the end of the day Clemens somehow prevailed. This is the way the series shaped up:

The Clemens-Saberhagen Log:

Jul 31, 1987	Boston 4, Kansas City 0	Clemens WP, Saberhagen LP
Jul 15, 1988	Boston 3, Kansas City 1	Clemens WP, Saberhagen LP
Apr 18, 1991	Boston 1, Kansas City 0	Clemens WP, Saberhagen LP
Sep 5, 1998	Toronto 4, Boston 3	Clemens WP, Saberhagen LP

On August 16, 1991, Clemens was matched against Saberhagen in a game played at Boston. Neither pitcher was around long enough (each went seven innings) to gain a decision. Phil Plantier's two-run homer off reliever Storm Davis won the game for Tony Fossas, who relieved Clemens. Reliever Davis was charged with the defeat.

Bret Saberhagen, one of the best pitchers in the majors during the latter stages of the 20th century, showed major league scouts how he just might succeed against the big boys in a Los Angeles high school championship game. Except for an error that permitted a base runner, his no-hitter was just about perfect that day. With an average fastball, a good delivery, and extraordinary control, he made his way through high school ball, not an inning of minor league ball and directly on to the Kansas City Royals. It soon became common knowledge that if you were going to get on base against Saberhagen, you'd better hit your way on.

His control was his "thing." Just how good he was about getting the ball over the plate is best illustrated in the following chart:

Among Bret Saberhagen's many accomplishments is his 7 to 0, no-hit victory over the White Sox on Aug. 26, 1991.

	Yrs	Innings Pitched	BB	BB/Gm
B. Saberhagen	1984–01	2562.2	471	1.65
G. Maddux	1986–01	3550.0	760	1.87
G. Swindell	1986–01	2200.1	496	2.03
M. Mussina	1991–01	2238.1	509	2.05
D. Wells	1987–01	2407.1	559	2.09
K. Tapani	1989–01	2265.0	554	2.20
C. Schilling	1988–01	2158.2	538	2.24
R. Johnson	1989–01	2776.1	768	2.49
J. Moyer	1985–01	2292.0	664	2.61
R. Clemens	1984–01	3887.0	1258	2.91

Each of the ten pitchers above has pitched at least 2000 innings, and you will note that Saberhagen and Clemens have logged the most years of service through the 2001 season, 18. Saberhagen and Maddux lead the parade of the hurlers above whose exceptional control has narrowed the hitter's opportunity to get on base by making him put the ball in play — or pay the price: back to the bench with the hated "K."

Over the span of the past century many of the game's great hurlers have relied primarily on their control to get them by. That list includes many of the greats reviewed in this book: Ed Walsh (1.87 BB/Gm), Babe Adams (1.29), Eppa Rixey (2.17), Juan Marichal (1.82) and Don Sutton (2.29), among others. It is worth noting that each of the Mound Maestros in this review were under three free passes per game pitched, the lowest figure belonging to Cy Young (1.49).

And on the matter of control, here's what Cy Young himself said: "Control is what kept me in the big leagues for 22 years!" Looking at Bret Saberhagen's record, which includes two Cy Young awards, a World Series MVP award, and a *TSN* Pitcher of the Year award, you know that he would agree with Mr. Young's outlook on throwing pitches to ML hitters. For these chaps control is the very essence of successful pitching.

Roger Clemens versus David Andrew Stieb (1957–)

Prior to the 1990 season, Californian Dave Stieb had no-hit glory within his grasp three times, only to have Dame Fortune look the other way. But on September 2, 1990, at Cleveland Stadium, a crowd of nearly 25,000 saw him record Toronto's first no-no, 3 to 0. The win moved his mark to a sparkling 17 and 5 on the season, and he would close out with an 18 and 6 mark. At 33, he no doubt felt that another season would bring him within striking distance of the 200-win mark. He couldn't know at that point that in less than a year's time his physical problems would eventually necessitate surgery for a herniated disc which would hasten the end of his career.

After December 1990 surgery, Dave Stieb began preparing for the 1991 season, and his '91 spring training regimen brought him along to the point where manager Cito Gaston gave him the ball for the season opener at Toronto's Skydome. Enter Roger Clemens. In that '91 opener Dave Stieb pitched through five innings, allowing four hits, while walking two and fanning two. Unfortunately, one of those four hits was a bases-jammed fourbagger by Jackie Clark that upped the Boston count to five against a lone run the Blue Jays scored in the second frame. Clemens? Well, Clemens was Clemens. He gave up that singleton in the second, and then retired after the eighth without another run being scored. The final score was 6 to 2, and Dave Stieb found himself on the short end of a 0–1 record as the season got underway. Interestingly, that opening day matchup with Roger Clemens was the only time the two met in a decade of AL competition between the Blue Jays and Bosox.

Dave Stieb lost his next start, but then ran off a four-game winning streak to post a 4 and 2 record by mid–May. The rest of the season, however, was a painful nightmare, and he wound up the '91 campaign with those four wins. For all practical purposes, that was the end of Dave Stieb's career, although, like many another before him, he tried several comebacks. But to no avail.

Unheralded Dave Stieb never won a Cy Young award, experienced very little success as a post-season pitcher, and somehow never quite captured the fancy of the media or baseball analysts. Be that as it may, this fellow could pitch as few others. A perfectionist, outspoken and fearless, he brought a moving fastball, slider, changeup and curveball — the complete package — plus 110 percent effort every time out. His ranking among pitchers on *TBE*'s Total Pitching Index is number 56. Perched among other greats like Robin Robert (at number 60), Eddie Plank (54), Dolf Luque (55) Addie Joss (61) Tommy John (63) and Dazzy Vance (50), he's keeping some pretty good company.

Roger Clemens versus Tommy "TJ" John (1943–)

Adversity is no stranger to professional athletes. The stress and strain of their profession, with its inordinate demands on strength and mobility, exact an enormous toll, not only on the body but also on the mental fabric of players who regularly push themselves to the limit — and often beyond. A pitcher's arm is his most valuable and, simultaneously, most vulnerable asset. Since the very beginning of professional baseball, many a promising career has been cut short by arm and shoulder injuries.

Tommy John knows all about that. Famously known as baseball's first bionic man, he underwent ligament transplant surgery midway in his career to restore his arm after he sustained an elbow injury while pitching in

Montreal. With absolutely no guarantee that he would be able to resume his career, he went under the knife. To make a well known story short, the final ending to Tommy John's tale was a successful, post-surgery, 14-year run that concluded a career many knowledgeable observers believe should one day put him in the Hall of Fame. Not every story can be expected to end that way, and many do not, but TJ wound up throwing baseballs at ML hitters for 26 seasons, a record for longevity surpassed by only one person, Nolan Ryan, whose 27-year record sets the standard.

During the final stages of his career, Tommy John

Equipped with his new bionic flipper at mid-career, Tommy John, a crafty southpaw, went on to a 26-year career.

encountered Roger Clemens twice, both times at Yankee Stadium. The games can hardly be classified as pitching classics. In the first of the two, on June 26, 1987, no less than 20 runs were scored in the first three innings. The Red Sox bombed John for four first-inning tallies and followed that with five more in the second.

Yankee bats, silenced the first two frames, came alive with a vengeance in the third, chasing home 11 marks to forge ahead 11 to 9. By the time those early inning fireworks subsided, both Clemens and John were long gone. The game then settled into a parade of relief pitchers who worked the game into extra innings. Finally, in the bottom of the tenth the Yanks pushed across the deciding tally to win 12 to 11. Neither of the starters was a pitcher of decision.

In 1987 managers Lou Piniella of the Yankees and John McNamara of the Bosox decided to try the Clemens-John matchup once more. This one, on a pleasant evening in June, was witnessed by 42,804, and it was much better than the slugfest the year before. TJ entered the game with a 4–1 mark, nursed along with spot starts to keep the Venerable One (by this time John was 44) in top starting shape. His counterpart, on his way to a second straight 20-game season, stood at 9 and 2.

Clemens mowed down the first nine hitters in succession. Tommy John, on the other hand, scraped by the first two stanzas with a run in each, trailing 2 to 0. Then, in the third, four consecutive singles convinced John's skipper that the bullets rattling through the infield were a harbinger of much worse ahead, so he lifted TJ, putting his bullpen to work. That ended the John-Clemens confrontation at a sum total of 3.2 innings, with the Yankees on the losing end of both John outings.

It was only a tiny sampling out of a career that amounted to 288 victories, 4710.1 innings pitched and a host of superior marks (he's 17th in innings pitched and 26th in shutouts, all time) accumulated over a quarter century of crafty, cunning hurling. The bionic arm had left its mark.

Roger Clemens versus James Edward "Jimmy" Key (1961–)

On October 26, 1996, Jimmy Key, a veteran of 13 years aboard the Big Show bandwagon, and with two rotator cuff surgeries behind him, faced Greg Maddux and the Atlanta Braves in the sixth game of the '96 Fall Classic. With 56,375 Gothamites on hand, he worked masterfully into the sixth inning to lead the dangerous Braves 3 to 2. In that pivotal sixth, manager Joe Torre, in his first year as a Yankee manager, came out to the mound, removed Key, and turned the game over first to Dave Weathers, and then to Graeme Lloyd. That, in turn, brought out the "heavy hitters" of the New York bullpen, Mariano Rivera and John Wetteland, who wound up with the Save behind Key's triumph, and put the World Series trophy into the Yankees' treasure house for the first time in 18 years. That was more than enough atonement for the talented southpaw who had dropped game two under the influence of a masterful Maddux effort, a seven-hit shutout, that put the Braves up two games to none. The tables were turned in game six, however, in a tilt that will go down in Jimmy Key's mind, and everyone else's, as a career highlight.

Jimmy Key was one of the best southpaw curveballers in the game's history. His hook, combined with a moving fastball and a thoroughgoing mastery of his craft, enabled him to win in double figures a dozen times. He was a consistent winner, first for Toronto's Blue Jays, and later for the Yanks and Orioles. Key's 1987 season, a campaign featuring league-leading numbers in ERA (2.76), Opponents' BA (.221) and Opponents On Base Percentage (.273), was strong enough to garner serious Cy Young attention. He finished second to one Roger Clemens, which brings us to the busiest series among those hurlers who made the Clemens Honor Roll. And we should note before getting into the particulars that Key beat Clemens five times, losing but two. Two other matches ended up in No Decisions. That's the best record among the Clemens competitors profiled in the Rocket's chapter.

The Clemens-Key Log:

Jul 2, 1986	Toronto 4, Boston 2	Key WP, Clemens LP
Sep 21, 1986	Boston 3, Toronto 2	Clemens WP, Key LP
Apr 11, 1987	Toronto 11, Boston 1	Key WP, Clemens LP
Sep 20, 1989	Boston 10, Toronto 3	Clemens WP, Key LP
Aug 11, 1993	New York 8, Boston 3	Key WP, Clemens LP
Jul 1, 1996	New York 2, Boston 0	Key WP, Clemens LP
Jul 16, 1996	New York 9, Boston 5	Key WP, Clemens LP

The first time these two met, Gary Lavelle came on in relief of starter Roger Clemens (ND) to beat Toronto on June 16, 1985. Reliever Steve Crawford was charged with the defeat.

Reliever Mark Eichhorn, closing out a monster rookie season, came to Key's rescue on September 26, 1986, to win a taut 12-inning battle, 1 to 0. Neither Key nor Clemens were pitchers of decision. Cal Schiraldi was the losing pitcher.

The pitching gem of this series occurred on July 1, 1996, when Clemens and Key faced one another before 27,734 at Yankee Stadium. Boston was limited to six singles, and the New Yorkers didn't fare much better against Clemens. Both moundsmen pitched through six innings, lining the scoreboard with 12 goose eggs. But substitute first baseman Mike Aldrete led off the seventh with a fourbase blow that proved to be all Jimmy Key needed to win his fourth game of the season. In relief, Mariano Rivera picked up his 12th Hold of the season, and John Wetteland mopped up with a hitless and scoreless ninth for his 26th Save as the Yanks downed Boston 2 to 0. Clemens, not quite as sharp as he usually was, walked seven, including former teammate Wade Boggs four times, though New York had only four hits in addition to Aldrete's game-winning smash.

The 1996 season for Roger Clemens was the last of four straight frustrating years during which he had slumped from his former intimidating stature to spend time as a mere mortal among pitchers struggling to get along. His 2 to 0 loss to Key was his seventh in a 10 and 13 season that showed only rare flashes of his overpowering mastery. The loss to Key was perhaps his best showing of the year, and before the year was out he had left Boston behind to start afresh with the Toronto Blue Jays. With something to prove, he engineered a complete turnaround, crafting two straight Triple Crown years that were the foundation pieces of Cy Young awards in both 1997 and '98. Those two magnificent years north of the USA's border left him 57 Ws shy of 300 victories, something he obsessed over as the years moved on.

As for Jimmy Key, 1996 was indeed a climax. The 1997 season found him in a Baltimore uniform, where he played the penultimate and final seasons of his career, pitching well but frequently in pain. 22 and 13 over a two year span with the O's, he was forced to retire in 1998, having drained the last ounce out of his arm — and career.

Before his last pitch as an Oriole, Jimmy Key found time to rebound from injuries and the disappointments of losses in a key game here and there (such as the one suffered on the last day of the 1987 season, when he lost a 1 to 0 heartbreaker to Frank Tanana that cost the Blue Jays a divisional title) to reach personal heights such as his World Series victory a decade later. He had become Toronto's winningest lefty, a winner in the 1992 All-Star game in Toronto, putting together an eight-game winning streak in 1987, beating the White Sox 5 to 0 on a one-hitter on May 22, 1986, and proudly wearing that 1996 World Series ring. And there is also that 5 and 2 record against one of the very best, Roger Clemens.

Roger Clemens versus Frank Viola (1960–)

Frank Viola was the World Series MVP in 1987, the 1988 Cy Young award winner, and the starting and winning pitcher of the 1988 All-Star Game. A St. John's University phenom, he was Minnesota's second pick in the 1981 draft, and he immediately set about justifying the Twins' faith in his ability. By 1984 he was an 18-game winner, and moved from there to establish himself as the game's premier portsider. Much like Kevin Appier and Chuck Finley, the other hurlers in this grouping, he was an intense, tough competitor who asked no quarter and gave none.

Moving over to the Senior Circuit in a mid-season 1989 trade, he became a 20-game winner for the New York Mets a second time in his career in 1990. In 1992, as a teammate of Roger Clemens, he came within one out of a no-hitter, as he beat Toronto at the Blue Jays' Skydome. That season with Boston he won 13, dropping 12.

Between 1985 and 1989 Frank Viola appeared a half dozen times against Roger Clemens but was successful against him only once. His one and five record against the Rocket set the stage for Clemens' winning record against the three hurlers. The three matched up with Clemens 17 times, and Clemens came away from those engagements with 12 wins, five losses and one No Decision, for a .706 winning percentage.

Roger Clemens versus Chuck Finley (1962–)

Chuck Finley, the second of this trio, another lefty, has won in double figures 11 times. Possessor of a bagful of breaking pitches that induce ground balls, the rangy Louisianan was successful in downing Clemens the first time they squared off, producing a real gem.

The California Angels met the Red Sox in Boston, with 32,417 of those wildly supportive New Englanders on hand to see Clemens & Co. take the Californians into camp. That wouldn't happen. Not the way Charley Finley pitched that night. He tore through seven innings unscathed until, with two out in the eighth, Jody Reed lined a single to center, breaking up a masterfully pitched no-hitter. In the ninth, Wade Boggs, Marty Barrett and Ellis Burks went down in order, and that enabled Finley to preserve his one-hitter, raising his season record to 7 and 2 at that point. The box score follows:

California Angels at Boston, May 26, 1989

California	AB	R	H	BI	Boston	AB	R	H	BI
Downing, dh	4	0	1	0	Boggs, 3b	4	0	0	0
Washington, rf	3	1	2	1	Barrett, 2b	3	0	0	0
Ray, 2b	4	0	1	1	Burks, cf	4	0	0	0
Anderson, pr	0	1	0	0	Greenwell, lf	3	0	0	0
White, cf	4	0	0	0	Evans, rf	2	0	0	0
Joyner, 1b	4	0	1	0	Rice, dh	2	0	0	0
Davis, lf	4	1	0	0	Esasky, 1b	2	0	0	0
L. Parrish, c	4	1	2	2	Reed, ss	3	0	1	0
Howell, 3b	4	0	1	1	Cerone, c	2	0	0	0
Finley (WP)	0	0	0	0	Clemens (LP)	0	0	0	0
					Murphy, p	0	0	0	0
					Stanley, p	0	0	0	0
Totals	35	5	9	5	Totals	26	0	1	0

Line Score: California 000 002 102 5–9–0
Boston 000 000 000 0–1–1

2BH: Washington, Ray; HR: L. Parrish; DP: California 1, Boston 2; BB: Finley 4, Clemens 1, Murphy 0, Stanley 0; K: Finley 5, Clemens 3, Murphy 0, Stanley 1; Umpires: Hirschbeck, Barnett, Ford and Kosc; Time: 2:26; Attendance: 32,417.

Finley's 1989 record wound up at a 16 and 9 reading, and he added two 18 and 9 seasons to that in 1990 and '91. His 5 to 0 conquest of the Red Sox in that scintillating one-hitter of his was the only shutout he threw that season. As the series between Chuck Finley and Clemens wore on, there would be no more of this one-hit, California-winning stuff where the Rocket was concerned. Clemens turned the next five outings into victories, beating the Angels 7 to 1, 4 to 1, 5 to 1, 6 to 0 (on a five-hitter) and, finally, 2 to 1 in their final engagement. That amounts to four runs in 45 innings. There's not much Chuck Finley or anyone else could do with those kind of rations.

Roger Clemens versus Kevin Appier (1967–)

Kevin Appier, a strapping 6'2" 200 pounder, came to the Royals as a first round draft choice in 1987. He came to Kansas City to stay in 1990 after having been bounced back and forth between minor league teams and the big club from '88 to '90, and in his first real taste of the Bigs, he put together a one-hitter at Detroit, won a dozen ball games, and took home *TSN*'s Rookie Pitcher of the Year award. One of those 12 victories was over Roger Clemens in a gem of a three-hit performance that beat the Red Sox 3 to 0. Unlike with Chuck Finley, however, there were more Appier-over-Clemens outings to come. In their next game Appier subjected Boston to a four-hit shutout. That made 18 straight stanzas of shutout ball against the Rocket and his pals. The next time they met Appier gave in a little and beat the Bosox by a 3 to 1 count. That made it three straight. There was a fourth straight humiliation, this time in 1993, and by a 7 to 2 score. Then, on April 6, 1996, the Royals once again chased Roger Clemens, beating the Sox 7 to 3, although neither Appier nor Clemens were pitchers of decision.

At that point Roger Clemens must have drawn the old line in the dirt. Enough already. On April 30, 1997, he lowered the boom on Kansas City with a 1 to 0 four-hitter. Pitching for Toronto in his first year away from Boston, Clemens won his fourth straight in what would wind up being a Cy Young year, and finally beat the Young Turk from Kansas City.

Frank Viola, Chuck Finley and Kevin Appier were three fine pitchers who had their fair share of success in the 1980s and '90s, and they are representative of the many workmanlike hurlers who have toiled in the Big League fields, in many instances barely known — except to teammates who know how to appreciate quality performance, if not the things that make for a constant parade of headlines, when they see it. The chronological listing of their encounters with Roger Clemens:

May 22, 1985	Boston 4, Minnesota 3	Clemens WP, Viola LP
May 20, 1986	Boston 17, Minnesota 7	Clemens WP, Viola LP
Sep 5, 1986	Boston 12, Minnesota 2	Clemens WP, Viola LP
Jun 1, 1987	Minnesota 9, Boston 6	Viola WP, Clemens LP
Aug 21, 1987	Boston 11, Minnesota 3	Clemens WP, Viola LP
May 26, 1989	California 5, Boston 0	Finley WP, Clemens LP
Jul 13, 1989	Boston 3, Minnesota 1	Clemens WP, Viola LP
Jul 20, 1990	Kansas City 5, Boston 0	Appier WP, Clemens LP
Aug 7, 1991	Kansas City 2, Boston 0	Appier WP, Clemens LP
Aug 28, 1992	Boston 7, California 1	Clemens WP, Finley LP
Apr 5, 1993	Boston 3, Kansas City 1	Clemens WP, Appier LP
Jun 2, 1993	Kansas City 7, Boston 2	Appier WP, Clemens LP
Jul 21, 1993	Boston 4, California 1	Clemens WP, Finley LP
Aug 17, 1996	Boston 6, California 0	Clemens WP, Finley LP
Aug 27, 1996	Boston 2, California 1	Clemens WP, Finley LP
Apr 30, 1997	Toronto 1, Kansas City 0	Clemens WP, Appier LP

On April 6, 1996, Kansas City beat Boston, 7 to 3. Neither Clemens nor Appier were pitchers of decision. Hipolito Pichardo, Kansas City reliever, was the winner, and Stan Belinda of the Red Sox was the losing pitcher.

The Rocket Man

Blowin' 'em away. William Roger Clemens has made a career of it. He has been an intimidator, a larger-than-life presence propped up out there 60'6" from home plate, readying one bolt of electricity after another, registering one K after another, and piling up enormous numbers that will make him a first ballot Hall of Famer when the time comes. By the time he's thrown his last pitch he will have been around at least a score of years, having won at least 300, and having elevated his name into one of the five top slots among pitchers in the game's history.

The Rocket Man.

Among the game's flamethrowers there have been only a dozen who have averaged 10 or more whiffs per nine innings in a single season. Except for Sandy Koufax and "Sudden Sam" McDowell, 10 of the 12 have been active during the 1980–2000 era. The Rocket Man is one of them, having logged 10.39 Ks per game in 1998. In three other seasons, 1997/9.95, 1988/9.92 and 1996/9.53, he came close, and as late in his career as 2001 he was still sittin' 'em down at the rate of 8.71 per game.

Those numbers drop, as might be expected, when tabulating Ks per game over the course of a career. The following is a list of some of the game's great flamethrowers and their career K/Gm numbers through the 2001 season:

	Career Ks/Gm
Amos Rusie	4.66
Lefty Grove	5.18
Walter Johnson	5.34
Bob Feller	6.07
Dazzy Vance	6.20
Roger Clemens	8.61
Sam McDowell	8.86
Sandy Koufax	9.28
Nolan Ryan	9.55
Pedro Martinez	10.53
Randy Johnson	11.18

The modern game is more than whiffing batters, however. That's nothing new. What is new is the development in the past 15–20 years of the pitch they used to call a forkball, today called the split-finger fastball, which causes the ball to drop suddenly as it hits the strike zone. Formerly used as a change of pace pitch, it is presently a part of the fastball portfolio because it is thrown at speeds of up to 95 mph by those who can master it. One other thing has entered the picture and has caused substantive changes in the approach to pitching, and that is the low strike zone. Pitches being called strikes today would have been called balls years ago, and that has added to the strategy of keeping the ball low — very low — thus causing a parade of infield ground balls. Among those who have adjusted to these developments are pitchers like Pedro Martinez, Greg Maddux and our Mr. Clemens. Each of the three has charted a personal route to Cooperstown. The talents they possess, the work ethic that goes into daily and grueling routines, and the adjustments they have made to their game because of health problems or changes in the pitching game or other circumstances is a key to the one thing they all realize: the price is great but the rewards are greater. They have counted the cost, as it were, and their careers show the results. A rocket may be an odd addition to a place like the Baseball Hall of Fame, but they're going to have to find room for a rocket named Clemens. That will dress the place up a bit, right?!

9. GREG MADDUX

Major League Totals	Won	Lost	Pct.
Through the 2001 Season			
Chicago, Atlanta (NL)	241	126	.657

Like sturdy bookends, they hold up either end of the 20th century masterworks in pitching, the fabled Christy Mathewson on the one end and his latter-day counterpart, Greg Maddux, on the other. To mention anyone in the same breath as Mathewson already bestows the highest of honors, much less intimating that a pitcher might perform on Mathewsonian levels. But here we have, as the grand old game moves into its third century of professional competition, a pair of pitching geniuses whose approach, record, personal lives, and incalculable contributions to the game, as well as their affect on it, are uncanny in their likenesses — so much so that, if not cast in the very same mold, the second was indeed fashioned by the same craftsman extraordinaire whose hands shaped the original.

Greg Maddux, at this writing within sight of the end of one of baseball's more awe-inspiring careers, will not match Matty's lifetime totals in sheer numbers of wins or shutouts or complete games. But the quality of the record he will leave behind sparkles like a rare gem. Like Mathewson before him, Maddux has ventured into higher elevations seldom explored beforehand. And the effect this has had upon his team has been such that, were he removed from the scene, that same juggernaut, the Atlanta Braves, would have been something far less than the dynasty it turned out to be in the 1990s. Maddux was the granite, the bedrock foundation piece on which it all rested. That strikes a similar chord with the Giants clubs of the 1900s and early 1910s. There were Joe McGinnity, Rube Marquard, Red Ames and others then, just as there

Another Matty, Greg Maddux.

have been Tom Glavine, Steve Avery, John Smoltz and others to go with Maddux, but without either Matty or Greg the magic vanishes into thin air.

In reckoning with the Mathewson-Maddux matchup there is more than the similarity in career numbers and rankings. Beyond those categories where there are striking similarities (categories that it is reasonable to compare, given the differences in games played and innings pitched, as well as the demands of the two dissimilar eras), there are also similarities in competitive fire tempered by a mental discipline that kept each at the cutting edge of efficiency. Both commanded a full range of pitching weapons, each under tight control, and each tailored to the demands of different hitters and different ball parks, marking their game as highly intellectualized. Though it might have taken a season or three to get the whole package in place, once there, it was immediately recognizable as worthy of Hall of Fame honors. And, as for the numbers, several of which bring the two together among the highest echelons of the game's elite, here are some that tell their own story with respect to "command of the game," superiority and legendary status:

	ERA	ADJERA	H/Gm	BB/Gm	K/Gm	OppOB%	OBA	ADJPW	Ratio	PFR
Mathewson	2.13/5	136/13	7.94/57	1.59	4.71	.273/11	.236/48	44.7/9	9.6/4	68/4
Maddux	2.83/76	145/6	8.10/87	1.99	6.37	.288/36	.241.84	48.9/7	10.3/22	82/2

Legend: ADJERA, Adjusted ERA; OppOB%, Opponents' On Base Percentage; OBA, Opponents' Batting Average; ADJPW, Adjusted Pitching Wins; PFR, Pitcher Fielding Runs. All numbers above for Maddux are through the 2000 season.

What do these statistics tell us? Allowing for the huge discrepancy in time, from one end of the century to another, and the differences in the game, these two titans are "in the same ballpark" when it comes to some of the game's more telling numbers. In some of the categories above they are remarkably close in rank. The rankings above all fall in the top 100 range, and in many instances are top 25 numbers. Finally, in the summative statistic

Total Pitcher Index, the 2000 listing ranked Mathewson at number four, with a 62.9 Index, and Maddux at number five (60.0). Before Maddux and Roger Clemens have retired, those rankings will change, but all three will remain among the top five pitchers, all time. (Clemens' numbers, equally impressive, suggest, at least in this author's opinion, that the Rocket, though an entirely different type of pitcher than Maddux, rates somewhere nearer Walter Johnson among the greatest, all time, than either Mathewson or Maddux.)

TBE's Top Ten includes each of the legends reviewed in this book and rates them, as of its 2001 edition, in this order: Johnson, Young, Alexander, Mathewson, Maddux, Grove, Clemens, Nichols, Spahn and, in the 10th spot, Seaver. We have been in the company of the best the game has so far had to offer. Greg Maddux graces that list, topping off the 20th century as the final Maestro under review here. In order to bring him into sharper perspective, he is matched against the following pitchers of his era, who are listed, as has been previously done, in chronological order according to their major league debut dates:

Name/HOF Year	Debut/ML Years
Don Sutton, 1998	Apr 14, 1966–1988
Nolan Ryan, 1999	Sep 11, 1966–1993
Dennis Martinez	Sep 14, 1976–1998
Orel Hershiser	Sep 1, 1983–2000
Jose Rijo	Apr 5, 1984–2001
Dwight Gooden	Apr 7, 1984–2001
Doug Drabek	May 30, 1986–1998
David Cone	Jun 8, 1986–2001
Randy Johnson	Sep 15, 1986–2001
Kevin Brown	Sep 30, 1986–2001
Curt Schilling	Sep 7, 1988–2001
Mike Mussina	Aug 4, 1991–2001
Pedro Martinez	Sep 24, 1992–2001
Mike Hampton	Apr 17, 1993–2001

Note: Tom Glavine was with Atlanta (1987–1992) while Maddux was with Chicago, but never appeared against him. If he had, he would have been included as one of the finest pitchers of the era.

Sutton, Ryan, the Hall and Mr. Maddux

Baseball's Hall of Fame has been an ever present part of the chapters describing the nine Mound Maestros in this review. That is to be expected in a story about the game's greatest hurlers. The careers, comparisons, matchups and "pitched battles" under scrutiny have, after all, involved the game's goliaths of the hill, moundsmen who have excelled far above the usual norms for success in the major leagues. Their exploits have, of course, been honored accordingly. Two such, Don Sutton and Nolan Ryan, are represented in the Greg Maddux review, having finished their careers as Maddux's career was getting underway. Because Maddux has not yet completed an already illustrious career, Sutton and Ryan are the only Famers to call on. That will change. Among the Maddux matchups there are at least two whose dossiers will receive prompt Hall of Fame attention. They are Randy Johnson and Pedro Martinez. The electors will be busy when these two, with Clemens and Maddux, are eligible. From among the remainder on the Maddux list, there will be strong support, further, for Orel Hershiser; and depending on the way their careers finally wind up, three more, Kevin Brown, Curt Schilling and Mike Mussina, will merit due consideration.

Greg Maddux versus Don Sutton (1945–)

It still surprises some that Don Sutton's last season, 1988, was his 23rd. During 23 major league campaigns he contributed better than 5000 innings to six balls clubs, three in each league. His last season was with the team for which he began his career, Los Angeles. It was the only year that there was a possibility of a Sutton-Maddux matchup, and that didn't take place. Consequently, while both made the Senior Circuit tour in 1988, Sutton was attending to "closing ceremonies" while Greg Maddux was just beginning to shift his career into high gear. The surprise mentioned above regarding Sutton's 23-year tenure in the Bigs was that he was around as long as he was. Those who wondered didn't reckon, however, with Don Sutton's work ethic and his super-abundant competitive fire. Those very characteristics were as much responsible for his longevity and ultimate election to the Hall as his more-than-adequate fastball, a slider, and two other pitches that were outstanding, his curve and his changeup. Sutton, you will remember, has also appeared in the Seaver and Clemens profiles.

Greg Maddux versus Nolan Ryan (1947–)

Debuting in 1966, Nolan missed, by less than a year, crossing paths with Warren Spahn. Between them, these two blanket a good deal of baseball history, covering the years between 1942 and '93, about a half-century. As baseball marks time, that's roughly five generations. Spahn's 23 seasons and Ryan's record-setting 27 seasons are rarities, of course. Both are due to exceptional talents, steely discipline, and a Sutton-like workout regimen that frustrated Father Time.

Before moving back over into the AL for the 1989 season with the Texas Rangers, "the Only Nolan" spent a number of productive seasons with the

Houston Astros (1980–88). It was during these years that Ryan encountered Greg Maddux. The first of these games (there were three in the Maddux-Ryan series) started on Tuesday, September 2, 1986, and was completed the next day in one of the more remarkable encounters of the season. In this particular game, managers Hal Lanier of the Astros and the Cubs' Gene Michael emptied the benches, using a NL record 53 players. Nolan Ryan got the start for Houston and pitched seven innings before leaving the game knotted at a 4–4 count at the end of seven frames. From that point the game wore on another seven innings before being halted by darkness. Resuming play the next day, the teams battled on through two more innings before Houston broke through with a three-run rally that should have iced the contest — but didn't. The Cubs, apparently unwilling to bid the game *adieu,* answered with a threesome of their own in the 17th inning. That inning is noteworthy, for it was in that stanza that Skipper Michael called Greg Maddux off the bench for his first major league appearance to run for slow-footed catcher Jody Davis. Three runs were already in, and Maddux, now perched on second base, represented the winning run. Catcher Mike Martin was sent in to pinch-hit for reliever Dave Gumpert. That move was frustrated when Martin grounded out to end the inning. Note that both Martin and Maddux stayed in the game as the Cubs' new battery.

Call it history in the making. This, then, is the way Greg Maddux's first ML inning unfolded: Shortstop Craig Reynolds led off with a grounder that Ryne Sandberg converted into Houston's first out. That brought up Billy Hatcher, a fellow not known for much else than his hitting. And hit is what Hatcher did. He found one of rookie Maddux's offerings to his liking and put it out of everybody's reach, sending the Astros into a one-run lead. The first hit off Greg Maddux in his ML career was not only for four bases, it won the game, as things turned out. Maddux got the next hitter on a pop-up, and then finished off the inning registering his first K, at the expense of reliever Danny Darwin. Because the Bruins failed to score in their half of the 18th, Greg Maddux was tagged with the loss, winding up with his first inning of work, first K, first homer and first boxscore designation as LP. Greg Maddux would never forget that day at Wrigley Field, nor watching the ball disappear into the seats. Welcome to the Big Time, Mr. Maddux!

Houston at Wrigley Field, Chicago, September 2, 1986

Houston	AB	R	H	BI	Chicago	AB	R	H	BI
Lopes, cf	5	1	2	0	D. Martinez, cf	4	0	0	0
Kerfeld, p	0	0	0	0	L. Smith, p	0	0	0	0
L. Anderson, p	0	0	0	0	Dayett, rf	5	0	1	0
D. Smith, p	0	0	0	0	Sandberg, 2b	7	1	1	0
Keough, p	2	0	0	0	Mumphrey, lf, cf	4	0	1	0

Knepper, p	0	0	0	0	Dernier, pr, cf	5	2	1	0
Doran, p	2	0	0	0	Moreland, rf, 1b	6	2	2	3
Pankovits, 2b	6	1	1	0	Durham, 1b	3	1	1	2
Solano, p	0	0	0	0	C. Walker, pr	0	0	0	0
Darwin (WP)	1	0	0	0	DiPino, p	0	0	0	0
Garner, 3b	3	0	1	0	Sutcliffe, p	0	0	0	0
Walling, ph, 3b	5	0	2	1	Sanderson, pr	0	0	0	0
G. Davis, 1b	4	1	2	1	Trillo, pr, 3b	3	0	0	0
Driessen, 1b	3	1	2	1	J. Davis, c	6	0	1	1
Bass, rf	8	2	3	1	G. Maddux, pr (LP)	0	0	0	0
J. Cruz, lf	8	0	1	1	Speier, 3b	3	1	2	1
Ashby, c	5	1	2	1	Hofmann, p	0	0	0	0
Robbie Wine, c	3	0	1	0	Matthews, ph, lf	3	0	1	0
Thon, ss	2	0	0	0	Dunston, ss	7	0	1	0
Reynolds, ph, ss	5	0	0	0	Moyer, p	1	0	0	0
Ryan, p	3	0	0	1	Francona, ph	1	0	0	0
A. Lopez, p	0	0	0	0	R. Davis, p	0	0	0	0
Puhl, ph	1	0	0	0	Bosley, ph, lf	4	0	0	0
T. Walker, cf	0	0	0	0	S. Trout, p	0	0	0	0
Gainey, cf	0	0	0	0	Cey, ph	0	0	0	0
Hatcher, ph, cf	4	1	1	1	D. Gumpert, p	0	0	0	0
M. Martin, ph, c	1	0	0	0					
Totals	70	8	18	8	Totals	63	7	12	7

Line Score: Houston   010 002 001 000 000 031   8–18–0
             Chicago   001 000 201 000 000 030   7–12–1

Home Runs: G. Davis (27), Hatcher (4), Moreland (9), Durham (15), Speier (6).

Houston	IP	H	ER	BB	K	Chicago	IP	H	ER	BB	K
Ryan	7	4	3	1	2	Moyer	6	9	3	2	2
Lopez	1	0	0	0	1	R. Davis	2	1	0	0	0
Kerfeld	0	1	1	0	0	L. Smith	1	2	1	1	1
Anderson	.1	0	0	1	0	DiPino	2	0	0	0	3
D. Smith	.2	0	0	1	1	Hofmann	3	1	0	0	2
Keough	5	1	0	3	4	Trout	2	1	0	0	1
Knepper	2	2	0	2	0	Gumpert	1	3	3	1	1
Solano	.1	3	3	1	0	Maddux	1	1	1	0	1
Darwin	1.2	1	0	0	1						
Totals	18	12	7	9	12	Totals	18	18	9	4	11

The final two games of the three-game set between Maddux and Ryan occurred within a span of five days in August of 1988. Neither of the two hurlers earned a decision in the two games. The first was played in Chicago and went down to the last of the ninth before the deciding marker, tallied on an inning-opening two-bagger by Rafael Palmeiro and a single by Vance Law, gave the Cubs a 3 to 2 victory. Another one-run decision followed the game on the 24th. Ryan and Maddux were again the starters and once again turned a tight ball game over to relievers. Ryan pitched through eight, and Maddux nine, leaving behind a 1 to 1 tie. Finally, in the 11th, this time at Houston, Vance Law came through with an extra-inning blow that put the go-ahead run on, and center fielder Mitch Webster later singled Vance home with what proved to be the winning run. Scott Sanderson picked up the win, and Larry Anderson, who surrendered the Webster and Vance singles, was saddled with the loss, 2 to 1.

Consequently, Nolan Ryan was involved in three one-run ball games, none of which could be accounted for in the win or loss column. The trio of games between Ryan and Maddux, then, stood at no wins and no losses for Ryan, despite having been a part of three one-run ball games, each of which went down to the final inning of play. For Greg Maddux it meant no wins against Hall of Fame rival Ryan, and the loss that got his career started on the wrong foot. What was to follow simply had to be better — much, much better.

Greg Maddux versus Jose Dennis "El Presidente" Martinez (1955–)

Nicaragua's first major league superstar was so popular in his native land that he could have been elected its president. That brought about the Latin American's nickname "El Presidente." He also cut a presidential figure on the mound, where the usual order of things was 1–2–3 and it's our turn to bat when Senor Martinez presided.

Dennis Martinez was around long enough to wear five different uniforms, win 245 ML ball games, and record 15 double-figure seasons in his 23-year career. The number 245 has some significance for Latin American baseball fans because it is a record, if only by a margin of one, for the most career victories by one of their heroes. (Juan Marichal formerly held that record at 244). Martinez' career victory total, and his Wins Above League (229.6), are both among the 50 best in baseball. But perhaps his most outstanding feature, emphasized by his number 12 all time ranking, was his fielding ability, which enabled him to amass 43 Fielding Runs during his career. That is not to say that he lacked the outstanding stuff to rank him among the better pitchers of his time, for, indeed, a searing fastball and a puzzling array of breaking pitches kept the hitters at bay.

Dennis Martinez' most outstanding achievement, however, did not have to do with numbers. Coping with alcoholism was a far more traumatic challenge for Martinez than dealing with the game's heavy lumbermen. By 1986 he was a ten-year Baltimore veteran who had won over 100 games—and on the brink of a unique and harrowing oblivion that only alcoholics experience. Though he had been traded to Montreal, he was at that point out of a

Dennis Martinez. They called him "El Presidente," Nicaragua's most famous ball player.

job, and it took Martinez until May of 1987 to get himself back into the game, steadied and sobered to a point where he might once again be successful in the only trade he knew. So the Latino, playing the American Game north of the border with Montreal's Expos, battled back to establish himself as one of baseball's stellar hurlers, and during the second half of his career more than doubled the productivity of his younger years as an accomplished master craftsman.

The Maddux-Martinez Log:

Sep 26, 1989   Chicago 3, Montreal 2   Maddux WP, Martinez LP

On September 23, 1986, Montreal beat Chicago 10 to 5. Greg Maddux, who made his fourth ML start, was the losing pitcher. Dennis Martinez (ND), who started, was followed by relievers Randy St. Clair, the winner, and Andy MacGaffigan (SV).

The Expos beat the Cubs 8 to 4 on July 26, 1988. Maddux and Martinez started (ND for either). The game went into the 11th frame tied at four. In the bottom of the 11th catcher Mike Fitzgerald, batting for reliever Neal Heaton (WP), lofted a bases-loaded home run into Olympic Stadium's seats to win the game, 8 to 4. Chicago reliever Jeff Pico was charged with the defeat.

In the final Martinez-Maddux matchup, Montreal beat Chicago 3 to 2, scoring an unanswered run in the top of the ninth on September 13, 1991. Martinez (WP) was relieved by Barry Jones, who earned the Save. Maddux (ND) was relieved by losing pitcher Bob Scanlon.

In the four-game series between these two moundsmen, each of which occurred during the Chicago phase of Maddux's career, Martinez earned one win, lost one and was involved in two No Decisions. Maddux won one, lost two and picked up one No Decision. The game Maddux did win in this set was his 19th, a number that would crop up four more times in Atlanta. It came during a season that stamped him as one of the NL's young luminaries. For Martinez it was a minor glitch in a year that saw him run an 11-game winning streak (a club record) in the midst of a 16 and 7 season. He was back.

Greg Maddux versus Orel Leonard Quinton "The Bulldog" Hershiser IV (1958–)

Proceeding right to the heart of matters, we go directly to Olympic Stadium where, on August 30, 1988, Orel Hershiser was scheduled to pitch for the Los Angeles Dodgers. Entering the game with a 17 and 8 record, he pitched with the kind of dominating effort that had marked most of what was turning out to be a brilliant season. The Expos managed a pair of runs in the fifth inning to narrow the score a bit, but "the Bulldog," so named by his skipper Tommy Lasorda for reasons that were apparent to anyone who saw this fellow at work, got by the inning without further damage and then shut Montreal down the rest of the way to raise his season mark to 18 and 8 and help bring his team a step closer to the NL's West Division crown.

Orel Hershiser's season had already drawn enough rave notices to put him in the vanguard of the Cy Young award parade. But as it turned out, the first 17 Ws were merely prelude. The main act was about to move to center stage. The last four innings of shutout ball in Montreal were followed in rapid and ever increasingly

A fierce competitor, Orel Hershiser pitched for pennant winners in both leagues.

suspenseful order by five straight goose egg games that raised his consecutive scoreless inning total to 49 straight. The record book was beckoning. In his final start of the season at San Diego he worked his way through another bunch of zeroes, 10 innings worth, maxing out at 59 straight. San Diego had a last laugh of sorts: in their half of the 16th of that record-setting game, they matched the lead run LA scored in the top half of the inning, and then added the winner, turning a 0–0 game into a 2 to 1 victory within the space of six outs. But the major item of business that day was the onset of Orel Hershiser's 59 consecutive shutout innings, which would eclipse another great Dodger's record by one, the 58 straight authored by the "Big D," Don Drysdale. Playoff and World Series MVP awards followed, capped finally by the 1988 Cy Young award. It was a once-in-a-career year, and though there were a number of other super years, this one was literally one for the book.

In 1988 Greg Maddux faced the Dodgers twice, but in neither game did he duel Orel Hershiser. Maddux that season was a winner in 18 out of 24 decisions, recording his first big season for the Cubbies. His ERA that season dropped from the five-plus ERAs he had registered in his first two years to a smart 3.18, and the combination of his devastating inside pitching plus his uncanny control of the strike zone were beginning to make their mark around the league. A Hershiser-Maddux matchup that summer would have been most interesting.

Four of the five Hershiser-Maddux matchups took place before the winter of the big Chicago gaffe. Although they had been known to throw caution and reason to the wind before, the Cubs organization outdid itself when it came time to get Greg Maddux's name on a new contract. The 1992 Cy Young award winner would have been more than content to spend his eighth big league season within "the Friendly Confines." Instead he signed on as a free agent with the Atlanta Braves because a series of crude interchanges with the people in the front office indicated beyond doubt that, Cy Young award or not, Mr. Maddux was not indispensable. The principal offender was the Cubs' CEO, Stanton Cook, who was known to have uttered those familiar GM words, "He'll [Maddux will] sign on *our* terms — not his or his agent's." It was easy, after all had been said and done, for Greg Maddux to leave Chicago for the Southland. All he did was to win a second straight Cy Young award — this time for Atlanta, where he helped the Braves win the NL's West Division title. Chicago, meantime, finished out of the running in the East. Might not Maddux have made a difference?

Thus it was that the fifth and final meeting between Orel Hershiser and Greg Maddux took place in Atlanta, where in an early season exhibition of superb pitching the Braves and Dodgers hooked up in a duel of aces on April 10, 1993. The game went into the tenth frame before the Dodgers pushed across a run, unanswered by the Braves, to win 2 to 1. Both Hershiser and

Maddux went nine innings, tied at one, before giving way to the bullpen. Hershiser got the W and reliever Jay Howell was tagged with the loss. Maddux didn't get that one, but he did come through with a 20 and 10 record before it was all over in '93. And this time there would be post-season play to make it that much more interesting.

The Maddux-Hershiser Log:

Apr 27, 1989	Chicago 1, Los Angeles 0	Maddux WP, Hershiser LP
May 7, 1989	Chicago 4, Los Angeles 2	Maddux WP, Hershiser LP
Jul 18, 1989	Los Angeles 4, Chicago 1	Hershiser WP, Maddux LP

In the inaugural match of this series on July 10, 1987, Los Angeles beat the Cubs 5 to 4. Neither Maddux nor Hershiser were pitchers of decision. This game was suspended, with two out in the bottom of the ninth, and completed the next day. Dodgers' reliever Matt Young was the winner, and Cub relief ace Lee Smith was charged with the loss.

The April 10, 1993, game, referred to above, and won by Los Angeles, was a 10-inning affair won by Hershiser. The loss went to Jay Howell. Maddux (ND) left after nine innings.

As has so often been noted, and so often happened, arm injuries are almost invariably a part of the pitcher's career. The strain and stress of throwing a baseball is, after all, enormous, and it does exact a frightful toll over the course of many seasons. Despite rigorous training and scrupulous attention to pitching mechanics, pitchers simply have to learn to live with what has been called "the sweet pain of success." Orel Hershiser was no exception. Less than two seasons after his career high point in 1988 he was down to a 1 and 1 record for the 1990 Dodgers. Where he had once blown hitters away with overpowering stuff, it was now his own arm that was blown out, and it took him several seasons to get back into a winning groove. By that time he was, like many before him, winning with his head as much as with his arm. Consequently, Orel Hershiser's final numbers read 200, not 300 victories, with all the other statistics normally associated with Hall of Fame careers adjusted accordingly.

That said, it should be noted that the five Maddux-Hershiser outings were occasions that brought out the best in both pitchers and ball clubs, with the closely contested ball games that one would expect when two master craftsmen duel. Though Greg Maddux won two, lost one and received two No Decisions against Hershiser, whose record was two, two and one, staff ace Maddux knew he had been in a real dogfight by the time it was all over. An afternoon like that, at crossed swords with "the Bulldog," is exactly what Mr. Maddux should have expected — and did.

Greg Maddux versus Jose Antonio (Abreu) Rijo (1965–)

The big Dominican, Jose Rijo, was a major league prospect at 15. That says something about precocity, and in young Rijo's case, it was even more significant inasmuch as the New York Yankees, no less, were interested enough to sign him to his first pro contract in 1980. Four years later, having made the Yankees' varsity squad, he debuted at Kansas City, taking over for reliever Bob Shirley in the third inning of a game in which the Royals had already battered the Yanks mercilessly, forging a 14 to 0 lead by the time the youngster entered the game with two away. And so he faced his first major league hitter, Greg Pryor, and promptly hung a K on him to end the inning. Not yet 19, the rookie threw his smoke at Kansas City the rest of the way, fanning four more and giving up a run in the seventh. Though the Yanks were whipped that day, they had seen enough on the hill to know that this fellow would be around for a while. There was some distance to travel between that first ML exposure and a polished, professional performance, but "the right stuff" was in place waiting to be molded.

Playing left field that day was Lou Piniella, who already in the 1984 season, which was to be his last, served the Yankee brass in a coaching capacity. The peppery Floridian, whose potent shillelagh, hot temper and competitive drive had already seen him through 18 seasons, had spent a decade in pinstripes and was about to be named the Yankee skipper. During the next couple of seasons, at the height of the Billy Martin off-and-on managerial era, he was himself in and out of the Yankee managing job, scouting, and various front office chores under Der Boss, George Steinbrenner. That kind of scenario was just not up to "Sweet Lou's" tastes or interests, so when Cincinnati's managing job opened up for the 1990 season, Piniella jumped at the chance, shifted gears and moved over to the NL.

It was in Cincinnati, where Jose Rijo had landed after some four seasons in the AL with New York and Oakland, that the former teammates caught up with one another. This time Piniella would be the skipper, and Rijo, by 1990 (when Piniella took over) a veteran on the Redleg's staff—at age 25, would be the ace of his pitching corps.

Between them, Rijo and Piniella produced a winner in 1990. Instantly. The Reds swept from a fifth place 1989 finish to the championship of the NL West with a five-game bulge over the second-place Dodgers. After besting the Pirates in the LCS (Rijo won game four), they went on to an improbable sweep of the heavily favored Oakland A's. Jose Rijo was the primary mover in that 1990 world series, winning two of the four games while allowing but a single run in 15.1 innings of near-flawless work in the Fall Classic. Jose Jr., with his mother, Rosie, and Rijo's father-in-law, Juan Marichal, were all proud rooters at that world series.

Reds ace Jose Rijo, who led Lou Pinniela's team to the 1990 world championship.

The year 1990 was also noteworthy from the standpoint of the Rijo-Maddux series, begun in 1988 when Greg Maddux prevailed over the Reds 6 to 3 in a game in which Rijo appeared as a reliever. During 1990 the Reds and Cubs met twice, and on both occasions Jose & Co. took the measure of the Bruins. The complete Rijo-Maddux series follows:

The Maddux-Rijo Log:

May 21, 1990	Cincinnati 4, Chicago 3	Rijo WP, Maddux LP
Sep 21, 1990	Cincinnati 6, Chicago 2	Rijo, WP, Maddux LP
Aug 15, 1993	Atlanta 1, Cincinnati 0	Maddux WP, Rijo LP
Aug 6, 1994	Atlanta 2, Cincinnati 1	Maddux WP, Rijo LP

This series began with a 6 to 3 Chicago victory on June 1, 1988. Maddux was the winning pitcher. Tom Browning started for the Reds and was charged with the loss. Rijo (ND) was used in relief.

Neither Maddux (ND) nor Rijo (ND) were around at the end of a 13-inning game on July 25, 1991, won by the Cubs 5 to 4. Relievers Heathcliff Slocumb (WP) and Tim Layana (LP) finished the game.

Relievers Tim Pugh (WP) and Mike Stanton (LP) were the pitchers of decision in a June 11, 1993, game won by Atlanta 6 to 5. Rijo (ND) and Maddux (ND) started the game.

On May 12, 1995, Cincinnati beat Atlanta 5 to 4. Maddux (ND) was the starting pitcher against Rijo (ND) in a game won by Jeff Brantley. Steve Bedrosian was charged with Atlanta's defeat.

After posting a 5 and 4 log in 1995, Jose Rijo, it appeared, was finished. But he resurfaced in 2001 to make spot appearances for his old team, the Reds, in 17 innings. There were 12 more strikeouts, always a Rijo trademark, in a career that featured 7.83 Ks per nine innings pitched, which ranks him 12th on the all time K/Gm list. His 227 whiffs in 1993, a career high, led the NL. Other league-leading marks included a .714 winning percentage in 1991 (his record that year was 15 and 6), a 9.8 Ratio, and a .274 opponents' BA.

Ranking in the top 100 among pitchers all time for hits per game, Jose Rijo shares a unique distinction with father-in-law Juan Marichal. Both have identical 8.09 marks, putting them on the same number 86 rung in the all time listing. Talk about a family affair!

Greg Maddux versus Dwight "Doc" Gooden (1964–)

Rangy Dwight Gooden, not yet 20, came down to September of the 1984 season sporting a 13 and 8 record. He had pitched two scoreless innings in the All-Star Game held at Candlestick Park in San Francisco, striking out the Americans in order in the fifth inning. Then came the final month of the season, and he salted away the Rookie of the Year award with a blistering finale that consisted of four more wins and a single, 2 to 1, loss to Philadelphia that left him with a final 17 and 9 mark. During that month he had gone the route five times, had hurled 24 straight scoreless innings and had fanned 62, at one time putting together two straight 16-K games. He had accomplished all this as the youngest hurler, ever, to play in an All-Star Game, as well as the youngest to win a strikeout title.

A year later he became the youngest Cy Young award winner. That season he won 24 and lost but four, won the ERA title with a 1.53 ERA, and added K laurels to further garnish his record with a Pitcher's Triple Crown. When you can do this as a player in the Big Apple, the whole world is your chocolate store. Dwight Gooden, who had quickly become "Dr. K," resident New York hero, was on top of the world. Young, willing and able, he was ready to try just about anything and everything.

Unfortunately, "everything" included the murky, debilitating world of drugs. And by the time he had found his way back to the daylight of a drug-free world, injuries began to plague him, so that between occasionally falling off the wagon and undergoing treatment to keep that marvelous K-machine of his in working order, the near limitless potential of the first few marvelous chapters of his career had diminished to the point where people no longer suggested that a Hall of Fame plaque was a foregone conclusion when his career came to an end.

Dwight Gooden, Dr. K, who was the youngest player ever to be named Rookie of the Year (1984).

Despite all that, consider this: during the time he was a recovering addict, and in spite of the many injuries he suffered, he still won 81 and lost only 55 between 1988 and '93, for a .596 winning percentage, including a sterling 19 and 7, 1990 season. A mean heater and a sharply dropping curveball came to his rescue on any day that his arm was up to it. The crosstown Yankees understood what a decent Gooden arm would mean to their pitching staff and, even as a well-traveled veteran, put him into pinstripes long enough for him to get into the ML's Big Dance during their pennant surge in the late '90s.

What might have been doesn't count for much in the record books, but even then it is worth noting that "Doc" has left behind at least one strong testimony to the dominating quality of his better days: a 7.37 K/Gm strikeout rate that ranks at number 23 on the all time charts. Another part of that record is the four-game series of matchups with another of his era's stalwarts, Greg Maddux. The two matched pitches four times, and it took Greg Maddux three tries before he was able to subdue Dwight Gooden. In the first three encounters Gooden won by scores of 13 to 6 (September 8, 1988, against the Cubs), 7 to 3 (on September 23, 1990) and (five days later, on the 28th), 7 to 1. Seven years later the two dueled at Yankee Stadium, where, on July 2, 1997, in an interleague game, the Braves throttled the Yanks 2 to 0 on a Maddux three-hitter. The box score of that game follows.

Atlanta Braves at Yankee Stadium, July 2, 1997

Atlanta	AB	R	H	BI	New York	AB	R	H	BI
Blauser, ss	3	1	1	0	Jeter, ss	4	0	0	0
Tucker, rf	2	0	0	0	Girardi, c	3	0	1	0
C. Jones, 3b	4	0	2	1	O'Neill, rf	3	0	0	0
McGriff, 1b	4	0	0	0	Fielder, dh	3	0	0	0
Klesko, lf	3	1	2	1	T. Marinez, 1b	3	0	0	0
D. Bautista, lf	0	0	0	0	Boggs, 3b	3	0	0	0
A. Jones, cf	4	0	0	0	Whiten, lf	3	0	1	0
Lockhart, dh	4	0	1	0	Curtis, cf	3	0	1	0
E. Perez, c	4	0	0	0	P. Kelly, 2b	2	0	0	0
Lemke, 2b	4	0	1	0	B. Williams, ph	1	0	0	0
Maddux (WP)	0	0	0	0	Gooden (LP)	0	0	0	0
					Lloyd, p	0	0	0	0
					Nelson, p	0	0	0	0
Totals	32	2	7	2	Totals	28	0	3	0

Line Score:	Atlanta	001	001	000	2–7–0
	New York	000	000	000	0–3–0

2BH: Blauser; HR: Kelsko; HPB: Klesko by Gooden; DP: Blauser, Lemke, McGriff; BB: Maddux 0, Gooden 3, Lloyd 0, Nelson 0; K: Maddux 8, Gooden 6, Lloyd 1, Nelson 2; Umpires: Hirschbeck, Hendry, Joyce and Hickox; Time: 2:09; Att: 36,606.

The victory was Maddux's eleventh (against three losses), and Gooden's first loss of the season. He had previously won three. Dwight Gooden was more than a worthy opponent that day. Unfortunately, he had run headlong into a Maddux year that produced a 19 and 4 record which brought a second place finish to Pedro Martinez' Cy Young award. During that season, a masterpiece by any yardstick, Maddux led the league in winning percentage, giving up but 20 free passes (14 unintentional), a career high point in control and efficiency, with a 2.20 ERA. His work on that summer afternoon at Yankee Stadium was indicative of the kind of season he was having, and he would wind things up with another eight conquests in nine tries.

On the other hand, Dwight Gooden wound up in 1997's LCS, as did

Maddux, having contributed a 9 and 5 record to the Yankees' divisional championship. His final record showed 194 wins, a late-career Yankee no-hitter against the Seattle Mariners on May 14, 1996, and a key to Mayor Rudy Giuliani's city, not as a Met, where he had recorded his most spectacular deeds, but as a vintage Yankee, who had found from deep down inside the craftsmanship, endurance and will to make it through nine innings of no-hit baseball.

On his best days, with all his stuff going, Dwight Gooden has to be named among the premier hurlers of the 20th century's last score of years. On those days he stands right up there with Roger Clemens, Randy Johnson and Pedro Martinez, all of whom grace the Maddux portfolio.

The Professor and the Aces

Perhaps it's the way he looks, bespectacled when not on the mound, and giving all the appearances of a "straight arrow," which he actually is; and perhaps it's because of his professorial precision when it comes to pitching a baseball; but Greg Maddux has often been cast in the mold of the Professor. He does fit the mold. Articulate, given to family matters, and always, ever and always, well prepared to "hold forth."

By the time a new century had dawned in the midst of his illustrious career, Professor Maddux had made the circuit long enough to know a thing or two about the pitching arts. Summing up Maddux's studied approach to his profession, Don Sutton ventured that both Sandy Koufax and Greg Maddux had a love for the *art* of pitching, even though it was the only similarity they shared. He added that it was the only similarity they *needed*, because it prompted them to be appreciative of their gifts and their craft, in turn causing them to work hard at it, always finding out more information and using it.

The outstanding characteristics of a Maddux game, given his distinctive approach, came down to informed and adaptive pitch selection, incredible control, and one of the better changeups in the game's history. A devastating combination, that. In the professor's words, deceptively simplistic, it all came down to this: "The best pitch you can throw is a comfortable pitch, the pitch that you believe in, even if it's the wrong pitch."

Of course, there were those who were around to challenge him right on down to the last out. Four of the best he faced are assembled in this profile. In David Cone, Kevin Brown, Doug Drabek and Randy Johnson, each of whom debuted in Greg Maddux's rookie season, 1986, the Professor faced his own "final exams." In the following chronological listing is a breakdown of the Maddux matchups with this quartet of latter day superstars, at least one of whom, Randy Johnson, is himself headed Cooperstown way.

The Professor and the Aces — A Matchup Log:

Jun 26, 1987 vs. Drabek	Pittsburgh 5, Chicago 2	B. Jones WP, Maddux LP
Aug 3, 1987 vs. Drabek	Pittsburgh 6, Chicago 4	Drabek WP, Maddux LP
Apr 16, 1988 vs. Drabek	Pittsburgh 4, Chicago 0	Drabek WP, Maddux LP
Sep 23, 1988 vs. Drabek	Chicago 5, Pittsburgh 3	J. Moyer WP, R. Kipper LP
Jun 5, 1989 vs. Cone	Chicago 15, New York 3	Maddux WP, Cone LP
Jun 21, 1989 vs. Drabek	Chicago 1, Pittsburgh 0	Maddux WP, D. Bair LP
Jun 26, 1989 vs. Drabek	Pittsburgh 2, Chicago 1	Drabek WP, Maddux LP
Apr 18, 1990 vs. Cone	Chicago 8, New York 5	Maddux WP, Cone LP
Jun 6, 1990 vs. Drabek	Pittsburgh 6, Chicago 1	Drabek WP, Maddux LP
Aug 4, 1991 vs. Cone	Chicago 8, New York 3	Maddux WP, Cone LP
Aug 9, 1991 vs. Cone	Chicago 5, New York 4	Maddux WP, Cone LP
Jul 27, 1992 vs. Drabek	Chicago 3, Pittsburgh 2	Maddux WP, Drabek LP
Aug 31, 1995 vs. Drabek	Atlanta 5, Houston 2	Maddux WP, Drabek LP
Aug 1, 1997 vs. Brown	Florida 3, Atlanta 2	J. Powell WP, M. Cather LP
Aug 11, 1997 vs. Brown	Atlanta 2, Florida 1	F. Heredia WP, M. Wohlers LP
Jun 7, 1998 vs. Drabek	Atlanta 9, Baltimore 0	Maddux WP, Drabek LP
Sep 2, 1998 vs. Johnson	Houston 4, Atlanta 2	Johnson WP, Maddux LP
May 30, 1999 vs. Brown	Los Angeles 5, Atlanta 4	P. Borbon WP, M. Remlinger LP

Through the 2001 season (Maddux was not paired with any of the pitchers above in 2000 or 2001), the record on the Professor and the Aces reads as follows:

	Won	Lost	No Decision
Maddux vs. the four aces	8	6	4
Doug Drabek	4	3	3
Randy Johnson	1	0	0
Kevin Brown	0	0	3
David Cone	0	4	0

A closer look at both the matchup games and the pitchers is in order. The games in which they were involved, in particular, shed some light on the kind of pitching domination, with an exception or two, going on. Note first that among the 18 games only three "got away" on either Greg Maddux or his opposing pitcher. Secondly, in 11 of these tilts the losing team scored two runs or less, with six of them showing a run production of either one or no runs at all. The best of these matchups follow in the review of each Maddux rival.

Greg Maddux versus Douglas Dean "Doug" Drabek (1962–)

The only good comment Bill James could offer about Doug Drabek, though it was a fine compliment indeed, was: "A better man than a Ballplayer."[46] But, considering some of the other personalities and their baseball accomplishments reviewed in his far-ranging dissertation about the game's best, that seems a bit shallow. Here was a pitcher who became the Pirates' ace and enjoyed five far-better-than-average seasons (1987–92), winning 92 ball games while leading his club to championship series playoffs three straight years (1990–92). The first year of that championship run he was the NL's Cy Young award winner, with a 22 and 6 record. During those days of the "Killer Bees," Bobby Bonilla and Barry Bonds, the Pirates, under foxy Jimmy Leland, squeaked by on undersized budgets, oversized desire and a sound pitching staff anchored by the likes of Drabek, John Smiley, Randy Tomlin, Bob Walk and reliever Stan Belinda.

In the space of one week during the 1989 season, Doug Drabek and Greg Maddux locked horns in an exceptional run of pitching mastery. In the first of these, on June 21, the two teams were helpless in the grip of Drabek and Maddux, both of whom threw one scoreless inning after another at each other. For strategic reasons Drabek was lifted after nine innings, during which he gave up five hits, equaled by five Ks, and no runs. Maddux rolled along just as effortlessly, matching Drabek goose egg for goose egg. In the 11th the Cubs broke the ice with a single tally off Doug Bair, who had relieved Drabek in the 10th inning. Cub manager Don Zimmer then brought on relief ace Mitch Williams, who tacked down Maddux's victory with his 18th of 36 Saves that season.

Just five days later Maddux and Drabek had at it again, this time in a night game at Wrigley Field. Before the dust had settled in the first inning, the Killer Bees had led the Pirates to a two-run start toward what turned out to be a 2 to 1 victory. In that one Doug Drabek gave up seven scattered hits and a single run in the fifth stanza, and though that narrowed his lead, he held on to beat the Cubs for his fifth win, while Maddux absorbed his seventh loss.

Doug Drabek was acquired by Pittsburgh from the Yankee organization, and in 1987 seemed to be headed absolutely the wrong way, posting a 1 and 8 record in the early going. But Jimmy Leland stuck with him, noting that he was striking out hitters at the rate of almost six per game, while his K/BB ratio was in the three-to-one range. Leland's patience paid off, as Drabek finished the season with 10 wins and only four losses, evening out his record at 11 and 12. By 1988 he was ready for heavy duty, and the winning seasons soon followed. Drabek wound up with better than 150 big league wins and a TPI that averaged almost two wins above league-average pitchers during his eight best seasons. Not your typical HOF numbers, but a fine professional nonetheless.

Greg Maddux versus David Brian "Dave" Cone (1963–)

In four tries, it just wasn't in the cards. The New York Mets succumbed to the artistry and wiles of Greg Maddux on June 5, 1989, at Wrigley Field.

David Cone was the losing pitcher. At Shea Stadium on April 18, 1990, the Cubs beat the Mets 8 to 5 with a 5-run seventh that chased losing pitcher David Cone. Twice in 1991 Cone squared off against the Professor and was chastened on both occasions with a few more lessons about pitching winning baseball. And the strange part about Cone's 0 for 4 against Maddux is that it happened to a pitcher of his stature, one of those high percentage winners who took on all comers no matter how good they were and beat them all. But not Greg Maddux.

There were more than a few orbital moments in David Cone's career, beginning with a 20 and 3 season that came during Orel Hershiser's big year in 1988. Hershiser was first in line for the Cy Young award, but not without heat from one Mr. Cone, who that year posted a 2.22 ERA and limited opposing hitters to a .213 BA. There were two 13-K games, a 19-K game against the Phils, and a game against Cincinnati's Reds in which he fanned the side on nine pitches, all in what might look like a so-so season at 14–14 in 1991, but was actually one of those rare examples of a pitcher who pitched well enough to have won more than 20—except that he didn't. Sometimes that's the way it is.

Mixing speeds, arm angles and deliveries, and never giving the same hitter the same look in his four or five at bats in a game, Cone was a classic improviser. The result was your classic strikeout pitcher. Through 16 seasons he not only won .611 percent of his games (his career record through 2001 was 193 and 123), but during that time he K'd batters at the rate of 8.30 per game.

That's a stiff enough pace to rank him among the top ten in the game's history. As late in his career as 1997, David Cone registered a 10.25 strikeout per game average. That's worthy of a number 27 rank for single season marks.

Cone's 1997 K-mark came between the 1996 and 1999 Yankee world series years when he beat Tom Glavine and the Braves 5 to 2 in game three of the '96 Classic, and Kevin Millwood and the '99 Braves in game two, 7 to 2, proof positive that he could win big games against the best. And in the 1992 All-Star game at San Diego, started by Tom Glavine (who was the losing pitcher) and continued by Greg Maddux (who was knicked for a pair of runs in two innings), David Cone came on for the Nationals and sat down the Americans without a run in his one-inning appearance. All of this nonetheless paled in comparison to his greatest pitching performance, which came during the 1999 season.

On a 95-degree afternoon at Yankee Stadium on July 18, David Cone dueled Javier Vazquez of the Montreal Expos in an interleague game. With Yankee mystique and tradition permeating the air, Don Larsen threw out the first pitch to Yogi Berra on a day set aside to honor Larsen's perfect world series game in 1956. David Cone, on that very day, threw a perfect game of his own. It was the 14th perfect game, including Larsen's masterpiece, of the century. The laconic Cone commented afterward, "You probably have a better chance of winning the lottery than having this happen." In that record performance he fanned 10, used but 88 pitches and didn't get to a three-ball count all day. On a day like that, not being able to beat Greg Maddux is no big deal, right?! Maddux himself would have agreed.

Greg Maddux versus James Kevin Brown (1965–)

In three tries neither Kevin Brown nor Greg Maddux could wrest a victory from one another. The two hooked up in three regular season ball games that went down to the last out, one of which was an extra inning affair, and in each of them the relief corps of their ball clubs was called on to finish out what these two veteran aces had started.

The Maddux-Brown Log:

On August 1, 1997, Florida beat Atlanta 3 to 2 in a 12-inning thriller. Jay Powell finished up as Florida's winner, and Mike Cather was charged with the Braves' loss.

Ten days later Brown took on Maddux once again in a game won by Atlanta, 2 to 1, behind relief ace Mark Wohlers. Felix Heredia received the loss for the Marlins.

The final Brown-Maddux face-off was played on May 30, 1999, when Brown, now with Los Angeles, started but was relieved by Pedro Borbon, who won the game 5 to 4. Mike Remlinger earned the loss for the Atlanta Braves.

Reviewed in the Clemens chapter, Kevin Brown, who moved over to Florida's Marlins in the NL for the 1996 season after a decade in the AL, recorded a splashy 92 and 45 (.672 winning percentage) for three different teams in the Senior Circuit between 1997 and 2001, despite several visits to the DL and the lost time that goes with recovering from injuries. It was during his peak NL stint that the lean "groundball pitcher," a man of many and severely breaking pitches, met the crack Atlanta pitching staff— not only during regular season play, but in the 1997 NLCS as well. As both clubhouse leader and the Marlin's staff ace, he took on the Braves' powerful duo of Maddux and Glavine and beat them both to propel Florida into world series play, where, despite Brown's two losses, the Marlins beat Cleveland in the 11-inning, seventh game barnburner that elevated the young Marlins to baseball fame and fortune under the much-traveled man of many managerial wiles, Jimmy Leyland.

A year later, this time in a San Diego Padres uniform, Brown clashed with the Braves one more time. At Atlanta he took on Tom Glavine just as he had the previous season. These pitchers can be a hitter's worst nightmare on any given day, and on this day, October 8, 1998, Kevin Brown filled the role to near-perfection, shutting down the Braves on a scorching three-hitter in the second game of the NCLS. But after three straight in the two series over the Braves' awesome 1–2 punch, he finally lost one, this time to the controversial rookie John Rocker, who came to John Smoltz's relief to beat the Padres in a game that the old master, Greg Maddux himself, finished with a ninth-inning flourish. Kevin Brown had entered that game in the seventh in relief of Mark Langston and retired the side, only to fall victim to a three-run shot by Michael Tucker the next frame. That cost the Padres — and Brown — the ball game by a final 7 to 6 margin.

Moving on to the Dodgers in 1999, the year Maddux and Brown dueled in the 5 to 4 Dodgers victory (above) that was earned by Pedro Borbon, Kevin logged a 41 and 19 record the next three seasons. He might not have been able to corner a Cy Young award, but his Los Angeles contract, calling for an incredible $105 million over a seven year stretch, made him the best paid pitcher in the history of the game, at least to that point. As 2002 approached, he was into the fourth of those seven years, and, probably more significantly, into his 37th year. Barring further lengthy stays on the DL he might conceivably push his career win–mark up toward the 250 level. And, with a strong finish, Cooperstown might not be entirely out of reach. A "Big Cy" would surely help!

Greg Maddux versus Randall David "Randy" Johnson (1963–)

Thinking it over, any seventh grader baseball nut, like his dad and most adults, might just be tempted to say, "Aw shucks!" over not having been able to see more than just one Big Unit-Greg Maddux game. But one game is the sum and substance of it. So we'll just have to take a closer look at it and savor that one confrontation. The game took place on September 2, 1998, during Randy Johnson's first weeks in the NL. He had been traded to Houston's Astros on July 31 of that year for two pitchers and Carlos Guillen in the biggest swap of the season, and promptly blew away his new NL opponents with five wins in his first six tries. Then, on September 2, his Houston team traveled to Atlanta, where the turnstiles clicked 46,238 times, and that evening the Big Unit whiffed 10 in eight innings (Bill Wagner came on for the Save in the ninth), gave up a run in the first inning on singles by Gerry Williams and Javey Lopez, and then settled in to pound his sizzlers past Atlanta's hitters through the next seven scoreless innings. The Braves' second and final run came on an Andrew Jones fourbagger in the bottom of the ninth off closer Wagner.

Meantime, Greg Maddux didn't fare quite as well. Touched for three dingers in the Braves' homer-prone ball park, he left the game after seven frames with a 4 to 1 deficit that turned out to be his 7th loss against 17 wins in a season that would find him at 18 and 8, and, after losing to the Padres in the NLCS, at home to watch the '98 Fall Classic. Randy Johnson, who couldn't pull his Astros far enough in the playoffs to make it to baseball's autumnal extravaganza, wound up in front of his TV also, for that matter. The box score of that historic Maddux-Johnson confrontation follows.

Houston at Atlanta, September 2, 1998

Houston	AB	R	H	BI	K	BB	Atlanta	AB	R	H	BI	K	BB
Biggio, 2b	4	1	2	2	2	0	O. Guillen, ss	4	0	1	0	0	0
Gutierrez, ss	4	0	1	0	1	0	G. Williams, rf	3	1	1	0	0	1
De. Bell, rf	4	0	1	0	0	0	C. Jones, 3b	4	0	0	0	3	0
Bagwell, 1b	4	1	2	1	1	0	Lopez, c	4	0	1	1	2	0
Alou, lf	3	0	1	0	0	1	A. Jones, cf	2	1	1	1	1	2
Everett, cf	4	0	0	0	0	0	Colbrunn, 1b	4	0	0	0	2	0
Berry, 3b	4	1	3	1	0	0	Klesko, lf	3	0	1	0	0	1
Spiers, pr	0	0	0	0	0	0	Graffanino, 2b	4	0	0	0	1	0
Bogar, 3b	0	0	0	0	0	0	Maddux (LP)	2	0	0	0	1	0
Ausmus, c	4	1	2	0	0	0	DeRosa, ph	1	0	0	0	1	0
R. Johnson (WP)	3	0	0	0	1	0	Rocker, p	0	0	0	0	0	0
B. Wagner, p	0	0	0	0	0	0	Charlton, p	0	0	0	0	0	0
							E. Perez, ph	1	0	0	0	1	0
Totals	34	4	12	4	5	1	Totals	32	2	5	2	12	4

Line Score: Houston   010   020   100   4–12–1
               Atlanta   100   000   001   2–5–0

2BH: Alou; HR: Biggio, Bagwell, Berry, A. Jones; SH: R. Johnson; SB: Bagwell, G. Williams 2, Klesko; DP: Atlanta 2; BB: R. Johnson 3, B. Wagner 1, Maddux 0, Rocker 1, Charlton 0; K: R. Johnson 2, B. Wagner 2, Maddux 3, Rocker 1, Charlton 1; Umpires: Darling, Rippley, Poncino and Winters; Time: 2:22.

One of the most dominant pitchers in the game, ever, Randy Johnson's strikeout record will leave power pitchers an awesome goal to shoot at. His name already appears on the single season K/Gm list in the number 3, 4, 5, 6 and 7 slots, and, going down the list a little farther, reappears at numbers 15, 17, 25 and 30. His best effort was a 12.56 per game K-rate in 1995. 364 strikeouts in 1999 rank 14th, and in 1995, when Johnson posted a .900 percent winning percentage, he took over fourth place in that single season category. The capstone to the Big Unit's brilliant career came in 2001 when, with Curt Schilling, he led the Arizona Diamondbacks to the world's championship over the Yankees in a spine-tingling world series that had him out there at the last out of game seven — a winner. Next stop: Cooperstown.

A Maddux Special: The Professor, Bags and Bonds

Interesting. Intriguing. Baseball's buffs are captivated by the prospect of great hitters facing great pitchers. In previous chapters we've had a peek at what it must have been like to sit in on a Walter Johnson vs. Babe Ruth or Ty Cobb matchup, and later, between Warren Spahn and Willie Mays or Stan the Man Musial. Every age has its share, and during Greg Maddux's career two of the game's best were Jeff Bagwell and Barry Bonds. In answer to what is usually the first question asked by fans everywhere, here is a listing of all six hitters and their batting averages against their three great pitching rivals:

	BA
Ruth vs. Johnson	.321
Cobb vs. Johnson	.367*
Mays vs. Spahn	.322
Musial vs. Spahn	.314
Bagwell vs. Maddux	.262
Bonds vs. Maddux	.243

You will not fail to notice the sharp drop-off in average between the first four superstars and the contemporary tandem of Bagwell and Bonds. While it would be unwise to draw any significance from these averages alone, it is worth noting that as time went on and slugging became an ever increasingly more important part of the game, hitters' averages in general declined. In the likes of Barry Bonds, Sammy Sosa, Jeff Bagwell, Mark McGwire and Frank Thomas, regarded as the best among the turn-of-the-century hitters, we have five hitters who epitomize the "Mr. Crunch" approach to latter day hitting. Only Thomas, among those five, will end his career with a .300 plus BA.

It is quite possible that Greg Maddux, on the other hand, may be even better than Walter Johnson or Warren Spahn were in handcuffing the good hitters. That makes a comparison of these career averages an interesting bit of information:

	Yrs	OBA	OB%	ERA
Walter Johnson	21	.227	.279	2.17
Warren Spahn	21	.244	.297	3.09
Greg Maddux[†]	16	.241	.282	2.84

Those career numbers all appear among the top 75 pitchers, with Johnson's numbers leading the way at number 27 for his Opponents' BA (.227)

---

*Ty Cobb's 368 plate appearances vs. Johnson is the ML career record for a hitter against one pitcher.
[†]Maddux statistics through the 2001 season.

and at number 21 OB% (.279). It remains to be seen just how well Maddux will fare at his career's terminus, but his numbers are odds-on favorites to wear well as the end of his brilliant career comes into view.

The very least that can be said for accomplished hitters like Jeff Bagwell and Barry Bonds is that they hit with more authority than Maddux's average normally allows. Of more significance in the head-to-head encounters between Maddux and the Bonds-Bagwell duo is what happened in these ball games that might have been decisive in winning or losing. Often one hit or a timely sacrifice fly with the winning run on is more important than a string of 2 for 3 or 3 for 5 days which pump up the old BA, but may mean no more than high average. A closer look, then, is in order. Here are some of the overall numbers.

1) *The Bonds-Maddux matchup:*

Games played	35
Chi/Atl games won	22
Maddux games won	19
Maddux games lost	13
Bonds vs. Maddux	.243 (27 for 111); 19 RBI, 6 HR
Bonds Factor*	8 games
Maddux Factor†	10 games in which he allowed 1 or 0 runs

All statistics for Maddux, Bonds and Bagwell include the 2001 season.

2) *The Bagwell-Maddux matchup:*

Games played	21
Chi/Atl games won	14
Maddux games won	14
Maddux games lost	2
Bagwell vs. Maddux	.262 (17 for 65); 11 RBI, 5 HR
Bagwell Factor‡	6 games
Maddux Factor§	5 games, allowed 1 or 0 runs

A closer look at these matchups reveals the upper hand Bagwell had over Bonds, though not by much, and that with respect to Greg Maddux, the Braves' future Hall of Famer quite clearly got the better of it with both hitters. Maddux's success against Houston, in particular, was striking. In that series of games he won 14 times and lost but two. The best games in the Bonds and Bagwell series against Maddux are listed in chronological order:

---

*In eight of the Bonds-Maddux games, Bonds contributed hits or home runs that either won the game for his team or put his team in a position to catch up or win outright.

†In seven of the 35 games played, Maddux shut out his opponent seven times, and in six of the games he allowed four hits or less.

‡Bagwell contributed decisive hits in six of the 21 games when Maddux was pitching.

§There were 5 games in which Maddux was in command of the game from the outset, allowing either 0 or 1 runs. In three other games Maddux's team won games in the late innings by one run when Maddux was called on to hold Houston at bay.

1) *The Bonds-Maddux matchup:*

June 21, 1989	The Cubs beat Pittsburgh 1 to 0 at Three Rivers Stadium in an 11-inning game in which Maddux gave up six hits. Bonds had two of them.
April 13, 1990	Bonds had two of the Pirates' three hits in a Maddux 2 to 0 shutout.
July 4, 1991	The Cubs finally prevailed at Wrigley Field in an 11-inning game, 9 to 8. Maddux went 7.2 innings, and Bonds had two RBIs on a two-run homer off Maddux.
June 1, 1994	Atlanta won at San Francisco 1 to 0 as the Giants had only six hits. Maddux pitched 8 innings. Bonds, 0 for 3, walked twice.
July 25, 1996	The Giants beat the Braves 4 to 3 on a 3-run homer by Bonds in the first inning off Maddux, who lost his eighth game. Atlanta had only three hits and was held scoreless until the ninth, when they scored three times to pull within a run of the Giants.

2) *The Bagwell-Maddux matchup:*

August 16, 1992	The Cubs beat Houston behind a Maddux 4-hitter, 1 to 0. Bagwell had no hits and a HPB in 3 official at bats.
May 28, 1995	Maddux shut down the Astros on one hit, a Bagwell home run in the eighth inning that ruined his bid for a no-hitter in a 1 to 0 victory at Houston. The box score follows.

Atlanta at Houston, May 28, 1995

Atlanta	AB	R	H	BI	Houston	AB	R	H	BI
Grissom, cf	5	0	1	0	Biggio, 2b	3	0	0	0
Blauser, ss	3	2	1	1	Thompson, rf	4	0	0	0
Jones, 3b	3	1	0	0	Gonzalez, lf	3	0	0	0
McGriff, 1b	4	0	2	2	Bell, cf	3	0	0	0
Justice, rf	3	0	0	0	Bagwell, 1b	3	1	1	1
Klesko, lf	2	0	0	0	Donnels, 3b	3	0	0	0
Kelly, lf	1	0	0	0	Eusibio, c	3	0	0	0
O'Brien, c	4	0	0	0	Stankiewicz, ss	2	0	0	0
Belliard, 2b	4	0	0	0	Magadan, ph	1	0	0	0
Maddux (WP)	3	0	1	0	Kile (LP)	0	0	0	0
					Veres, p	0	0	0	0
					Hartgraves, p	0	0	0	0
					Miller, ss	0	0	0	0
					Cangelosi, ph	1	0	0	0
Totals	32	3	5	3	Totals	28	1	1	1

Line Score:					
	Atlanta	000	000	201	3–5–1
	Houston	000	000	010	1–1–1

3BH: McGriff; HR: Bagwell, Blauser; SB: Thompson; DP: Atlanta 1; BB: Maddux

1, Kile 7, Hartgraves 0, Veres 0, Jones 0; K: Maddux 7, Kile 5, Hartgraves 0, Veres 0, Jones 3; Umpires: Bell, Rapuano, Runge and Layne; Time: 2:19; Att: 25,526.

June 3, 1995	Houston beat the Braves at Atlanta, 2 to 1, in an 11-inning game that Maddux started (ND, 8 IP). Paul Byrd relieved Maddux and received credit for the win. Bagwell's dinger in the fifth inning gave the Astros the lead, and his single, followed by Tony Eusibio's hit in the 11th, gave Houston its winning run.
August 27, 1997	In another extra-inning game, Paul Byrd (LP) once again relieved Maddux (ND) and surrendered the winning run to Houston on a Bagwell homer in the 13th. The final score was 4 to 3. Bagwell had a 2 for 5 day.
June 16, 1999	Greg Maddux fired a three-hitter at the Astros and beat them in Houston 3 to 1, shutting down Bagwell, who had an 0 for 4 day.

To conclude this look at some of the game's top hitters, then and now, here is a comparison chart of some of the game's more significant numbers for all six of the superstars reviewed. The pitchers, Walter Johnson, Warren Spahn and Greg Maddux, come up for further scrutiny at the conclusion of the Maddux review. The statistics are taken from the 2001 *TBE*. The second line for each player below indicates his rank in a specific category among the top 100 players, all time.

	Yrs	GP	Runs	HR	HR%	RBI/Gm	OB +SLG	BW	ISO Power	FR	TPR
Babe Ruth	22	2503	2174	714	8.50	.88	1164	124.2	.348	5	108.9
		40	3	2	2	5	1	1	1		1
Willie Mays	22	2992	2062	660	6.07	.63	944	84.1	.256	180	95.9
		7	6	3	26		23	7	16		2
Ty Cobb	24	3035	2246	117	1.01	.64	945	104.0	.146	54	92.0
		4	1			99	2.2	3			4
Barry Bonds	15	2143	1584	451	6.63	.66	982	68.0	.278	169	89.4
		40	17	9	75		9	14	7		5
Stan Musial	22	3026	1949	475	4.07	.64	977	97.8	.228	-38	71.4
		5	7	19		91	11	4	44		15
Jeff Bagwell	10	1476	1073	310	5.80	.74	975	44.9	.248	80	45.2
				81	35	23	13	44	25		32

Reading the career numbers above: HR%— Number of home runs per 100 at bats; OB + Slg — On Base Percentage plus Slugging Average; BW — Batting Wins. The number of victories a batter contributes to his team above the wins of a league-average player (0). During his career, then, Babe Ruth contributed 124 wins above the number of a league-average player; ISO Power — Isolated Power. Slugging Average minus BA. A good measure of a hitter's success percentage in scoring runs. Babe Ruth was successful roughly two times in five opportunities, the best mark in the game's history; Fielding Runs — A linear weights measure of runs saved beyond the number of runs a league-average player was able to save his team through his defensive play; TPR — Total Player Rating.

Greg Maddux versus Curtis Montague Schilling (1966–)

It took jumbo-sized Curt Schilling four and one-third seasons to get his first call as a starting pitcher. He made the most of it. In a mid–May game in Philadelphia, skipper Jim Fregosi gave him the ball for an evening skirmish with Houston's Astros. Pitching six scoreless innings, he surrendered nary a run, gave up but three hits, fanned four and walked two hitters, leaving the game ahead 4 to 0. It mattered little that Jeff Bagwell came on in the

Co-winner of the 2001 World Series MVP award, Curt Schilling.

eighth to send one of reliever Barry Jones' pitches into orbit with two men on. Bagwell's shot merely brought the Astros to within one, and it didn't cost Curt his first starting win. That evening in 1992 brought an abrupt end to his days in the pen. From that point onward the games he would lose in his career would be lost on his own account as SP. That suited Curt Schilling just fine.

Schilling followed his 1992 "debut" with a 16 and 7 log in 1993, despite time on the DL because of a bone spur in his right elbow. It was the beginning of a three year off-and-on period, during which he treaded water with an 18 and 23 record, spending a good deal of time on rehabilitation sorties. Finally, in 1997 he hit his stride as he enjoyed three strong seasons while moving into the staff leadership spot as the team's ace. By this time he was 30 and in full command of his pitching game, a knowledgeable starter whose diligence and studious approach to the game began paying big dividends.

The biggest dividend came during the 2001 post-season championships from which he emerged as a Co-MVP with Randy Johnson in the world series that dethroned the Yankees as world champs. The award capped a 22 and 6 season that was further polished with the glitter of 39.1 innings of championship play in which he gave up but six earned runs en route to world series laurels.

The big fellow throws his fast one in the neighborhood of 95 mph, and sometimes faster, depending on the situation and just how steamed up he might be. And the way Schilling goes about his job, with both a *joie de vivre* and an awareness of what each outing means in the perspective of the game itself, hitters know just what that means every time he takes the hill. The net result has been a stretch of five seasons that has deposited his name on that very prestigious and very short list of the ML's premier hurlers.

Three relief appearances against Chicago, and another against Atlanta, preceded Schilling's first start against Greg Maddux. Through the 2001 season the two had vied as starters on seven occasions, Maddux emerging with a 3 and 2 record, and Schilling at 4 and 3. The record follows.

The Maddux-Schilling Log:

Jun 21, 1993	Atlanta 8, Philadelphia 1	Maddux WP, Schilling LP
May 11, 1994	Atlanta 4, Philadelphia 2	Maddux WP, Schilling LP
Apr 5, 1998	Philadelphia 2, Atlanta 1	Schilling WP, Maddux LP
Aug 2, 2000	Arizona 2, Atlanta 0	Schilling WP, Maddux LP
Sep 7, 2000	Atlanta 4, Arizona 0	Maddux WP, Schilling LP

May 1, 1991: Cubs 11, Astros 8; Maddux WP, Jim Deshaies LP, Schilling RP-ND May 6, 1991: Cubs 4, Astros 3; Maddux WP, Jim Deshaies LP, Schilling RP-ND Apr 20, 1992: Cubs 8, Phils 3; Maddux WP, Kyle Abbott LP, Schilling RP-ND May 15, 1993: Braves 5, Phils 3; Maddux WP, Adam West LP, Schilling RP-ND May 7, 1995: Phils

5, Braves 4; Schilling WP, S. Bedrosian LP, Maddux SP-ND Apr 10, 1998: Phils 1, Braves 0; Schilling WP, M. Cather LP, Maddux SP-ND

Curt Schilling's 2-hitter against the potent Atlanta Braves on April 10, 1998, has to rank as one of that season's best-pitched ball games, and certainly the best of the Maddux-Schilling matchups. 30,311 were on hand to watch these two aces duel right on down to the bottom of the ninth, when reliever Mike Cather, who had come on for Maddux to start the ninth, issued walks to Gregg Jeffries and Scott Rolen. Catcher Mike Lieberthal's single then scored Jeffries with the winning run. Maddux had pitched well, giving up five hits and walking none through eight innings. But Schilling was flatout better, pitching masterfully all the way while doling out two scattered singles, one to Chipper Jones and another to Tony Graffanino. The victory in that early April game left him at 2 and 0. He finished the season with a 15 and 14 record. Greg Maddux went on to an 18 and 9 season.

As these two moved deeper into the ranks of the NL's elite hurlers, they offered their faithful fans four superb evenings, beginning with a ball game that Schilling won just five days before his April 10, 2-to-0 masterpiece. On April fifth he beat the Braves 2 to 1 on a five-hitter, one of these a Chipper Jones fourbagger that scored Atlanta's only run. In that game Greg Maddux gave up only five hits himself. The two '98 tilts were followed by two more gems in 2000, both of which were shutouts. The first of these, a 6-hitter by Schilling, brought the Diamondbacks home a winner; and in the second, the old wizard, Mr. Maddux, silenced Arizona bats with a 4-hit, 2-to-0 blanking. The fans got just what they expected from both, superb pitching and a great night at the ball park.

Greg Maddux versus Mike Mussina (1968–)

Mike Mussina, profiled in the Rogers Clemens chapter, pitched in two All-Star games, hurling scoreless innings in the 1993 game at San Diego and at Fenway Park in 1999. Both times his AL club won. He was not so fortunate in two other brushes with the NL. On those occasions he ran into the Professor, Mr. Maddux, who presided over Atlanta victories, the first at Baltimore's expense in 2000 and the second at Yankee Stadium, where he lost again, 4 to 1. Both losses came in interleague competition.

Mussina, as has been noted, turned in one of baseball's more striking records during the 1990s and on into the first years of the 21st century. Deploying two- and four-seam fastballs that hit the strike zone in the '90s, along with a complete arsenal of breaking balls (like his sharp curve and a curve ball that is thrown with a knuckle on the ball, causing it not only to dip and sway, but to move away from the hitter just as it crosses the plate), he is a highly effective workman whose K-to-BB ratio is above normal (in 2001 Mike maxed at a career high 5.10). His 7.03 K/Gm stat is right up there with the very good ones. Outstanding control (2.05 BB/Gm) and gold glove fielding are still other features of his game that caused George Steinbrenner to dip deeply into Yankee coffers to bring big Mike to New York for the 2001 season. It was a sound investment that paid off in a 17 and 11 season that was a significant contribution to another Yankee pennant.

One of those eleven 2001 losses came at the hands of Maddux, Atlanta & Co. on June 10 in a game in which Maddux threw a wet blanket over the Yankee Stadium proceedings, allowing but seven scattered safeties and a second inning run that momentarily tied up the game. A two-run fifth turned out to be enough for the Braves, who went on to ruin an otherwise splendid day in the Big Apple for 41,392 Yankee fans.

At Baltimore's Camden Yards on July 13, 2000, before better than 40,000 Oriole fans, the Professor once again held class, dealing a 6 to 3 loss to Mussina's Orioles in a game that was tied 3 to 3 going into Atlanta's turn to bat in the seventh inning. At that point the Braves scored one li'l ol' lousy run that Baltimoreans somehow knew would be enough — and it was. In fact, manager Bobby Cox was confident at that point to let his ace finish the seventh and then retire, his 11th scalp tucked away at the season's midpoint. Before the season had seen its last out, Maddux added another eight wins to chalk up his fifth 19-win season and garner serious consideration for yet another Cy Young award.

There remain several seasons of "taking care of business" for Mike Mussina if he is to cross the line from very good to great — great enough, that is, to be considered for Hall of Fame laurels. Even to be considered one of those who *might* be recognized for such laurels is an honor, to say nothing of the privilege of joining that tiny three-plus percent of major leaguers who have played the grand old game. If that should happen to Mike Mussina, it would be in recognition of a consummate professional who, without exaggerated fanfare, has *earned* baseball's highest honor.

Greg Maddux versus Pedro Martinez (1971–)

Pedro Martinez, entering his 11th ML season in 2002, is at a point where, ultimate baseball honors within reach notwithstanding, there is some doubt as to whether he can stand up under the stress he puts on his pitching arm. There is only one way the Dominican can pitch — and, by his own choosing, that is all out. Further, by his own admission, he simply cannot "let up" and pace himself through big leads or the bottom end of the batting order, even though on rare occasions he has done just that and has fared just as well as others. For Pedro it's full throttle all the way. Long entrenched habits being what they are, it remains to be seen just how far this brilliant meteor can race across the big league horizon.

That said, it is by no means outside the realm of possibility that Pedro Martinez will wind up among pitchers of rare distinction. He has already put a pair of Cy Young awards into his trophy case, and just a cursory glance at some of the pitchers' numbers tables will show how exceptionally well he has performed. An example or two: As of the turn of the century he stood atop the career winning percentage list at .691; he was second to Nolan Ryan with only 6.73 hits allowed per nine innings; his 9.6 Ratio ranked fourth; he was 3rd and 10th, respectively, in Opponents' BA and Opponents' OB%; and his 10.38 Ks/Gm stands right behind Randy Johnson's 10.95 in first place. Additionally, his single game strikeout percentage of 13.20 for 1999 tops that list, and a miniscule 7.22 Ratio for the 2000 season ranks third.

Martinez switched over to the AL after the 1997 season. Montreal lost its superstar simply because they could no longer afford him. The Boston vault, one of the deepest in ML baseball, emptied enough of its treasure to bring the man with the Big K to Fenway Park for the 1998 season, and since that time he has won 83 times while dropping only 20 games for an astounding .806 winning percentage.

While in the NL, Pedro Martinez fell victim to Greg Maddux three times, once in 1994 and twice in 1995. On May 6, 1994, Pedro's Expos had the door slammed in their faces with a 5 to 0 blanking at Montreal. A second-inning, solo fourbagger by Fred McGriff was really all that Maddux needed to beat the Expos as he scattered seven hits around to keep Montreal under control for his fifth win of the season. The loss dropped Martinez to 1 and 3 at that point, but he recovered sufficiently to round out his record at 11 and 5 that season.

The Maddux-Martinez wars resumed the next season with another pair of games, each resulting in another Maddux victory, one at Montreal on June 15, 1995, by a 2 to 0 margin on a two-run fourbagger by Panamanian Roberto Kelly, and the other, again at Montreal, on August 4, 1995, when the Braves pushed across four early tallies and then outlasted the Expos 4 to 3. After that win Maddux moved to a 12 and 1 reading in a season that found him next to unbeatable. His 19 and 2 record, along with equally eye-popping numbers across the board, led to another of his Cy Young awards. The immovable object and the irresistible force had come head to head, and Pedro found that immovable objects can indeed be moved, provided the irresistible force is named Greg Maddux. Alas, like so many others who had that same experience, Senor Martinez found the Cooperstown-bound Braves star good enough when he had to be. But that needn't, nor did it, diminish Martinez' excellence in any way. Should he hold up, he should, all said and done, be able to enter the same Valhalla Maddux is primed for. It will be interesting to see how all of that evolves.

Greg Maddux versus Michael William "Mike" Hampton (1972–)

Mike Hampton is one of the junior members of the superstar pitchers' firm that has thus far been on display. He enters the 2002 season with but 10 ML seasons under his belt, a lesser number of years by several than the norm among the many extraordinary pitchers in this 20 century review of greats vs. greats. But he's been around long enough to post some outstanding numbers, thus meriting a Maddux matchup.

Hampton's major league decade began in Seattle. He was the Mariners'

Mike Hampton, a solid ball player who shares the NL single season record for homers by a pitcher (7 in 2001).

sixth round selection in the 1990 June draft, later that year starting his professional career as a 17-year-old with Tempe in the Seattle organization. Seventeen. That's a tender age for a professional pitcher — unless you happen to be Mike Hampton.

Brimming with competitive fire and unbounded faith in his God-given talent for throwing a baseball, Hampton looked the odds directly in the eye and came out firing. And after sufficient improvement, including a 1991 no-hitter for San Bernadino, he was added to Seattle's pitching staff under their new manager, Lou Piniella, in 1993. In need of more seasoning, he spent a good deal of that season making several trips between the Bigs and Seattle's minor league affiliates, though he did win his first ML ball game in April in a relief role against the Yankees. With a four-run outburst that came during Hampton's scoreless, 2.2 relief stint, Seattle beat the Bronx Bombers 6 to 4. First ML victories being what they are, replete with significance and lasting memories, one can just imagine Mike Hampton savoring that moment of moments.

That April victory, however, was to be his only AL conquest. Before that season ended, there were three losses to round out his first ML season, after which he was traded to Houston, where he spent his next six years.

It was in Houston that Hampton picked up the professional gloss that enabled him to step into the upper echelons of the NL's hurlers. During those years he developed not only physically, but as a complete craftsman, dressing up his repertoire with a biting, two-seam fastball, a very effective changeup, and his outpitch, a cut-fastball. In that six year period of time (Hamp's work was limited to 41.1 innings and a 2 and 1 record in 1994, his first year with the Astros) from 1994 to '99, he turned in a .633 winning percentage, winning 69 and losing 40. The climax came in 1999 when his 22 and 4 record won him the Players Choice NL Pitcher Award, as well as runner-up honors in the Cy Young voting to Randy Johnson.

Although he didn't pitch against Greg Maddux during his exceptional 1999 campaign, he did engage the Braves' ace righthander in three other seasons.

The Maddux-Hampton Log:

Sep 18, 1996	Atlanta 6, Houston 2	Maddux WP, Hampton LP
Apr 2, 1997	Houston 4, Atlanta 3	Hampton WP, Maddux LP
Sep 18, 2000	Atlanta 6, New York	Mets 3 Maddux WP, Hampton LP

In the race to the divisional championship in 2000, literally every game was vitally important. That season the Braves won the championship by one game over Hampton's Mets, and on September 18 the Mets faced the front running Braves three games off the pace. Greg Maddux picked that day to shut down the visiting New Yorkers with seven innings of shutout baseball before turning the game over to Bobby Cox' relief corps. The Mets took the first opportunity they had in the top of the eighth to narrow the score to 6 to 3, but failed to muster enough timely hits and went to a four game deficit, saddling their ace with a 13 and 10 record at that point. The season ended with the Mets trailing the Braves by one game.

However, the 2000 season was not yet over. The NL post-season playoffs were next on the docket. In the first round divisional playoffs favored Atlanta met St. Louis' pesky Cardinals and, quite unbelievably, lost three straight in the best-three-of-five series, as the Cards fired an ominous shot across the Braves' bow with a first-inning bombardment against Greg Maddux, of all people, that netted six and forecast the Braves' doom right there. Meanwhile, the Mets disposed of San Francisco's Giants three games out of four, with Mike Hampton setting the pace in a 5 to 1 opening game victory. Hampton won the first game of the NLCS, and the Mets again emerged victorious, winning the NL pennant and moving on to the World Series with the Yankees and a renewal of the old subway series New Yorkers reveled in. But this time the Mets train didn't make it to the station. The Yankees won the big prize, beating the Mets four games out of five. Mike Hampton also lost in his only Series appearance at Yankee Stadium.

Mike Hampton moved on to the Colorado Rockies in 2001 to pitch for his third team in three seasons, and, at the top of his game, won seven of his first eight decisions by the end of May. And then the old injury bug bit him with a groin injury that hampered him virtually the rest of the season, as he finished out the year with a very ordinary 14 and 13 record. Not yet 30, Mike Hampton has the potential to record a number of top-drawer seasons before he turns in his uniform the last time. By this time a knowledgeable pitcher, his name will appear a number of times among those listings reserved for the game's best. He has already worked himself into a spot among the top 150 pitchers with a career TPI now on its way to the 20 mark. It's reasonable to assume that Mike Hampton will wind up among the top 100 with a few other of the game's great lefthanders, like Eddie Plank, Tommy John, Harry Brecheen, Billy Pierce and his contemporary, Tom Glavine.

Masterful Maddux

Past Master [for pass*ed* master]: One who has complete control and mastery of his art, an expert. Applied to baseball, the definition would read: One who has completely mastered his chosen profession, baseball, and therefore qualifies for membership in the Hall of Fame. One who will bring such qualifications to the BBWAA when the time comes is Masterful Gregory Alan Maddux.

During those halcyon years of 1992–1995, when the Master ran away with the voting for the Cy Young award, his numbers included an 18-game winning streak *on the road*, a 19 and 2, 1995 record, and a record-setting third straight season leading his league in complete games, as well as league leaderships in a host of pitching categories. Looking all that over, some wag out there among the beat writers who cover the game said at the midpoint of the 1995 season, "Maddux is a shoo-in to win his fourth straight Cy Young award, but I'm not sure Cy Young could ever have won a Greg Maddux award."

With his baffling speed changes, a variety of pitches that bob and weave through the strike zone, and impeccable control, Maddux has worked his way, with a string of incredibly brilliant seasons, to the top of his profession. Among his contemporaries, only Roger Clemens can match him in "Oh, my goodness" comments as we pore over the many and astounding numbers in almost every facet of his record. Like the Spahns and Johnsons before him, he has endured to run up those numbers not just four or five times, but, once established in his own groove, in a consistent run of brilliance year in and year out.

If he chooses to make the run at it, Greg Maddux will achieve his 300th victory sometime during the 2004 or '05 season. But unlike many others whose address is now at Cooperstown, he has never been one to hang on the numbers. What has always been important to him has been how his team has fared. Beyond that, he is even more interested in how his family is doing, a rather rare concern in these latter days of superegos among the game's superstars. But, just as his pitching is a rare example of artistry, so is he a *rara avis* in a highpowered world of hype and spotlights.

During the 2001 season Maddux ran together a string of 72.1 innings without issuing a base on balls, establishing a new record for NL pitchers. In so doing, he underscored the most striking feature of his work as one of the game's premier moundsmen — his control over the thin edges of the strike zone. Given his studied approach to every opponent and each hitter as an individual, that kind of control translates into a tight grip on the progress of every game he works. About the only thing left for an opposing pitcher, if he wants to beat the Master, is to out–Maddux Maddux. Just try. Very few have succeeded, and those who have, usually paid the price the next time around. You could look that one up, too!

10. Fall Classics

Not every great pitcher gets into a World Series. Fewer get to match pitches with Hall of Fame pitchers who appear in post season, championship play. Today's pitchers, a bit more fortunate in that respect than their forerunners, whose play was limited to one best-of-seven series that decided the baseball championship of the world, have more opportunities, since divisional and league championships have been inaugurated to precede the grand climax of the World Series. But there are some great classics involving a number of the heroes we have reviewed, despite the limited opportunities. In the following pages that story unfolds, however briefly each is sketched, beginning with Christy Mathewson (Cy Young appeared only in the 1903 World Series and did not face any Famers in the three games in which he worked), and continuing with Pete Alexander, Lefty Grove, Warren Spahn and Tom Seaver. Walter Johnson, like Cy Young, did not pitch against Famers during World Series play. Roger Clemens and Greg Maddux, contemporary hurlers in the more elaborate post-season playoffs of the present day, are presented in keeping with the expanded series of opportunities. Among their contemporaries are several who will receive serious consideration for a Cooperstown plaque in the future. Clemens and Maddux, therefore, are profiled in cameos against the best of the game's present and recently retired pitchers.

Christy Mathewson

World Series class starts with the "Big Six." In the 1905 Fall Classic's second series, a renewal of 1903's inaugural that featured Big Bill Dineen, Cy Young and their victorious Red Sox teammates, it was Christy Mathewson who set a still unsurpassed record that marked him, at 25 and in his fifth full ML season, as the very best in the business. In his first World Series game he threw a four-hit shutout at Connie Mack's mighty Athletics. He repeated with the second verse of the "same song" in game number three. Again the A's touched him for only four hits and another string of goose eggs on the scoreboard. The third time out the Athletics "improved" their offensive attack, stroking six hits, but still unable to send a runner across home plate.

Fast forward to 1911, when Matty next appeared, once again against the A's. This time the A's finally scored a run. It came in the first game of the Series and gave the Mackmen a momentary 1 to 0 lead in the second inning. Mathewson's string was broken, then, at 28 straight innings of scoreless World Series pitching. That was the A's' only run that day, by the way, and before that game was over McGraw's Giants had scored two, enough to win the Series opener, 2 to 1.

Philadelphia's Athletics finally caught up with Mathewson in game four of the 1911 series when Albert "Chief" Bender, who lost the 1911 Series opener, beat the Giants 4 to 2, breaking out with a 10-hit effort that finally chased New York's titanic ace. Bender, who met Mathewson three times (the two dueled in the 1905 Series' fifth game), consequently came out on the short end of their three-game rivalry.

Matty's other Hall of Fame World Series opponent was the worthy southpaw "Gettysburg Eddie" Plank. The best portsider in the game until Lefty Grove came along, Plank was a stern match for Matty. He was Matty's equal as a brainy, crafty pitcher, and he had the stuff to keep the A's' infield busy with ground balls aplenty. The two squared off in that Mathewson masterpiece on October 9 at Baker Bowl in Philadelphia. It turned out to be Mathewson's first of his three shutouts. They didn't meet again until the 1913 World Series, when the Giants and A's went nine innings of scoreless ball before the New Yorkers hung a three-spot on Plank in the top of the 10th to bring Mathewson home a 3 to 0 winner in game two. But in game five at the Polo Grounds the Athletics put it all together behind Plank's sturdy two-hit effort, winning the game by a 3 to 1 margin, and the Series title with it. That left the record of these two magnificent Famers at Mathewson's two wins to Plank's one.

It would be difficult to point to one of those six Mathewson games as the Classic Among Classics, but the vote for the award from this corner goes to Christy Mathewson's first World Series game played at Baker Bowl on October 9, 1905.

New York Giants		000	020	001	3–10–1
Philadelphia A's		000	000	000	0–4–0

Pitchers	NY	Mathewson (WP): 9-IP, 0-BB, 6-K
	Phl	Plank (LP): 9-IP, 3-ER, 2-BB, 5-K

Extra Base Hits: NY 2, Phl 3
Stolen Bases: NY 3
Time: 1:46; Att: 17,955

Grover "Pete" Alexander

Pete Alexander's first World Series appearance was in 1915 against Boston's Red Sox of Hooper-Lewis-Speaker fame, and he was so dejected by the outcome of that Series that he wrote an article about how *he* lost the Series. But there would come another time, even though it would come at a point in his career when his pitching was craft and guile, and smoke and mirrors, because time and Jim Barleycorn had taken its toll on him. But that didn't stop Rogers Hornsby from insisting that the Cardinals bring Ol' Pete to St. Louis from Chicago, where he had outlived his welcome in manager Joe McCarthy's clubhouse. So the deal was made in June of 1926, and within a scant several months he was the toast of the baseball world, having disposed of the mighty Yanks in game seven of the '26 Series amid the tension and drama of that famous seventh-inning Tony Lazzeri strikeout.

Interestingly, his sixth game conquest in that 1926 Series is often forgotten. In that game "Old Low and Away" silenced the big sticks in the New York batting order enough to enable the Cardinals to get into the seventh game on the strength of his complete game victory. Earlier, in game two, he had paced the Cards to a 6 to 2 victory. Consequently, the disappointment of his 1915 Fall Classic experience was counterbalanced by his overpowering 1926 effort. Had there been a vote for Series MVP at that time, it would have gone to Pete in unanimous approval.

In World Series warfare Alexander vied with two of Cooperstown's Famers who appeared in the 1926 and '28 Series. In 1926 it was Waite Hoyt who started on the hill for New York in that historic seventh game. Hoyt worked the first six innings of that game, leaving it with his Yankees behind 3 to 2. Manager Miller Huggins brought Famer Herb Pennock on for the seventh inning, and Pennock finished the game for the Yankees, though Hoyt was the losing pitcher.

Contrariwise, the 1928 World Series was a bitter pill for the Cardinals. The Yankees put the embarrassment of the '26 Series behind them and thrashed the Cardinals in four straight. First of all they whipped Ol' Pete in game two at Yankee Stadium, pounding him for eight tallies on six hits in a 9 to 3 massacre. The Cardinals lost their third straight in St. Louis, and then the Yankees, in no mood to tolerate any comeback momentum whatsoever, stripped the Cardinal gears with a 7 to 3 win that gave them the 1928 crown. The last pitcher standing for the Cardinals, though wobbly, was Grover Cleveland Alexander, who gave up the last three Yankee runs in २⅔ innings of relief work against Waite Hoyt, who had gone all the way for his second series win.

There could be but one selection for the Classic Among Classics Award insofar as Pete Alexander is concerned, and that would be the Series-winning game seven in 1927.

St. Louis Cardinals	000	300	000	3–8–0
New York Yankees	001	001	000	2–8–3

Pitchers   StL   Haines (WP): 6⅔ IP, 5-BB, 2-K
                Alexander (SV): 2⅓ IP, 1-BB, 1-K
           NY   Hoyt (LP): 6-IP, 0-BB, 2-K
                Pennock: 3-IP, 0-BB, 0-K

Extra Base Hits: NY 2, StL 0
Time: 2:15; Att: 38,093

Robert Moses "Lefty" Grove

Connie Mack began to put together his last Athletics juggernaut in 1924. The next season he brought Mickey Cochrane, Jimmie Foxx and Lefty Grove to Philadelphia to join Al Simmons already there. By 1927 and '28 they had become a real pain in the neck for New York's perennial champions, and in 1929 overtook them to win the first of three straight AL pennants. Mack's pitching staff had developed into a formidable weapon by that time, anchored by baseball's greatest southpaw, Lefty Grove. And when the A's' pitching couldn't overpower or out-finesse their opponents, it seemed that the Foxx-Cochrane-Simmons conglomerate would make up for it with a withering long distance attack that would break down fences and ball games for the venerable Mack.

Sometimes irrational, sometimes just plain unbearable, but always an odds-on favorite to keep the A's on the winning side of the ledger or very close to it, Lefty Grove would be a logical choice to open any big-time Series. But for reasons known only to Connie Mack, Grove was not used in a starter's role in the 1929 Series, though he came back to start the A's off in both the 1930 and '31 Classics. In those latter two Series Grove encountered two of the NL's most gritty and fiery pitchers, Famers Burleigh Grimes and Jesse Haines.

Grimes and Grove appeared as adversaries in the opening game of the 1930 Fall Classic at Shibe Park in Philadelphia. Cochrane and Simmons hit homers in that one as the A's kept pecking away, run by single run, to beat the Cardinals and "Old Stubblebeard" 5 to 2. Next, Grove took on Jesse Haines on a pleasant Sunday afternoon at Sportsman's Park, St. Louis, only to find that Haines and his Cardinal playmates were bent on evening the Series, which they did, disposing of the A's 3 to 1, as Jesse nailed down the Mackmen with but four safe blows and a complete game victory.

But Lefty got even the very next game, coming back as a reliever to haunt the Red Birds with two glittering innings of relief work, and when Jimmie Foxx found one of Grimes' pitches to his liking, he crushed it for a two-run shot, ending the string of scoreless innings in the game and sending the St. Louisians to a 2 to 0 defeat. Grove got the win in relief of workhorse George Earnshaw, who had gone seven strong innings, giving up but a pair of hits. Though he had pitched well, that Foxx boomer put an end to any hopes Burleigh Grimes might have had of another World Series victory.

Burleigh Grimes came back in the 1931 Cardinals victory over the A's to beat Lefty in game three by a 5 to 2 score at Philadelphia, holding the Athletics scoreless until the bottom of the ninth, when an Al Simmons' fourbagger accounted for the only two runs the Mackmen could muster. This time he was in the driver's seat all the way in a game that put the Cards two up in the Series. In the Grove vs. Grimes-Haines matchups, then, Grove emerged with a 2 and 2 record, Haines 0–1, and Grimes 1 and 2.

From among those games the choice for the Classic Among Classics Award goes to Grove's victory in relief of the A's' 2–0 win in the fifth game.

Philadelphia		000	000	002		2–5–0
St. Louis		000	000	000		0–3–1
Pitchers	Phl	Earnshaw: 7-IP, 3-BB, 5-K				
		Grove (WP): 2-IP, 1-BB, 2-K				
	StL	Grimes (LP): 9-IP, 3-BB, 7-K				

Extra Base Hits: Phl 1, StL 1
Time: 1:58; Att: 38,144

Warren Spahn

After Johnny Sain beat Bob Feller in the first game of the 1948 World Series in a 1 to 0 game that was a classic in and of itself, the Braves looked forward to nailing down a 2–0 Series lead before heading to Cleveland, where the Fall Classic's third game would be played at the Indians' cavernous Lakefront Stadium. Warren Spahn, at 27 already established as one of the better southpaws to come along in quite some time, took on Bob Lemon, whose heavy, breaking pitches and overall athletic ability had provided the makings of his first big summer. Lemon that year came full bloom with a no-hitter, was elected to the AL All-Star Team, and won 20 games. He took on Spahnie at Braves Field on October 7, winning 4 to 1 while outlasting Spahn, who was tagged with the loss, and two relievers. Spahn learned something in that game, and that was that Fall Classic games are indeed played at another level, the kind of situation when ball players are called on to turn it up another notch. Being the cerebral type, Spahnie tucked it all away for another day. That came sooner than most expected, when in the fifth game of the '48 Series he was summoned from the bullpen in the fourth inning to stay the hand of the Tribe in the midst of a four-run rally that moved them ahead of the Braves, 5 to 4. All he did was pitch 5⅓ innings of one-hit ball, walking one and fanning seven, as his Boston colleagues went on to an 11 to 5 mauling of the frisky Indians. In that game he faced both Feller and another Famer, the Ancient of Days himself, Satch Paige. Spahnie had learned well.

A decade later baseball's winningest lefty took on one of the game's craftier portsiders, a pitcher habituated to victory, especially in the big-money ball games. That chap was Whitey Ford, and, in one of those classic duels, he beat the Braves and Spahn, 3 to 1. Even though he came back to take a gritty come-from-behind victory in game four of the Series at County Stadium in Milwaukee, Spahn festered over that Ford victory for a year.

In 1958 Spahn found his vindication in a second straight Braves-Yankees World Series, beating the Yanks twice in games involving Stengel's ace, Mr. Ford. Alas, where he was on a world's championship team in 1957, his Milwaukee club was a loser in 1958. Still another confrontation with the old Yankee warrior Ford in game six, which the Braves lost (though neither Spahn nor Ford were pitchers of decision), pushed his team right to the edge as the Yanks evened the Series at three games each. The New Yorkers won it the next day with a 6 to 2 triumph.

Though he would go on for another eight seasons, embellishing his Hall of Fame credentials with another four 20-game seasons and still more "mosts" in a record-crammed career, there would be no more Fall Classics for Warren Spahn. He would enter the Hall with a World Series record of 4 and 3, and a 2.89 ERA.

The Classic Among Classics Award for Warren Spahn is his two-hit, 3 to 0 shutout over the Yankees in game four of the 1958 Fall Classic.

	Milwaukee	000	001	110	3–9–0
	New York	000	000	000	0–2–1

Pitchers	Mil	Spahn (WP): 9-IP, BB-2, K-0	Extra Base Hits: Mil 4, NY 1
	NY	Ford (LP): 7-IP, BB-1, K-6	Time: 2:17, Att: 71,563
		Kucks: 1-IP, 1-BB, 0-K	
		Dickson: 1-IP, 0-BB, 0-K	

Tom Seaver

In 1969 the World Series became the pot at the far end of the rainbow, its colorful arc having been lengthened by a post-season playoff in both leagues that qualified the winners for berths in the annual Fall Classic. The rainbow was stretched even farther as the years moved on to its present elimination tournament of Divisional, and then League Championship playoffs before engaging the leagues' respective winners in the seven-game World Series.

It was Tom Seaver's privilege to start this new order of things with the first NL Championship Series game on October 4, 1969, at Atlanta, where his Mets subdued the Braves 9 to 5 in a game the New Yorkers broke open with an eighth-inning five-spot that chased Hall of Famer Phil Niekro, pinning the loss on Atlanta's knuckleballer. Seaver, who worked seven innings, was the winner. The Mets, mildly surprising the baseball world, went on to beat the Braves in that series, three games to none. But, as has been voluminously reported time and again, that was nothing compared to their followup, a stunning victory in the World Series over prohibitively favored Baltimore that made them the Miracle Mets. Tom Seaver's hand in that miracle was a victory in game four, a pulsating, ten-inning affair won by the Mets, 2 to 1. That one more than atoned for Seaver's opening game loss.

In 1973 Tom Terrific was granted one more opportunity to mix it with a Hall of Fame pitcher. In that Series he met Jim "Catfish" Hunter and the Oakland Athletics, opening up the New York part of the Series in the first of three games at Shea Stadium after the A's and Mets had split the first two games in Oakland. In a game that neither legend finished, Oakland finally pushed across the winning tally in the top of the eleventh at the expense of reliever Harry Parker. Paul Lindblad, with help from relief ace Rollie Fingers, one of three relief specialists who possesses a Hall of Fame plaque, earned the 3 to 2 win.

In game six back in Oakland, Seaver and Hunter crossed swords again, but this time both were pitchers of decision, the victory going to Catfish Hunter in another tight duel that Hunter won, with the final touches administered once again by bullpen ace Fingers. Seaver, the loser in the 3 to 1 tilt that enabled the Athletics to move on to the deciding chapter of the 1973 saga, had pitched well, only to have his aces trumped by even better Oakland hurling. The A's, behind Kenny Holtzman (WP) and the usual string of Oakland relief specialists, won the final game — and the Series — by a 5 to 2 count.

Tom Seaver's Classic Among Classics Award is conferred for his complete-game, extra-inning victory over the Baltimore Orioles in the 1969 World Series. Though it didn't come at the expense of a Famer, it was nonetheless a determined exhibition of championship pitching in which he held the dangerous Orioles to a single run, which didn't come until the top of the ninth. The Mets' money man was there when he was needed.

| Baltimore | 000 | 000 | 001 | 0 | 1–6–1 |
| New York | 010 | 000 | 000 | 1 | 2–10–1 |

Pitchers	Balt	Cuellar: 7-IP, 0-BB, 5-K	Extra Base Hits: Balt 0, NY 2
		Watt: 2-IP, 0-BB, 2-K	Time: 2:33
		Hall (LP): 0-IP,* 1-BB, 0-K	Att: 57,367
		Richert: 0-IP,† 0-BB, 0-K	
	NY	Seaver (WP): 10-IP, 2-BB, 6-K	

Roger Clemens and Greg Maddux

Between them, Roger Clemens (19) and Greg Maddux (26) have appeared in 45 post-season playoff games,[47] all as starters, as befits their superstar status. For those prone to keeping records, Maddux will probably wind up at or very near the top of the list for post-season appearances and starts,[48] having benefited from a lengthy starring role with the Atlanta Braves' perennial playoff and World Series teams.

As one might expect, it has been no bed of roses for these two Hall of Fame–bound pitchers in postseason play. The level of intensity and focus in these pressurized encounters rises dramatically with each inning as the teams vie for supremacy and championships. But each of these stars have risen to the occasion with stellar pitching, and their most outstanding efforts along the way have been recognized with our World Series Classic Among Classics Award. Further, one of their games in divisional and league championship play has been designated as a Playoff Gem and cited accordingly.

The complete post-season record for Clemens and Maddux follows:

	Clemens (W-L-ND)	Maddux (W-L-ND)
Divisional Series	2–1–2	4–2–4
League Championship	3–4–1	3–8–0
World Series	3–0–3	2–3–0
Career Post-Season Record	8–5–6	9–13–4

Among the outstanding hurlers Clemens and Maddux met during post-season games were Dwight Gooden, Jimmy Key, Curt Schilling, Pedro Martinez, Randy Johnson, Mike Hampton and Hall of Famer Don Sutton, whom Clemens met twice in the 1986 ALCS, once as a starter in game four, and again as a reliever in that ALCS final game. Each of these pitchers has been noted in the preceding chapters of this book.

Orel Hershiser, mentioned above, took on Greg Maddux in game one of the 1995 World Series between Hershiser's Cleveland Indians and Maddux's Atlanta Braves. In that game Maddux got the Braves off to a great start, allowing Mike Hargrove's Indians only three baserunning opportunities as he shut down heavy hitting Cleveland with only a pair of singles in a

---

*Pitched to two batters in the 10th.
†Pitched to one batter in the 10th.

complete-game, 3 to 2 victory. The only other Indians base runner got on base because of an Atlanta error. This game, called by manager Hargrove "one of the best-pitched games I have ever seen," was a vintage piece of Maddux moundsmanship, deserving of our Classic Among Classics Award.

Cleveland	100	000	001	2–2–0
Atlanta	010	000	20x	3–3–2

Pitchers Clv Hershiser (LP): 6-IP, 3-BB, 7-K
Assenmacher: 0-IP, 1-BB, 0-K
Tavarez: 1⅓-IP, 1-BB, 0-K
Embree: ⅔-IP, 0-BB, 2-K
Atl Maddux (WP): 9-IP, 0-BB, 4-K

Extra Base Hits: Cleveland 0, Atlanta 1
Time: 2:37
Att: 51,876

On September 30, 1997, the Houston Astros challenged the Atlantans in the first game of the NL's Division Series. Manager Bobby Cox sent Greg Maddux to the mound in hopes of getting the important first game victory. Maddux didn't fail him. Working on the slimmest of margins and an impotent Braves attack that registered only two hits off 19-game winner Darryl Kile, the Professor proceeded to strangle Houston's offense attack by scattering the seven hits he surrendered while holding the Astros scoreless. The Braves won the series opener 2 to 1 and went on to sweep the series. Maddux's victory, which set the tempo for Atlanta's run at another pennant, was his best game in 21 post-season Divisional Series or NLCS tries, and therefore rates the Playoff Gem Award.

Roger Clemens' World Series Classic Among Classics was his conquest of the New York Mets in the 2000 Subway Series, ending in a deceptive 6 to 5 score that might suggest a free-swinging ball game with numerous scoring opportunities. There were indeed scoring opportunities, as well as some free swinging, but not while the Rocket was doing his stuff. In fact, aside from an outburst he himself precipitated with the severed end of Mike Piazza's sundered bat, the game proceeded in tense but steady progress toward a Yankee victory that was played out before a rather hushed house, so deadening was the effect of Clemens' masterful performance. In eight intimidating innings Clemens threw 112 pitches, 78 of which were explosive strikes and only two of which were singles. He left the game after he had put eight zeroes in place, leading 6 to 0. Then, at the expense of relievers Nelson and the usually parsimonious Mariano Rivera, the Mets staged a five-run rally that set up the game's frenzied finale. But the Mets fell one run short and the Yankees prevailed, 6 to 5.

New York (NL)	000	000	005		5-7-3
New York (AL)	210	010	11x		6-12-1

Pitchers NY (NL) Hampton (LP): 6-IP, 5-BB, 6-K
Rusch: ⅓-IP, 0-BB, 0-K
White: 1⅓-IP, 1-BB, 1-K
Cook: ⅓-IP, 0-BB, 0-K

NY (AL) Clemens (WP): 8-IP, 0-BB, 9-K
Nelson: 0-IP, 0-BB, 0-K
Rivera: 1-IP, 0-BB, 1-K

Extra Base Hits: New York (AL) 5, New York (NL) 2
Time: 3:30
Att: 56,059

Roger Clemens authored one of the most dominating post-season playoff performances in the game's history on October 14, 1999, just eight days prior to his Classic Among Classics Award–winning game on October 22. A line drive double by the Mariners' Al Martin in the seventh inning was the only hit Clemens gave up. He sat down 15 M's via the strikeout route with fastballs that shattered the air at speeds of up to 98 mph. Seattle never came close to being in the ball game as the Mariners' stunned faithful watched this masterpiece unfold.

It was almost the first no-hitter in playoff history. The Rocket's effort that day ranks, consequently, as worthy of a Playoff Gem Award.

Classics Among Classics: A Footnote

At the Huntington Avenue Grounds, home of the Boston Pilgrims, the fledgling American League's first entry into the modern World Series, Cy Young threw the first pitch on Thursday, October 1, 1903. One of the fabled Mound Maestros profiled in this book, his World Series exploits were not included because he didn't face a Hall of Fame pitcher in his only World Series. Some years later, in 1924 and '25, Walter Johnson had a similar World Series experience. That does not mean that these two Cooperstown titans did not pitch well in the Fall Classic. We pause, therefore, in concluding this World Series overview, to include a gem or two crafted by these legends.

Cy Young. Pittsburgh's Pirates, behind Charles "Deacon" Phillippe, beat the Pilgrims and Young in that opening game of the inaugural World Series by a score of 7 to 3. But Old Cy, by 1903 a crafty veteran on his way to the record book, came back in that Series to beat William "Brickyard" Kennedy in game five at Pittsburgh's Exposition Park with a beauty of a six-hitter. Boston won that day, pounding out four triples, one by Young himself, as they beat the Pirates 11 to 2 to get back into the Series, though trailing at that point three games to two. Four days later, on October 10, he bested Deacon Phillippe in another complete-game victory, 7 to 3, to even his account with Phillippe and to put the Pilgrims in a position to win the Series, which they did three days later in Boston. Young's 11 to 2 win over Brickyard Kennedy was his best World Series game by a hair's breadth over the important 7 to 3 win at Phillippe's expense, and it came at a point in that first Series when Boston desperately needed it.

Walter Johnson

By 1924 the World Series had become a Fall Classic, and Walter Johnson, in his waning years, had become a national hero for whom everyone was rooting. Never having appeared in a World Series, the 18-year veteran was just about everybody's sentimental favorite as his Washington Senators took on the mighty men of John McGraw, the New York Giants. For baseball buffs there was only one game in that Series, even though "the Big Train" had opened up the festivities by losing a heartbreaker, as far as Senator fans were concerned, to Artie Nehf, 4 to 3 in 12 innings of spine-ting ling baseball. Both pitchers went all the way, and both covered themselves with glory. In game five Johnson went down again, this time by a 6 to 2 count. Finally, when the seventh and deciding game rolled around, Sir Walter was called on once again, this time out of the bullpen, to subdue the Giants during the final four innings of the game. The Senators pulled it out with an incredible turn of good fortune and a hippety-hop single over third baseman Freddie Lindstrom's head that won the game and the series — and a World Series ring for America's Mr. Johnson.

Ranking the closest possible second to Johnson's relief win in 1924 is his six-hit shutout masterpiece against the Pirates in 1925. On October 11 of that year, in game four of the Series, he beat Pittsburgh 4 to 0 to put the Senators within a game of the 1925 championship with his second Series conquest. But this time there were no seventh-game miracles. After the Pirates had come from behind a 3 to 1 deficit in games to even matters, they kept right on rolling with a 9 to 7, seventh-game victory that beat a tired Johnson and the Senators for the World's Championship.

Those two World Series brought about a 3 and 3 Johnson record. That mattered little then, and it matters little now, so it seems. After all, the great Walter Johnson had already burned his name into the record books, and a World Series win or loss would not change his number one place in the hearts of baseball fans.

NOTES

Introduction

1. Linn, Ed. *The Great Rivalry: The Yankees and the Red Sox, 1901–1990*. Boston: Houghton Mifflin, 1990 (Introduction, p. ix).
2. The list may be found on p. 2317 of the 2001 edition of Total Sports' *Total Baseball Encyclopedia*, by John Thorn, Pete Palmer, Michael Gershman and David Pietrusza, with Sean Lahman and Greg Spira. TPI: Total Pitcher's Index, a sabermetric statistic representing the sum of a pitcher's Pitching Runs (p. 2501), is further explained on page 1309 as a statistic expressed in wins beyond league average that a pitcher contributes to his team during the course of the season. Walter Johnson heads this list with a career total of 91.4, followed by Cy Young with 78.0 and Pete Alexander with 64.6.
3. Exceptions have been made for Clemens and Maddux, who are still active.

1. Cy Young

1. The Clutch Pitching Index is a sabermetric figure that calculates a pitcher's performance with respect to the number of runs he might be expected to give up over the course of a season as compared to the actual number of runs he surrendered. An average pitcher's CPI would be in the 100 range. Expected runs are figured on the basis of the pitcher's opposing at bats, hits, walks, and hit batsmen.
2. The Wins Above League (WAL) statistic states a hurler's Pitching Wins above the league average for a given season. Ed Walsh, with 33.8 WAL in 1908, recorded the greatest number in the 20th century.
3. The Ratio statistic indicates how many players reached base via basehits, walks and HPB per nine innings pitched. Less than 11–12 per game is outstanding, usually limiting a team to two runs or less.

2. Christy Mathewson

1. Pitcher's Defense, which is expressed as Pitcher Runs, is a linear weights measure used by sabermetricians to calculate how many runs a pitcher can save his team over the course of a season beyond that of a league-average pitcher (average is 0). The Pitcher's Runs, Pitcher's Wins and Pitcher's Defense categories are all related. Number one in PD is Ed Walsh (84), followed by Greg Maddux (81), Carl Mays (74) and then Mathewson, with 69. These four would have to be listed as the game's top defensive pitchers.
2. The Pitching Wins statistic is derived from Pitching Runs, another linear weights measure which calculates runs saved beyond that of a league average pitcher (average is 0) over the course of a season. In turn, one tenth of that number is approximately the number of Pitching Wins a pitcher contributes to his team. All time leaders include Walter Johnson, with 77, number 1; Cy Young, 73, number 2; Lefty Grove, 58, number 3; Roger Clemens, 54, number 4; and Grover Alexander, 51, number 5.
3. The Clutch Pitching Index figures the number of expected runs a pitcher allows over the number of runs that were actually scored against him. Expected runs are calculated on the basis of the pitcher's opposing at bats, walks and hit batsmen. Pitchers like Eddie Lopat gave up a lot of hits but were hard to score on. This statistic sorts out pitchers who allowed the same number of hits as other pitchers but who were scored on less, thus indicating that they were tough in the clutch, preventing runs, and able to win where others couldn't.
4. "Rube" Waddell was a teammate of Phillippe and Wagner with the 1899 Louisville Colonels, won the NL's ERA title in 1900 with a 2.37, and started out the 1901 season in Pittsburgh before exhausting manager Fred Clarke's patience. So Clarke released him. Waddell then finish ed the season with the Chicago Cubs before being picked up by Connie Mack for the 1902 season. Imagine Waddell, Phillippe and Wagner on the same ball club. Clarke couldn't — and shipped him.
5. To check Blengino's insights further, see *Baseball's Top 100*, by John Benson and Tony Blengino, Diamond Library, Wilton, Conn., 1995.

3. Walter Johnson

1. The quote is taken from an article Johnson helped write for *The Baseball Magazine*, October 1929 issue.
2. The nickname Barney, used almost exclusively by very close friends, came about because of a speeding ticket Johnson received on the day he purchased a new car. The Barney reference related to the speed king of the day, Barney Oldfield.
3. The first Bender-Mathewson matchup came on October 14, 1905, at the Polo Grounds, when Christy Mathewson completed his world series shutout trifecta with a 2 to 0 conquest of The Chief and his Philadelphia teammates.
4. The final Ruth tally comes to .321, forged on 44 hits in 137 at bats. There were 17 doubles and two triples to go with his 10 home runs against Walter Johnson.
5. Because Babe Ruth became a position player in 1920, the Ruth-Johnson comparison seasons postdate the 1920 season.
6. From an interview with the Christy Walsh Syndicate, April 11, 1925.

5. Lefty Grove

1. The information used here was taken from a chapter entitled "The Most Dominant Starting Pitchers of All Time: The Relative Control Power Factor," in *Baseball's Top 100: The Best Individual Seasons of All Time*, by John Benson and Tony Blengino, Diamond Library, Wilton, Conn., 1995 (pp. 307–316).

2. The complete Grove-Johnson game by game pitching log is detailed in the Walter Johnson chapter.

3. A seventh Famer, Al "Chief" Bender, appeared in the one game covered in the previous profile on Bender, Johnson and Wynn.

4. Nemec, David; Matt Greenberger, Dan Schlossberg, Dick Johnson, Mike Tully, Paul Adomites and Pete Palmer. *The Players of Cooperstown*. Lincolnwood, Ill.: Publications International, 1998.

5. The feat was duplicated for the second and final time by the 1971 Baltimore Orioles' Mike Cuellar, Pat Dobson, Jim Palmer and Dave McNally.

6. In *Baseball When the Grass Was Real*, by Donald Honig, Simon and Schuster, New York, 1975. Taken from Honig's *A Donald Honig Reader* (1988), p. 31.

7. Sabermetrician Bill James, one of baseball's foremost analysts, wrote *The Politics of Glory* in 1994 (Macmillan Co., New York). His treatise analyzed Hall of Fame selections and qualifications.

8. Here are some of the HOF Fame pitchers who won fewer games than Ferrell: Lefty Gomez (189), Koufax (165), Joss (160), and Diz Dean (150). Among those HOFers whose winning percentage was less than Ferrell's are: Jack Chesbro (.600), Walter Johnson (.599), Herb Pennock (.598), Warren Spahn (.597), Mickey Welch (.594) and Bob Gibson (.591).

6. Warren Spahn

1. This book, published by Harcourt, New York, 2000, contains in-depth studies not only of great pitching personalities, but of the battle of wits between pitchers and hitters.

2. Reichler, Joe. *Baseball's Great Moments*. New York: Crown Publishers, 1981 (p. 13).

3. Juan Marichal's profile is also a part of the Warren Spahn story, following the Bob Gibson review coming up shortly.

4. Newcombe's 1949 All-Star game appearance was the first of four in his career, and in it he followed Warren Spahn, who opened the game for the NL, to the mound. It was the only time the two appeared together in the same game.

5. Klapisch, Bob, and Pete Van Wieren. *The World Champion Braves: 125 Years of America's Team*. Atlanta: Turner Publishing, 1996 (p. 72).

7. Tom Seaver

1. Mazer, Bill, with Stan and Shirley Fischler. *Bill Mazer's Amazin' Baseball Book: 150 Years of Baseball Tales and Trivia*. New York: Zebra Books, Kensington Pub. Corp., 1991 (p. 246).

2. *A Quality Start:* Starting Pitcher records at least six innings, giving up no more

than three earned runs. *Hold:* Recorded when the reliever enters a Save situation, gets at least one out, and leaves the game with his team ahead. *Save:* Recorded when the reliever enters the game ahead, pitches at least one inning and his team three runs ahead (or less) with the potential tying run on base, at bat or on deck. A Save may also be awarded for three or more outstanding innings of relief (scorer's discretion).

3. Christy Mathewson averaged 35.9 starts per season in his career; Tom Seaver: 32.4; Roger Clemens 30.1; Carl Hubbell 28.1; Whitey Ford 27.4; and Billy Pierce 24.0.

4. The only time Perry was actually "caught grease-handed" was on August 23, 1982, when, as an "Ancient Mariner" pitching for Seattle, he was nailed, thumbed and suspended for ten days. A tsk-tsk, $250 fine was assessed to complete Perry's humiliation. Humiliation? Gaylord Perry loved it!

5. James, Bill. *The New Bill James Historical Baseball Abstract.* New York: Free Press, 2001 (pp. 286–287).

6. The Win Shares Method is fully explained on pages 331–338 of his book. One of its basic purposes is to rate and rank players and performance, enabling James to formulate his own listing of the game's best pitchers, third basemen, and other players.

7. *Op. cit.*, pp. 287–288.

8. Both Famers played for many managers during their 20-year careers. In Seaver's case it was nine, including two hitches, one in each league, with John McNamara. Carlton matched that with a pair of turns under Pat Corrales, who managed Carlton teams with Philadelphia in the NL and Cleveland in the Junior Circuit, plus another dozen skippers in his 24-year career. The two hurlers came within a couple of weeks of being teammates in Chicago when the White Sox, in 1986, had both on the roster but not quite at the same time.

9. On July 14, 1970, Palmer and Seaver opened the All-Star game at Riverfront Stadium, Cincinnati, as their leagues' starting pitchers. Each worked three innings, giving up no runs, but one hit, and turning a scoreless game over to the next hurlers. The NL won that game in the bottom of the 12th, 5 to 4. In 1977, at Yankee Stadium, they met once again in the 1977 All-Star game. This time Palmer, again the AL starter, was the loser. Seaver pitched the sixth and seventh innings of the NL win.

10. The Encyclopedia was edited by David Pietrusza, Matthew Silverman and M. Gershman, Total Sports Illustrated, New York, 2000 (p. 927).

11. The dates in parentheses are major league debut dates.

12. Honig, Donald. *The Greatest Pitchers of All Time.* New York: Crown Publishers, 1998 (p. 151).

13. Nemec, David and Saul Wisnia. *100 Years of Major League Baseball.* Lincolnwood, Ill.: Publications International, 2000 (p. 343).

8. Roger Clemens

1. Clemens debuted on May 15, 1984, just a few days before Jim Palmer retired.

2. Myers, Doug, and Mark Gola. *The Louisville Slugger Complete Book of Pitching.* Lincolnwood, Ill.: McGraw-Hill/Contemporary Books, 2000 (p. 72).

3. *Op cit.*, page 313.

10. Fall Classics

1. The records cited for Clemens and Maddux include the 2001 season.
2. Both Clemens and Maddux may add more appearances and other records to their postseason log before their careers are completed.

Appendix A: Ratings from the Total Pitcher Index

This listing presents those pitchers who have appeared in this book either as one of the primary players discussed (Cy Young or Christy Mathewson, for example) or as one of the top 250 pitchers according to the Total Pitcher Index ranking whose record against them was reviewed. The list as of the 2001 season:

1)	Walter Johnson	91.4	26)	Pedro Martinez	34.9
2)	Cy Young	78.2	26)	Jim Palmer	34.9
3)	Greg Maddux	64.7	26)	Gaylord Perry	34.9
4)	Grover Alexander	64.6	29)	Don Drysdale	34.6
5)	Christy Mathewson	62.9	30)	Phil Niekro	33.8
6)	Roger Clemens	60.1	31)	Steve Carlton	33.7
7)	Lefty Grove	59.7	35)	Bert Blyleven	30.7
7)	Kid Nichols	57.5	36)	Wes Ferrell	30.5
9)	Warren Spahn	50.2	37)	Bob Feller	30.2
10)	Tom Seaver	48.7	38)	Fergie Jenkins	29.8
12)	Ed Walsh	44.9	40)	Juan Marichal	29.5
13)	Bob Gibson	43.7	42)	Bucky Walters	29.0
14)	Carl Hubbell	41.1	44)	Mike Mussina	28.7
16)	Amos Rusie	39.8	45)	Clark Griffith	28.5
17)	Hal Newhouser	39.3	46)	Tommy Bridges	28.0
18)	Whitey Ford	39.2	46)	Red Ruffing	28.0
19)	Bob Lemon	38.4	48)	Brett Saberhagen	27.7
21)	Randy Johnson	37.1	49)	Dazzy Vance	27.4
21)	Ted Lyons	37.1	51)	Red Faber	27.2
23)	Carl Mays	36.6	52)	Stan Coveleski	27.0
24)	Mordecai Brown	35.3	53)	Eddie Plank	26.9
25)	Kevin Brown	35.1	54)	Dolf Luque	26.8

57)	Eppa Rixey	26.7		122)	Curt Schilling	18.1
59)	Robin Roberts	25.9		124)	Ed Reulbach	17.8
60)	Addie Joss	25.8		126)	Dwight Gooden	17.7
60)	Urban Shocker	25.8		130)	Jack Taylor	17.3
62)	Tommy John	25.6		130)	Larry French	17.3
63)	Eddie Cicotte	25.4		135)	Babe Ruth	17.2
66)	Harry Brecheen	25.0		136)	Early Wynn	17.1
67)	Rick Reuschel	24.7		144)	Harry Howell	16.6
68)	Rube Waddell	24.4		148)	Frank "Noodles" Hahn	16.0
70)	Jimmy Key	24.2		150)	Jose Rijo	15.7
73)	Burleigh Grimes	23.7		153)	Sam Leever	15.4
75)	Dave Cone	23.4		155)	Steve Rogers	15.3
77)	Fred Fitzsimmons	22.9		156)	Charles "Babe" Adams	15.2
81)	Dizzy Dean	21.8		158)	Waite Hoyt	15.1
83)	Orel Hershiser	21.4		158)	Deacon Phillippe	15.1
83)	Mariano Rivera	21.4		168)	George Mullin	14.5
89)	Vic Willis	21.2		170)	Albert "Chief" Bender	14.4
94)	Nolan Ryan	20.7		181)	Mike Hampton	13.9
96)	Sandy Koufax	20.5		189)	Dennis Martinez	13.6
101)	Guy "Doc" White	20.1		193)	Jim Bunning	13.4
102)	Wilbur Cooper	20.0		196)	Don Sutton	13.2
103)	Lefty Gomez	19.9		238)	Jack Chesbro	10.9
107)	Kevin Appier	19.7				
108)	Murry Dickson	19.5		*Other Hall of Famers*		
109)	Mel Harder	19.4		Herb Pennock		6.8
110)	Chuck Finley	19.3		Jesse Haines		6.8
113)	Joe McGinnity	18.8		Jim "Catfish" Hunter		6.0
117)	Ron Guidry	18.5		Leroy Satchel Paige		3.9
117)	Luis Tiant	18.5		Richard Rube Marquard		-2.3
119)	Don Newcombe	18.4				

Appendix B: Selected Career Statistics

Selected career statistics* are listed for the elite pitchers presented in this book. The Legend:

K/Gm — BB/Gm   Strikeouts and walks issued per nine innings pitched.

Rat   Ratio, a statistic that shows how few or many base runners per nine innings pitched the pitcher must contend with. The lower the number, the more efficient the pitcher. Pedro Martinez' 9.6 ties him with Christy Mathewson for fourth best, all time.

PD   Pitcher Defense. A measure of the pitcher's fielding contribution to his team's defense. Maddux's career 86 rates him as the best all time.

PB   Pitcher as Batter. The pitcher's contribution to the team's offense. Walter Johnson's career 99 rates fourth all time.

TPI   Total Pitcher Index. A cumulative statistic that rates a pitcher in a given year. Career TPI is the sum of the pitcher's individual seasons.

	W-L-W%	CG	K	K/Gm	BB/Gm	Rat	ERA	OBA	PD	PB	TPI
Young, 22 yrs	511-316,.618	749	2803	3.43	1.49	10.4	2.63	.252	19	-22	78.0
Mathewson, 17 yrs	373-188,.665	435	2507	5.03	1.70	9.6	2.13	.236	68	59	62.9
Johnson, W, 21 yrs	417-279,.599	531	3509	5.34	2.07	9.9	2.17	.227	-23	99	91.4
Alexander, 20 yrs	373-208,.642	437	2198	3.81	1.65	10.2	2.56	.250	31	24	64.6
Grove, 17 yrs	300-141,.686	298	2266	5.18	2.71	11.6	3.06	.255	-15	-37	59.7
Spahn, 21 yrs	363-245,.597	382	2583	4.89	2.71	10.8	3.09	.244	9	88	50.2
Seaver, 20 yrs	311-205,.603	231	3640	6.85	2.62	10.2	2.86	.226	13	28	48.7
Clemens, 18 yrs*	280-145,.659	116	3717	8.61	2.91	11.5	3.10	.229	2	1	60.1
Maddux, 16 yrs*	257-146,.638	102	2523	6.39	1.93	11.0	2.84	.241	86	15	64.7

*Statistics through 2001 season

BIBLIOGRAPHY

Adair, Robert K. *The Physics of Baseball*. New York: Harper & Row, 1990.
Alexander, Charles C. *Ty Cobb*. New York: Oxford University Press, 1984.
Allen, Lee. *One Hundred Years of Baseball*. New York: Batholomew House, 1950.
Blake, Mike. *Baseball Chronicles*. Cincinnati: Betterway Books, 1994.
Broeg, Bob, and J. Vickery. *St. Louis Cardinal Encyclopedia*. Indianapolis: Masters Press, 1998.
Curran, William. *Big Sticks: The Batting Revolution of the Twenties*. New York: William Morrow, 1990.
Dewey, Don, and N. Alcocella. *The Biographical History of Baseball*. New York: Carroll and Graf, 1995.
Durso, Joseph. *Baseball and the American Dream*. St. Louis: Sporting News, 1986.
Einstein, Charles. *The Baseball Reader*. New York: Lippincott and Crowell, 1980.
Frommer, Harvey. *Shoeless Joe and Ragtime Baseball*. Dallas: Taylor, 1992.
Gibson, Bob, with Lonnie Wheeler. *Stranger to the Game*. New York: Viking, 1994.
Golenbock, Peter. *Wrigleyville*. New York: St. Martin's, 1999 ed.
Hart, Stan. *Scouting Reports*. New York: Macmillan, 1995.
Honig, Donald. *The Greatest Pitchers of All Time*. New York: Crown Publishers, 1998.
James, Bill. *The New Bill James Historical Baseball Abstract*. New York: Free Press, 2001.
Kaese, Harold, and R. G. Lynch. *The Milwaukee Braves*. New York: Putnam, 1954.
Kahn, Roger. *The Head Game*. New York: Harcourt, 2000.
Kaplan, Jim. *Lefty Grove: American Original*. Lincoln: Bison Books, 2000.
Kavanagh, Jack. *Walter Johnson: A Life*. Lanham: Rowman and Littlefield, 1995.
Kelley, Brent P. *100 Greatest Pitchers*. Greenwich, CT: Bison Books, 1988.
Klapisch, Bob, and Pete VanWieren. *The World Champion Braves*. Atlanta: Turner Publishing, 1996.
Koppett, Leonard. *Concise History of Major League Baseball*. Philadelphia: Temple University Press, 1998.
Lanigan, Ernest. *The Baseball Cyclopedia*. The Baseball Magazine Publishing Company, 1922.
Lieb, Fred. *The Boston Red Sox*. New York: G. P. Putnam's Sons, 1947.

Linn, Ed. *The Great Rivalry.* New York: Ticknor and Fields, 1991.
Mack, Connie. *My 66 Years in the Big Leagues.* John C. Winston Co., 1950.
Mathewson, Christopher. *Pitching in a Pinch.* New York: Grosset and Dunlap, 1912.
Mazur, Bill, with Stan and Shirley Fischler. *Bill Mazur's Amazing Baseball Book.* New York: Kensington Publishing, 1990.
McCulloch, Ron, ed. *Baseball Roots.* Toronto: Warwick Pub., 2000.
McGraw, John J. *My Thirty Years in Baseball.* New York: Boni and Liveright, 1923.
Meany, Tom. *Baseball's Greatest Pitchers.* New York: Barnes Pub., 1951.
Mercurio, J. *Chronology of Major League Baseball Records.* New York: Harper's, 1989.
Myers, Doug, and Tom Gola. *The Louisville Slugger Complete Book of Pitching.* Lincolnwood, Ill.: Contemporary Books, 2000.
Neft, David, Richard Cohen and Michael Neft. *The Sports Encyclopedia: Baseball 2002.* New York: St. Martin's Griffin, 2002.
Nemec, David, and S. Wisnia. *100 Years of Major League Baseball.* Lincolnwood, Ill.: Publishers International, 2000.
Nemec, David, and M. Greenberger, Dan Schlossberger, R. Johnson, M. Tully, P. Adomites, and Pete Palmer. *The Players of Cooperstown.* Lincolnwood, Ill.: Publishers International, 1998.
Neyer, Rob, and E. Epstein. *Baseball Dynasties.* New York: W. W. Norton, 2000.
Okrent, Dan, and H. Lewine. *The Ultimate Baseball Book.* New York: Hilltown Press, 2000.
Pietrusza, David, and M. Silverman and M. Gershman, eds. *Baseball: The Biographical Encyclopedia.* Kingston: Total Sports Illustrated, 2000.
Povich, Shirley. *The Washington Senators.* New York: Putnam, 1954.
Ritter, Lawrence. *The Glory of Their Times.* New York: Macmillan, 1966.
Rogers, C. Paul, with Bill Werber. *Memories of a Ball Player.* Lincoln: SABR/University of Nebraska Press, 2001.
Romig, Ralph. *Cy Young.* Philadelphia: Dorrance and Co., 1964.
Seaver, Tom, with Marty Appel. *Great Moments in Baseball.* New York: Carol Publishing Group, 1992.
Seymour, Harold. *Baseball: The Early Years.* New York: Oxford, 1960.
Shouler, Ken. *The Real 100 Best Baseball Players of All Time...and Why!* Lenexa: Addax Publishing Group, 1998.
Smith, Ron. *Baseball's Greatest Players.* St. Louis: Sporting News, 1998.
Solomon, Burt. *The Baseball Timeline.* New York: Avon Books, 1997.
Sullivan, George. *Pitchers: 27 of Baseball's Greatest.* New York: Atheneum Press, 1994.
Thomas, Henry W. *Walter Johnson: Baseball's Big Train.* Lincoln: University of Nebraska Press, 1998.
Thorn, John, and J. Holway. *The Pitcher.* New York: Prentice-Hall, 1987.
Thorn, John, Pete Palmer, and Associates. *Total Baseball.* 1989–2001 editions, New York: Time Warner and Total Baseball, 1989–2001.
Voight, David Quentin. *American Baseball* (vols. 2 and 3), University Park: Pennsylvania State University Press, 1983.
Zimbalist, Andrew. *Baseball Billions.* New York: Basic Books, 1992.
Zoss, Joel, and John S. Bowman. *The National League: A History.* New York: Smithmark Publishers, 1995.

Periodicals

Daily News, New York
Enquirer, Cincinnati
Globe, Boston
Herald, Boston
Inquirer, Philadelphia
Journal, Milwaukee
Journal-Constitution, Atlanta
Post, Washington, D.C.
Post-Dispatch, St. Louis
The Sporting News, St. Louis
Sun-Times, Chicago
Times, New York
Tribune, Chicago
USA Today Baseball Weekly, Arlington, Va.

Baseball Guides

The Sporting News: Complete Baseball Record Book
The Sporting News: Baseball Guide
The Sporting News: Baseball Register
USA Baseball Weekly: Almanac
Who's Who In Baseball Magazine Company: Who's Who in Baseball
Stats, Inc.: Major League Handbook
Baseball America: Almanac

INDEX

Aaron, Henry (Hank) 128, 206, 216, 252
Abbatichio, Ed (Batty) 49
Abbott, Kyle 337
Acocella, Nick 112
Adams, Babe 27, 53, 131, 133–135, 143, 146–147, 156, 299
Agganis, Harry 115
Agosto, Juan 265
Aldrete, Mike 303
Aldridge, Vic 147
Alexander, Grover (Pete) 2, 7, 8, 17, 35–36, 39, 41, 61, 69–71, 73, 84, 92, 105, 115, 129–157, 160–161, 199, 202–203, 208, 217–219, 240, 272, 284, 311, 345, 347–348
Allen, Johnny 166–167
Allen, Rich 221, 228
Altobelli, Joe 258
Altrock, Nick 30
American Association 149, 205
American League (Junior Circuit) 7–9, 23, 25, 90, 124, 155, 164, 170, 175, 181, 190–191, 194, 203, 207, 246, 250, 255–259, 262, 264, 273, 277, 286, 288, 338, 340, 349, 354
Ames, Leon (Red) 58, 92, 136, 309
Anderson, Larry 315
Anson, Adrian (Cap) 9, 44
Appier, Kevin 282, 304–306
Appleton, (Jablonowski) Pete 185
Appling, Luke 107, 170
Arizona Diamondbacks 288, 331, 338
Armas, Tony 283

Ashburn, Richie 229
Ask, Ken 139
Assenmacher, Paul 353
Atherton, Keith 273
Atlanta, GA 252, 284–285, 318, 330
Atlanta Braves 251, 284, 302, 309–344, 351–353
Auker, Eldon 195
Autry, Gene 264
Averill, Earl 160
Avery, Steve 310
Ayers, Yancy (Doc) 105

Babe Ruth World Series Award 274
Bader, Lore (King) 103
Bagby, Jim, Jr. 195
Bagwell, Jeff (Bags) 218, 331–337
Bailey, A. L. (Sweetbreads) 138
Bair, Doug 326–327
Baker, Frank 86
Baker, Tom (Rattlesnake) 152
Baker Bowl, Philadelphia 346
Baltimore, MD 238
Baltimore Orioles 14–15, 218, 258–259, 290, 294–297, 303–304, 315, 338–339, 351
Bancroft, Dave (Beauty) 135, 244
Bankhead, Dan 223
Bannister, Floyd 265
Barrett, Marty 305
Baseball Research Journal 232
Bastille Day 59
Baumgartner, Stan 125, 174

371

Baylor University 121
BBWA (Baseball Writers Association of America) 203, 233, 248, 263, 343
Beckley, Jake 135
Bedrosian, Steve 322, 338
Belinda, Stan 306–327
Belinger, Clay 296
Bell, Herman (Hi) 148
Bell, James (Cool Papa) 125
Belle, Albert 113
Bench, Johnny 249
Bender, Albert (Chief) 3, 7–8, 23, 28–30, 41, 48, 69, 73, 79, 90–92, 103, 161–164, 181, 188, 227, 284, 288, 346
Bennett, Dennis 228
Bentley, Jack 99
Benz, Joey (Blitzen) 93, 99
Berra, Lawrence (Yogi) 190, 224, 328
Biloxi, MS 82
Birmingham, AL (baseball club) 74
Bjarkman, Peter 54
Black Sox 98, 106, 141, 170
Blades, Ray 205
Blake, John (Sheriff) 139
Blengino, Tony 75, 161
Bluege, Oswald (Ozzie) 122
Blyleven, Bert 137, 188, 241, 246, 257, 262, 265–267, 273, 282, 284, 292–293
Bocabella, Bobby 211
Boehler, George 135
Boggs, Wade 293, 303, 305
Bolling, Milt 216
Bonds, Barry 218, 327, 331–335
Bonilla, Bobby 327
Boone, James (Dan'l) 105
Borbon, Pedro 326, 329
Bostock, Lyman 115
Boston, AL (Pilgrims, Carmine, Red Sox) 15–17, 19, 27, 29–30, 33, 42, 50, 80, 87, 90, 96, 108–111, 123–125, 158, 169, 173–174, 176, 179–181, 183, 193, 242, 246, 263, 272–273, 275, 282–308, 340, 347, 354–355
Boston, NL (Rustlers, Beaneaters, Braves) 18, 27, 36, 43–44, 48, 50, 68, 136, 141, 200–203, 206, 209, 223, 349–350
Bowman, Doctor (NY Giants trainer) 215
Boyer, Ken 205, 207
Bradford, PA 200
Bragan, Bobby 233

Brantley, Jeff 322
Braves Field (Boston) 349
Braxton, Garland 175
Brazle, Alpha 207, 210
Brecheen, Harry (The Cat) 199, 202, 206, 208–210, 343
Brennan, Bill 70, 135
Brett, George 244, 278
Bridges, Tommy 162, 185, 187–188, 192–195
Brock, Lou 244
Brodie, Steve 13
Broken Bow, OK 210
Brooklyn–Los Angeles Dodgers 27, 65, 69, 74, 114, 136, 139–140, 145, 147–148, 152–153, 169, 174, 201, 210, 220–223, 226–228, 230, 232, 241, 243, 246, 257–258, 260–263, 268, 274, 317–320, 329–330
Brower, Frank 107
Brown, Clint 190
Brown, Kevin 282, 284, 288–290, 311–312, 325–325, 329–330
Brown, Mordecai 2, 8, 27–28, 40–41, 48, 57, 61–65, 69, 131–133, 156, 222, 291
Brown, Phil 232
Brown, Walter (Jumbo) 183–184, 192–195
Browning, Tom 322
Buckeye, Garland 189
Bucknell University 41
Buffalo, NY 200
Buffalo Bisons 227
Buhl, Bob 211, 215, 224, 234
Bunning, Jim 7, 202, 227–229, 235, 241–242, 246
Burdette, Lou 234
Burks, Ellis 305
Burns, Tommy 44
Burns, William (Bill) 71
Bush, Joseph (Bullet Joe) 76, 91, 102–103, 112
Byrd, Paul 335
Byrne, Bobby 70

Cain, Merritt (Sugar) 183, 190, 192
Camden Yards, Baltimore 287, 297, 339
Camnitz, Howie 53
California (Anaheim) Angels 263, 268, 304–305
Candlestick Park, San Francisco 211, 248, 322

Index 373

Cantillon, Joe 92
Caraway, Pat 173
Cardello, Joe 144
Carlisle, PA (Indian School) 90
Carlton, Steve 2, 78, 80, 137, 198, 202, 217, 222, 234–236, 240–241, 254–258, 261–262, 281–284, 288
Carlyle, Roy (Dizzy) 163
Carter, Gary 271
Cather, Mike 326, 329, 338
Cepeda, Orlando 244
Chalmers, George 70–71
Chambers, Cliff 206
Chance, Frank 7, 27, 65, 244
Chaney, Larry 136
Chapman, Ben 185
Chapman, Ray 115
Charlotte, NC 164
Cheeves, Virgil (Chief) 138, 143
Chesbro, John (Happy Jack) 7–8, 16–17, 41, 43, 57, 59–61, 79, 84–85, 188
Chicago AL (White Sox, Pale Hose) 7–10, 20, 23, 25, 28, 30–33, 66, 79, 90, 92–93, 105–108, 121–123, 164, 170–174, 176–179, 258, 263, 265–266, 276–278, 298, 304
Chicago NL franchises 7, 9, 27, 44, 47, 49, 63, 69, 98–100, 112, 132–139, 148, 201, 211, 225, 234–235, 239, 242, 254, 259–260, 267–268, 311, 313–314, 316–318, 320–321, 324, 327–329
Chicago Tribune 163
Cicotte, Eddie (Knuckles) 79, 98–100, 171
Cincinnati NL (Reds, Redlegs) 18, 54–56, 69, 71–74, 81, 113, 137–139, 141–143, 147–148, 170, 223, 252, 256, 264, 267, 270–271, 320–322, 328
Clancy, Jim 273
Clark, Jackie 300
Clarke, Fred 53, 57
Clarkson, John 8, 78
Clemens, Roger (The Rocket) 1, 3, 7, 61, 78, 125, 144, 158, 160–161, 240, 273, 280–308, 310–312, 325, 329, 338, 344–345, 352–354
Cleveland AL 5, 18, 20, 23–25, 30–31, 35, 42, 90, 92, 103–105, 164, 169, 179, 187, 189–190, 194, 218, 258, 265–266, 290, 292–293, 329, 349–350, 352–353

Cobb, Ty (The Georgia Peach) 92, 94–98, 114, 133, 158, 164, 171, 213, 217–218, 244, 332, 335
Cochrane, Mickey (Black Mike) 164, 192, 348
Cocrehan, Eugene 141
Coffman, George (Slick) 195
Cole, Leonard (King) 27
Colorado Rockies 343
Collins, Eddie 22, 87, 90, 107, 162, 164
Collins, Jimmy 13
Collins, Phil 155
Columbus, OH, Redbirds 205
Comeback of the Year Award 278
Comiskey, Charles 9, 33
Comiskey Park, Chicago 92, 112, 179, 258, 263, 274
Concorde 125
Cone, David 282, 296, 311, 325–329
Conley, Gene 206–207
Connally, George (Sarge) 163
Connolly, Tom 15
Cook, Dennis 354
Cook, Stanton 318
Cooley, Duff 43
Coolidge, President Calvin 116
Coombs, John (Colby Jack) 90–91, 103
Cooper, Wilbur 33
Cooperstown, NY 33, 46, 74, 76, 98, 112, 127, 137, 157, 186, 191, 218, 229, 235, 237–239, 248, 259–260, 263, 289, 308, 325, 330–331
County Stadium, Milwaukee, WI 201, 215, 226, 350
Coveleski, Harry 164
Coveleski, Stan 74, 80, 103–105, 137, 162, 165, 169–170
Cox, Bobby 284, 340, 344, 353
Crawford, Samuel (Wahoo Sam) 55
Crawford, Steve 303
Criger, Lou 11, 14, 16, 22, 24
Cromartie, Warren 272
Cronin, Joe 158
Crosley Field, Cincinnati 219, 220
Cross, Monte 22
Crutcher, Richard (Dick) 143
Cuellar, Mike 351
Cullop, Nick 117
Culp, Ray 228
Cvengros, Mike 122–123
Cy Young Award 222–223, 226, 233, 236, 240, 244, 248–251, 254, 258,

262, 269, 273, 276–281, 290, 292, 299–300, 303–304, 306, 317–318, 323–324, 327–328, 339–340, 343–344

Dangerfield, Rodney 250
Darwin, Danny 313
Davis, George 229
Davis, Harry 29
Davis, Jody 313
Davis, Joel 273
Davis, Storm 298
Dawley, Bill 273
Deal, Charlie 138
Dean, Jerome (Dizzy) 61, 76, 80, 137, 184, 280
Deane, Bill 223
Delehanty, Ed 115
Delehanty, Jim 26, 94
Deshaies, Jim 337
Detroit Tigers 7, 25–27, 54, 90, 92, 94–98, 133, 164, 169, 176, 185, 192–198, 228, 241, 273–274, 306
Dewey, Don 112
Dexter, Charlie 47
Dickey, William M. (Bill) 174, 192
Dickman, Emerson 192
Dickson, Murry 202, 205–207, 209–210, 218, 350
DiMaggio, Joe 187, 192, 278
Dinneen, William (Big Bill) 16, 44, 345
Doerr, Bobby 209
Donovan, William (Wild Bill) 76
Douglas, Phil 136
Drabek, Doug 311, 325–327
Dreyfuss, Barney 57
Driessen, Dan 271
Drysdale, Don 202, 218, 223–227, 232, 241, 318
Dugan Josoph (Jumpin' Joe) 112
Dumont, George 108
Dumovich, Ray 139
Duren, Ryne 77
Durocher, Leo (The Lip) 259
Dyer, Eddie 208–210
Dygert, Jimmy 30
Dykes, Jimmy 192, 223

Earnshaw, George (Moose) 173, 176, 349
Ebbets Field, Brooklyn 153, 221–222
Eckersley, Dennis (The Eck) 2
Eckert, Commissioner William 238

Ehmke, Howard 123, 167, 178
Eichhorn, Mark 303
Elberfeld, Norman (Kid) 90
Eller, Horace (Hod) 143
Embree, Alan 353
Emslie, Bob 73
Eskenazi, Jerry 241
Everett, Carl 296
Exposition Park, Pittsburgh 354

Faber, Urban (Red) 80, 105–108, 123, 162–166, 170–173, 178, 272
Falkenberg, Fred (Cy) 26
Farr, Steve 265
Federal League 64, 73, 132
Feller, Bob (Bullet Bob, Rapid Robert) 76–77, 125, 144, 162, 184–185, 198, 218, 280, 284, 307, 349–350
Fenway Park, Boston 124, 163, 194, 292, 338, 340
Ferrell, Rick 174, 185
Ferrell, Wes 158, 162, 174, 184–185, 188, 194
Filligim, Dana 136
Fingers, Rollie 351
Finley, Chuck 199, 282, 288, 304–305
Fisk, Carlton 244, 258, 266, 272
Fitzgerald, Mike 316
Fitzsimmons, Fred (Fat Freddie) 131, 152–153, 156
Flagstead, Ira 163
Flaskamper, Ray (Flash) 121
Fletcher, Scott 288
Flick, Elmer 89
Florida Marlins 290, 329
Fogel, Horace 61
Forbes Field, Pittsburgh 49, 114
Ford, E. (Whitey) 3, 48, 61, 100, 125, 198, 211, 217, 231, 140, 284, 350
Fossas, Tony 298
Foster, Eddie 87
Fox, Nelson (Lil' Nell) 229
Foxx, Jimmie (Double X) 158, 164, 175, 179, 187, 192, 197, 348–349
Francis, Ray 175
Franco, John 2
Frazee, Harry 112
Fregosi, Jim 336
Frseno, CA 279
Friend, Bob 219
Frisch, Frank (The Fordham Flash) 154
Frisella, Danny 248

Index

Galesburg, IL 157
Gallivan, Phil 173
Galvin, Jim (Pud) 7–8
Garagiola, Joe 207
Garciaparra, Nomar 221
Garman, Mike 246
Garrett, Wayne 247
Gaston, Cito 300
Gaston, Milton 173, 178–179
Gehrig, Lou 121, 160, 174, 181, 183, 192–193, 278
Gehringer, Charley 125, 160
Genewich, Joe 153, 155
Georgia Tech University 289
Germany 129
Gessler, Harry (Doc) 90
Gibson, George 53
Gibson, Bob 61, 78, 144, 149, 202, 222, 226, 229–231, 240–241, 244–266, 280, 288, 292
Gibson, Josh 190
Giuliani, Rudy 325
Glavine, Tom 199, 310–311, 328–329, 343
Gola, Mark, 289
Gold Glove Award 294
Goldsmith, Harold (Hal) 155
Goldstein, Isadore 195
Gomez, Vernon (Lefty) 48, 51, 125–127, 137, 162, 181, 187, 190–192, 199, 217
Gonzalez, Fernando 250
Gooden, Dwight 2, 61, 187, 282, 302–325, 352
Goshen, OH 52–53
Goslin, Leon (Goose) 160, 167
Gossage, Richard (Goose) 2, 77–78, 280
Gott, Jim 273
Graffanino, Tony 338
Graham, Kyle 136
Grant, Eddie (Attorney) 70
Greenwell, Mike 287
Gregg, Vean 126
Grich, Bobby 266
Griffey, Ken, Sr. 252
Griffith, Clark (The Old Fox) 7, 8–10, 79–82, 87
Griffith Stadium, Washington D.C. 77
Grim, Bob 223, 230
Grimes, Burleigh 41, 74, 131, 145–148, 156, 1162, 174, 244, 348–349
Grimsley, Jason 291

Groom, Bob 35, 87
Grove, Ethel 168
Grove, Robert (Lefty) 61, 74, 76, 78, 80, 82, 100, 125, 137, 144, 158–199, 201–203, 217, 240, 259, 265, 280, 284, 307, 311, 345–346, 348–349
Guidry, Ron (Louisiana Lightning) 51, 282
Guillen, Carlos 330
Gumpert, Dave 313

Haddix, Harvey 218–219
Hafey, Charles (Chick) 135
Hahn, Frank (Noodles) 41, 54–56
Haines, Jesse (Pop) 131, 148–152, 156, 188, 348
Hall, Dick 351
Hallahan, William (Wild Bill) 129, 176
Hampton, Mike 199, 311, 341–343, 352, 354
Hands, Bill 267
Harder, Melvin (Mel) 162, 187–190, 194
Hargrove, Mike (The Human Rain Delay) 250, 352–353
Harmon, Bob (Hickory) 133
Harridge, Will 190
Harris, Stanley (Bucky) 113, 123, 169, 193
Harrison, Jim 168, 175
Harriss, William (Slim) 127, 164–165
Hart, Jim Ray 248
Hartford (CT) Bees 201
Hartnett, Leon (Gabby) 148
Hatcher, Billy 313
Hayes, Jack Minter (Jackie) 122
Heaton, Neal 316
Heilmann, Harry 97
Hendix, Claude 149
Henke, Tom 2, 274
Henry, Frank (Dutch) 147, 178
Heredia, Felix 326, 329
Hernandez, Keith 289
Hernandez, Roberto 2
Hershiser, Orel (Bulldog) 2, 227, 311–312, 317–319, 328, 352
Hickman, Jim 226
Hilldebrand, George 121–122
Hodges, Gil 248
Hogue, Bobby 223
Holloway, Ken 189
Holt, James (Red) 165
Holtzman, Ken 351

Honig, Donald 129
Hooper, Harry 135, 347
Hornsby, Rogers 144, 149, 347
Houston Astros 257, 264, 313–314, 330, 333–336, 342, 353
Houston Buffaloes 210
Howell, Harold (Handsome Harry) 7, 8, 12–15, 133
Hoyt, Waite (Schoolboy) 48, 80, 118–121, 162, 166, 174–176, 193–195, 347–348
Hubbell, Carl (The Meal Ticket) 61, 80, 131–132, 153–154, 156, 198, 202–205, 209, 217, 272
Hubbes, Ken 115
Hudlin, Willis 190
Huggins, Miller 81, 116, 118, 167, 175, 347
Hughes, Thomas (Long Tom) 93
Hume, Tom 255, 262
Hunter, Jim (Catfish) 48, 125, 351
Huntington Grounds, Boston 13, 354
Hutton, Tom 271

Illinois State Amateur Baseball Association 218

Jackson, Vincent (Bo) 268
James, Bill 186, 250, 283, 326
James, Bob 265, 273
Jay, Joey 218, 223, 230
Jeffries, Gregg 338
Jenkins, Fergie 202, 234–236, 241, 246, 259–260, 262
John, Tommy (TJ) 100, 106, 199, 262, 269, 282, 300–302, 343
Johnson, Ban 112
Johnson, Bob 266
Johnson, Earl 190
Johnson, Randy 51, 61, 78, 82, 100, 125, 144, 199, 223, 265, 280–282, 284, 286–288, 299, 307, 311–312, 325,- 326, 330–331, 337, 340, 342, 352
Johnson, Sylvester 139
Johnson, Walter (The Big Train, Barney) 1, 3, 7–8, 27–28, 34–35, 37, 61, 76–128, 130, 132–137, 144, 146, 155–156, 158, 160, 162, 164, 167, 169, 175, 178, 199, 202, 213, 217, 240, 259, 265, 280, 284, 288, 307, 310–311, 332, 335, 344, 354–35
Jones, Andrew 330
Jones, Barry 316, 326, 337

Jones, Chipper 338
Jones, Samuel (Sad Sam) 173, 175
Joss, Adrian (Addie) 7–8, 23–25, 33. 40, 63, 79–80, 88–90, 115, 300
Judge, Joe 108, 121

Kaat, Jim 199, 166
Kahn, Roger 202
Kahoe, Mike 83
Kaline, Al 238
Kansas City, MO 149, 264
Kansas City, Western League 44
Kansas City Athletics 164, 207
Kansas City Royals 278, 298–299, 305–306, 320
Kaplan, Jim 168
Karl, Andy 206
Kaufmann, Tony 139
Keefe, Tim (Sir Timothy) 8, 269
Keister, Jim (Wagon Tongue) 13
Kelley, Brent 251
Kelley, Joe 135
Kelly, Michael (King) 244
Kelly, Roberto 340
Kennedy, William (Brickyard) 354–355
Kennett Square, PA 100–101
Kentucky, Commonwealth of 227
Kerr, Dickie 171
Kerrigan, Joe 291
Key, Jimmy 199, 241, 257, 272–273, 277, 282, 284, 288, 302–304, 352
Kile, Darryl 353
Kipper, Bob 326
Kline, Chuck 144
Kling, Johnny 53, 132
Kolp, Ray 139
Koosman, Jerry 264
Koppett, Leonard 247–248
Korean War 222
Koufax, Sanford (Sandy) 48, 61, 78, 80, 184, 190, 199, 202, 217–218, 223–227, 230–233, 243, 262, 280, 307, 325
Krakauskas, Joe 187, 190
Kranepool, Ed 229
Krause, Lew, Sr. 173, 179
Kremer, Ray 148
Kruk, John 287
Kucks, Johnny 350

Lajoie, Larry 89
Lake Erie 187
Lancaster Roses 169

Landis, Judge Kenesaw Mountain 98
Langston, Mark 330
Lanier, Hal 313
Lanier, Max 210
Larsen, Don 328
Lasorda, Tommy 317
Lavelle, Gary 274, 303
Law, Rudy 274
Law, Vance 314–315
Layana, Tim 210
Lazzeri, Tony 149, 192
Leach, Tommy (The Wee) 53
League Park, Cincinnati 54, 73
League Park, Washington D.C. 89
LeBourveau, Bevo 138
Leever, Sam 41, 51–54, 57–58
Leibrandt, Charlie 272, 282
Leifeldt, Albert (Lefty) 53, 133
Lelivelt, Jack 90
Lemon, Bob 51, 224, 231, 349
Leonard, Emil (Dutch) 187
Leonard, Walter (Buck) 190
Lewis, George (Duffy) 112–113, 347
Leyland, Jimmy 327, 329
Lieberthal, Mike 338
Lincoln, President Abraham 7
Lindberg, Dick 33
Lindblad, Paul 351
Lindsey, Jim 152
Lindstrom, Fred 355
Link, Fred 30, 35
Linn, Ed 1
Linzy, Frank 248
Lisenbee, Horace (Hod) 107–108, 123
Little, Bryan 274
Lloyd, Graeme 302
Lockmann, Carrol (Whitey) 267
Lockwood, Claude (Skip) 267–268
Lombardi, Vic 207
Lonaconing, MD 126, 175
Lopat, Eddie 190
Lopez, Javey 330
Los Angeles, CA 298
Lou Gehrig Memorial Award 236
Louisville Colonels 46, 57
Lundgren, Carl 57
Luque, Adolfo (Dolf) 131, 138, 141–143, 147, 156, 187, 300
Lyle, Albert (Sparky) 255
Lynch, Mike 51
Lyons, Ted 80, 106–108, 121–123, 162, 166, 171, 176–179, 272

MacGaffigan, Andy 316
Mack, Connie 8, 10–12, 20–23, 28–30, 44, 46–47, 75, 87, 90–91, 103, 126–127, 158, 164, 167, 169, 172, 174–176, 193, 346, 348
Mackey, Raleigh (Biz) 266
Maddux, Greg 2, 7, 61, 128, 160–161, 218, 236, 240, 269, 277, 282, 284, 288, 299, 302, 309–345, 352–354
Maglie, Salvatore (Sal, The Barber) 218, 224
Mahaffey, Art 228
Mahaffey, Roy 173, 190, 192
Mamaux, Al 148
Mantle, Mickey 219
Marberry, Fred (Firpo) 117–118, 126
Marichal, Juan 80, 202, 206, 215, 220, 230, 235, 238–239, 350
Marlin Springs, TX 33
Marquard, Rube 7–8, 36–37, 41, 68–69, 92, 131, 134–136, 146–147, 153, 156, 188, 243, 309
Martin, Albert (Al) 354
Martin, Albert (Billy) 320
Martin, Mike 313
Martina, Joseph (Oyster Joe) 117
Martinez, Jose Dennis 315–317
Martinez, Pedro 1, 282, 284, 290–293, 307–308, 311–312, 324–325, 339–340, 352
Martinez, Tino 292
Mathews, Eddie 206
Mathewson, Christy 7, 8, 17, 19, 27, 39–76, 81, 84, 91, 128, 130, 132, 133, 135–137, 146, 154–156, 160, 161, 199, 202, 217, 222, 224, 236, 240, 259, 272, 279, 284, 288, 291, 309, 310, 311, 345, 346
Maye, Lee 227
Mays, Carl 80, 99, 111
Mays, Willie 98, 211–218, 233, 279, 332, 335
Mazer, Bill 238
McCaffery, E.V. 251
McCaffery, R.A. 251
McCarthy, Joseph (Marse Joe) 174, 190–191, 347
McCovey, Willie 215, 248
McDaniel, Lindy 230
McDowell, Samuel (Sudden Sam) 77–78, 280, 307
McFadden, Barney 73
McGinnity, Joe (Iron Man) 7–8, 15–16,

41, 43, 54, 57–58, 65, 188, 224, 244, 309
McGraw, John 15, 39, 68, 81, 113, 142, 147, 153–154, 227, 346, 355
McGraw, Tug 246, 262
McGriff, Fred 340
McGwire, Mark 332
McInnis, John (Stuffy) 87
McKain, Hal 173, 178
McKeithan, Keith 195
McKeon, Joel 273
McLean, Larry 70
McMahon, Don 230
McNally, Dave 224
McNamara, Joe 275, 301
McQuaid, Herb 175
McWeeney, Don (Buzz) 148
Mendoza, Ramiro 291
Meriden, CT 33
The Merkle Game 63–64
Mertes, Sam 43
Meusel, Bob 118
Meyers, John (Chief) 70
Michael, Gene 313
Milan, Clyde (Deerfoot) 86, 113
Miljus, John (Jove) 185
Miller, Edmund (Bing) 188
Miller, Frank (Bullet) 136
Milnar, Al 190
Milwaukee, WI 207, 216, 230, 233–234
Milwaukee Braves 202, 206, 215, 220, 230, 235, 238–239, 350
Milwaukee Brewers (AL) 44, 290
Milwood, Kevin 328
Minnesota Metrodome (H. H. Humphrey Metrodome) 273, 276, 293
Minnesota Twins 225, 269–271, 290–291, 301, 315–317, 328, 340
Missouri 207
Mize, John (The Big Cat) 203, 208
Mobile, AL 54
Moeller, Danny 87
Mogridge, George 117
Monday, Rick 260
Moore, Wilcy 167
Moran, Pat 71
Morgan, Harry 20
Morrell, Bill 170
Morris, Jack 241, 257, 272–274, 282
Montreal Expos 259, 269–271, 290–291, 301, 315–317, 328, 340

Montreal Royals 221
Moyer, Jamie 299, 326
Mullin, George 7–8, 36–37, 41, 68–69, 92, 131, 134–136
Municipal Stadium, Cleveland (Lakefront Stadium) 187, 293, 299, 349
Munson, Thurman 115
Murphy, Danny 21–22
Murphy, Johnny 174, 184
Murray, John (Red) 70
Murtaugh, Danny 211
Musial, Stan (The Man) 98. 209, 211–218, 230, 332, 335
Mussina, Mike 282, 284, 288, 294–297, 299, 311–3122, 338–339
Myer, Bill 200
Myers, Doug 288

National League 8, 18, 42, 45, 61, 69, 112–114, 136, 139, 144, 155, 191, 203, 206–209, 211, 219, 231, 246, 250, 257, 259, 262, 265, 267, 271, 278, 286, 288, 290, 304, 317, 327, 329–330, 338, 340, 342, 348
Naymick, Mike 190
Negro Leagues 135, 217
Nehf, Artie 355
Nelson, Jeff 353–354
Nemec, David 279
New York (San Francisco) Giants 15, 18, 42, 44–46, 53, 55, 57–59, 61–63, 65, 69, 72–73, 82, 91, 134–137, 142, 147, 152–153, 181, 201–205, 211, 215–216, 222, 232–235, 246–249, 268, 334, 343, 346, 355
New York Mets 226–229, 231, 235, 238–272, 279, 304, 323–325, 327, 342–343
New York Times 17, 27, 47, 70, 120, 167–168, 175, 241–242, 247
New York Yankees (Highlanders, Bronx Bombers) 14–17, 81, 91, 94–98, 112–114, 116, 118–121, 149, 164, 168, 174–183, 190–192, 195, 207, 221, 231, 253, 284, 290–291, 294, 296–297, 320, 328, 331, 339, 342–343, 347–348, 350–351
Newark, NJ 33
Newcombe, Donald (Newk) 77, 202, 209, 218, 221–223
Newhouser, Harold (Prince Hal) 194–199

Newsom, Louis (Bobo) 185
Nichols, Charles (Kid) 8, 37, 41, 78, 160
Niekro, Joe 235
Niekro, Phil 202, 233–236, 241, 250–253, 257, 261, 281–284, 351
Nixon, Trot 1
North Carolina 184

Oakland Athletics 320, 351
Ogden, Warren (Curly) 117, 170
Olympic Stadium, Montreal 316
O'Neill, Steve 174
Orsatti, Ernie 155
Ott, Melvin (Mel) 154, 203

Page, Joe 209
Paige, Leroy (Satchel) 135, 217, 350
Palmeiro, Rafael 314
Palmer, Jim 61, 224, 241, 257–25, 281–284, 288
Palmer, Pete 48, 251, 269, 273
Parker, Harry 351
Parnell, Mel 199
Pearson, Monte 192
Pegler, Westbrook 125
Pennock, Herb (The Knight of Kennett Square) 43, 80, 100–103, 112, 120, 162, 165–169, 188, 347–348
Perkins, Broderick 250
Perry, Gaylord 137, 202, 224, 234–235, 241, 249–250, 261
Peterson, Jim 173
Pettitte, Andy 282
Pfiester, J. (Jack the Giant Killer) 63
Philadelphia Athletics 9–12, 20–23, 28–30, 78, 90–92, 101–103, 144, 158–159, 346–349
Philadelphia Phillies 36, 55, 67, 69–71, 73, 85–55, 103, 125–127, 132–159, 206, 218–220, 228–229, 234–236, 241–242, 254–257, 322, 336
Phillippe, Charles (Deacon) 41, 48–49, 51, 53–54, 57–59, 133, 187, 354–355
Phillips, Tom 103
Phillips, William (Silver Bill) 73
Piazza, Mike 221, 353
Pichardo, Hipolito 306
Pico, Jeff 316
Pierce, Billy 61, 100, 199, 343
Piniella, Lou 301, 320, 342
Pipgras, George 183, 192
Pipp, Wally 113

Pittsburgh Pirates (Corsairs) 18, 27, 48–54, 57–59, 65, 69, 74, 133–135, 139–141, 145–148, 153, 176, 206–207, 228, 241, 292, 320, 327, 334, 354–355
Plank, Edward (Gettysburg Eddie) 7–8, 20–23, 28, 57, 61, 79, 85–88, 90, 92, 103, 137, 199, 202, 217, 269, 300, 343, 346
Plantier, Phil 298
Players' Choice Pitcher's Award (NL) 342
Players League 42
Playoff Gem Award 353–354
Polo Grounds (Coogan's Bluff) New York 42–43, 49–58, 69, 90, 136, 147, 203–204
Porter, Chuck 263
Povich, Shirley 77
Powell, James (Jay) 325, 329
Price, Joe 270
Providence, RI 227
Pruiett, Charles (Tex) 30
Pryor, Greg 320
Pugh, Tim 322

Quinn, Jack 113, 167, 173, 178, 183

Radbourne, Charley 8
Reed, Jody, 305
Rees, Stan 117
Regan, Phil 290
Reichler, Joe 213
Remlinger, Mike 326, 329
Reulbach, E. (Big Ed) 41, 51, 57, 65–68, 76, 266
Reuschel, Rick 241, 267–268
Reynolds, Craig 313
Rice, Grantland 80
Rice, Sam 107, 113
Richard, J.R. 78, 280
Richert, Pete 351
Richie, Lew 27
Rickey, Branch 205
Ridzik, Steve 207
Rijo, Jose 311, 320–322
Rijo, Mrs. Rosie 320
Ripken, Cal, Jr. 128, 258, 286
Rivera, Mariano 291, 302–303, 353–354
Riverfront Stadium, Cincinnati 252
Rixey, Eppa 41, 71–72, 131, 137–140, 142, 146–147, 156, 299

Rizzuto, Phil 253
Roberge, Nert 273
Roberts, Robin 2, 45, 137, 202, 206, 218–220, 222, 231–232, 240, 269, 300
Robinson, Frank 223
Robinson, Jackie 244
Robinson, Wilbert 69, 115, 127
Rocker, John 330
Roe, Elwin (Preacher) 210
Roenicke, Gary 258
Rogers, Kenny 282
Rogers, Steve 241, 269–271
Rolen, Scott 338
Rommel, Eddie 51, 164, 170, 173–174, 178, 183
Rookie of the Year Award (BBWAA) 240, 322
Royals (Kaufmann) Stadium, Kansas City 266
Ruffing, Charley (Red) 80, 123–125, 166, 174, 179–184, 192
Rupert, Colonel Jake 124, 181
Rusch, Glendon 354
Rush, Robert (Bob) 224
Rusie, Amos (The Hoosier Cannonball) 8, 41–42, 72–73, 76–78, 144, 240, 265, 280, 307
Russell, Allan 103, 122
Russell, Ewell (Reb) 99
Russell, Jack 120
Ruth, George Herman (Babe, The Bambino, The Sultan of Swat) 9, 80, 93–98, 108–113, 118, 125, 128, 160, 164, 192–193, 210, 213, 217–218, 222, 278, 332, 335
Ryan, Nolan 48, 61, 78, 80, 241, 244, 257, 261, 263–265, 281–284, 92, 301, 307, 311–315, 340
Ryba, Mike 179

Saberhagen, Brett 241, 257, 272, 278, 282, 284, 298–299
SABR (Society for American Baseball Research) 161, 168
Safeco Park, Seattle 286
Sain, Johnny 208–209, 237, 341
St. Clair, Randy 315
St. John's University 304
St. Louis Browns 13, 23, 83, 86–88, 92, 115–118, 179
St. Louis Cardinals 43, 45–46, 50, 61, 134, 139, 145–153, 176, 205–206, 210, 214–215, 228–231, 245–246, 254, 257, 266–267, 343, 347–349
Sallee, H. (Slim) 133
San Bernadino, CA 342
San Diego, CA 249
San Diego Padres 250, 318, 328–329, 338
San Francisco, CA 322
San Francisco Giants 211, 215–216, 246–269, 343
Sandberg, Ryne 313
Sanderson, Scott 315
Santo, Ron 188, 266
Sarasota, FL 272
Sarmiento, Manny 270
Scanlon, Robert (Bob) 316
Schalk, Ray 107, 171, 272
Schilling, Curt 223, 299, 311–312, 331, 336–338, 352
Schiraldi, Calvin 303
Schourek, Steve 292
Schultz, Howie 210
Score, Herb 280
Scott, Everett 112
Scott, James (Death Valley Jim) 93
Seattle Mariners 287–288, 325, 341–342, 354
Seaver, Thomas (Tom Terrific) 2–3, 61, 160–161, 222, 227, 233–235, 238–279, 288, 292, 312, 345, 350–351
Segui, Diego 246
Seibold, Harry (Socks) 155
Sellbach, Albert (Kip) 43
Sewell, Luke 81–82
Sewell, Truett (Rip) 207
Seymour, James (Cy) 49
Shamokin, PA 104, 106
Shang, Wally 112
Shanks, Howie 120
Shannon, William (Spike) 49
Shatzkin, Mike 115
Shaw, Jim 99, 103, 105, 117
Shawkey, Bob 103, 116–117, 120, 124, 175, 181
Shea, Frank (Spec) 208
Shea Stadium, New York 227–228, 241–242, 256, 259, 328, 351
Sheely, Earl 107
Sherdel, William (Wee Willie) 139, 153
Sherry, Larry 224
Shibe Park, Philadelphia 91, 126, 165, 188, 193, 348

Index

Shocker, Urban 80, 99, 115–118, 269
Shore, Ernie 112–113
Shore, William (Bill) 178
Short, Chris 228
Shotton, Burt 221
Sid Mercer Award 236
Simmons, Al 164, 175, 192, 348–349
Simmons, Curt 220, 239
Sisk, Doug 255
Sisler, George 116, 164
Skydome, Toronto 277, 300, 304
Slaughter, Enos 206, 244
Slocumb, Heathcliff 322
Smalley, Roy, Jr. 276
Smiley, John 327
Smith, Earl 120
Smith, Lee 319
Smith, Ron 217
Smoltz, John 228, 310, 330
Snodgrass, Fred 70
Sorrell, Vic 195
Sotheron, Alan 86
Sosa, Sammy 332
South End Grounds, Boston 18, 132
South Park High School, Buffalo, NY 200
South Side Grounds, Chicago 92
Southern League 54
Spahn, Edward 200
Spahn, Warren 2–3, 61, 98, 160–161, 198, 200–237, 241, 246, 249, 269–270, 284, 290, 312, 332, 335, 344–345, 349–350
Sparks, Tully 55, 66
Speece, Byron (By) 117
Spence, Stan 208
The Sporting News (TSN) 76, 125, 217, 251, 283
The Sporting News All Star Team 236
The Sporting News Pitcher of the year Award 299
The Sporting News Rookie of the Year Award 269, 306
Sportsman's Park, St. Louis 145, 177, 348
Springfield, IL 218
Stahl, Chick 115
Stanky, Eddie 210
Stanton, Mike 292, 322
Steinbrenner, George 320, 339
Stengel, Charles D. (Casey) 207, 211, 350
Stewart, John (Stuffy) 121

Stieb, Dave 241, 257–258, 272, 274–276, 282, 284, 298–299
Stottlemyre, Mel 231
Suehsdorf, Adie 115
Sutton, Don 7, 153, 188, 241, 246, 257–260, 263, 273, 281–284, 299, 311–312, 325, 352
Swan, Craig 246
Sweetland, Les 155
Swindell, Greg 299

Taft, President William Howard 86–87
Tanana, Frank 304
Tannehill, Jesse (Powder) 35, 57, 198
Tapani, Kevin 299
Tavarez, Julian 353
Taylor, Jack (Brakeman) 41, 44–46, 57, 66
Tekulve, Kent 2
Tempe, AZ 342
Terry, William (Memphis Bill) 144, 152
Terry, Zebulon (Zeb) 148
Texas Rangers 260, 264–265, 284, 289–290, 312
Thomas, Frank 332
Thomas, Thomas (Tommy) 173, 190
Thorn, John 48, 251
Three Rivers Stadium, Pittsburgh 334
Tinker, Joe 132
Todt, Phil 164
Tomlin, Randy 327
Toronto Blue Jays 253, 273–277, 299–300, 302–304, 306
Torre, Joe 227, 252, 284, 290, 302
Trachtenberg, Leo 121
Tracy, MO 205
Tri-State League 169
Trout, Paul (Dizzy) 194
Tucker, Michael 330
Tulsa University 269
Turley, Bob 110
Twentieth Century Limited 112
Twitchell, Wayne 270

University of Southern California 238
University of Virginia 72

Valentine, Ellis 270
Valenzuela, Fernando 221
Van Atta, Russ 184
Vance, Arthur (Dazzy) 2, 61, 74, 76, 80, 114–115, 131, 143–145, 156, 187, 280, 300, 307

Vangilder, Elam 118
VanHaltren, George (Rip) 43
Vasquez, Javier 328
Vaughn, Irving 163
Veterans Committee, HOF 135, 137, 170, 176
Viola, Frank 241, 257, 272–273, 276–277, 282, 304, 306
Vitt, Oscar 94

Wabash, IN 25
Wagner, Charles (Broadway) 192
Wagner, Honus (Hans) 53, 57
Wagner, William (Bill) 330
Wakefield, Tim 291–292
Walberg, Rube 164, 173–174, 183–184, 190, 192
Walk, Robert (Bob) 327
Walsh, Edward (Big Ed) 7–8, 23, 28, 30–33, 61, 63, 79–80, 92–93, 137, 187, 299
Walsh, Edward, Jr. 31
Walters, William (Bucky) 186, 266
Waner, Paul 144
Ward, John Montgomery 40, 227
Warneke, Lon 266
Warner, John 55–56
Washington Senators (Nationals) 9, 34–35, 81, 89–90, 92, 116, 158, 162, 164–165, 169–170, 185, 194, 355
The Washington Star 85
Watt, Eddie 351
Weathers, Dave 302
Weaver, Earl 3
Weaver, George (Buck) 107
Webster, Mitch 315
Weeghman Park, Chicago 61
Welch, Mickey 8
Wells, David 282, 299
Welzer, Tony 183
Werle, William (Bill) 207
West, Adam 338
West Side Grounds, Chicago 20, 27, 64
Western Association (League) 44, 54
Wetteland, John 2, 302–303
Wheat, Zachary (Zack) 140
White, Ernie 210
White, Frank 278
White, Guy (Doc) 7–8, 19–20, 28, 30, 92, 133, 137, 187, 199
Wilhelm, Hoyt 2, 251

Wilkes-Barre, PA 33
Williams, Albert 258
Williams, Alva (Buff) 87
Williams, Claude 171
Williams, Gerry 330
Williams, Smoky Joe 280
Williams, Stan 224, 327
Williams, Ted 183, 187, 190
Williamsport, PA 294
Willis, Vic 8, 41, 48–51, 53–54, 57–58, 153, 229
Wilson, Enrique 296
Wilson, Jack 195
Wilson, John (Black Jack) 184
Wilson, Leon (Hack) 144
Wilson, Willie 278
Wiltse, George (Hooks) 49, 51, 53–54, 58, 71, 92, 136
Win Shares 251, 266, 283
Winter, George 27
Wise, Rick 267
Wisnia, Saul 279
Wohlers, Mark 326, 329
Wolfgang, Mellie 99
Wood, Wilbur 199, 250
Woodland, WI 23
World Series games 345–355
World War I 69, 129
World War II 177, 200, 202
Wright, Wayne (Rasty) 117
Wrigley Field, Chicago 138, 142, 150, 208, 230, 313, 318, 327, 334
Wyatt, Whitlow 173
Wynn, Early 162, 188, 190, 224, 226, 232, 244

Yawkey, Tom 174, 193
Yeager, Joe 27
Young, Denton (Cy) 2, 5–39, 41–42, 46, 57, 61, 69, 76, 79–80, 84–88, 90, 105, 131–133, 137, 155, 158, 160–161, 201–202, 217, 263, 284, 299, 311, 344–345, 354–355
Young, Matt 319
Youngs, Ross 115, 190

Zachary, Tom 102–103, 117
Zahniser, Paul 105, 117
Zimmer, Don 327
Zmich, Ed 51

www.ingramcontent.com/pod-product-compliance
Lightning Source LLC
Chambersburg PA
CBHW051204300426
44116CB00006B/437